A School Frozen in Time ①

Art by Naoshi Arakawa

Story by Mizuki Tsujimura

Contents

WARNING: This volume contains references to suicide. If you or someone you know has suicidal thoughts or feelings, you are not alone, and there is free, 24/7 help.

National Suicide Prevention Lifeline offers specific resources and confidential support for those in crisis or emotional distress. You can call 1-800-273-TALK (8255) or go to SuicidePreventionLifeline.org at any time for free, 24/7 help when you or anyone you know needs help.

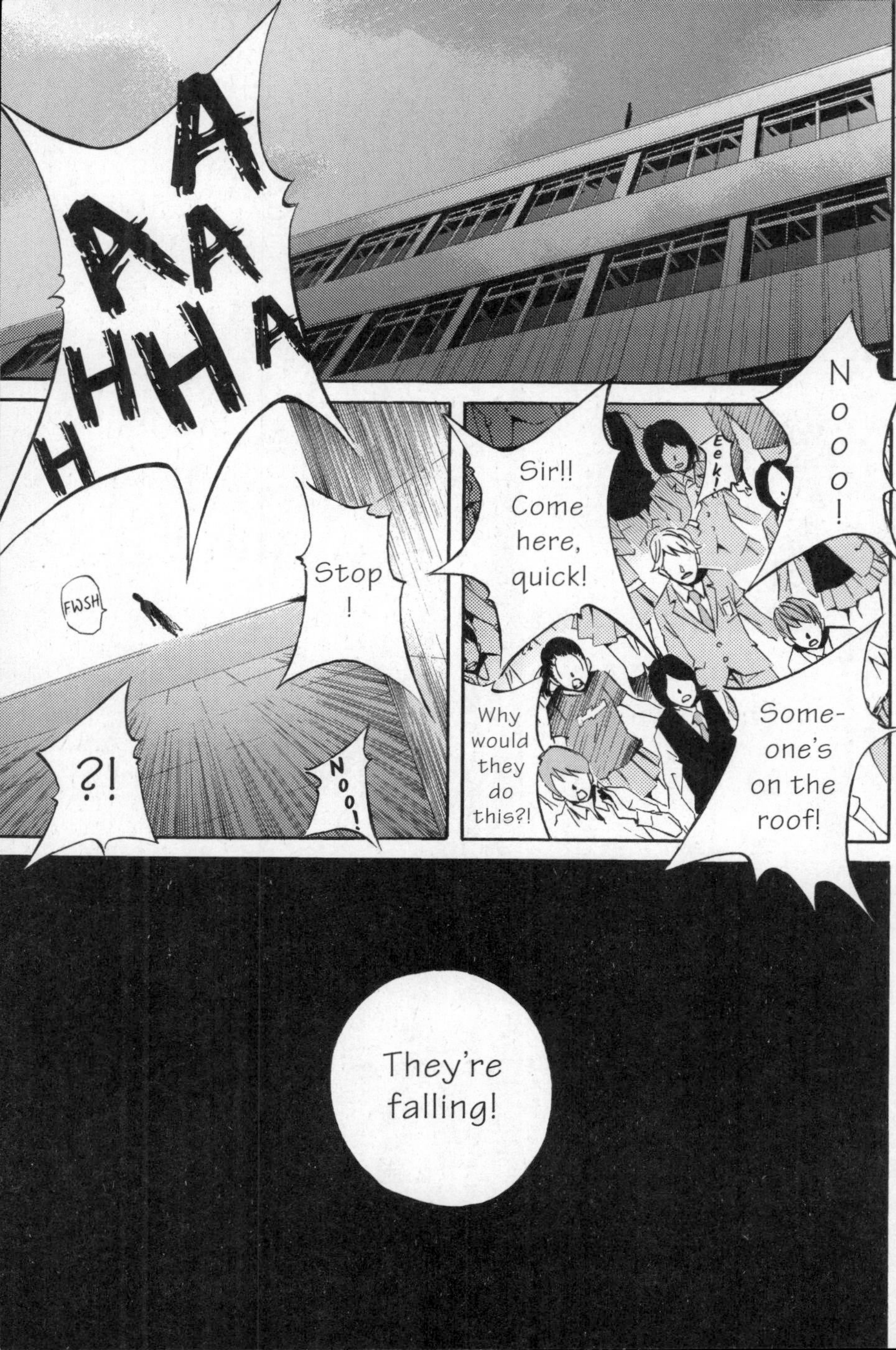
AAAAHHH
Nooo!
Sir!! Come here, quick!
Eek!
Some-one's on the roof!
Why would they do this?!
Stop!
FWSH
?!
Noo!
They're falling!

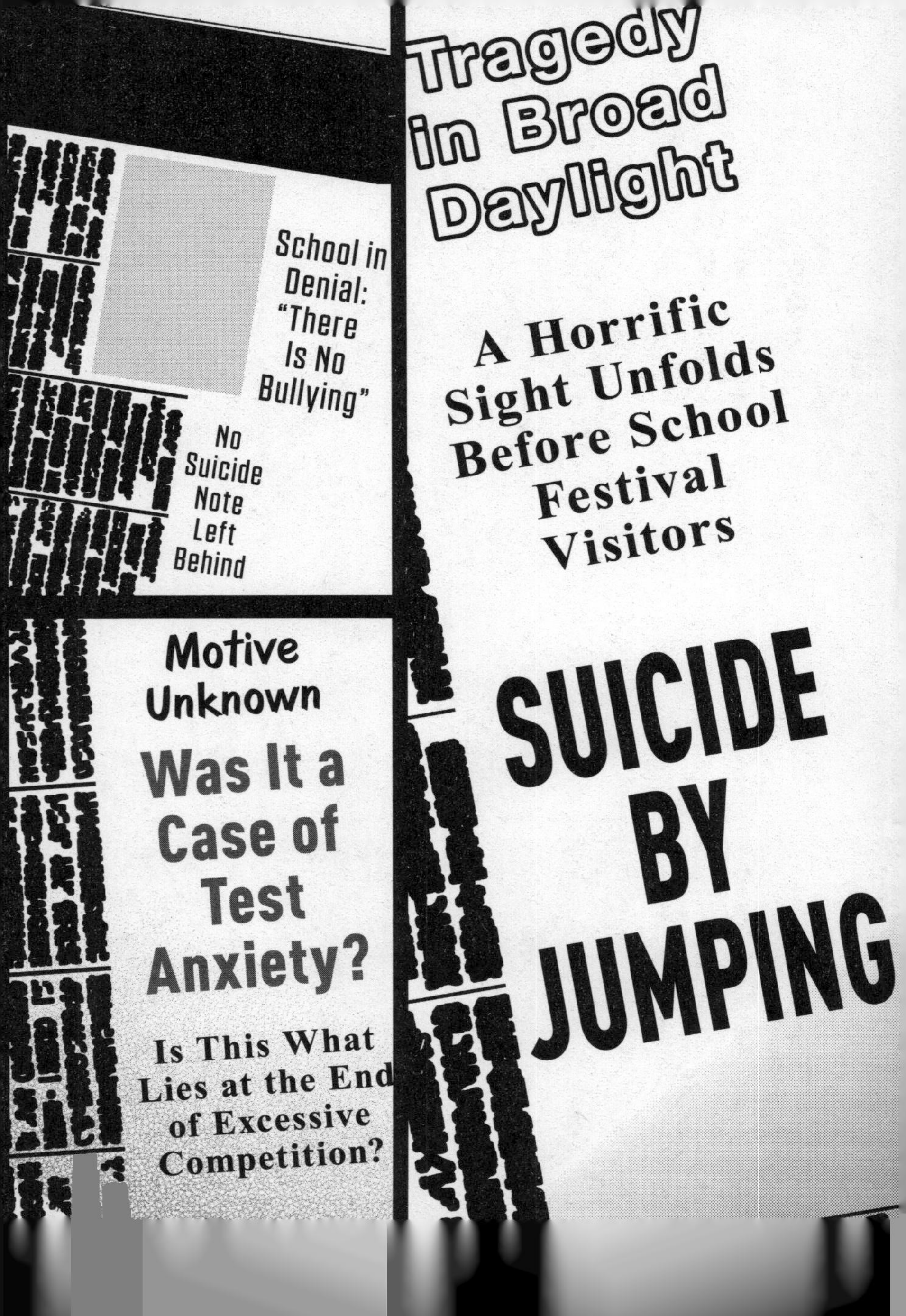
Tragedy in Broad Daylight
A Horrific Sight Unfolds Before School Festival Visitors
SUICIDE BY JUMPING
School in Denial: "There Is No Bullying"
No Suicide Note Left Behind
Motive Unknown
Was It a Case of Test Anxiety?
Is This What Lies at the End of Excessive Competition?

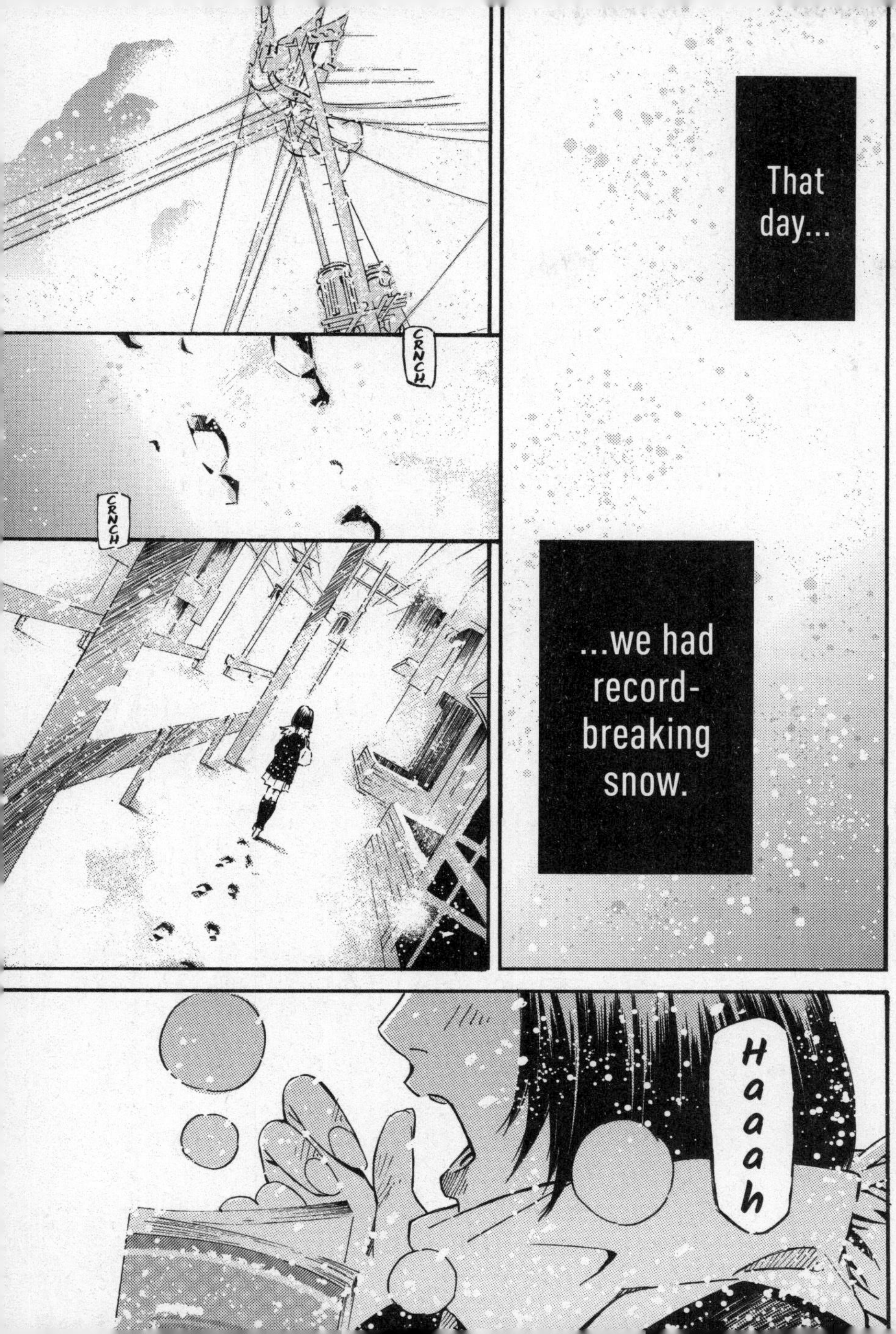
That day...
...we had record-breaking snow.
CRNCH
CRNCH
Haaah

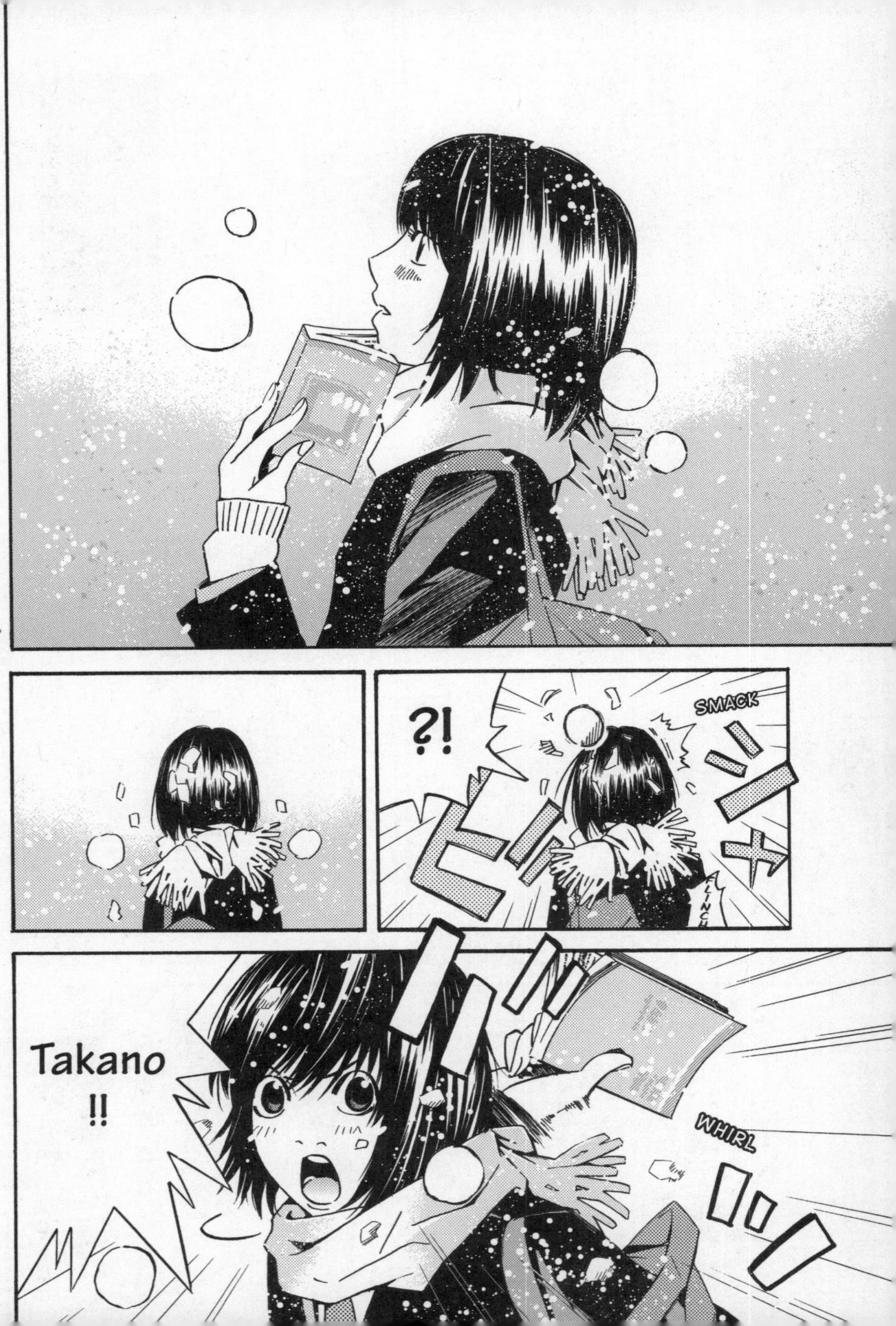
SMACK
?!
FLINCH
Takano !!
WHIRL

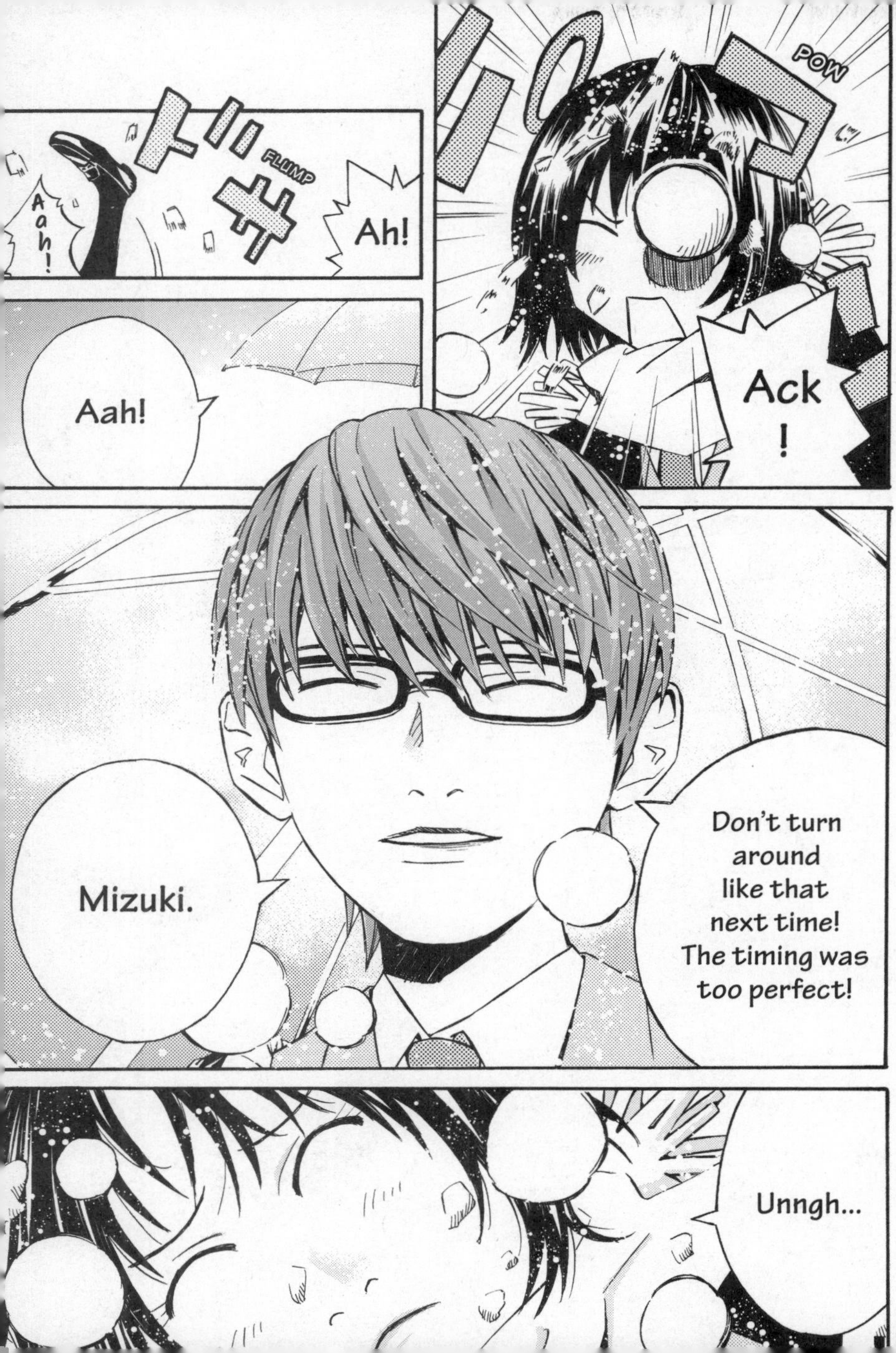
POW
Ack!
Ah!
FLUMP
Aah!
Aah!
Don't turn around like that next time! The timing was too perfect!
Mizuki.
Unngh...

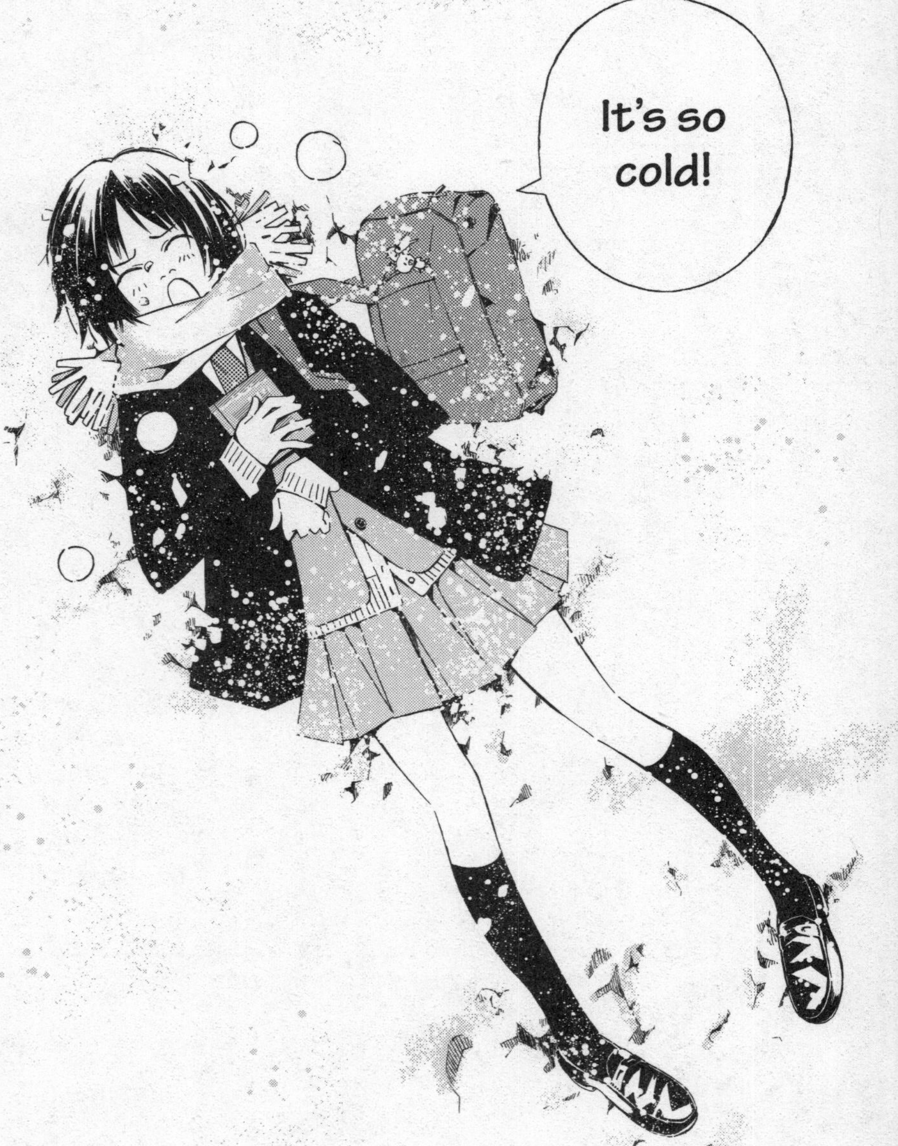
It's so cold!

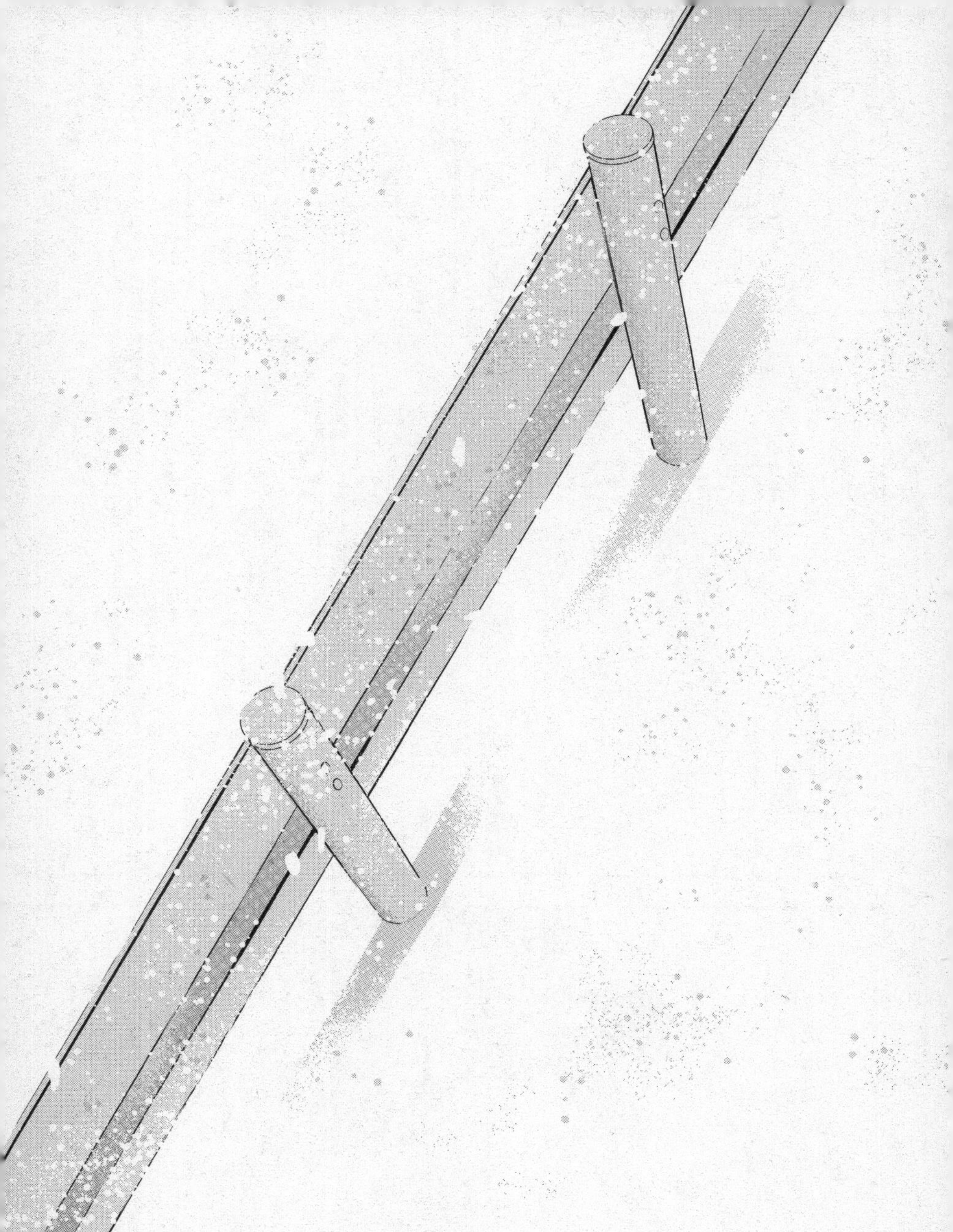

Chapter 1 A School Day

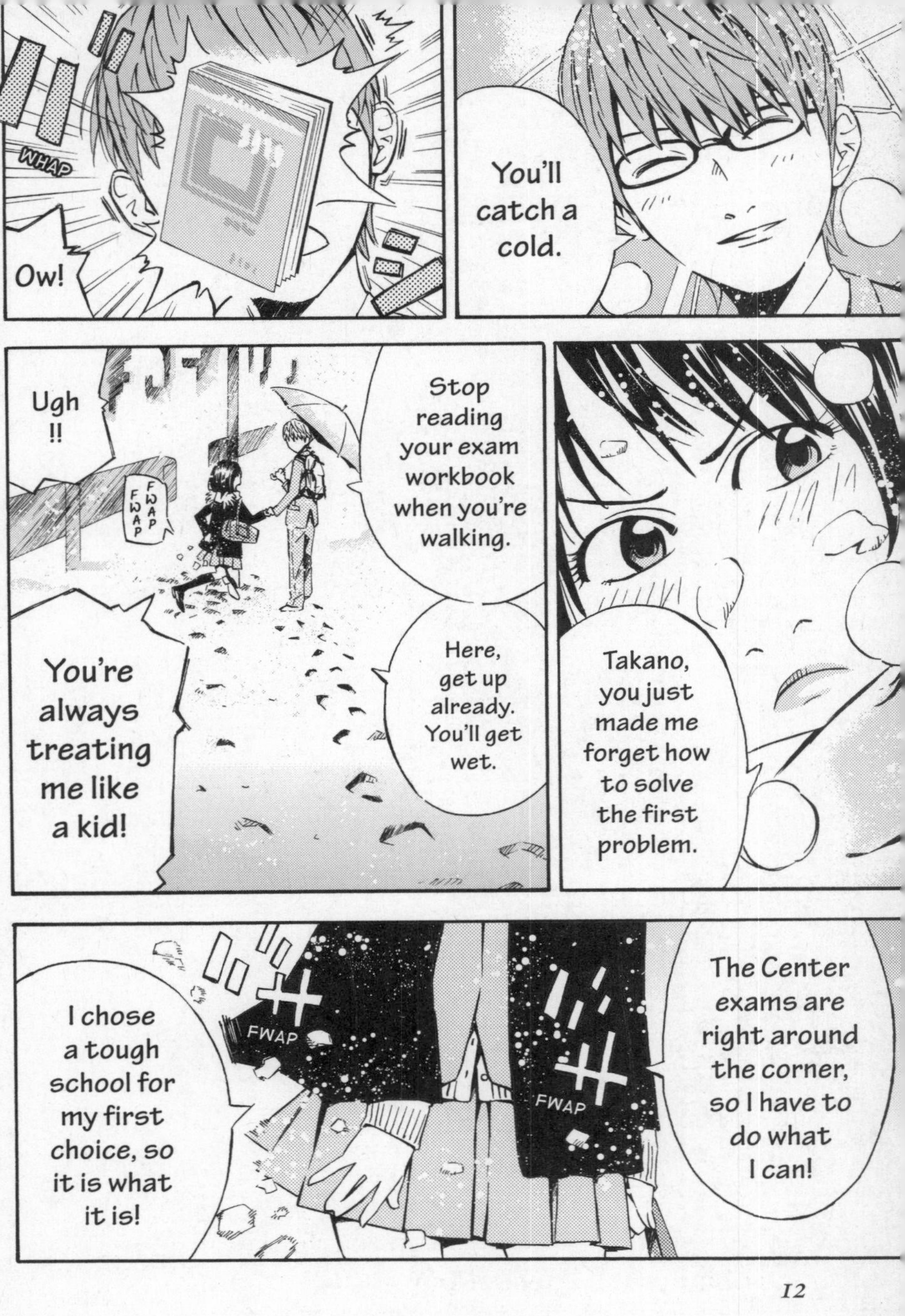
You'll catch a cold.
WHAP
Ow!
Takano, you just made me forget how to solve the first problem.
Stop reading your exam workbook when you're walking.
Here, get up already. You'll get wet.
Ugh !!
FWAP FWAP
You're always treating me like a kid!
The Center exams are right around the corner, so I have to do what I can!
FWAP
FWAP
I chose a tough school for my first choice, so it is what it is!

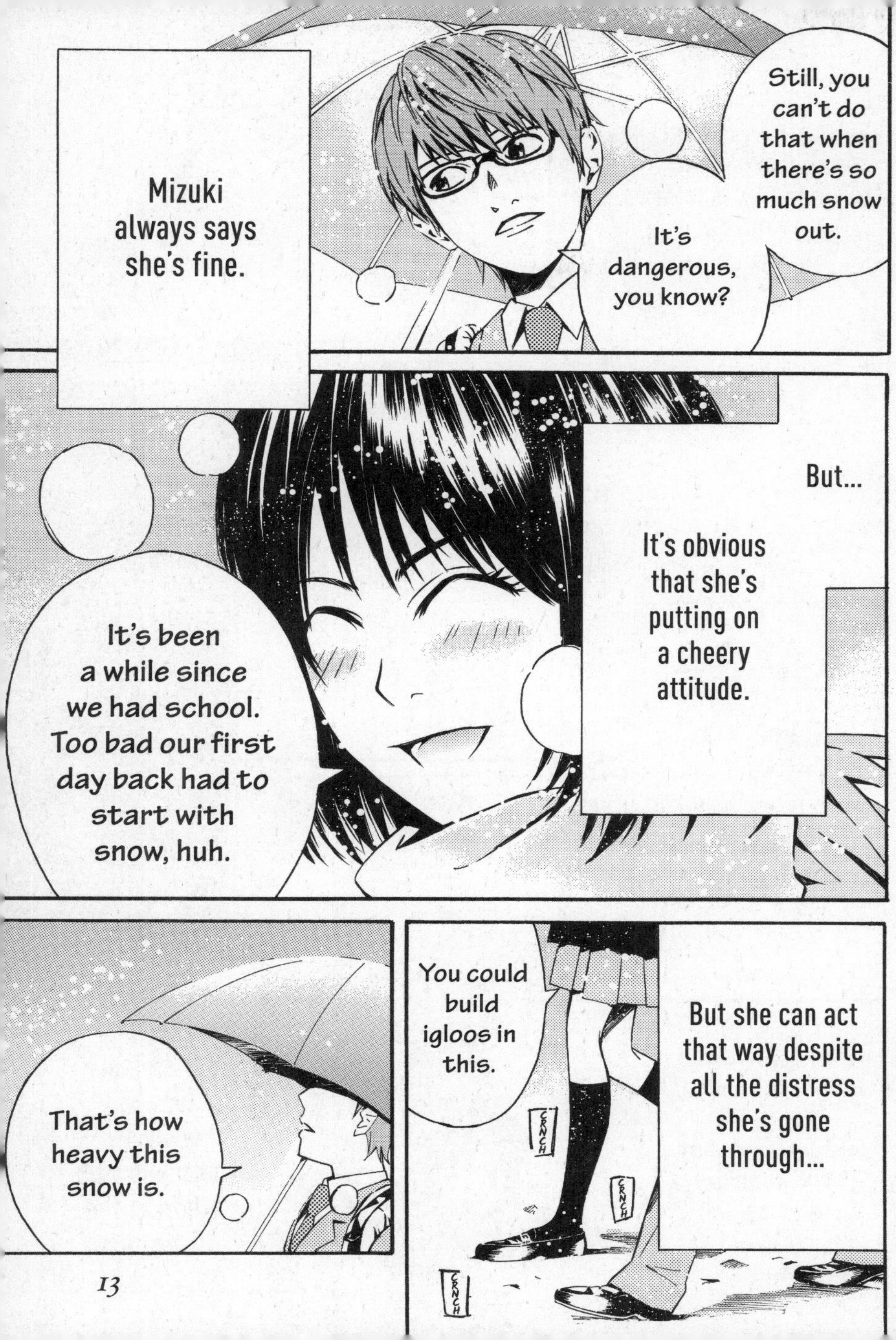
Still, you can't do that when there's so much snow out.
It's dangerous, you know?
Mizuki always says she's fine.
But...
It's obvious that she's putting on a cheery attitude.
It's been a while since we had school. Too bad our first day back had to start with snow, huh.
But she can act that way despite all the distress she's gone through...
You could build igloos in this.
CRNCH
CRNCH
CRNCH
That's how heavy this snow is.

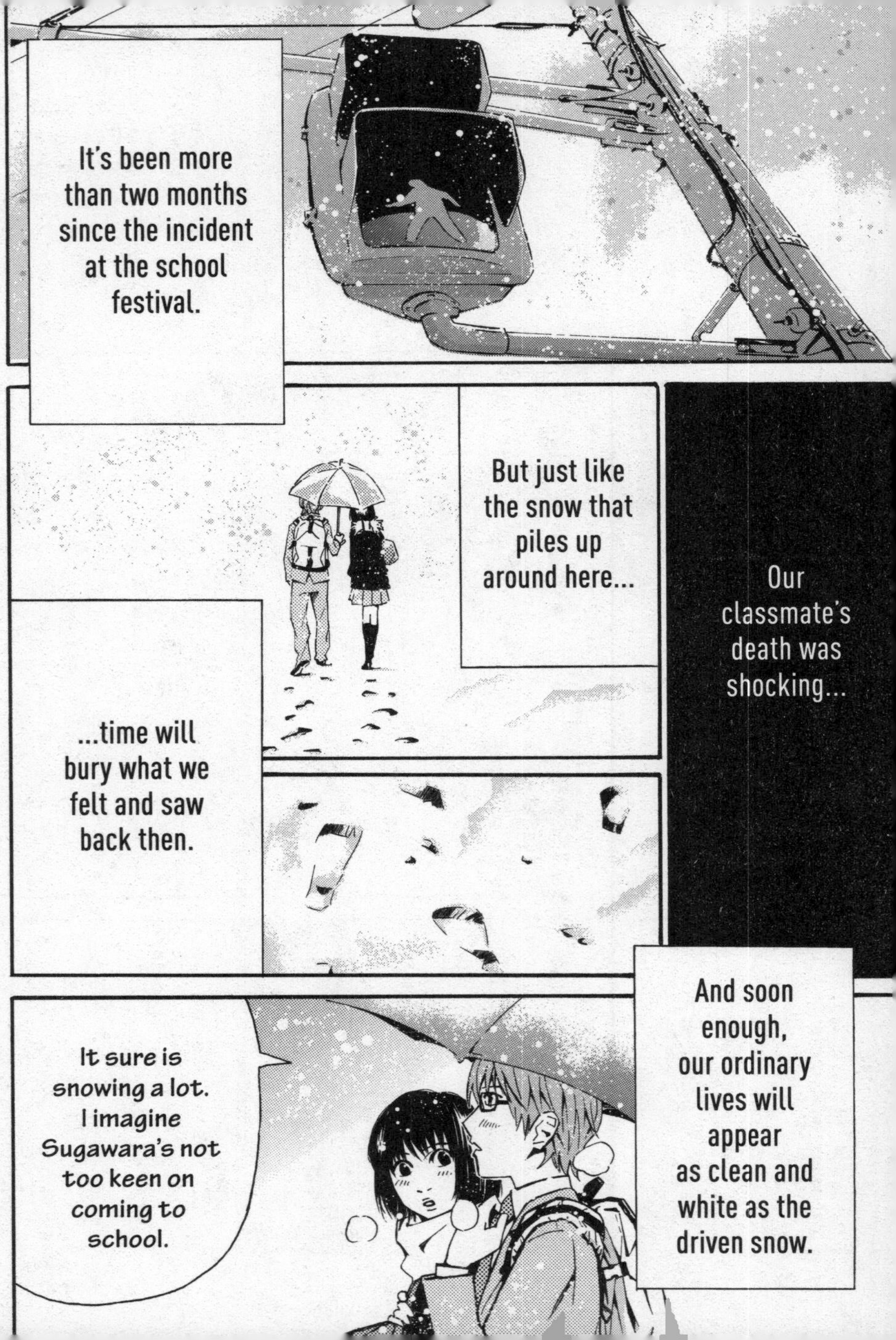
It's been more than two months since the incident at the school festival.
Our classmate's death was shocking...
But just like the snow that piles up around here...
...time will bury what we felt and saw back then.
And soon enough, our ordinary lives will appear as clean and white as the driven snow.
It sure is snowing a lot. I imagine Sugawara's not too keen on coming to school.

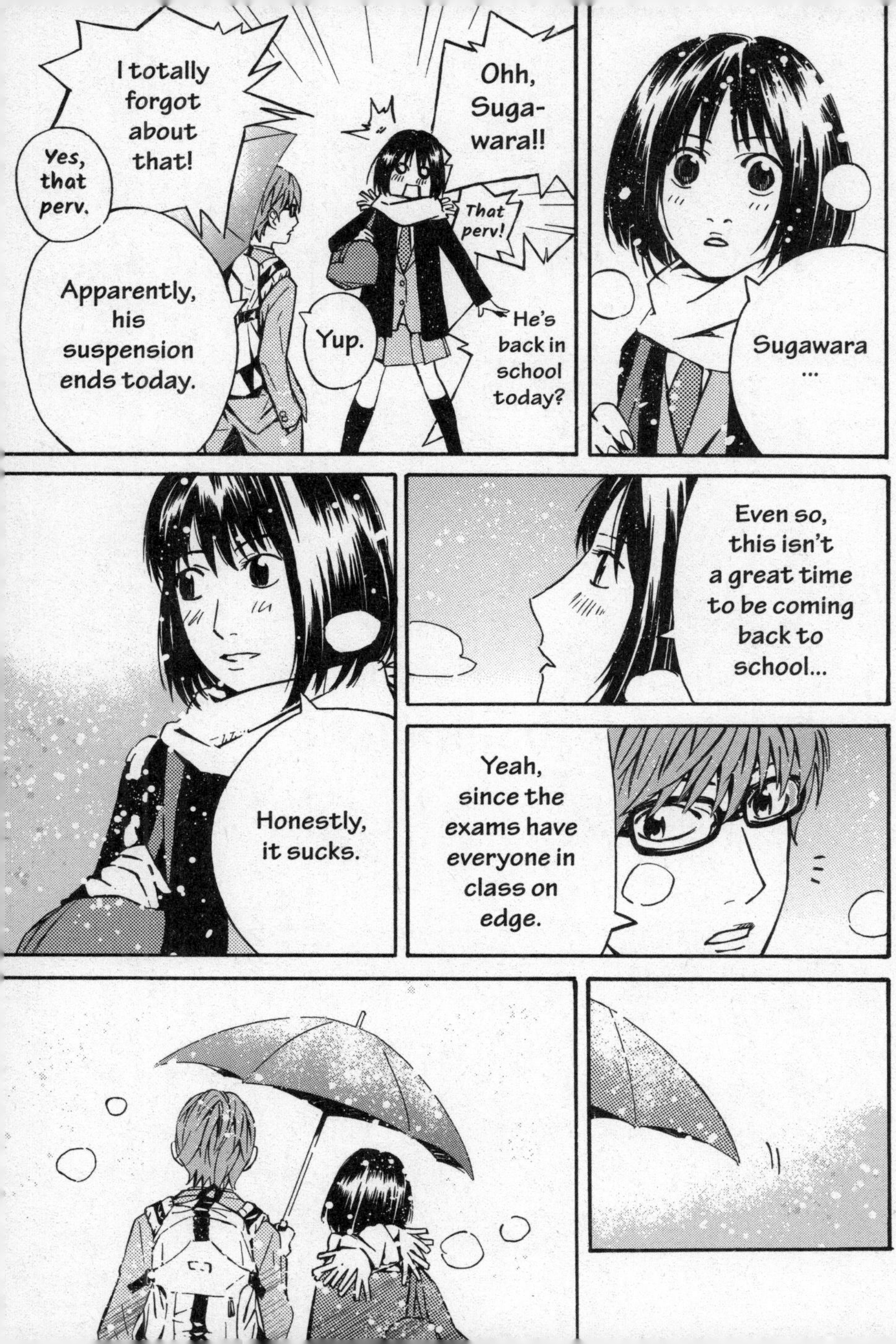
Sugawara ...
Ohh, Suga-wara!!
That perv!
I totally forgot about that!
Yes, that perv.
He's back in school today?
Yup.
Apparently, his suspension ends today.
Even so, this isn't a great time to be coming back to school...
Yeah, since the exams have everyone in class on edge.
Honestly, it sucks.

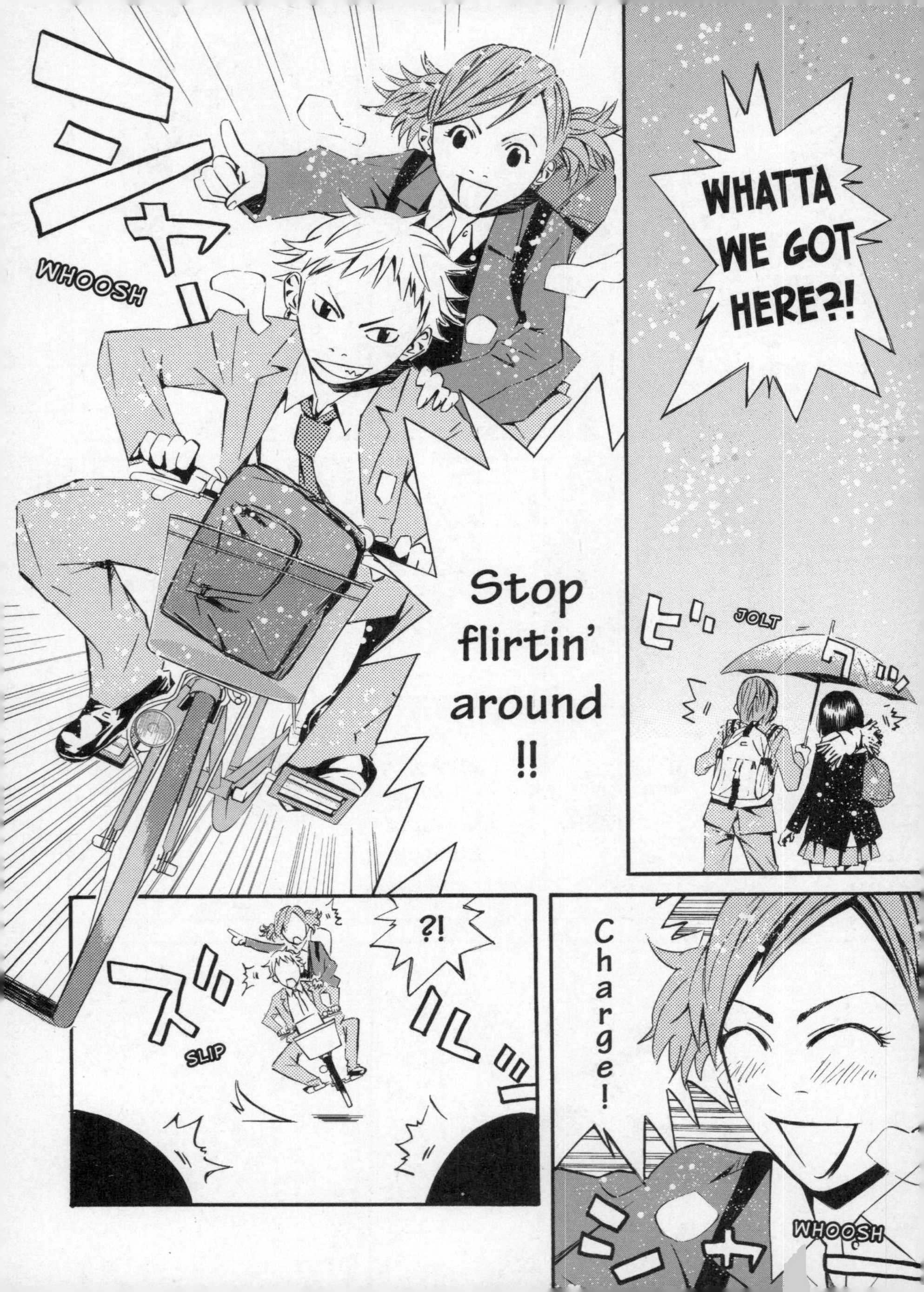
WHATTA WE GOT HERE?!
JOLT
WHOOSH
Stop flirtin' around !!
Charge!
WHOOSH
?!
SLIP

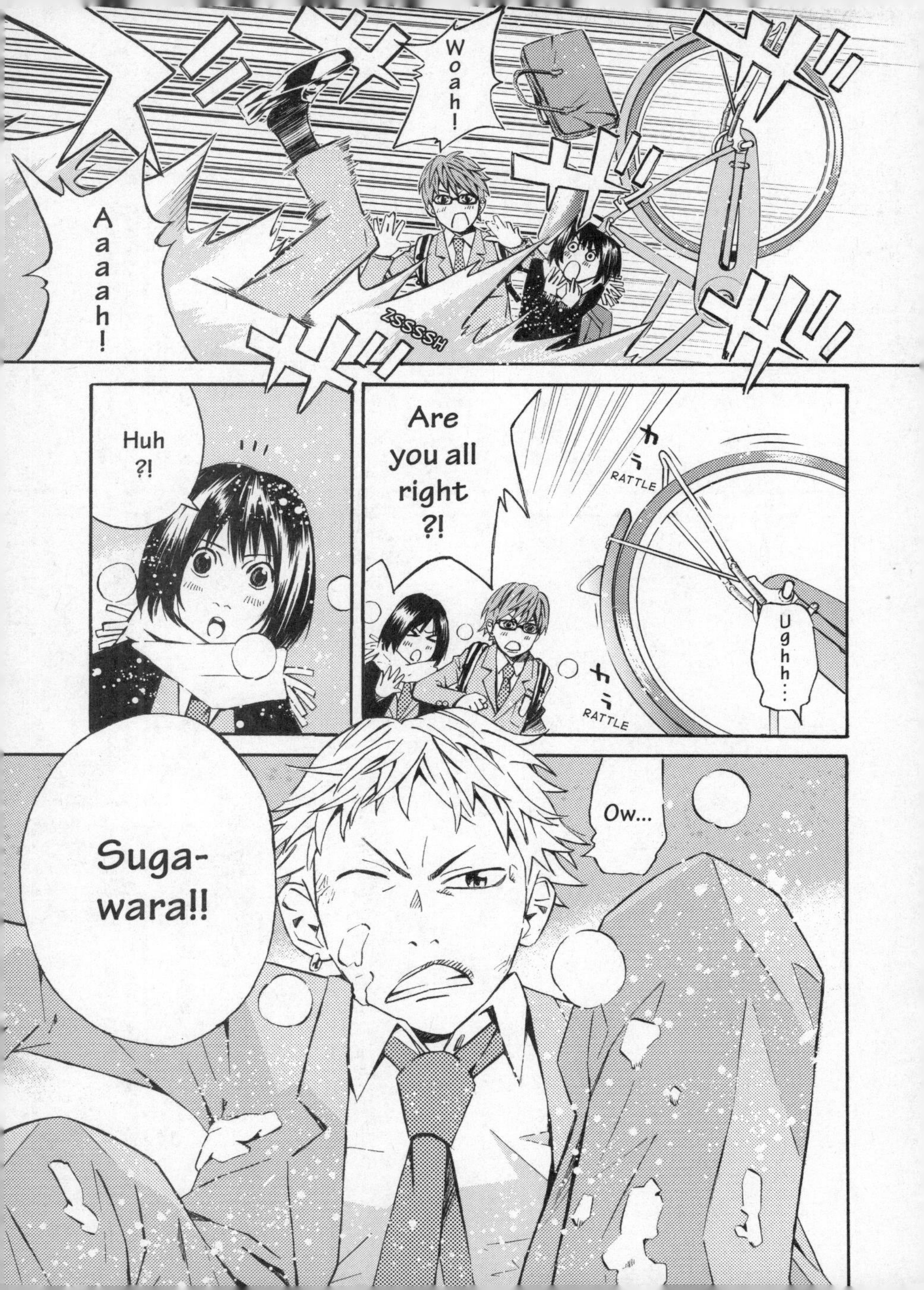
Woah!
ZSSSSH
Aaaaah!
RATTLE
Are you all right?!
Ughh...
RATTLE
Huh?!
Ow...
Suga-wara!!

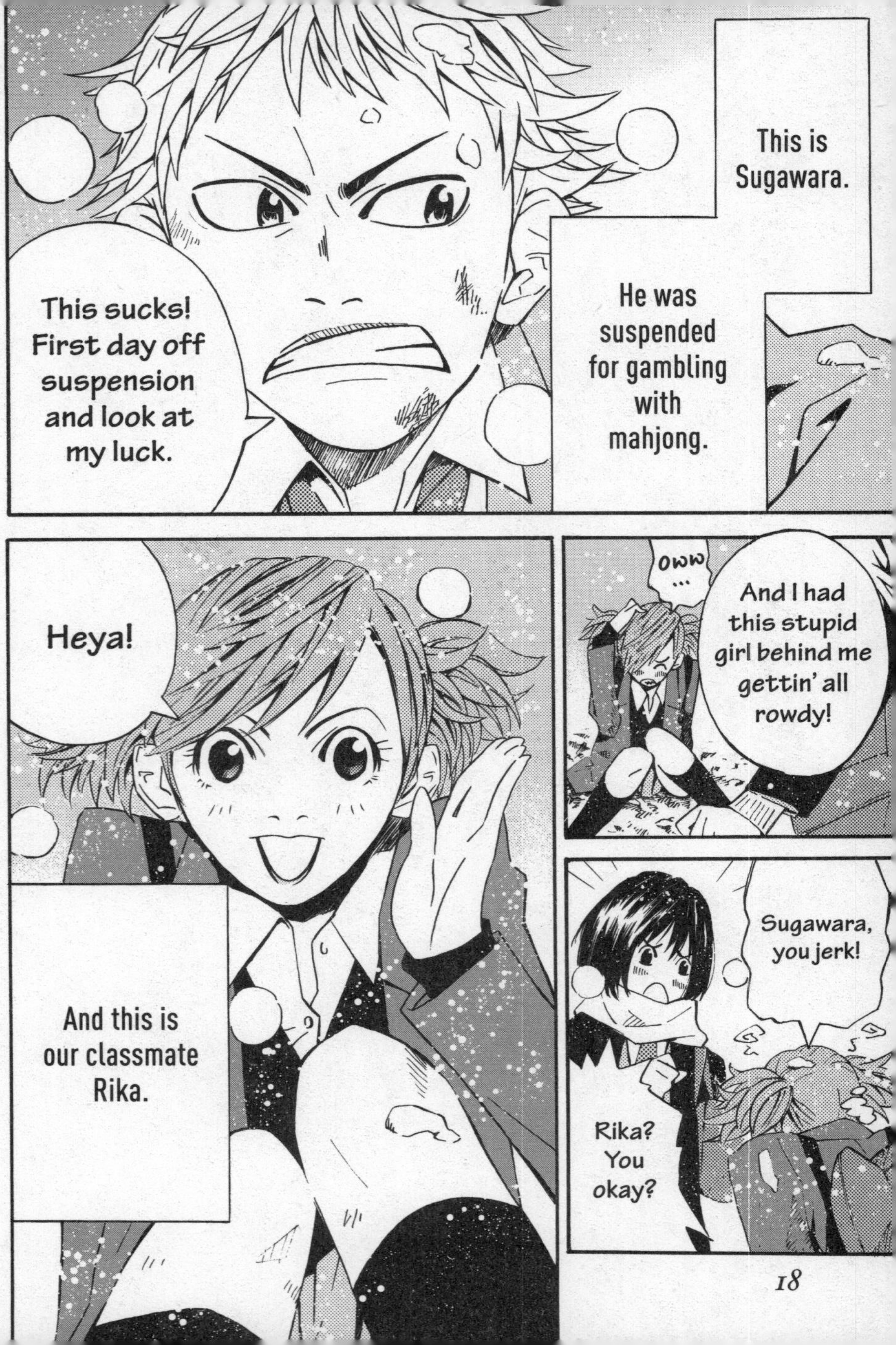
This is Sugawara.
He was suspended for gambling with mahjong.
This sucks! First day off suspension and look at my luck.
And I had this stupid girl behind me gettin' all rowdy!
Oww...
Sugawara, you jerk!
Rika? You okay?
Heya!
And this is our classmate Rika.

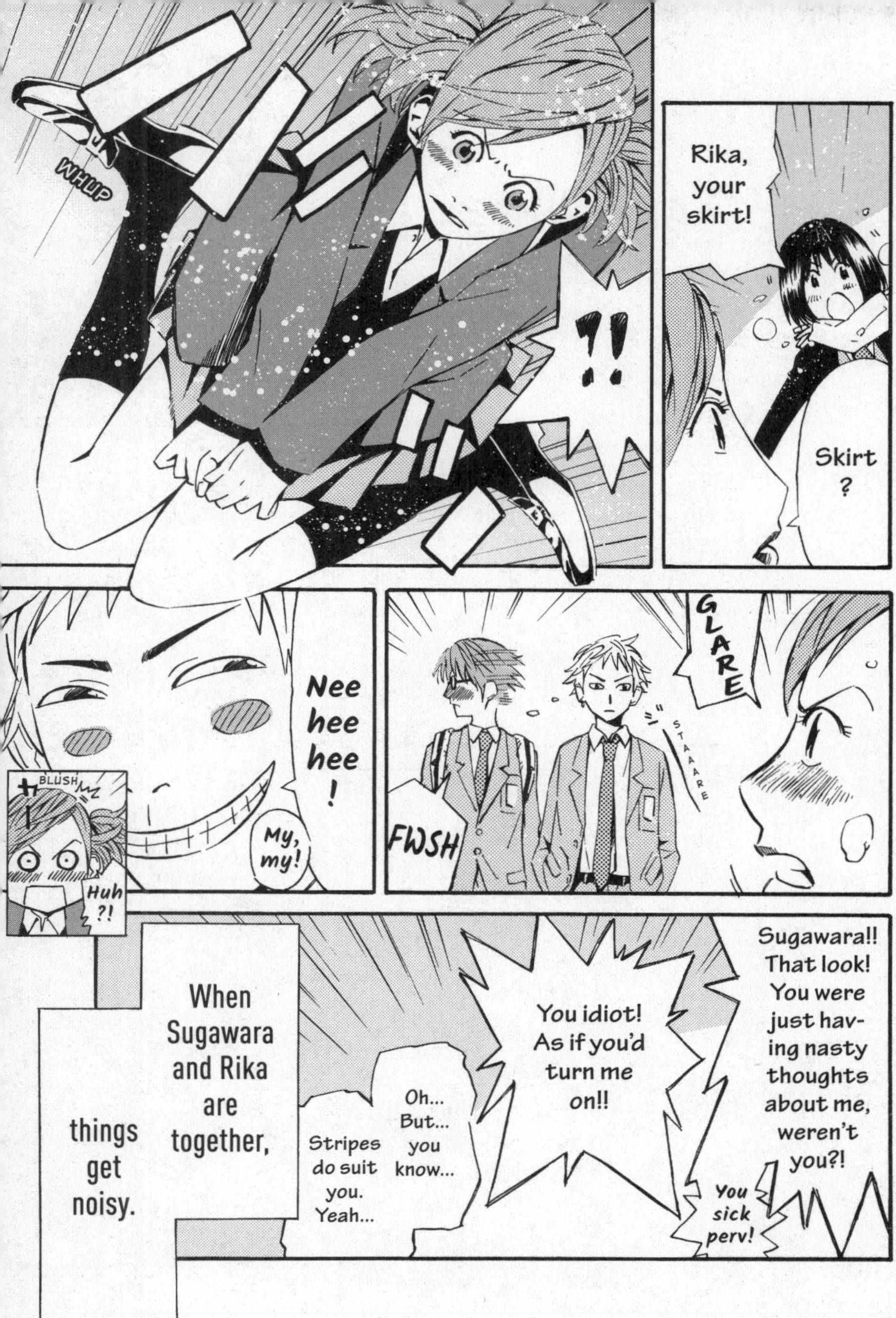
Rika, your skirt!
Skirt ?
?!!
WHLUP
GLARE
STAAARE
FWSH
Nee hee hee!
My, my!
BLUSH
Huh ?!
Sugawara!! That look! You were just hav-ing nasty thoughts about me, weren't you?!
You sick perv!
You idiot! As if you'd turn me on!!
Oh... But... you know...
Stripes do suit you. Yeah...
When Sugawara and Rika are together,
things get noisy.

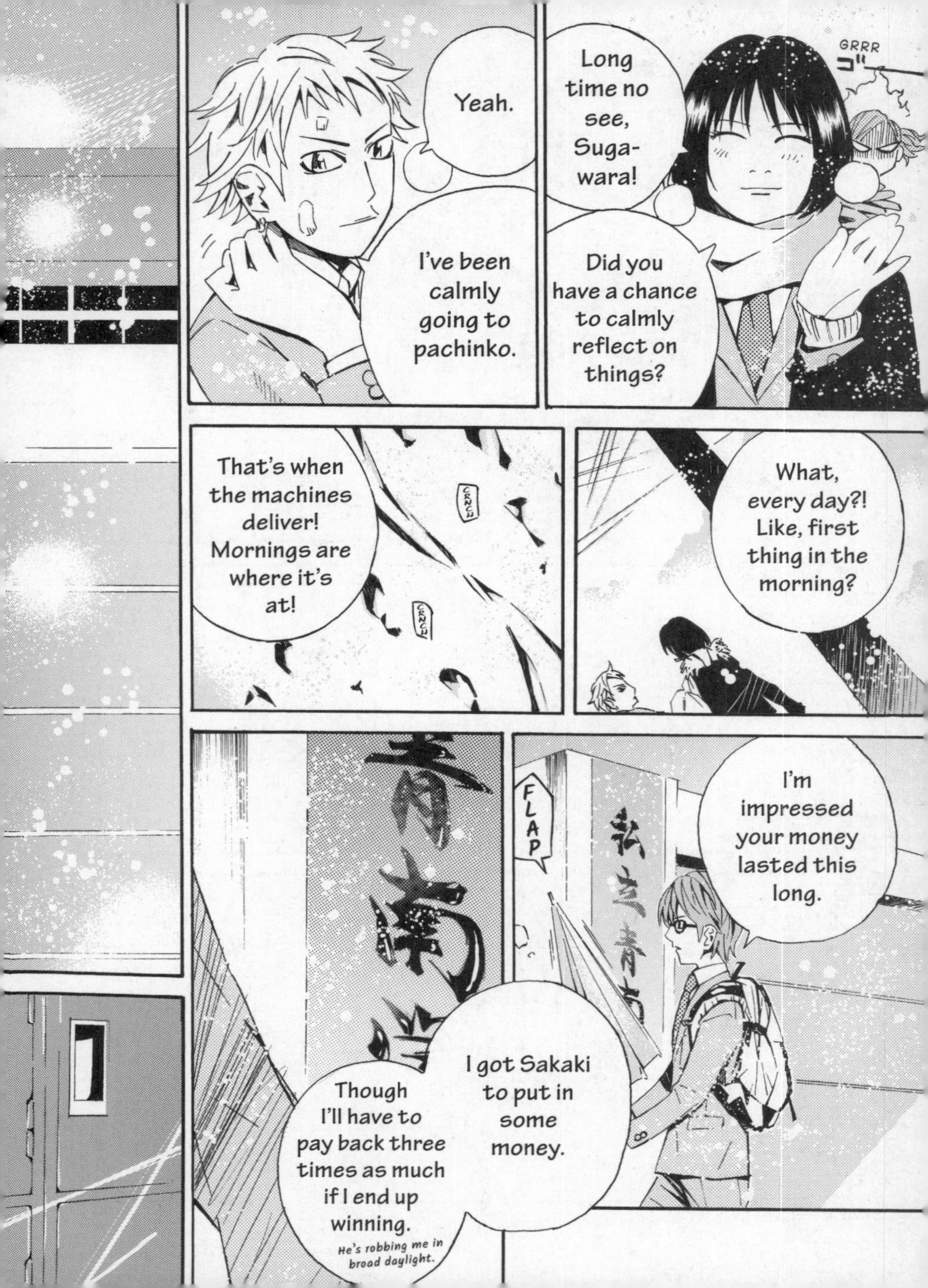
GRRR
Long time no see, Suga-wara!
Did you have a chance to calmly reflect on things?
Yeah.
I've been calmly going to pachinko.
What, every day?! Like, first thing in the morning?
That's when the machines deliver! Mornings are where it's at!
CRNCH
CRNCH
I'm impressed your money lasted this long.
FLAP
I got Sakaki to put in some money.
Though I'll have to pay back three times as much if I end up winning.
He's robbing me in broad daylight.

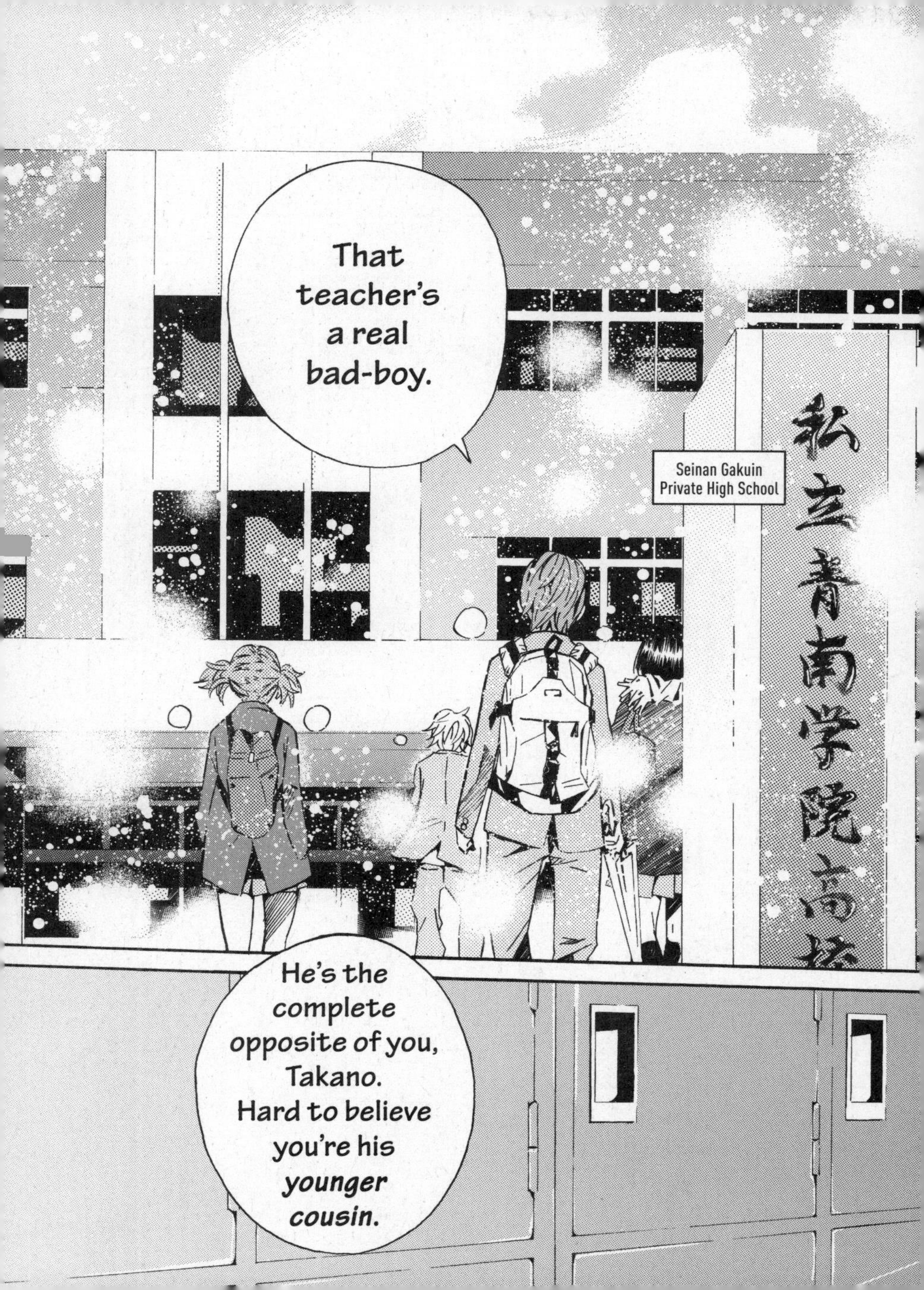
That teacher's a real bad-boy.
私立青南学院高
Seinan Gakuin Private High School
He's the complete opposite of you, Takano. Hard to believe you're his *younger cousin*.

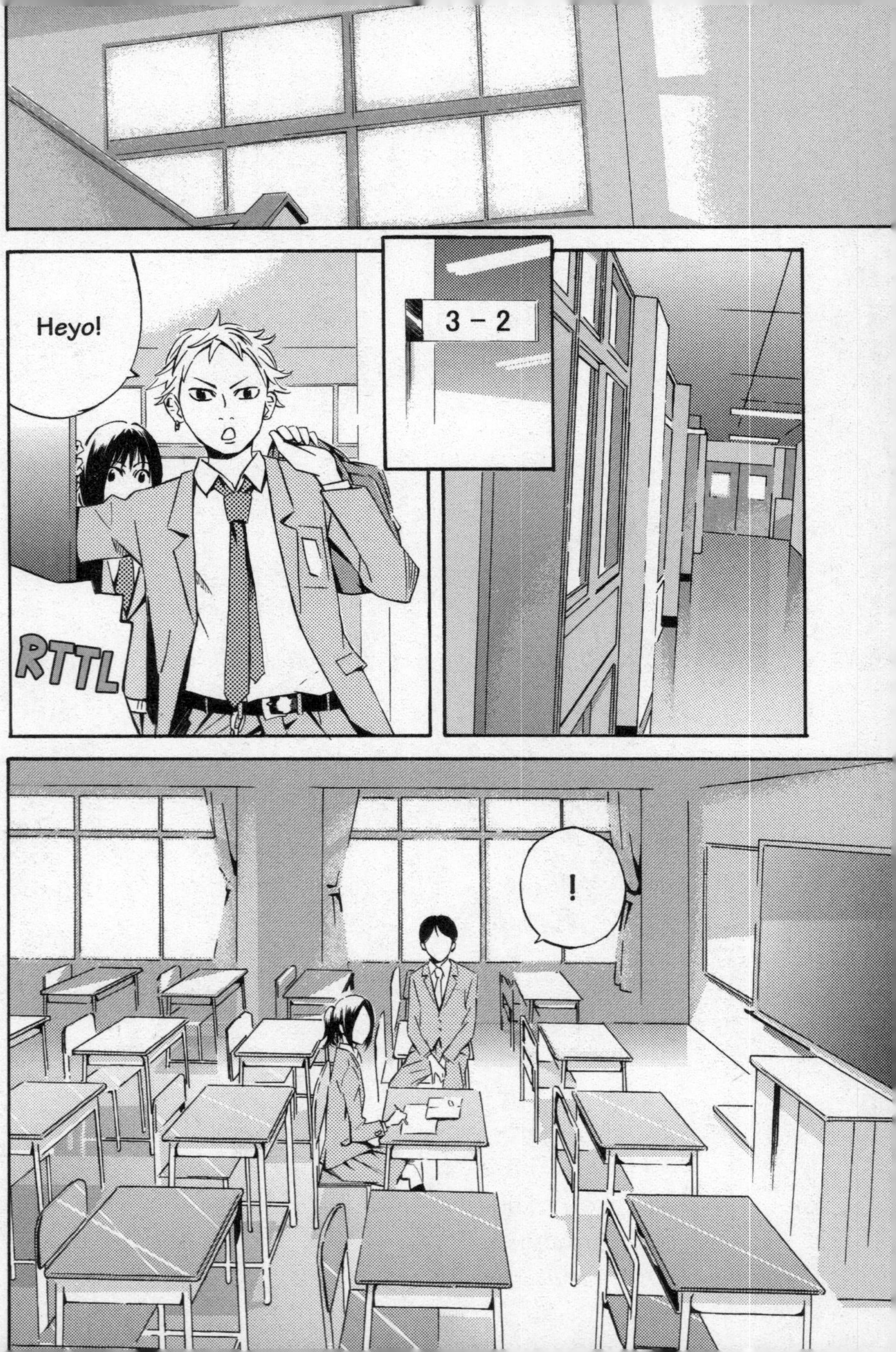
3 – 2
Heyo!
RTTL
!

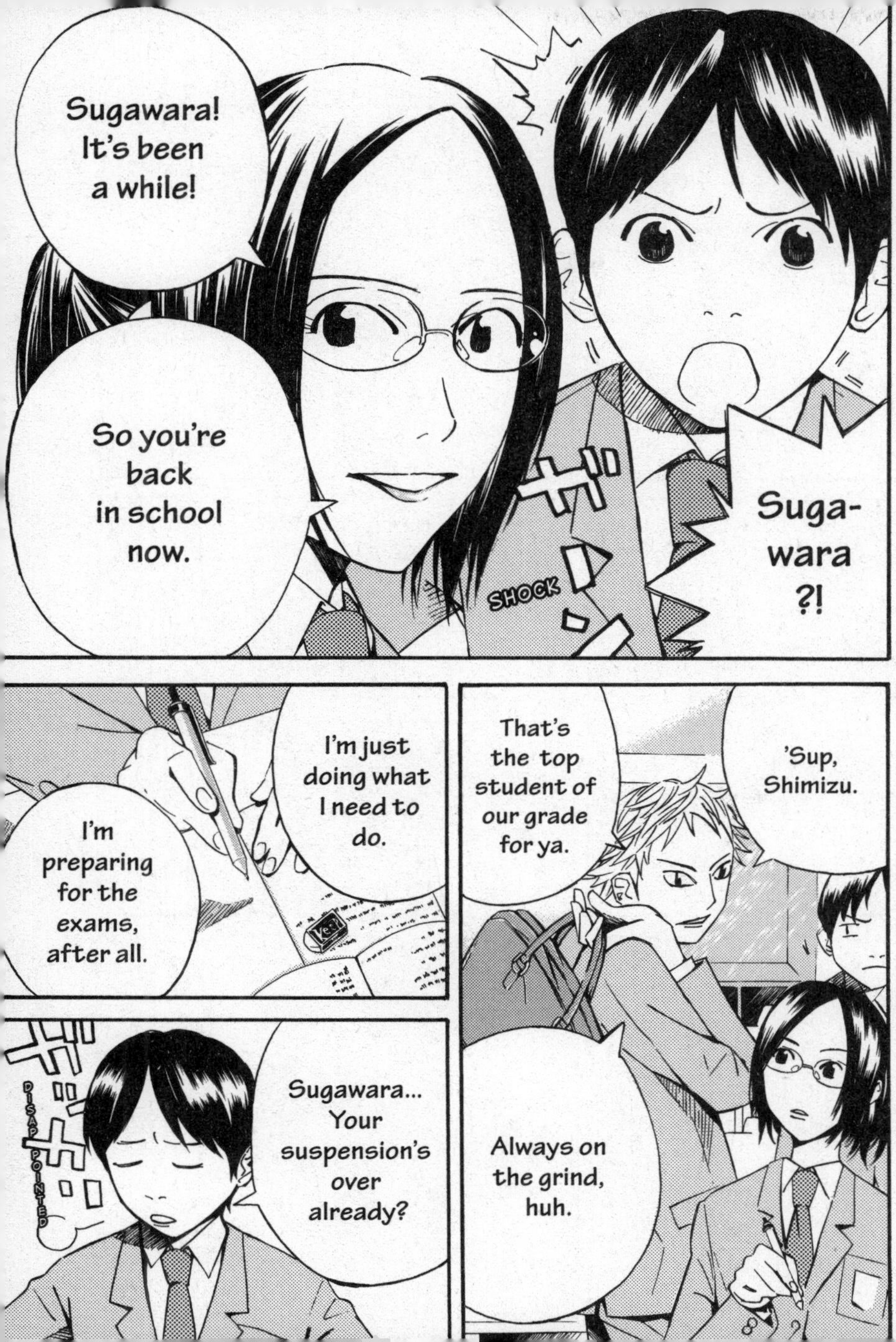
Sugawara! It's been a while!
So you're back in school now.
Suga-wara ?!
SHOCK
'Sup, Shimizu.
That's the top student of our grade for ya.
Always on the grind, huh.
I'm just doing what I need to do.
I'm preparing for the exams, after all.
Sugawara... Your suspension's over already?
DISAPPOINTED

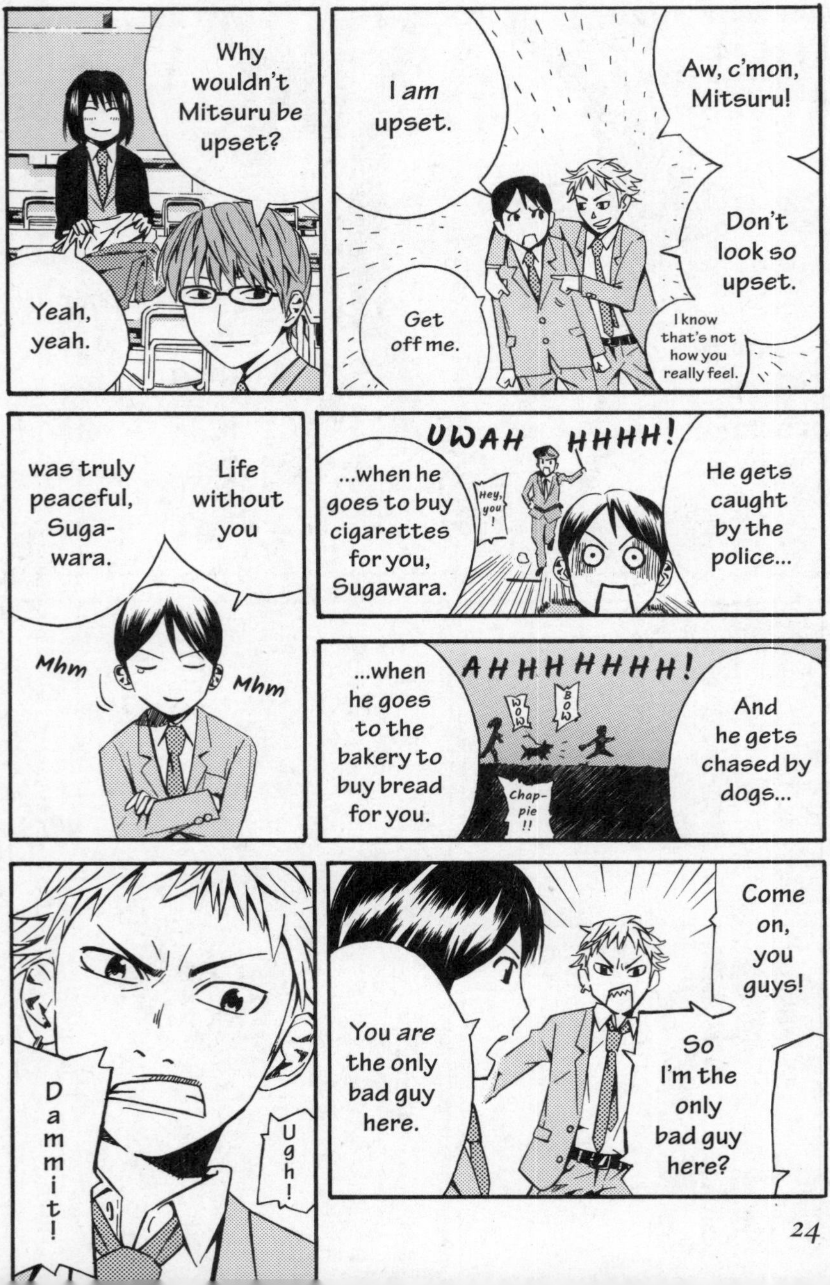

Aw, c'mon, Mitsuru!
I *am* upset.
Don't look so upset.
I know that's not how you really feel.
Get off me.
Why wouldn't Mitsuru be upset?
Yeah, yeah.
He gets caught by the police...
UWAH HHHH!
Hey, you!
...when he goes to buy cigarettes for you, Sugawara.
And he gets chased by dogs...
AHHHHHHH!
BOW
WOW
Chap-pie!!
...when he goes to the bakery to buy bread for you.
Life without you
was truly peaceful, Sugawara.
Mhm
Mhm
Come on, you guys!
So I'm the only bad guy here?
You *are* the only bad guy here.
Ugh!
Dammit!

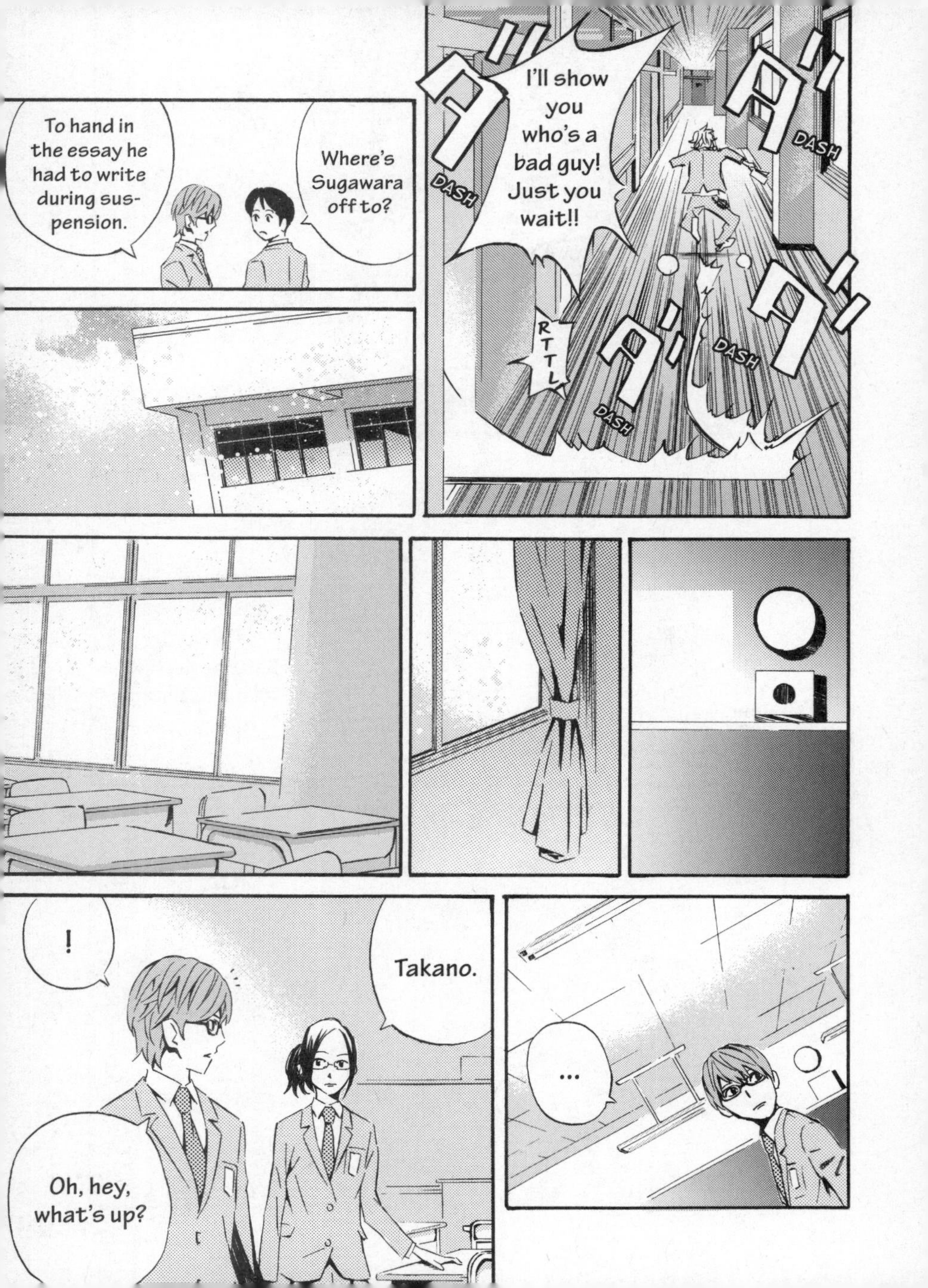

ダッ
DASH
I'll show you who's a bad guy! Just you wait!!
ダッ
DASH
ダッ
DASH
ダッ
DASH
RTTL
Where's Sugawara off to?
To hand in the essay he had to write during suspension.
...
Takano.
!
Oh, hey, what's up?

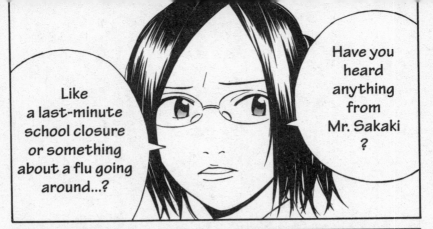

Have you heard anything from Mr. Sakaki ?
Like a last-minute school closure or something about a flu going around...?
We would've gotten a call through the phone tree if something happened.
There's been nothing.
I see what you mean, though. It's been bothering me, too.

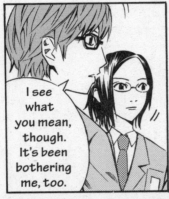

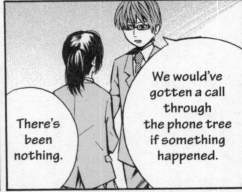

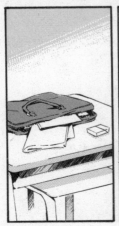

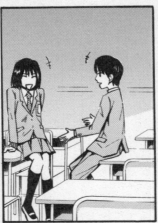

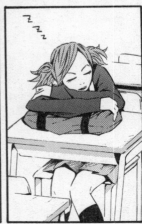

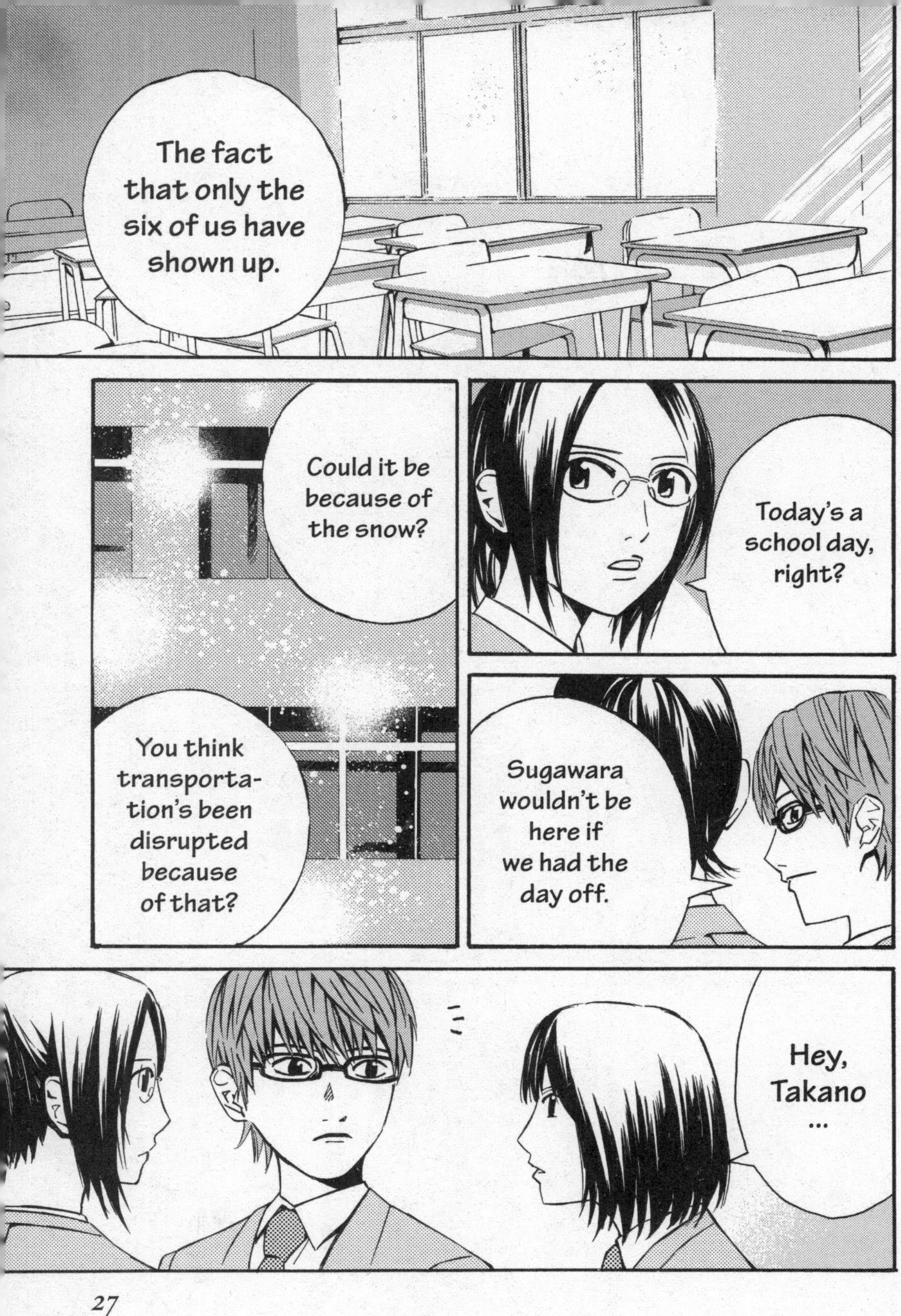
The fact that only the six of us have shown up.
Today's a school day, right?
Sugawara wouldn't be here if we had the day off.
Could it be because of the snow?
You think transportation's been disrupted because of that?
Hey, Takano ...

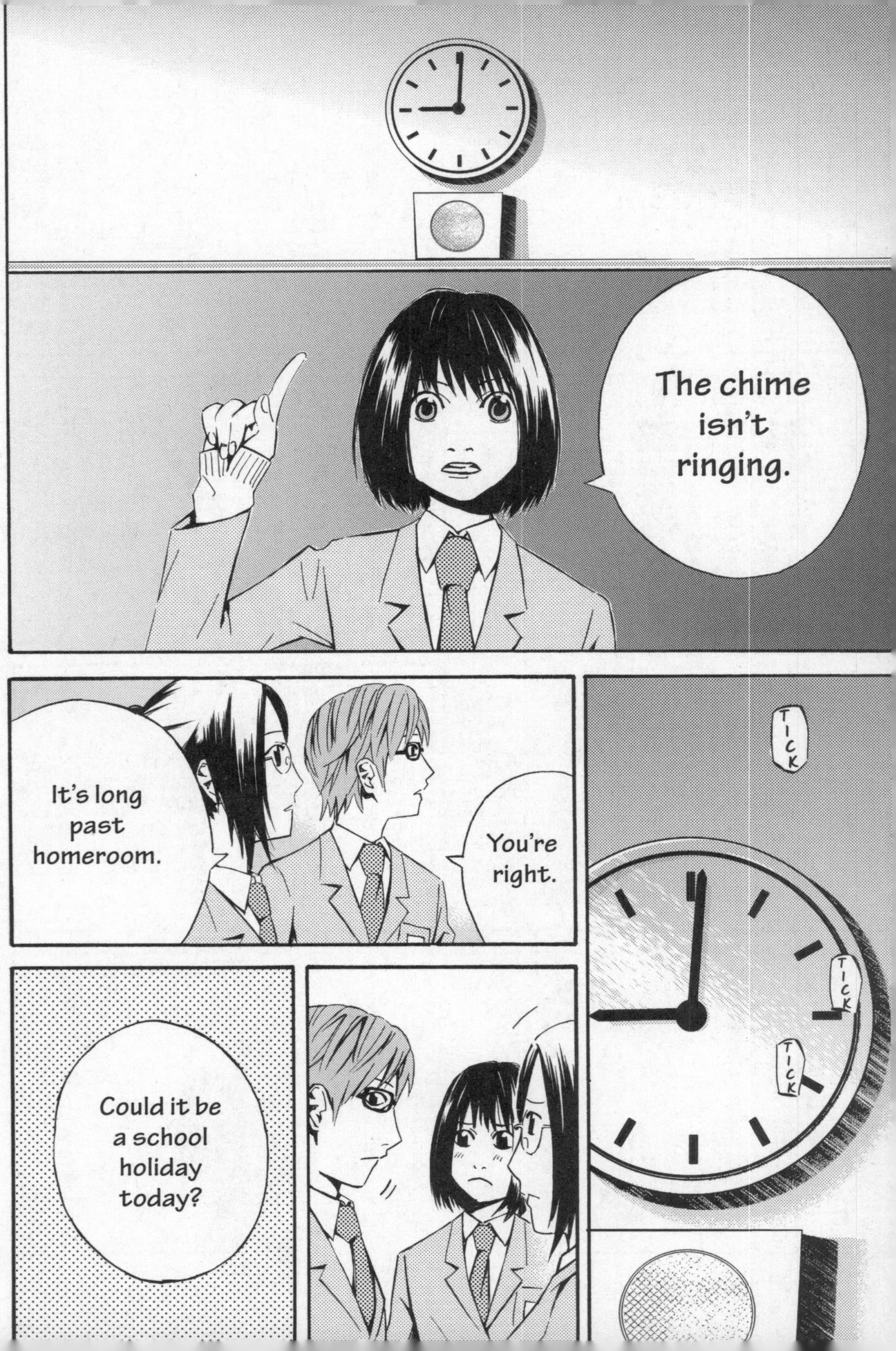
The chime isn't ringing.
TICK
TICK
TICK
You're right.
It's long past homeroom.
Could it be a school holiday today?

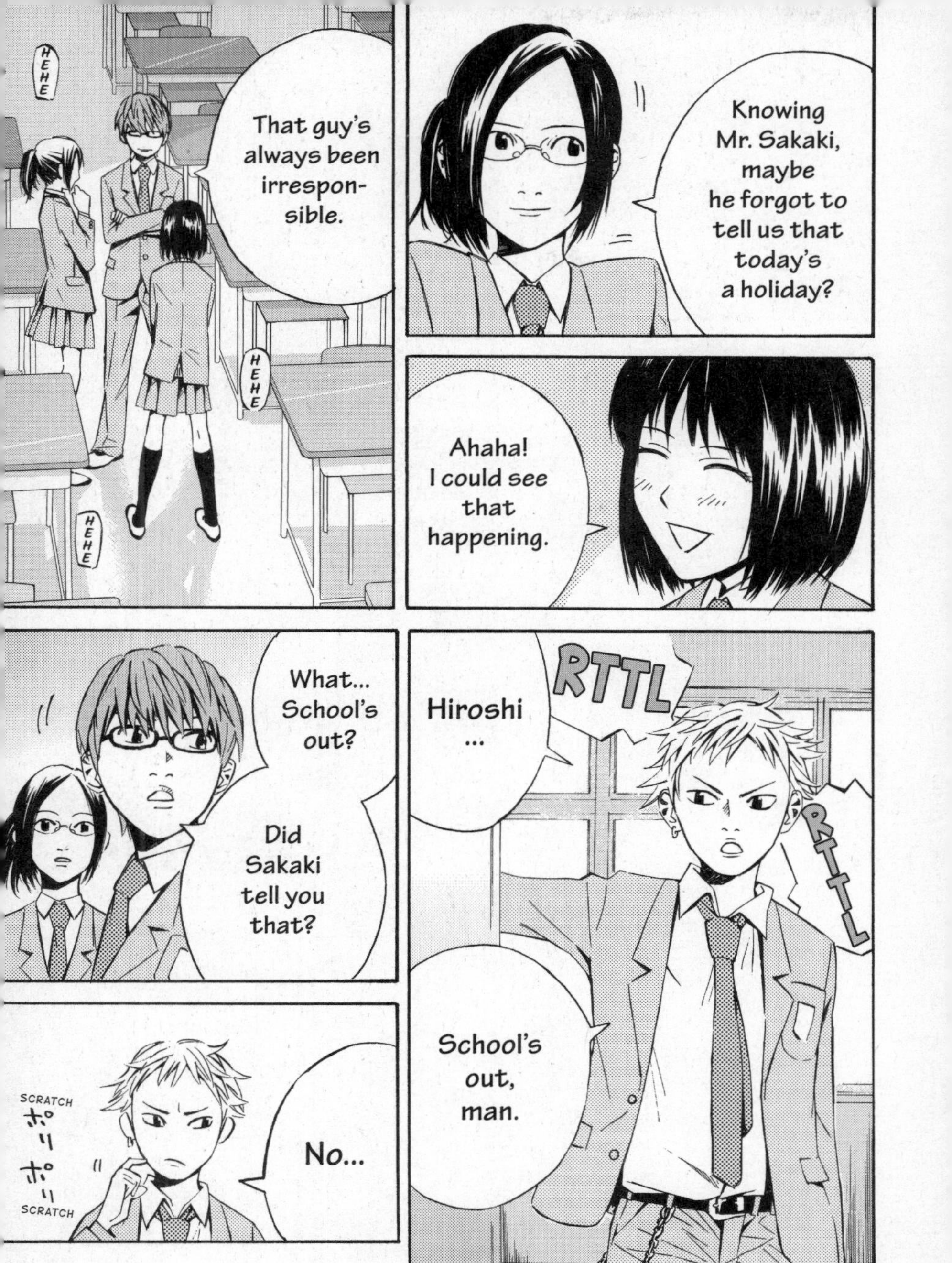
Knowing Mr. Sakaki, maybe he forgot to tell us that today's a holiday?
Ahaha! I could see that happening.
That guy's always been irrespon-sible.
HEHE
HEHE
HEHE
RTTL
Hiroshi ...
School's out, man.
RTTL
What... School's out?
Did Sakaki tell you that?
No...
SCRATCH
ポリ
ポリ
SCRATCH

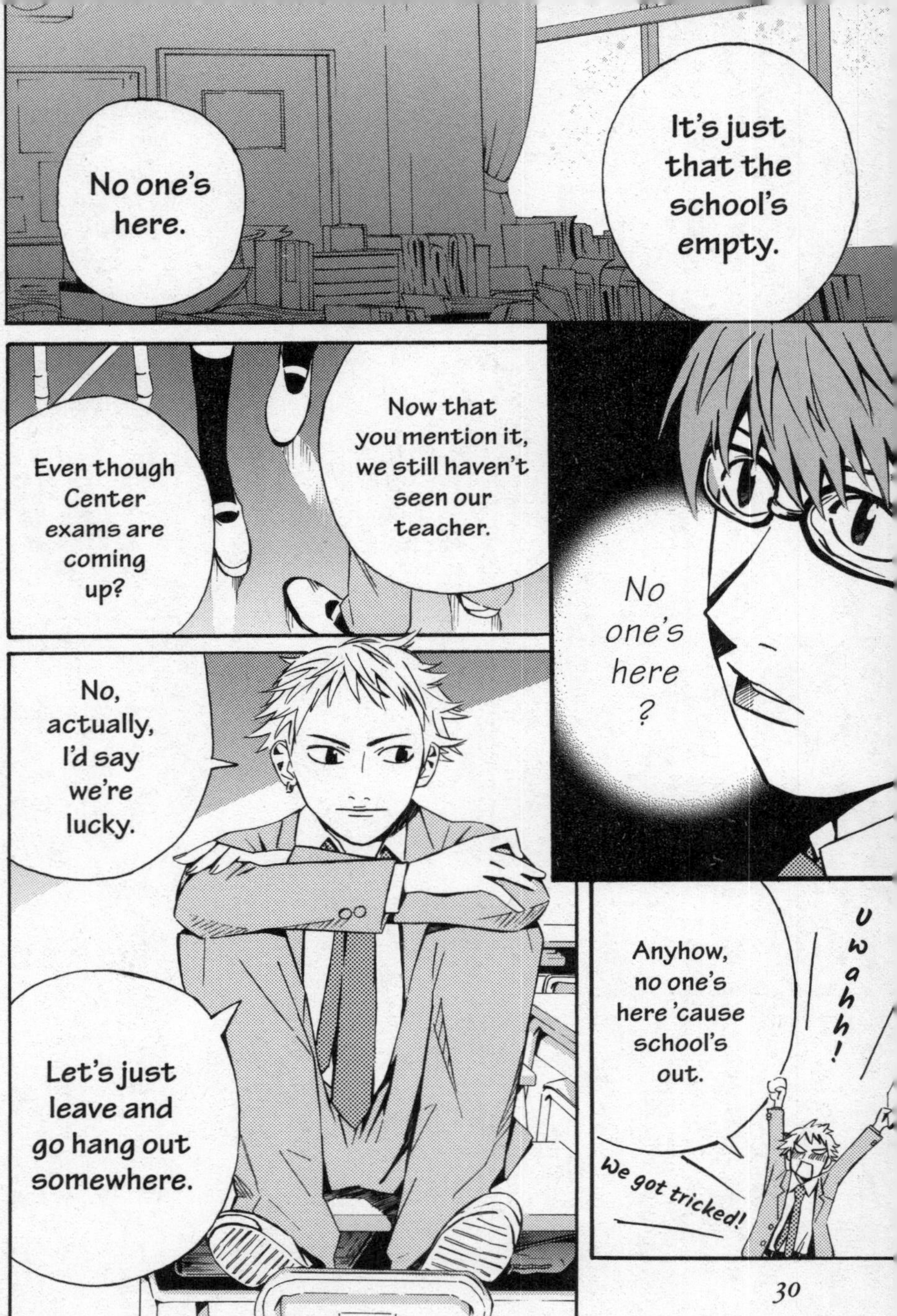
It's just that the school's empty.
No one's here.
No one's here?
Now that you mention it, we still haven't seen our teacher.
Even though Center exams are coming up?
No, actually, I'd say we're lucky.
Let's just leave and go hang out somewhere.
Anyhow, no one's here 'cause school's out.
Uwahh!
We got tricked!

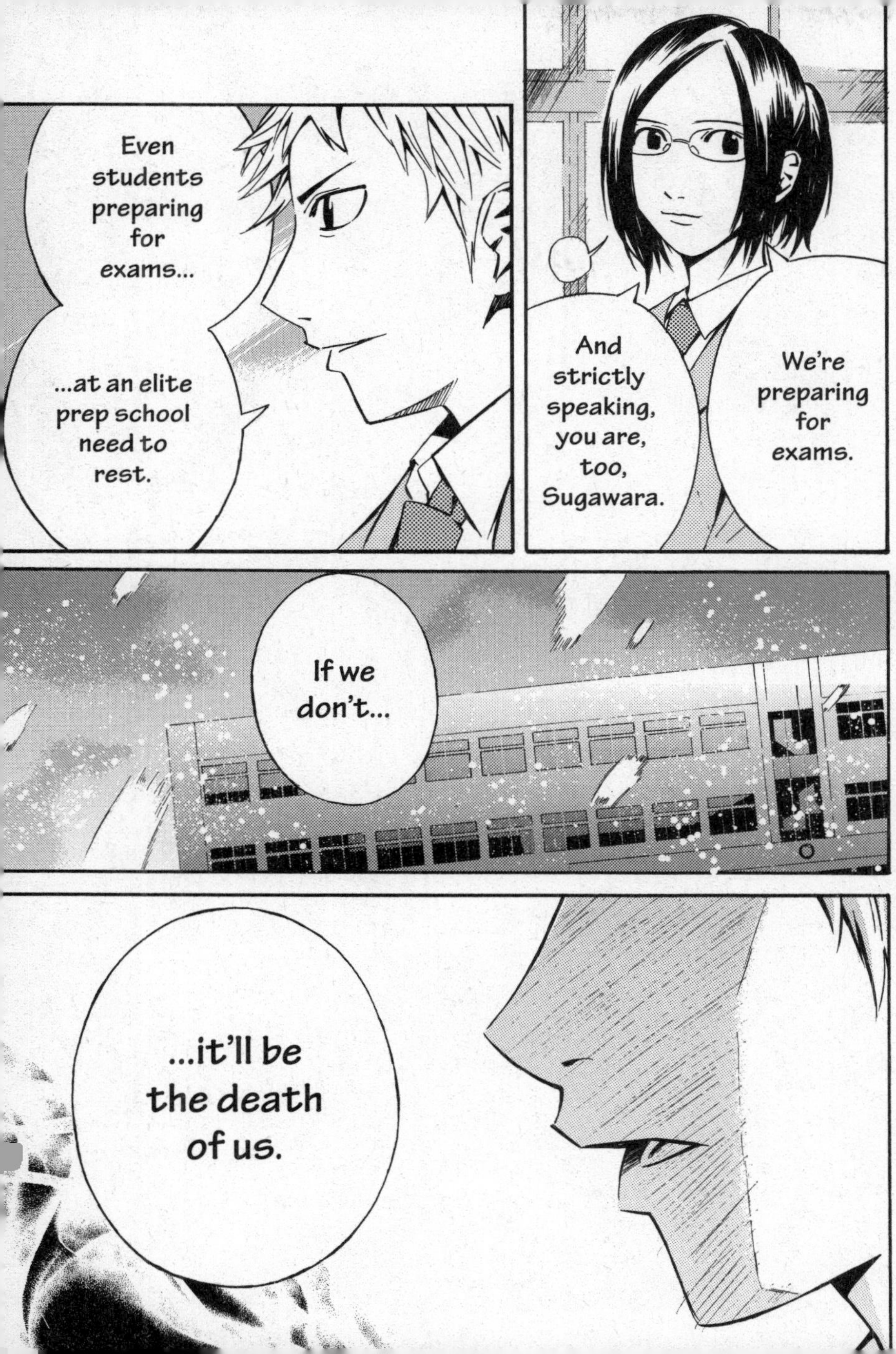
We're preparing for exams.
And strictly speaking, you are, too, Sugawara.
Even students preparing for exams...
...at an elite prep school need to rest.
If we don't...
...it'll be the death of us.

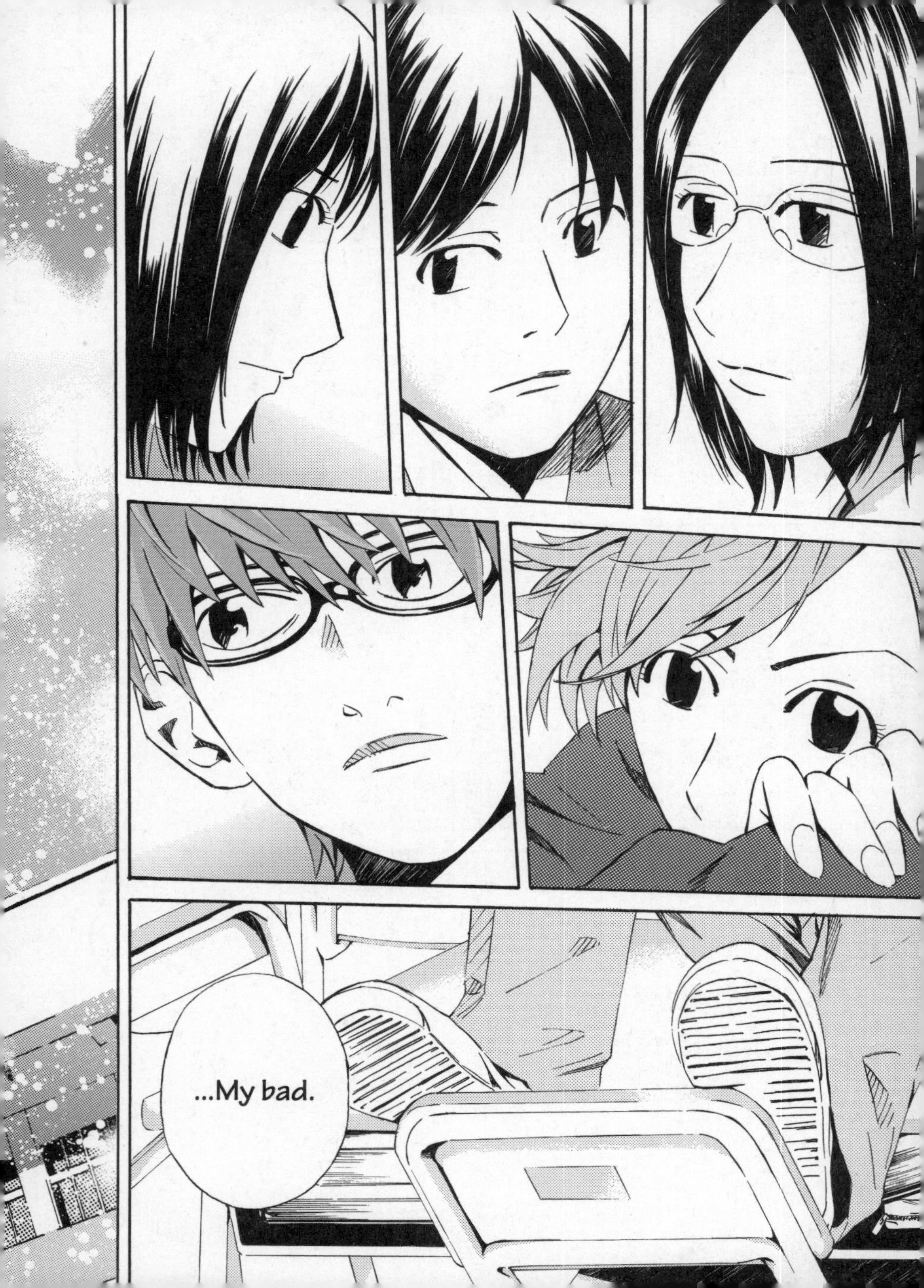
...My bad.

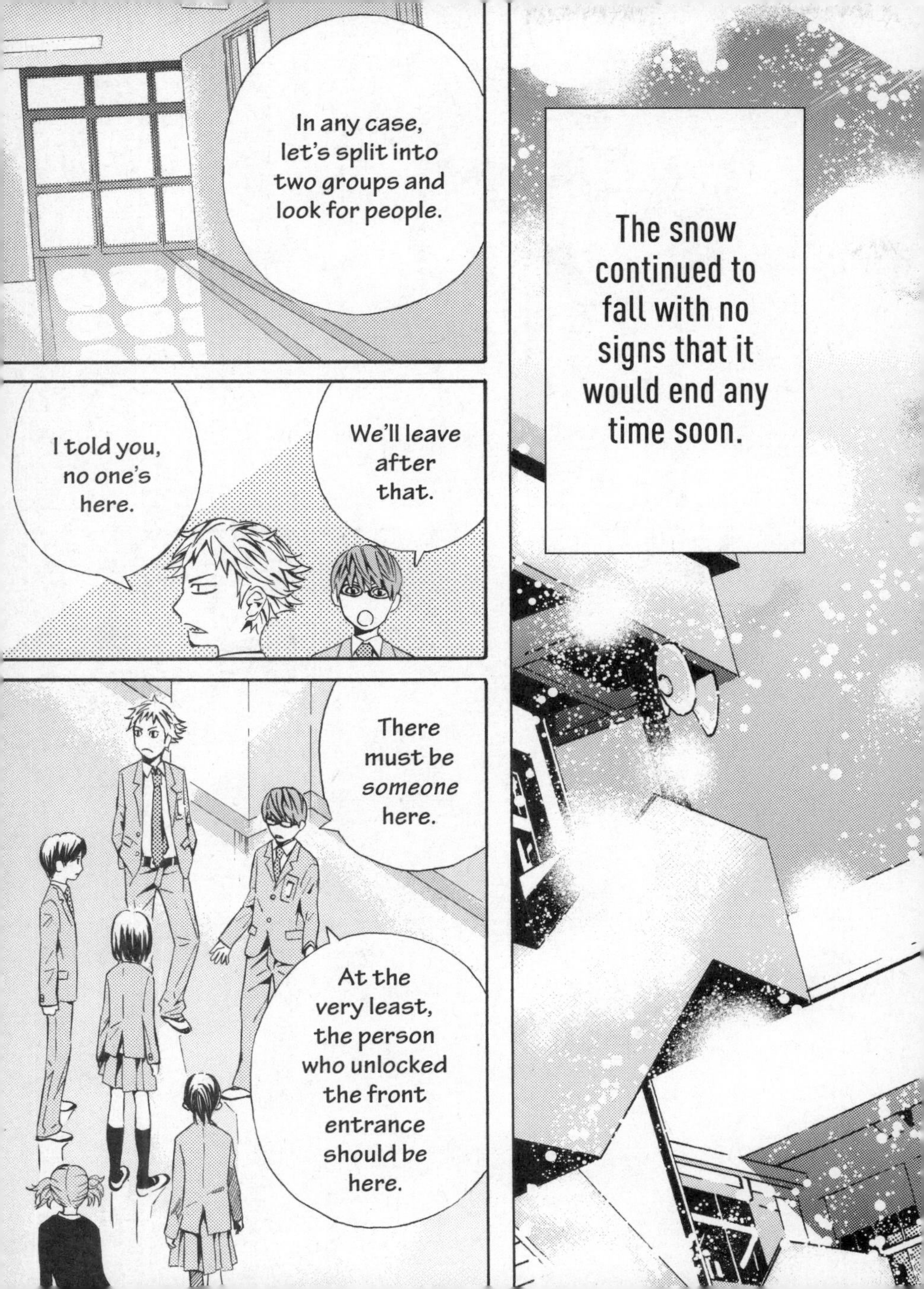
The snow continued to fall with no signs that it would end any time soon.
In any case, let's split into two groups and look for people.
We'll leave after that.
I told you, no one's here.
There must be *someone* here.
At the very least, the person who unlocked the front entrance should be here.

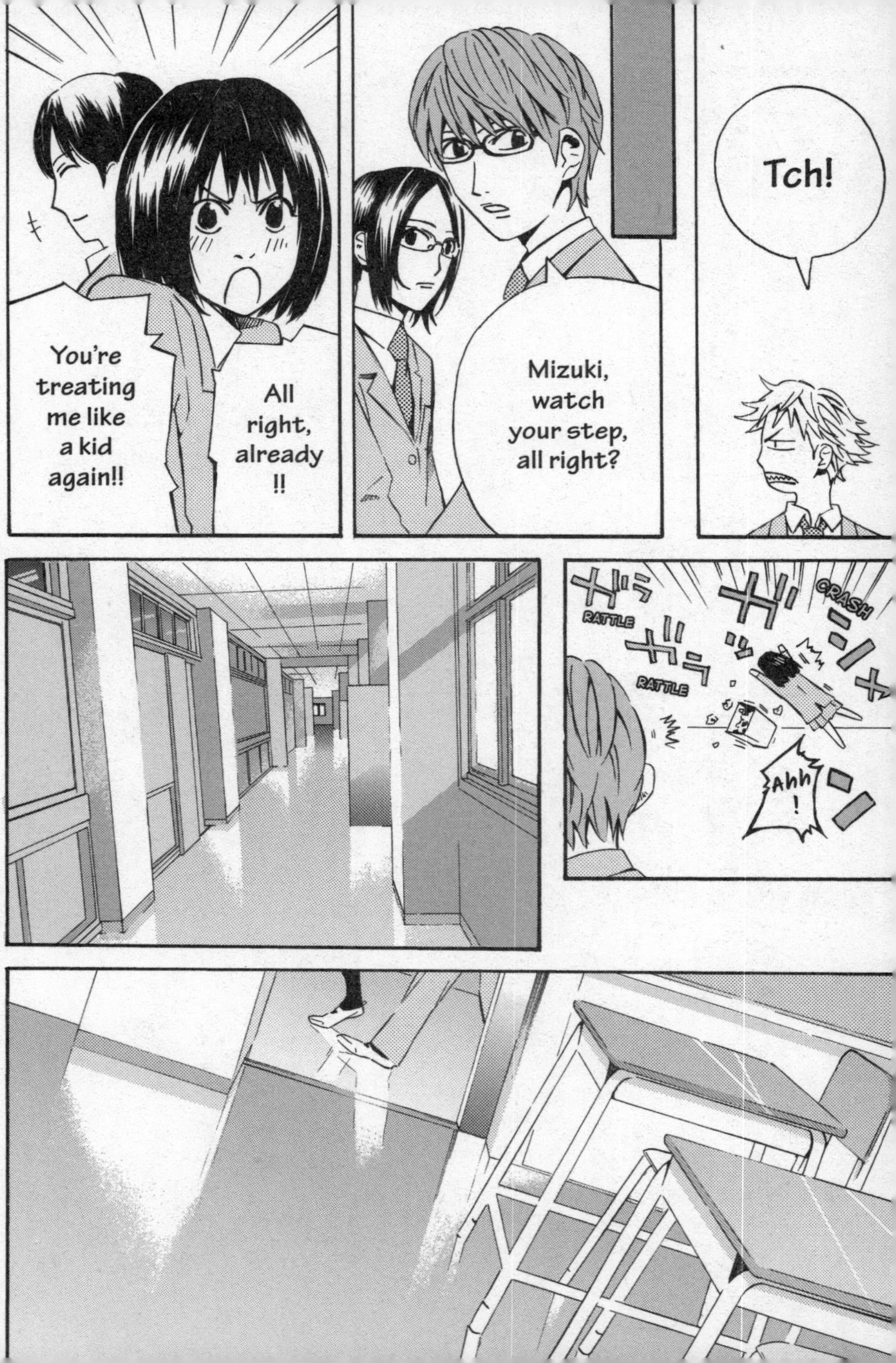
Tch!
Mizuki, watch your step, all right?
All right, already!!
You're treating me like a kid again!!
CRASH
RATTLE
RATTLE
Ahh!

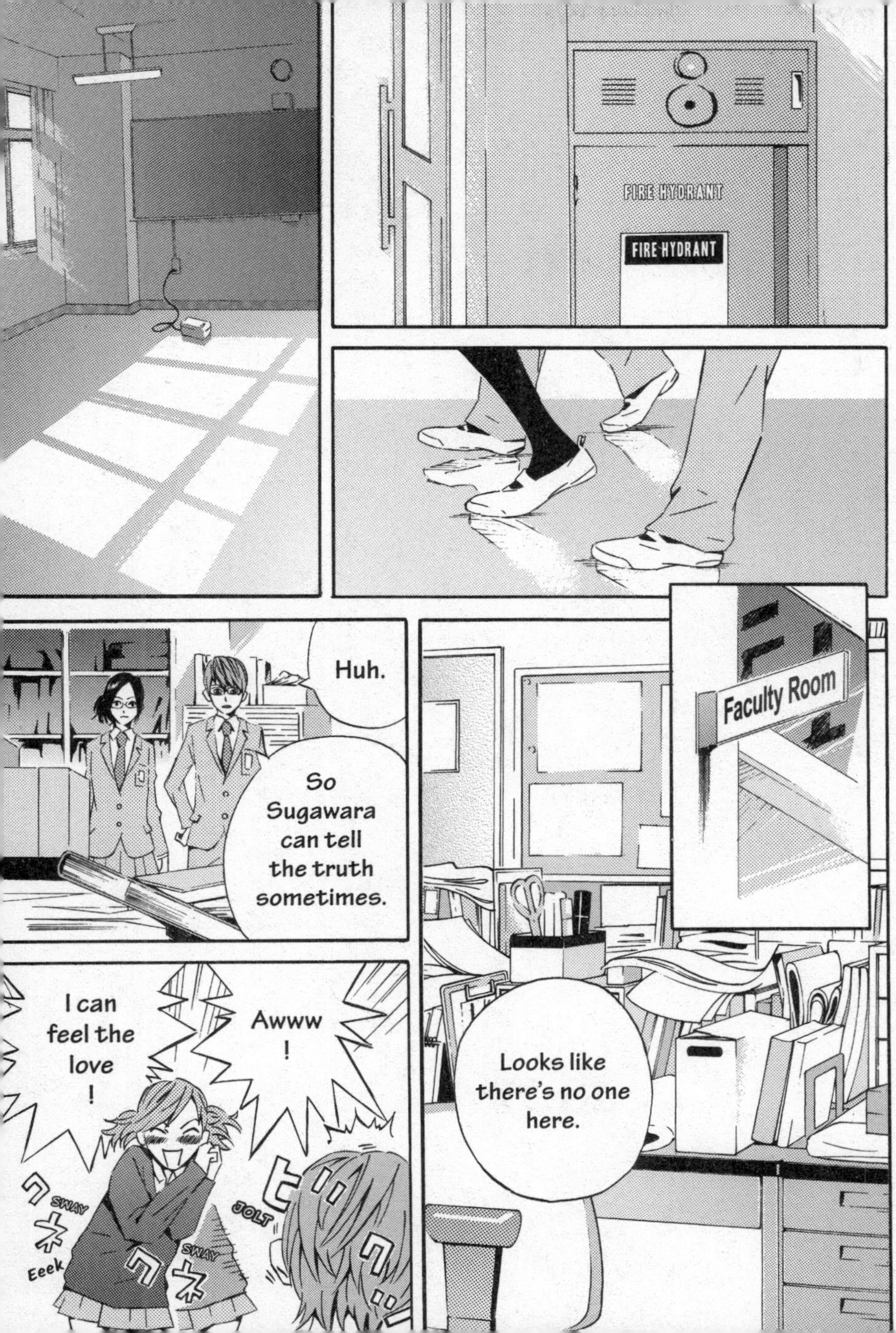
FIRE HYDRANT
FIRE HYDRANT
Faculty Room
Looks like there's no one here.
Huh.
So Sugawara can tell the truth sometimes.
Awww!
I can feel the love!
JOLT
SWAY
SWAY
Eeek

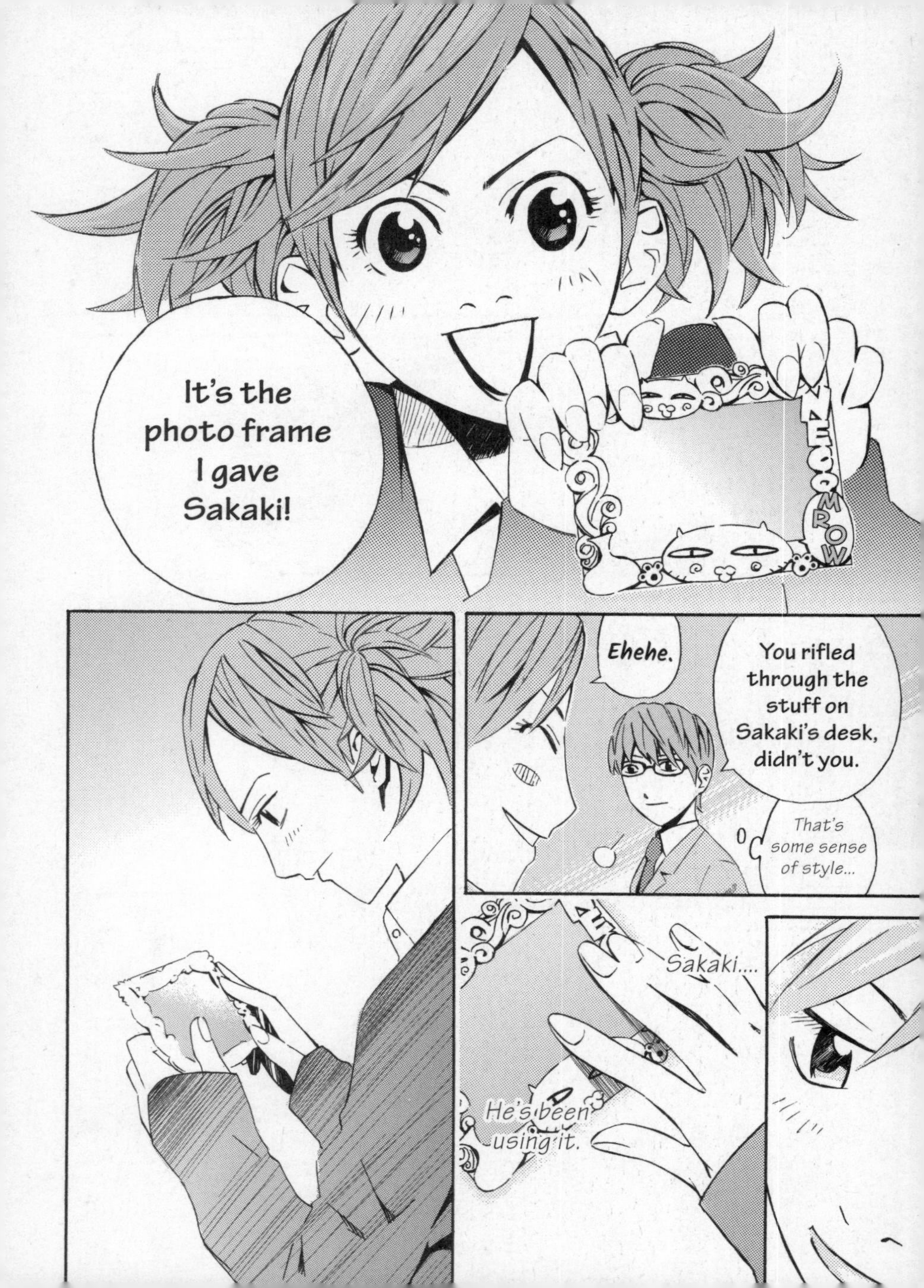
It's the photo frame I gave Sakaki!
You rifled through the stuff on Sakaki's desk, didn't you.
Ehehe.
That's some sense of style...
Sakaki....
He's been using it.

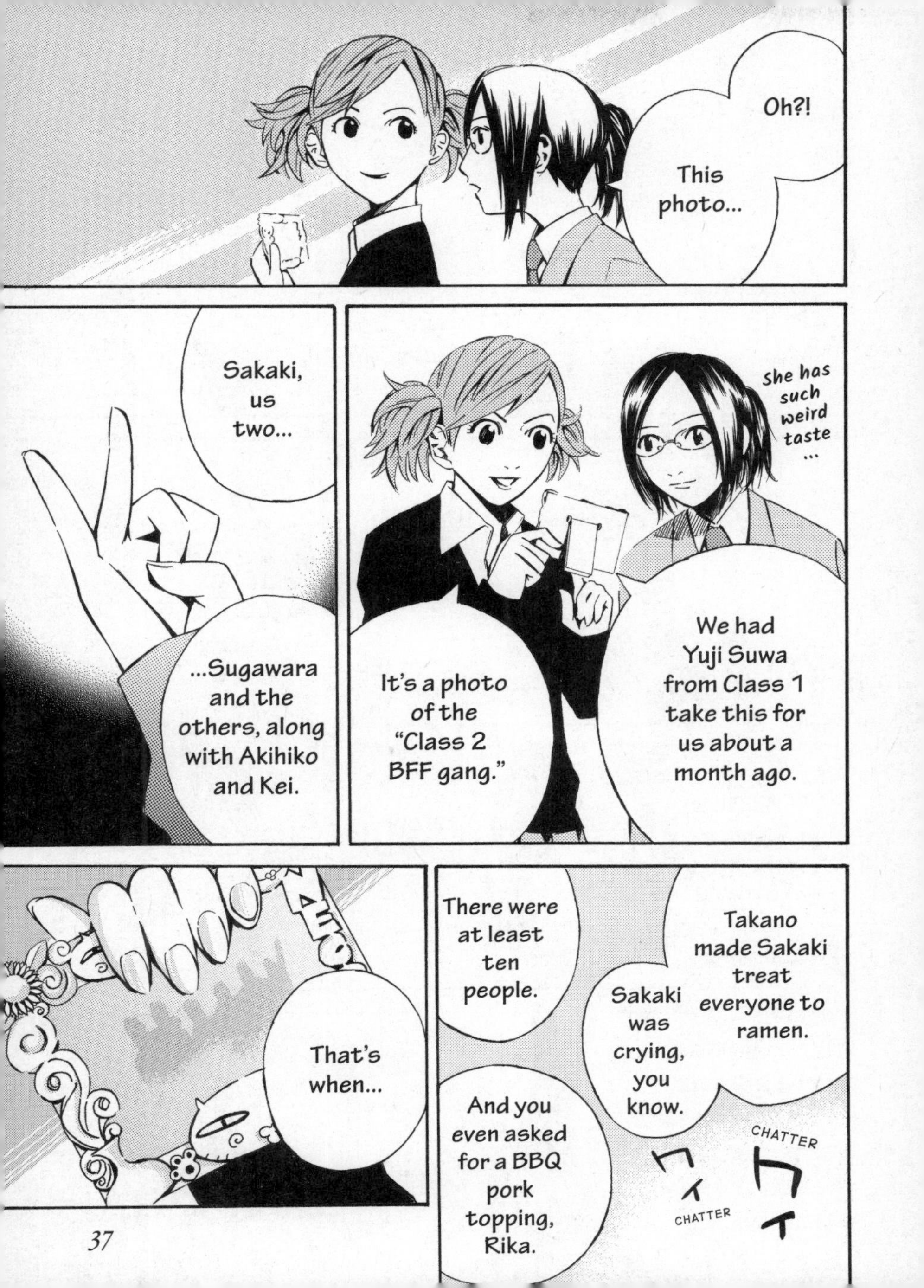
Oh?!
This photo...
she has such weird taste ...
We had Yuji Suwa from Class 1 take this for us about a month ago.
It's a photo of the "Class 2 BFF gang."
Sakaki, us two...
...Sugawara and the others, along with Akihiko and Kei.
Takano made Sakaki treat everyone to ramen.
There were at least ten people.
Sakaki was crying, you know.
CHATTER
CHATTER
And you even asked for a BBQ pork topping, Rika.
That's when...

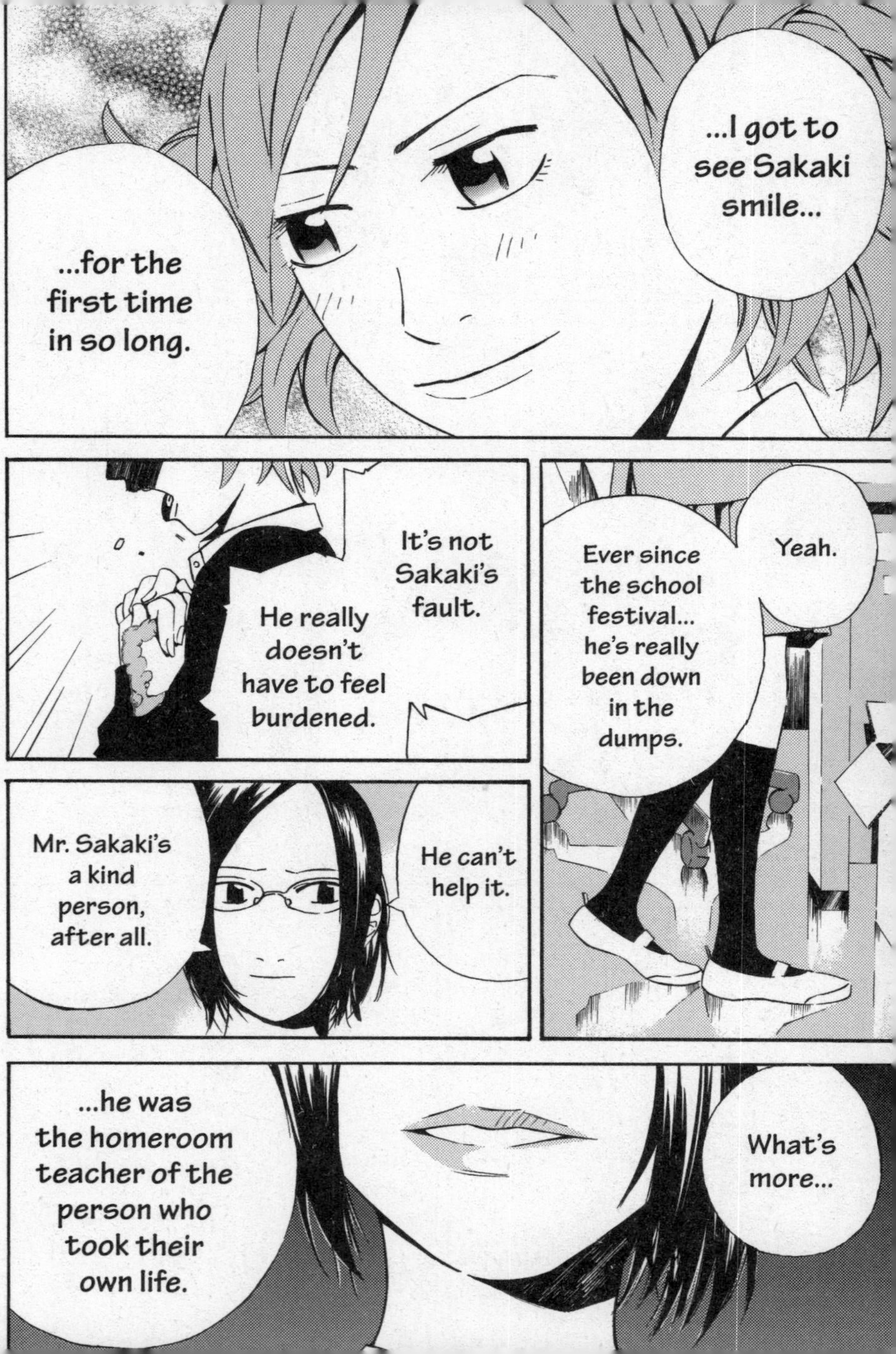
...I got to see Sakaki smile...
...for the first time in so long.
Yeah.
Ever since the school festival... he's really been down in the dumps.
It's not Sakaki's fault.
He really doesn't have to feel burdened.
He can't help it.
Mr. Sakaki's a kind person, after all.
What's more...
...he was the homeroom teacher of the person who took their own life.

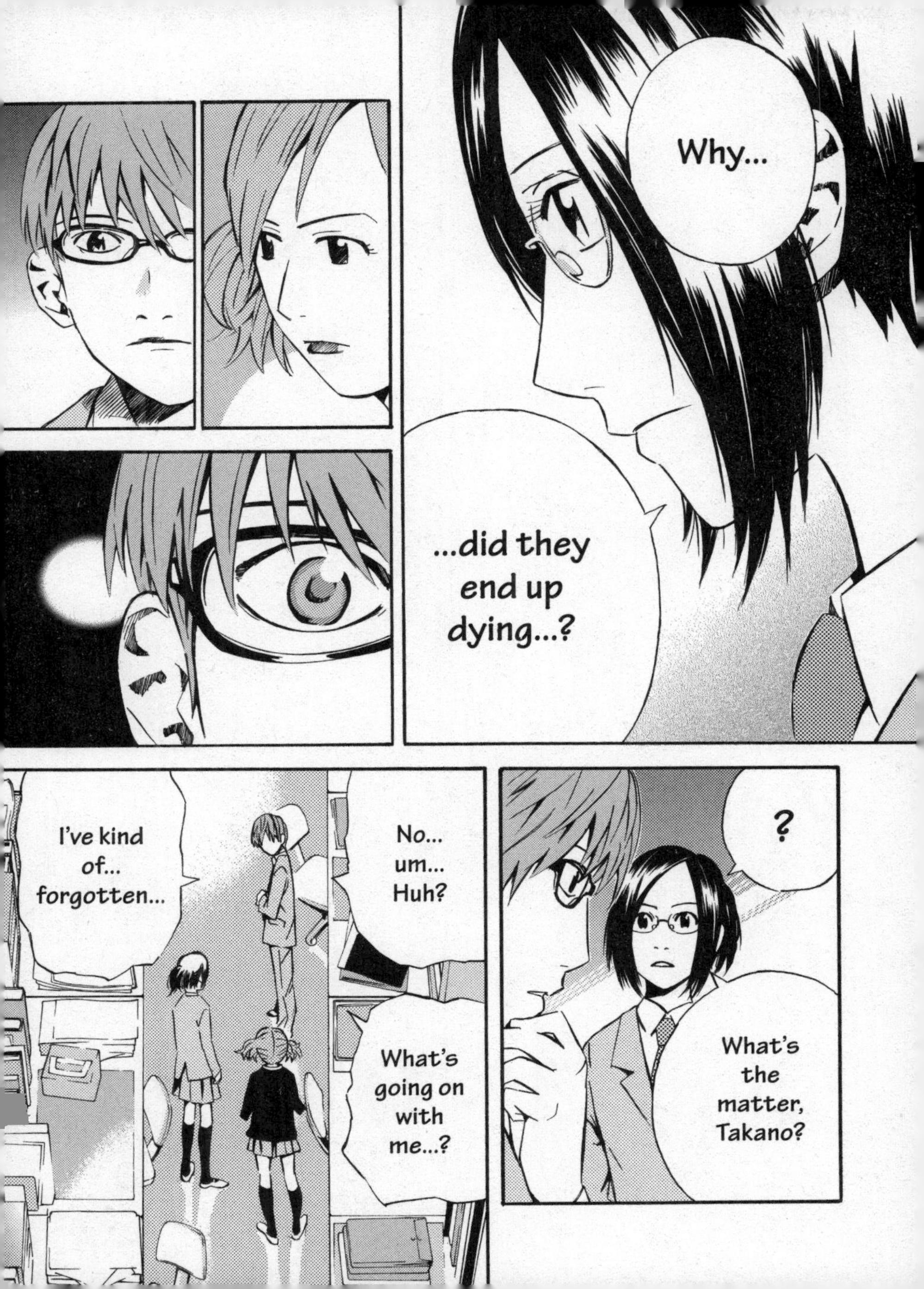
Why...
...did they end up dying...?
?
What's the matter, Takano?
No... um... Huh?
I've kind of... forgotten...
What's going on with me...?

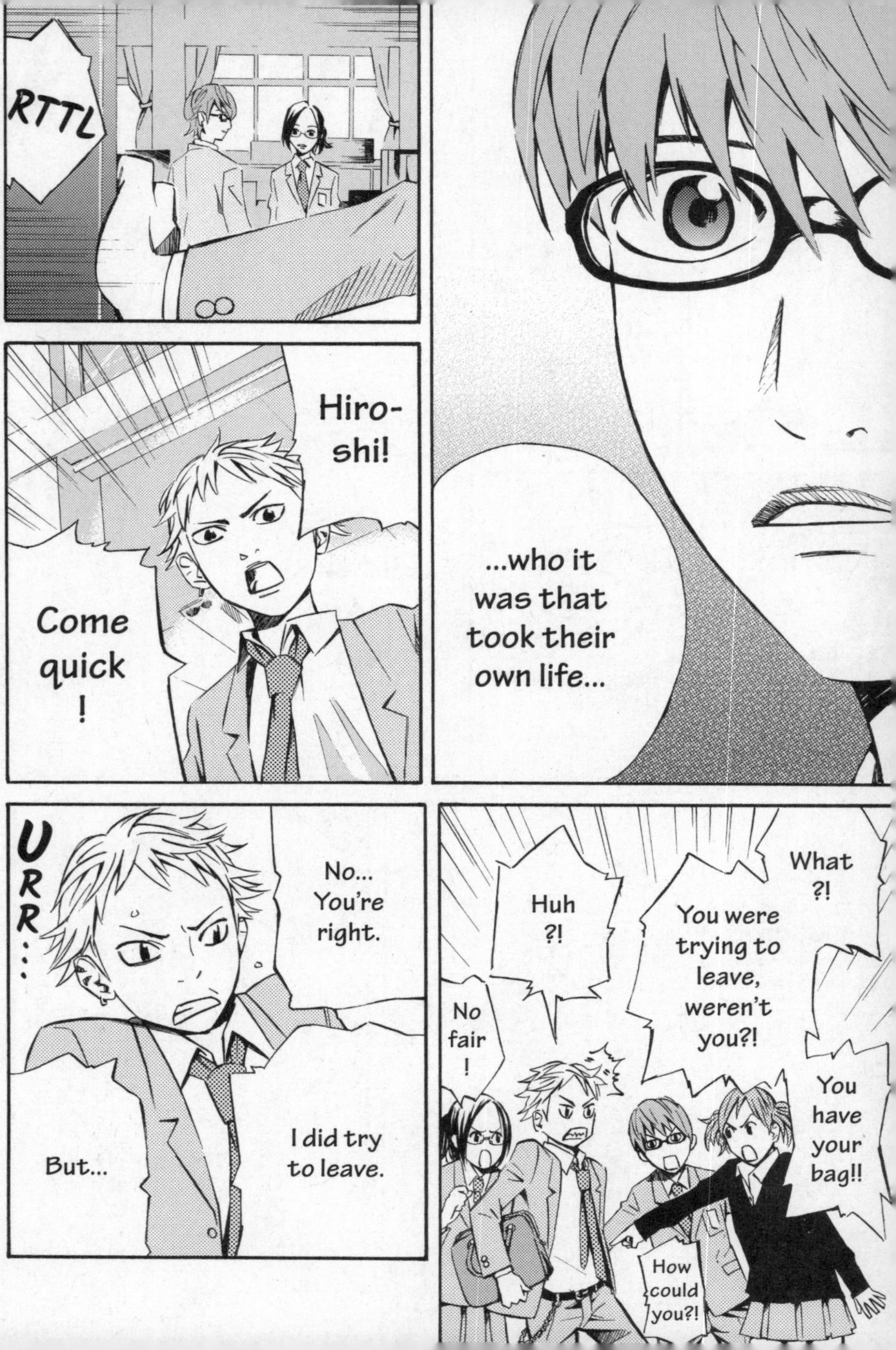
...who it was that took their own life...
RTTL
Hiro-shi!
Come quick!
What?!
You were trying to leave, weren't you?!
Huh?!
You have your bag!!
No fair!
How could you?!
No... You're right.
URR...
I did try to leave.
But...

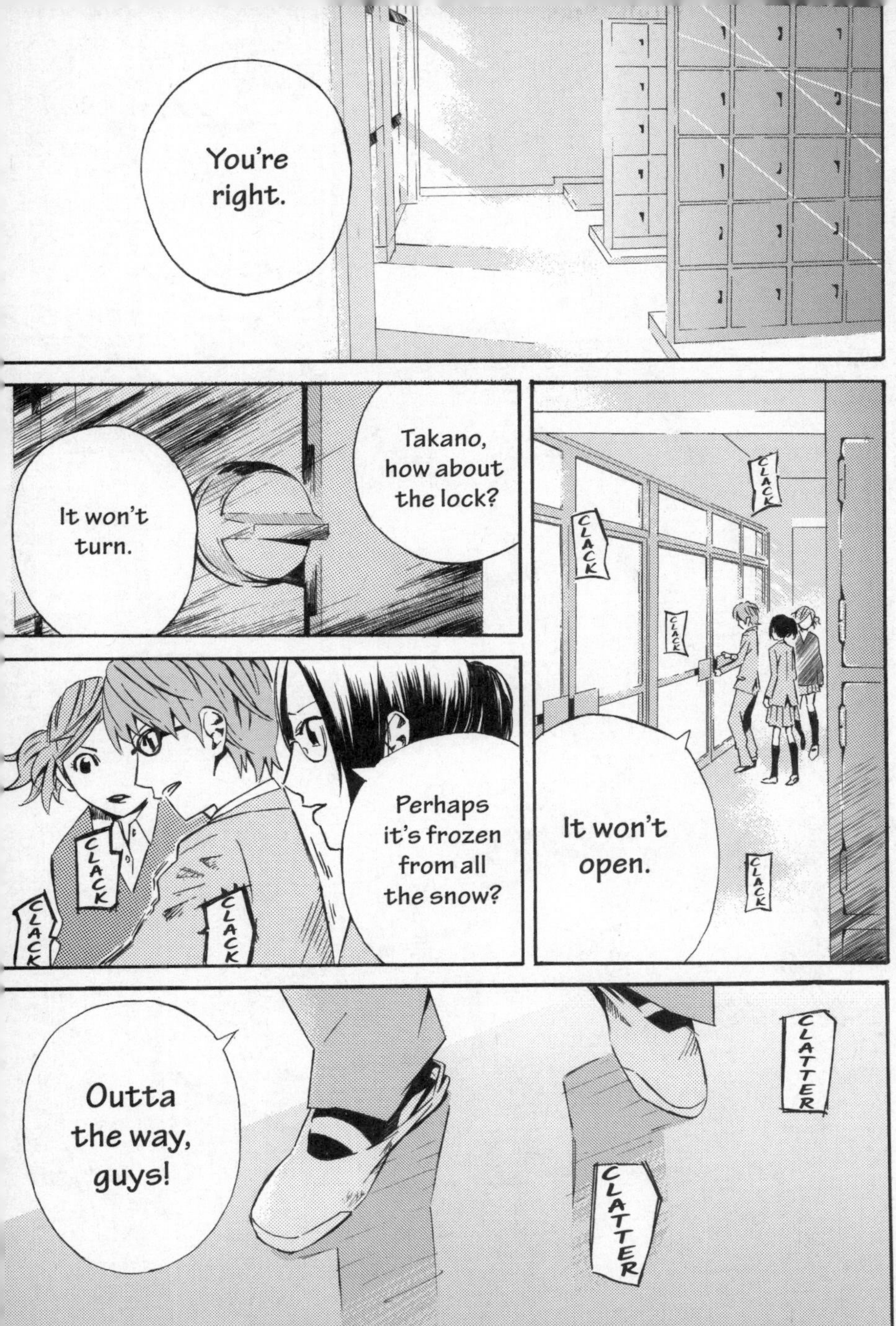
You're right.
CLACK
CLACK
CLACK
It won't open.
CLACK
Takano, how about the lock?
It won't turn.
Perhaps it's frozen from all the snow?
CLACK
CLACK
CLACK
CLATTER
CLATTER
Outta the way, guys!

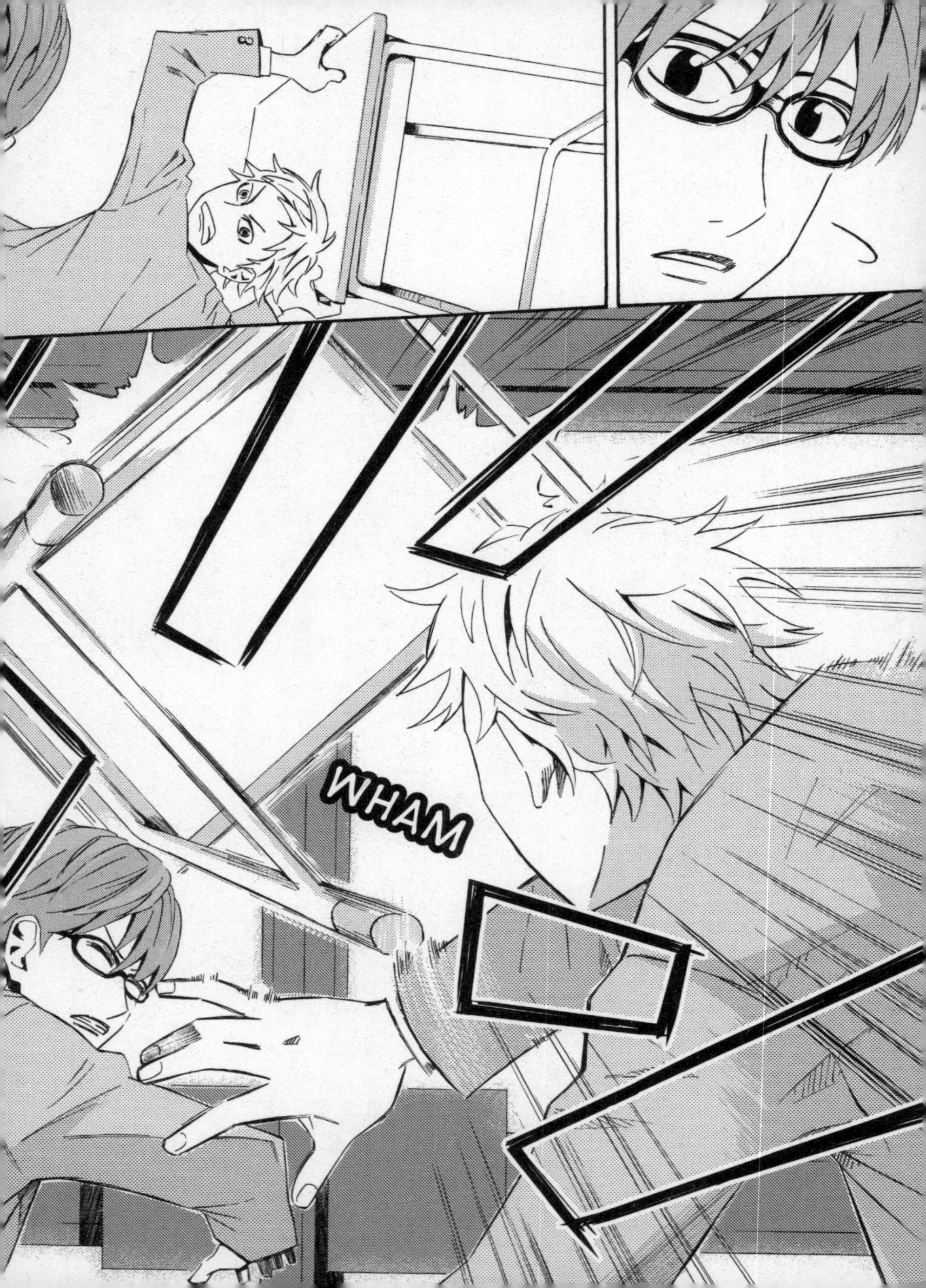
WHAM

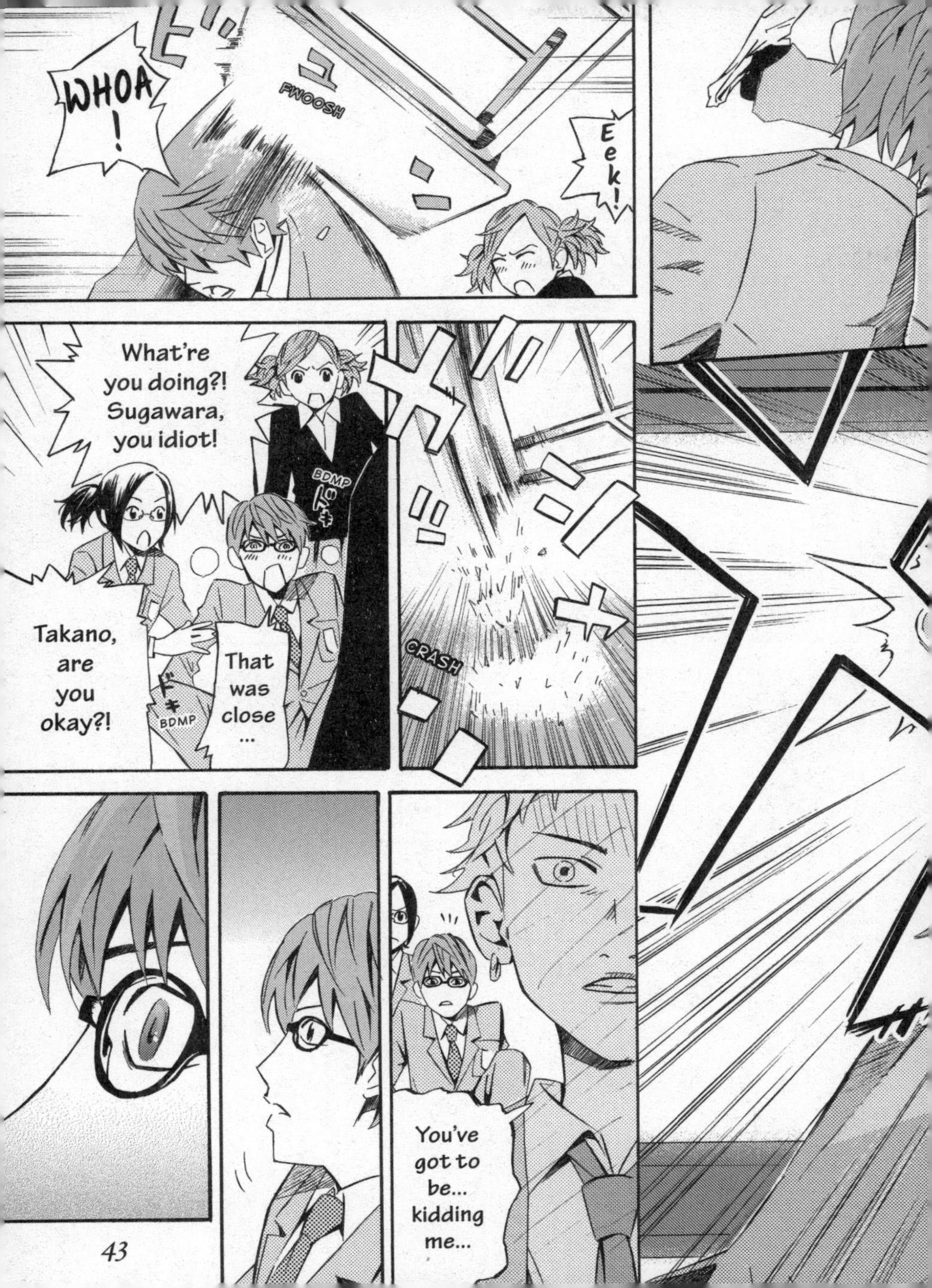
Eek!
FWOOSH
WHOA!
CRASH
What're you doing?! Sugawara, you idiot!
BDMP
That was close...
Takano, are you okay?!
BDMP
You've got to be... kidding me...

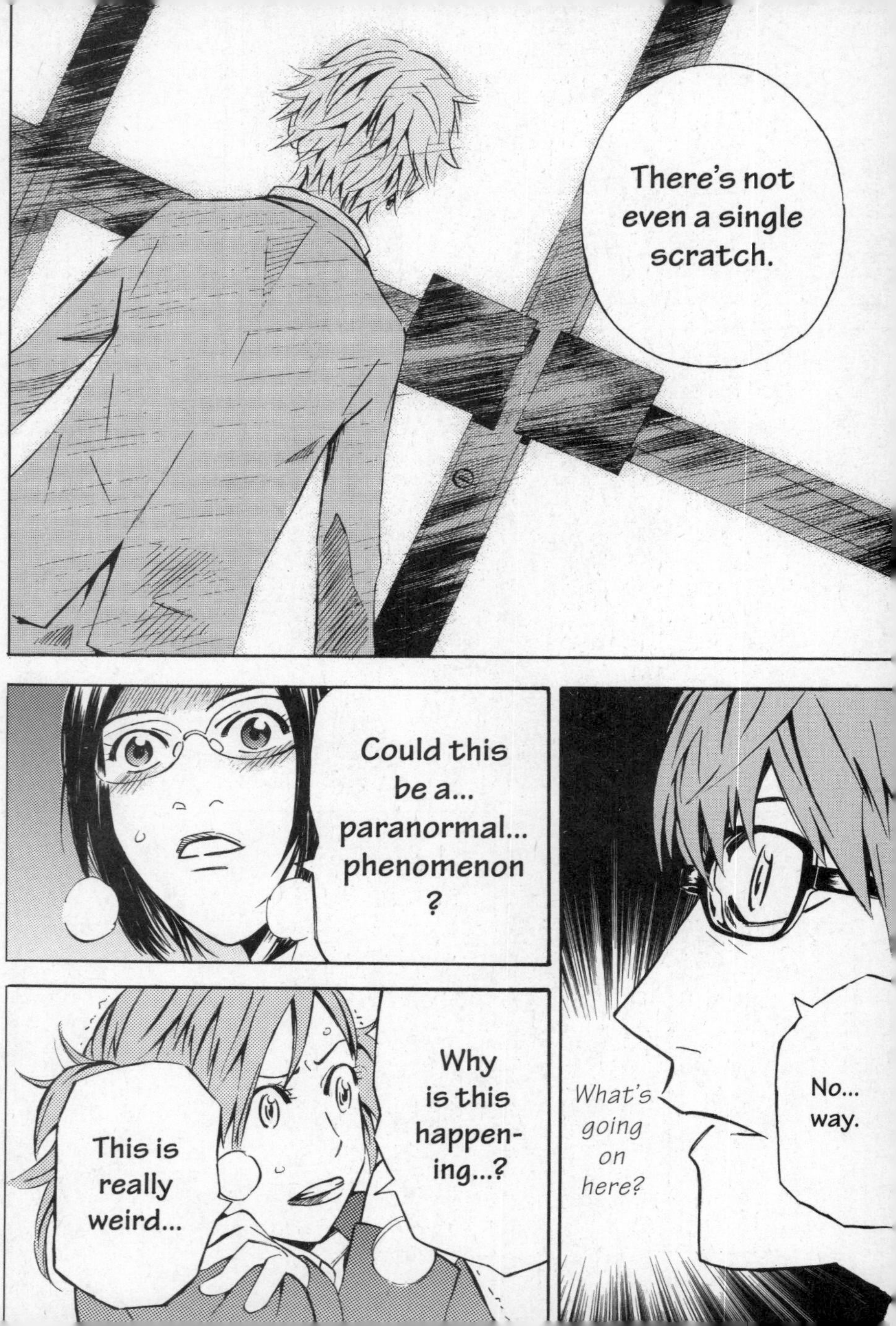
There's not even a single scratch.
No... way.
What's going on here?
Could this be a... paranormal... phenomenon?
Why is this happening...?
This is really weird...

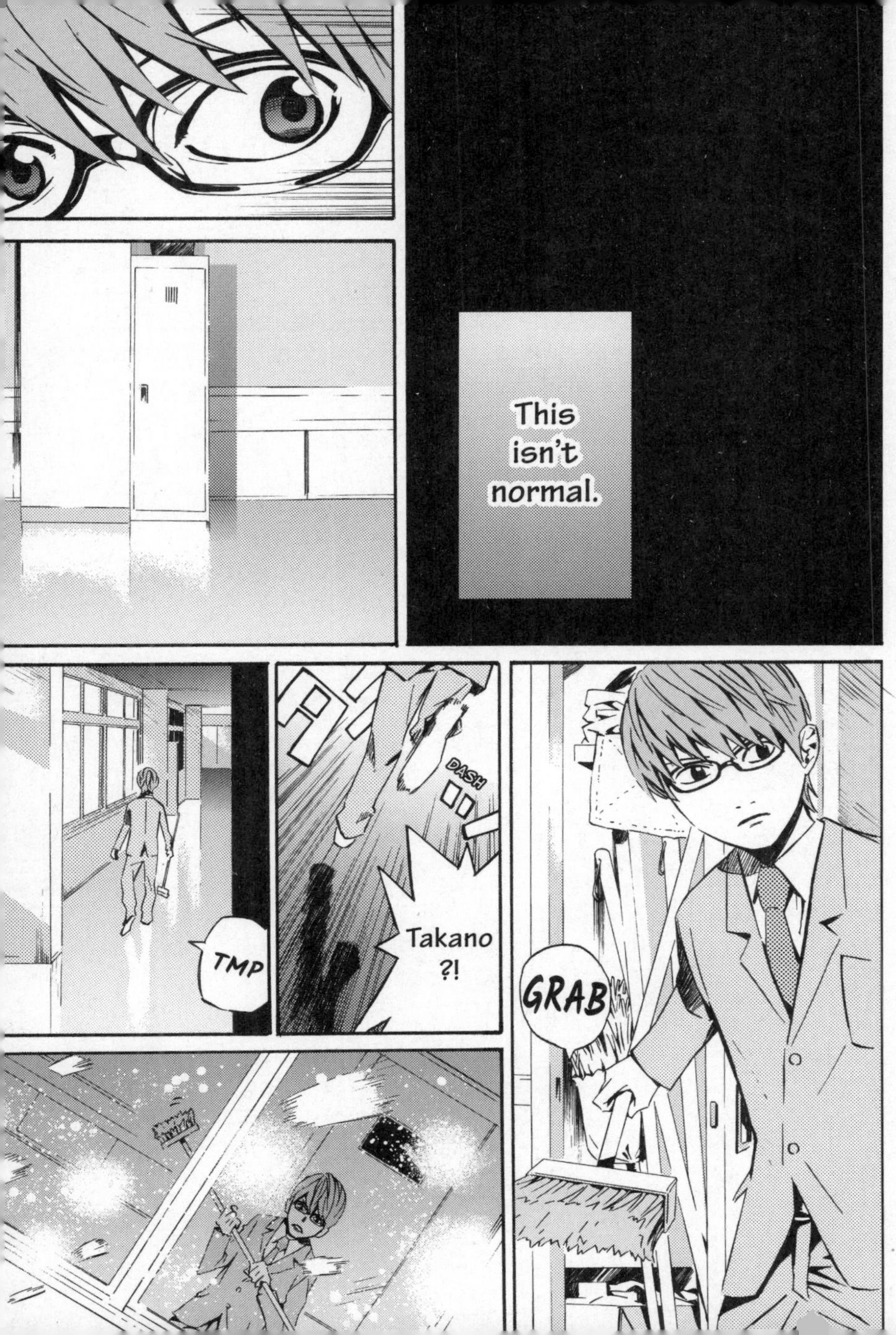
This isn't normal.
GRAB
DASH
Takano ?!
TMP

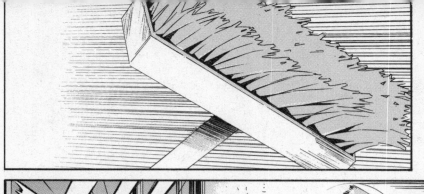

GA-KRAK

Even here...

CLATTER

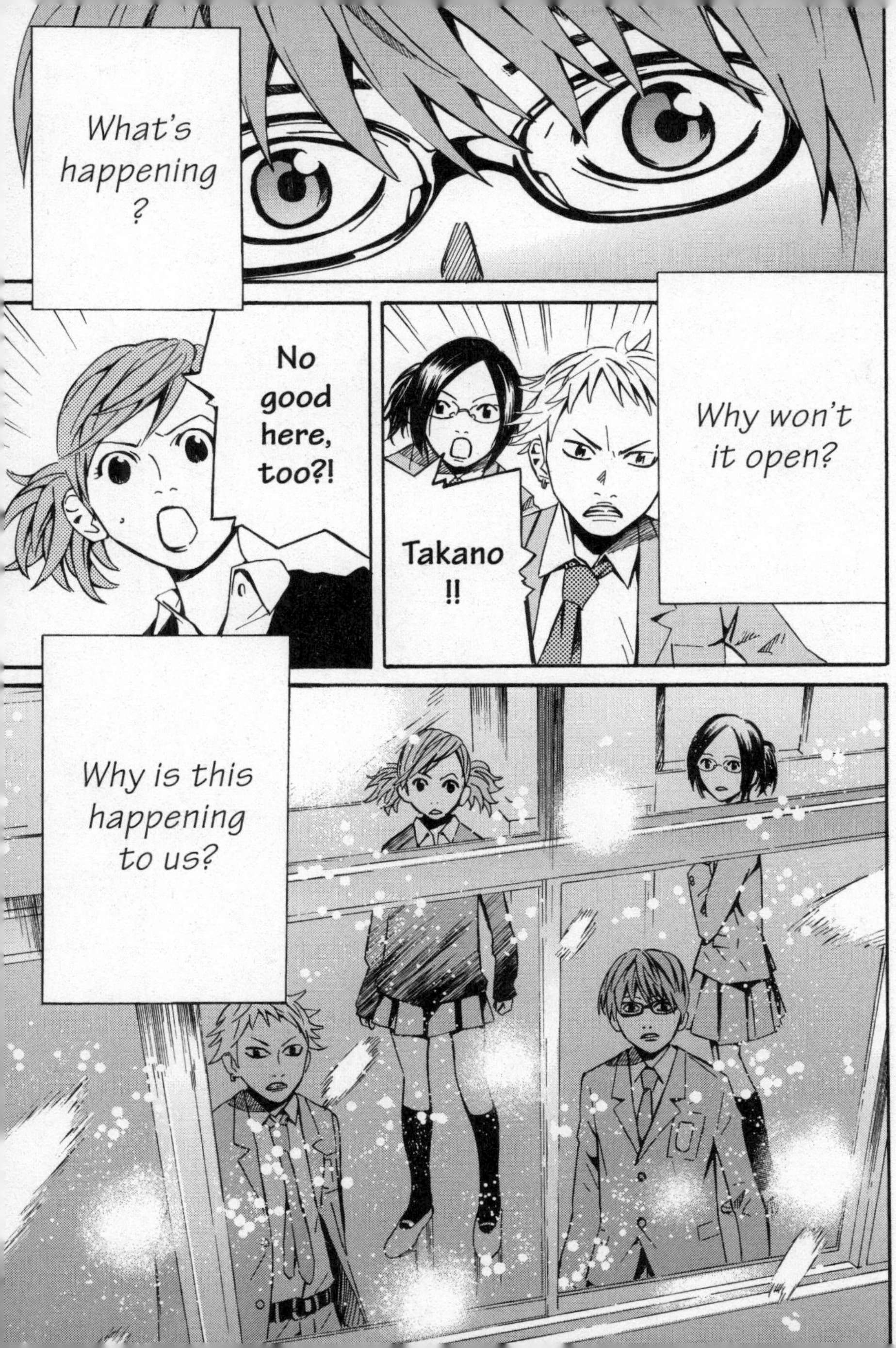
What's happening ?
Why won't it open?
Takano !!
No good here, too?!
Why is this happening to us?

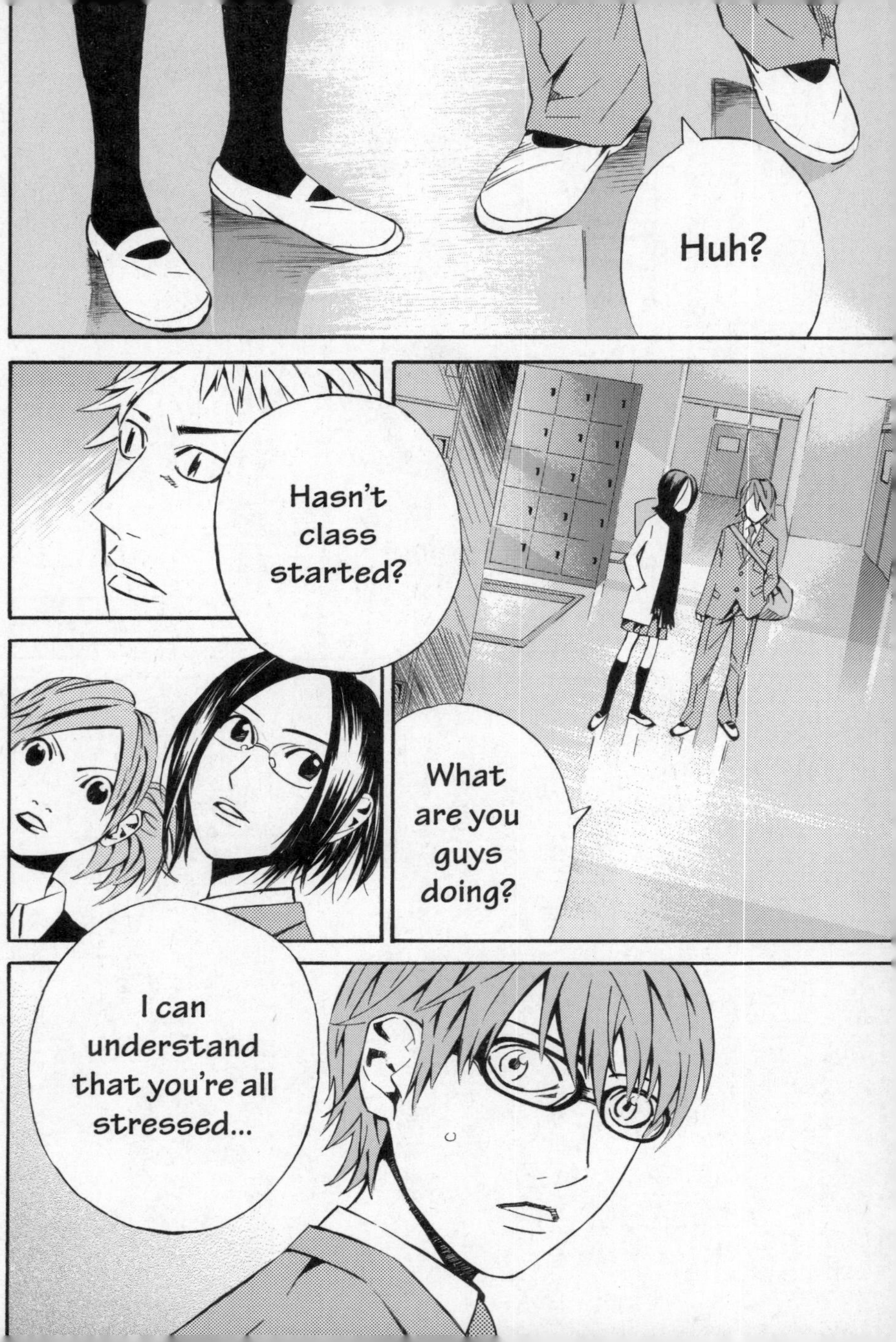
Huh?
What are you guys doing?
Hasn't class started?
I can understand that you're all stressed...

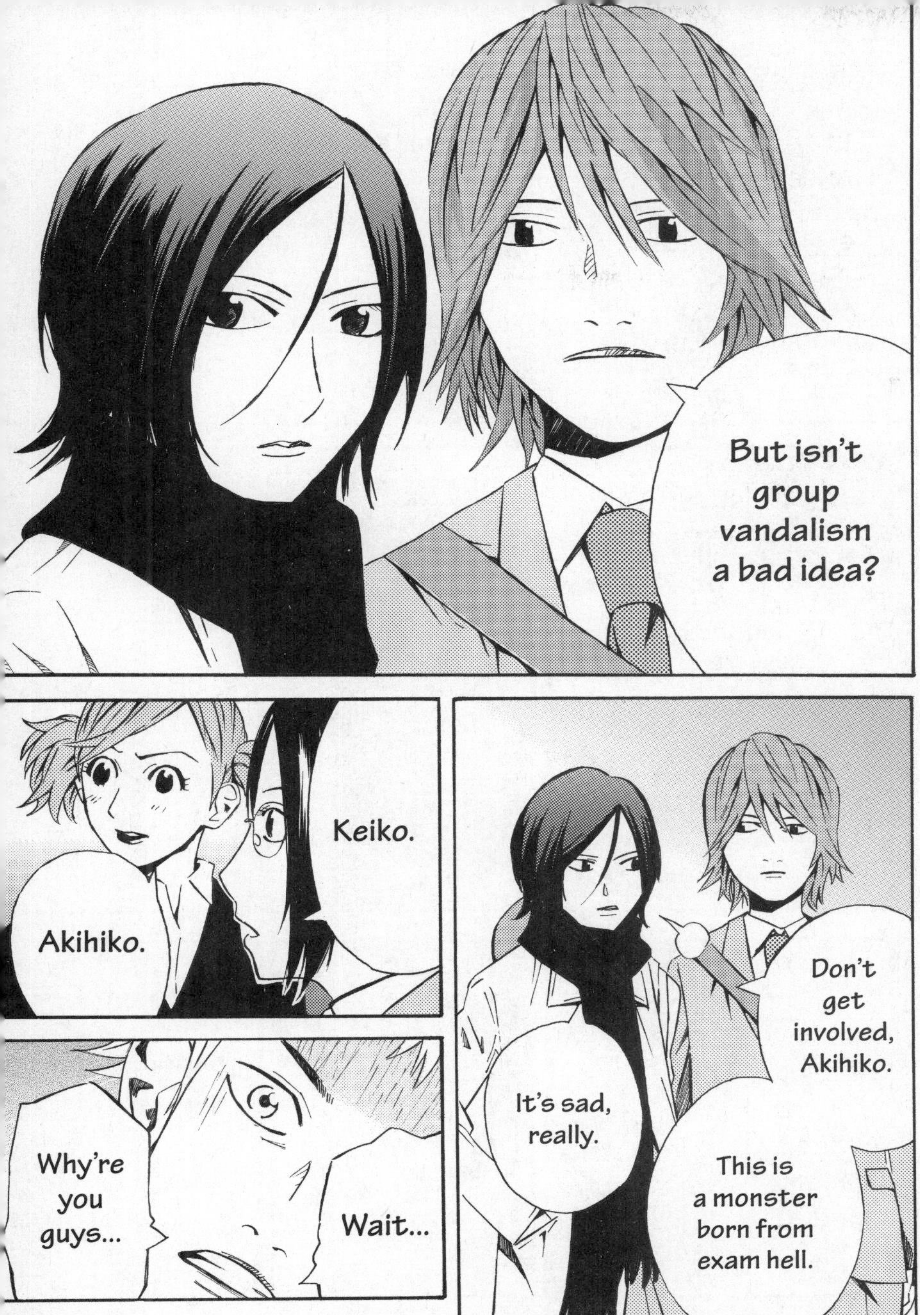
But isn't group vandalism a bad idea?
Don't get involved, Akihiko.
It's sad, really.
This is a monster born from exam hell.
Keiko.
Akihiko.
Wait...
Why're you guys...

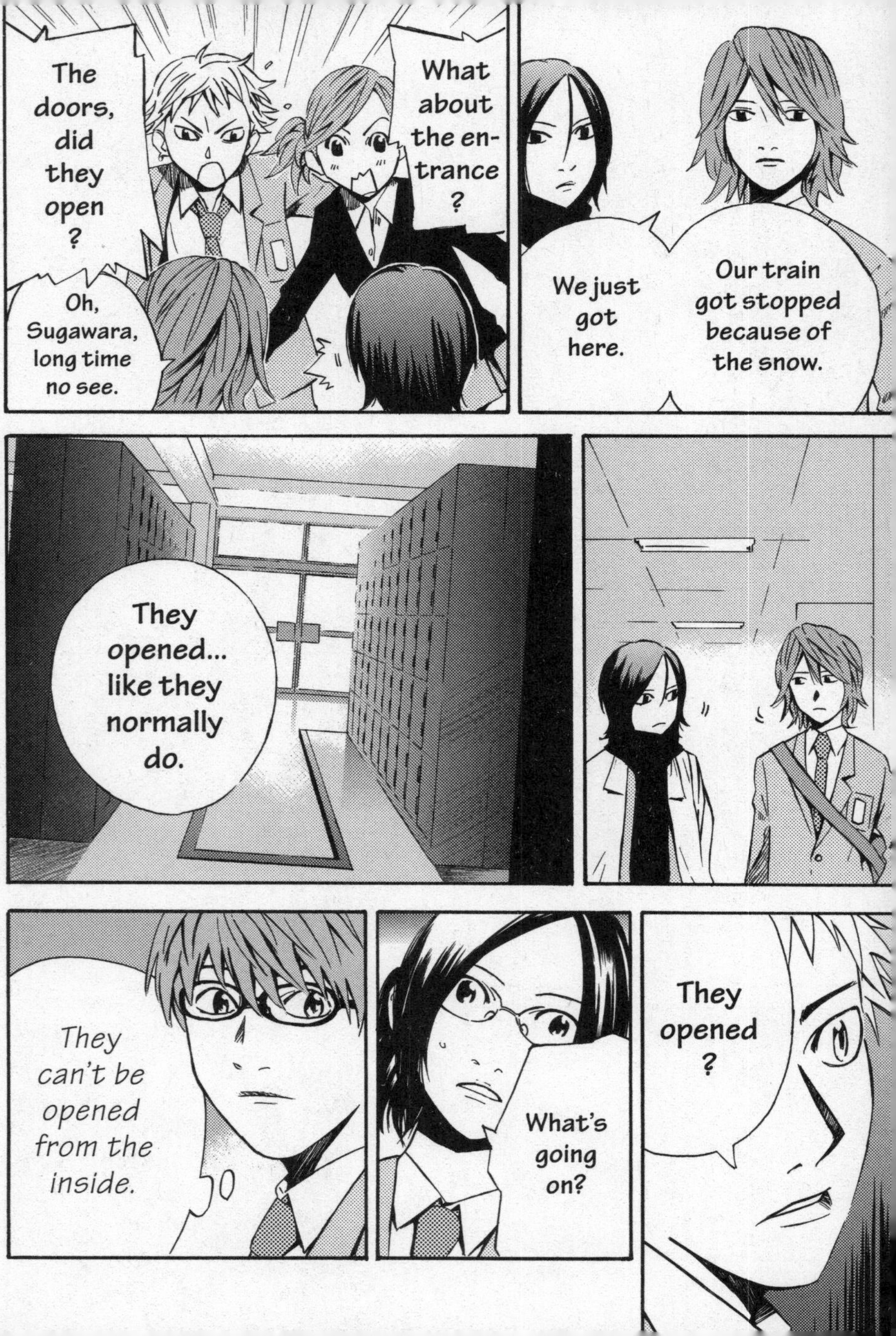
Our train got stopped because of the snow.
We just got here.
What about the entrance?
The doors, did they open?
Oh, Sugawara, long time no see.
They opened... like they normally do.
They opened?
What's going on?
They can't be opened from the inside.

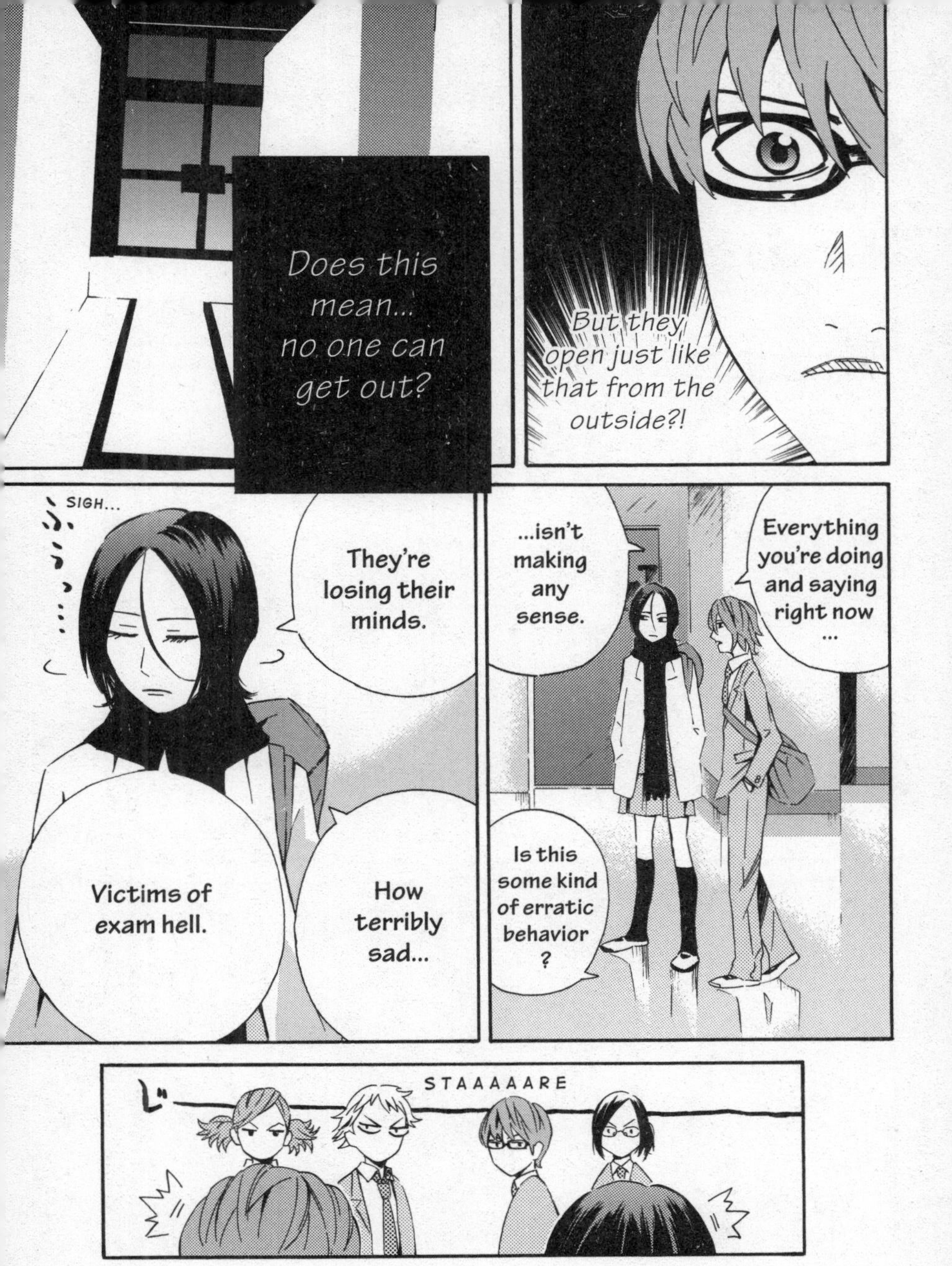
But they open just like that from the outside?!
Does this mean... no one can get out?
Everything you're doing and saying right now ...
...isn't making any sense.
Is this some kind of erratic behavior ?
SIGH...
ふぅ……
They're losing their minds.
How terribly sad...
Victims of exam hell.
STAAAAARE
じー

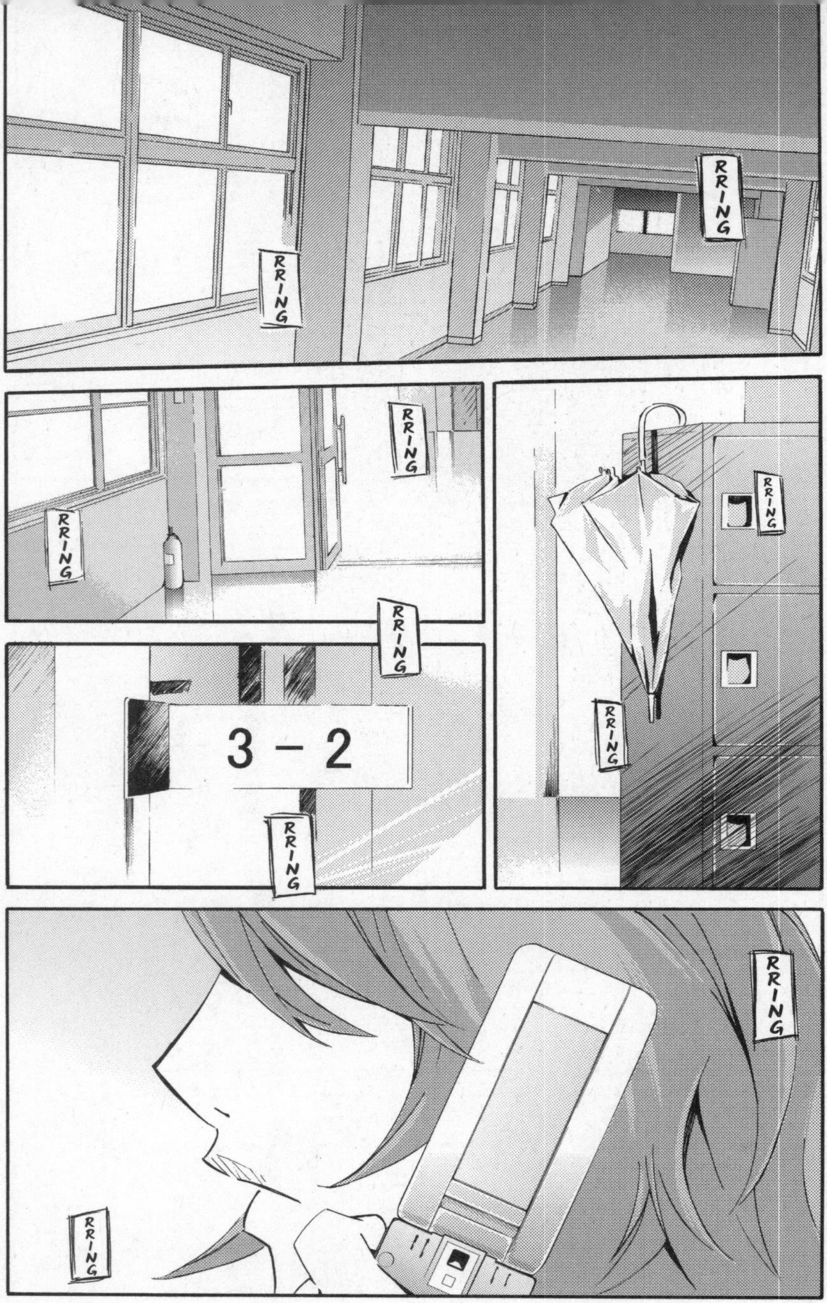
RRING
RRING
RRING
RRING
RRING
RRING
RRING
3 – 2
RRING
RRING
RRING

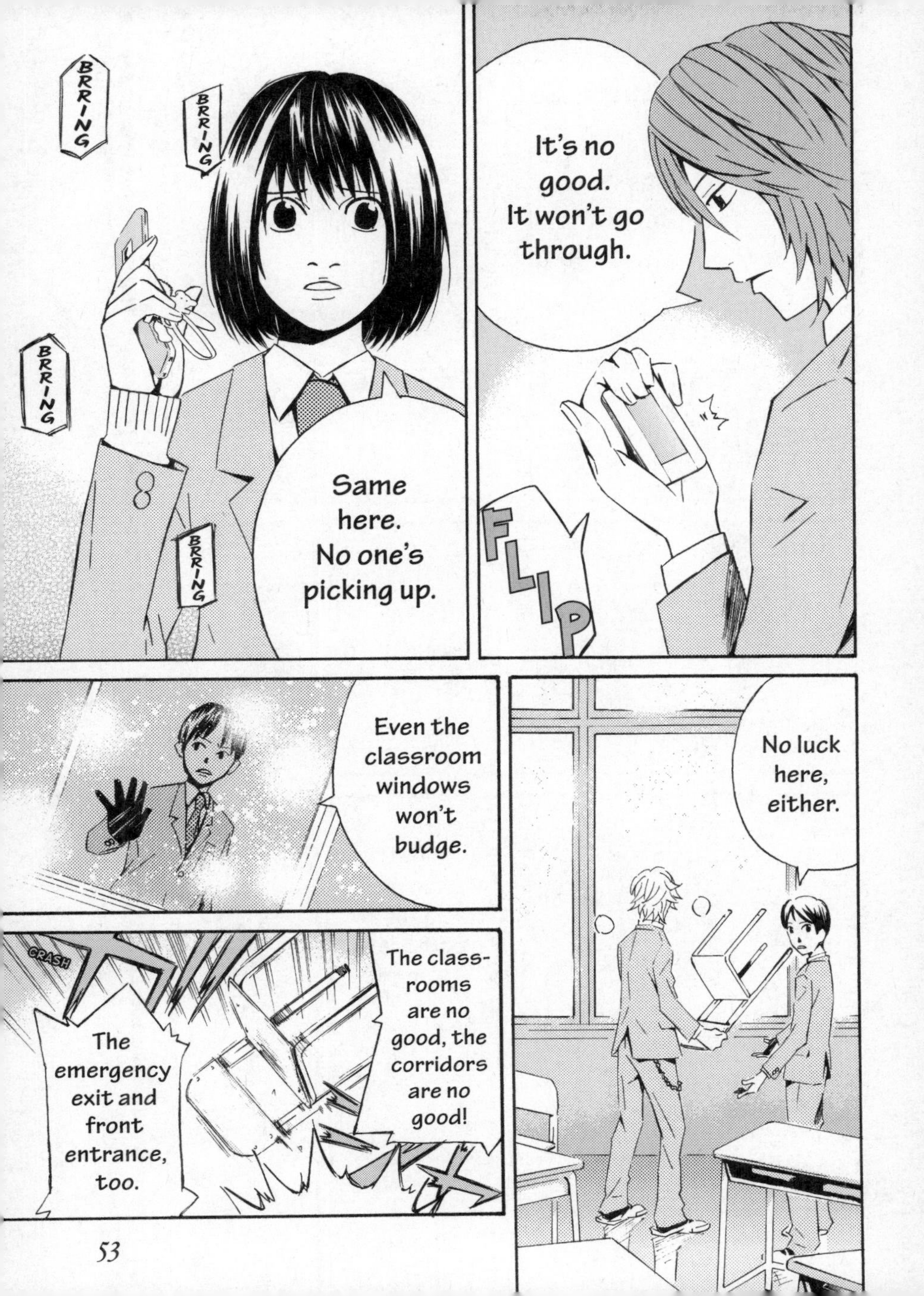
It's no good. It won't go through.
FLIP
BRRING
BRRING
BRRING
BRRING
Same here. No one's picking up.
No luck here, either.
Even the classroom windows won't budge.
The class-rooms are no good, the corridors are no good!
CRASH
The emergency exit and front entrance, too.

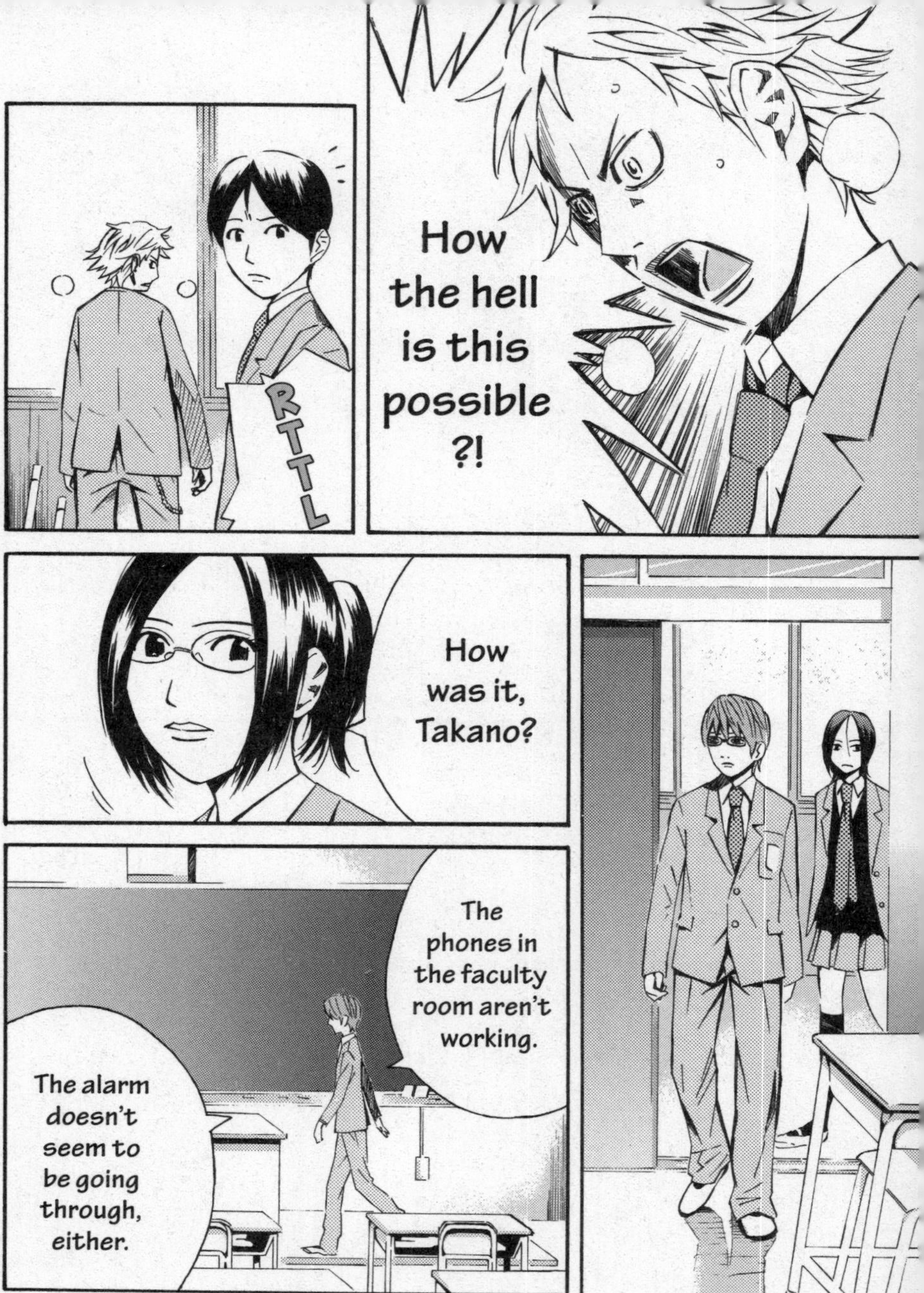
How the hell is this possible ?!
RTTL
How was it, Takano?
The phones in the faculty room aren't working.
The alarm doesn't seem to be going through, either.

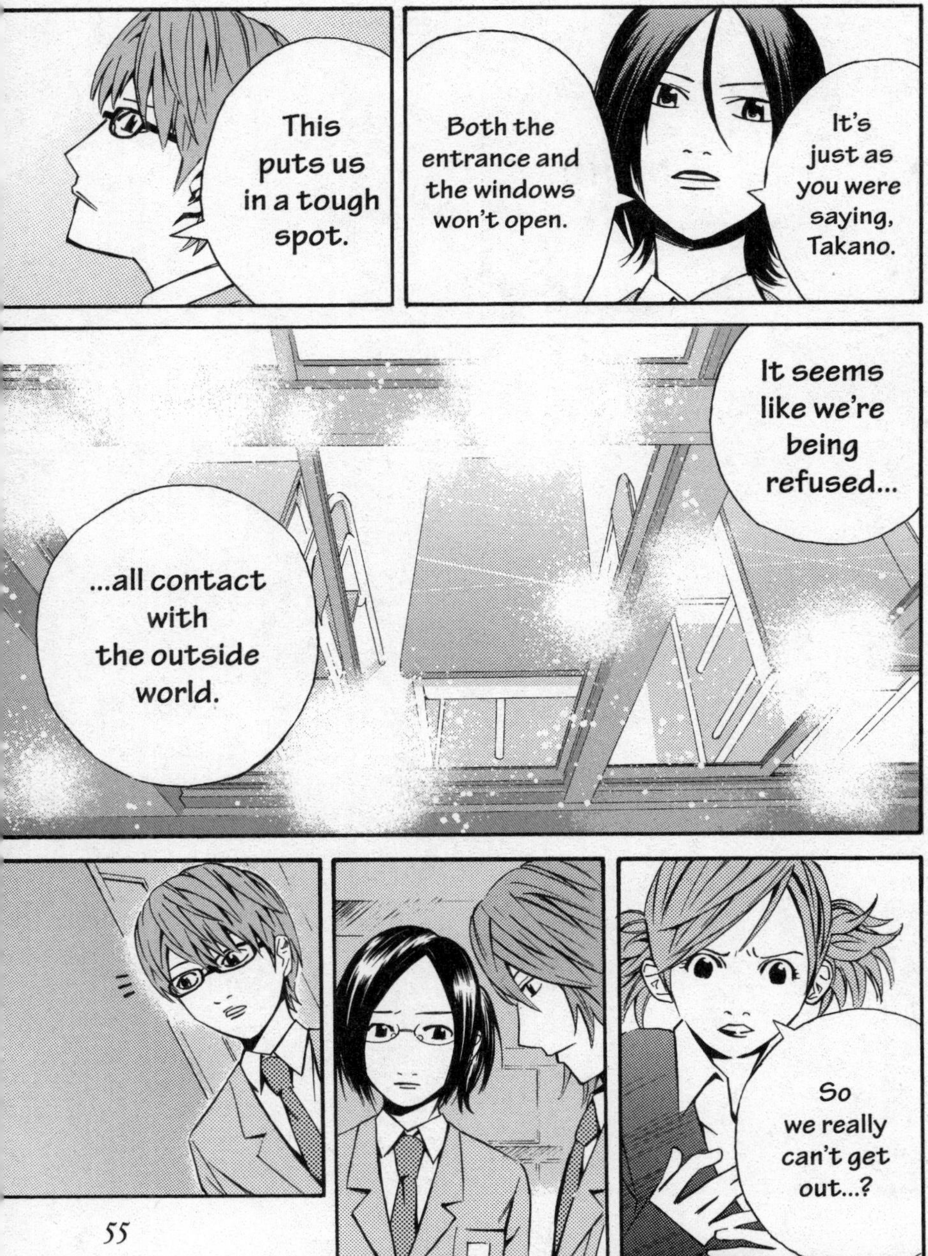
It's just as you were saying, Takano.
Both the entrance and the windows won't open.
This puts us in a tough spot.
It seems like we're being refused...
...all contact with the outside world.
So we really can't get out...?

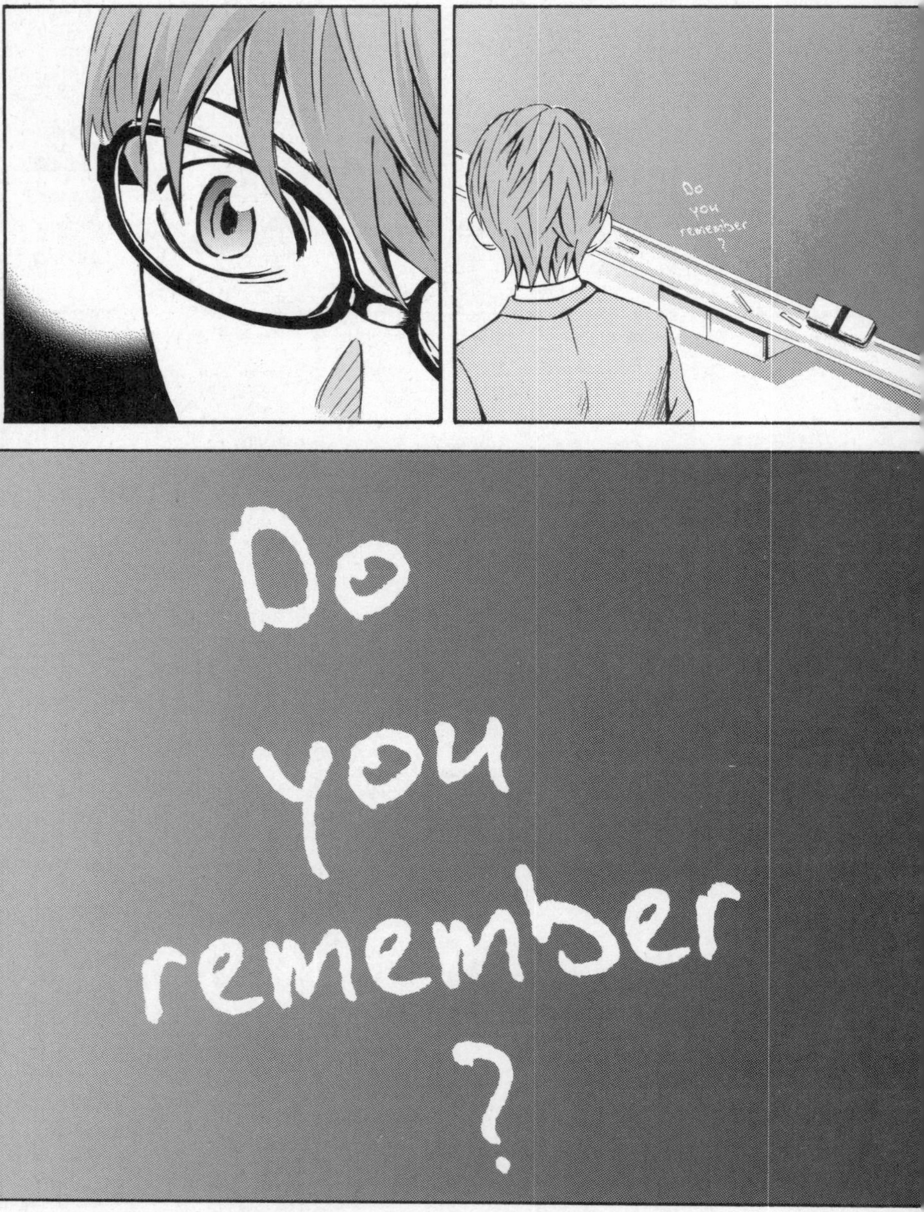
Do you remember ?
Do you remember ?

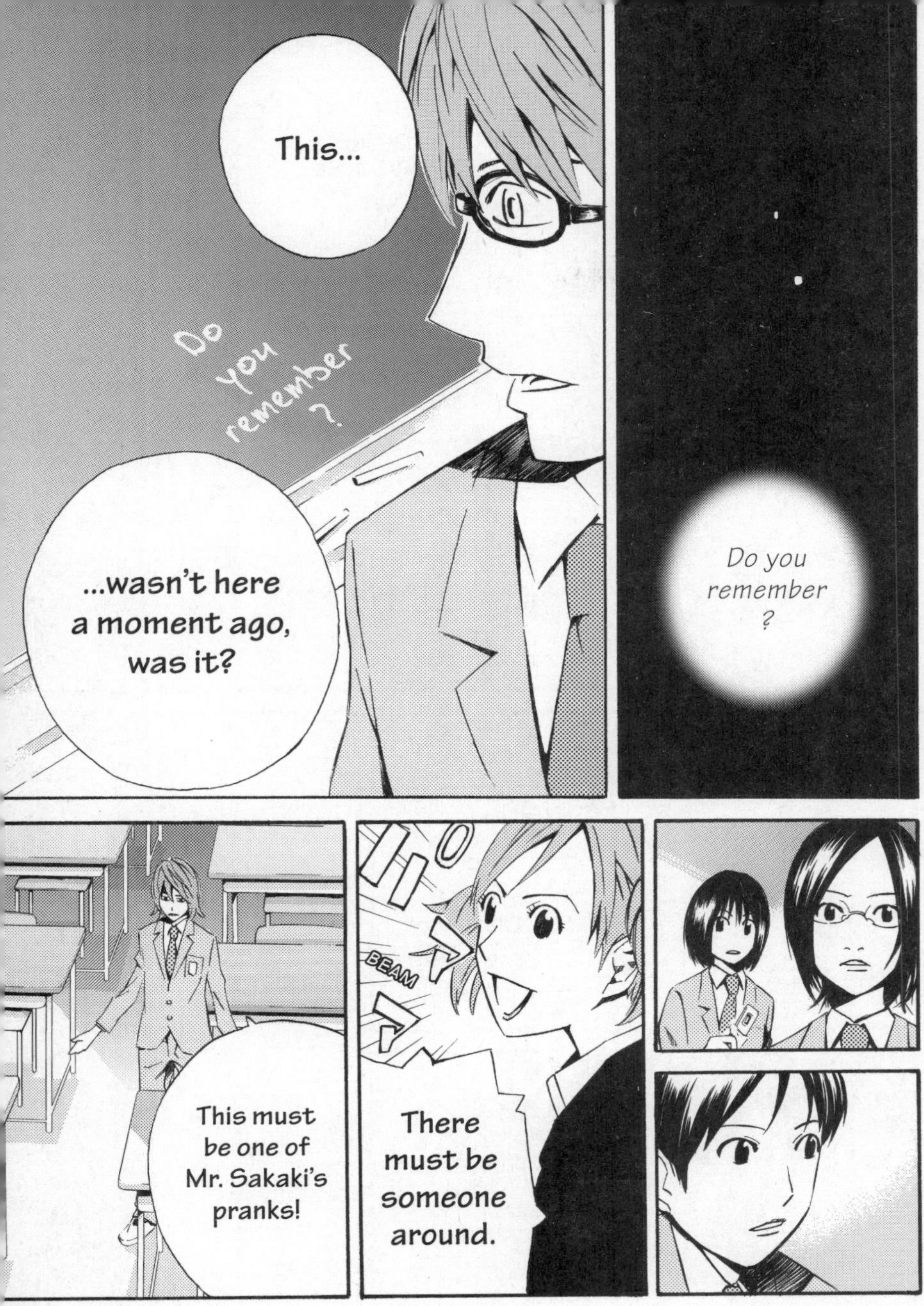
Do you remember ?
This...
Do you remember ?
...wasn't here a moment ago, was it?
BEAM
There must be someone around.
This must be one of Mr. Sakaki's pranks!

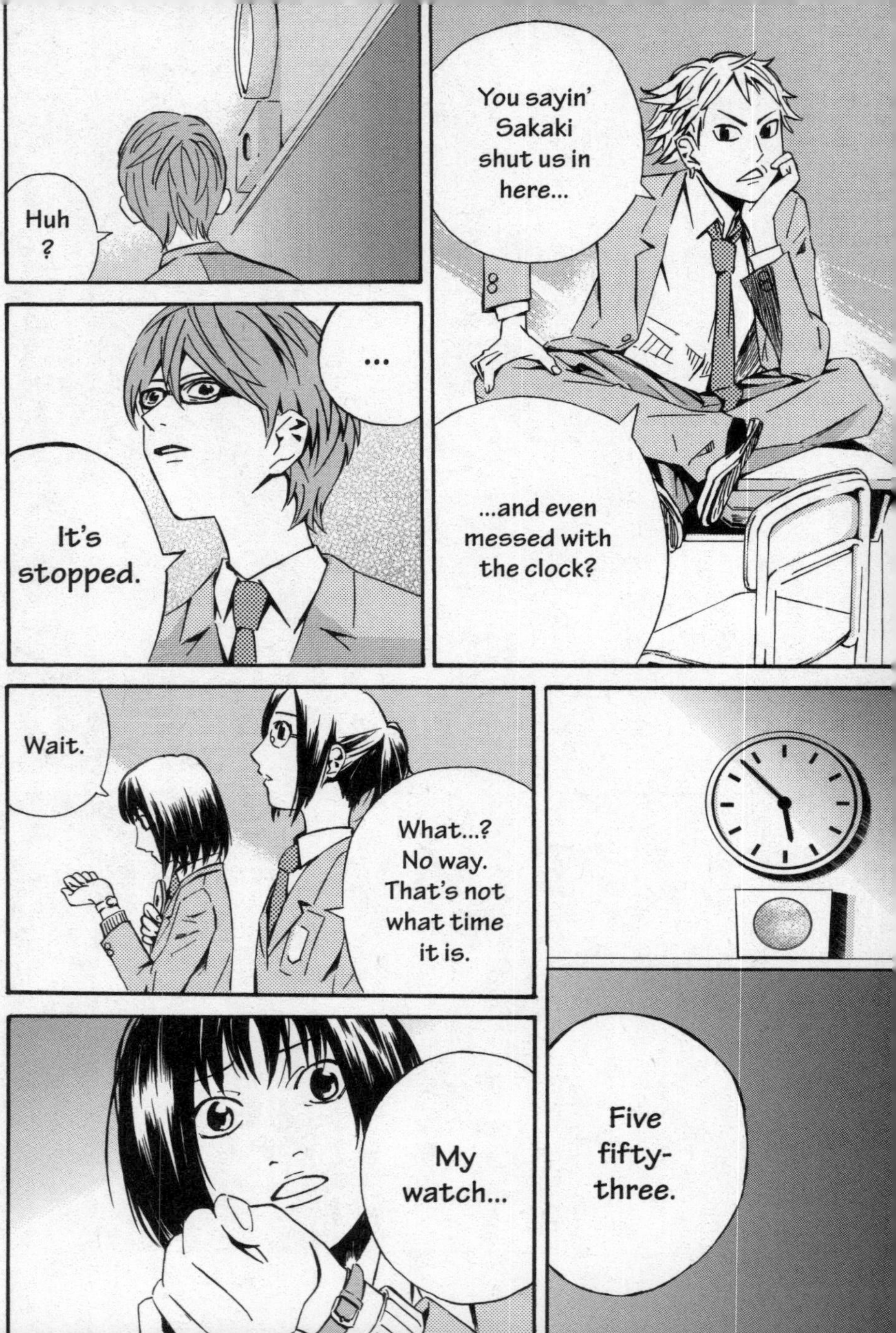
You sayin' Sakaki shut us in here...
...and even messed with the clock?
Huh?
...
It's stopped.
Wait.
What...? No way. That's not what time it is.
Five fifty-three.
My watch...

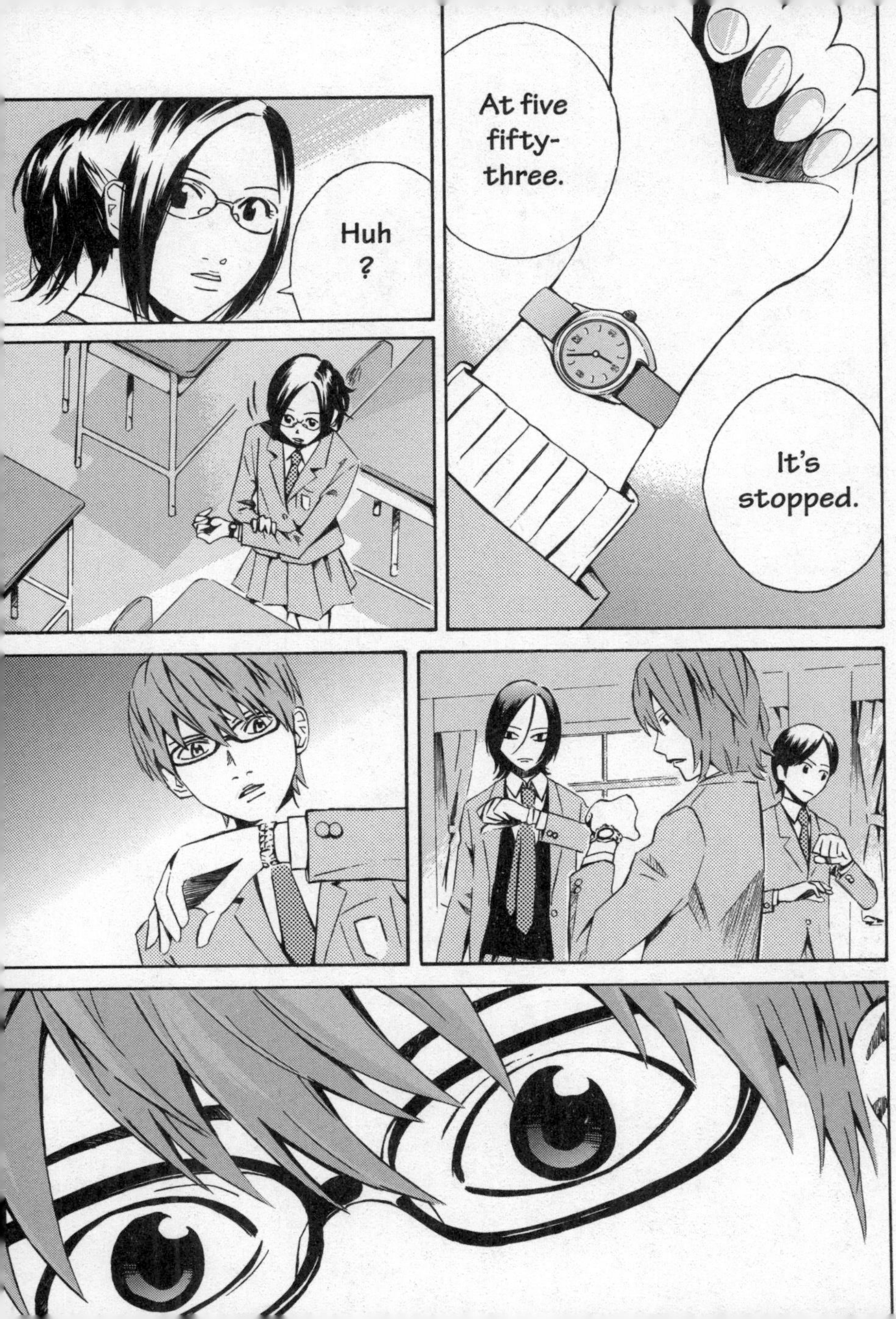
At five fifty-three.
It's stopped.
Huh?

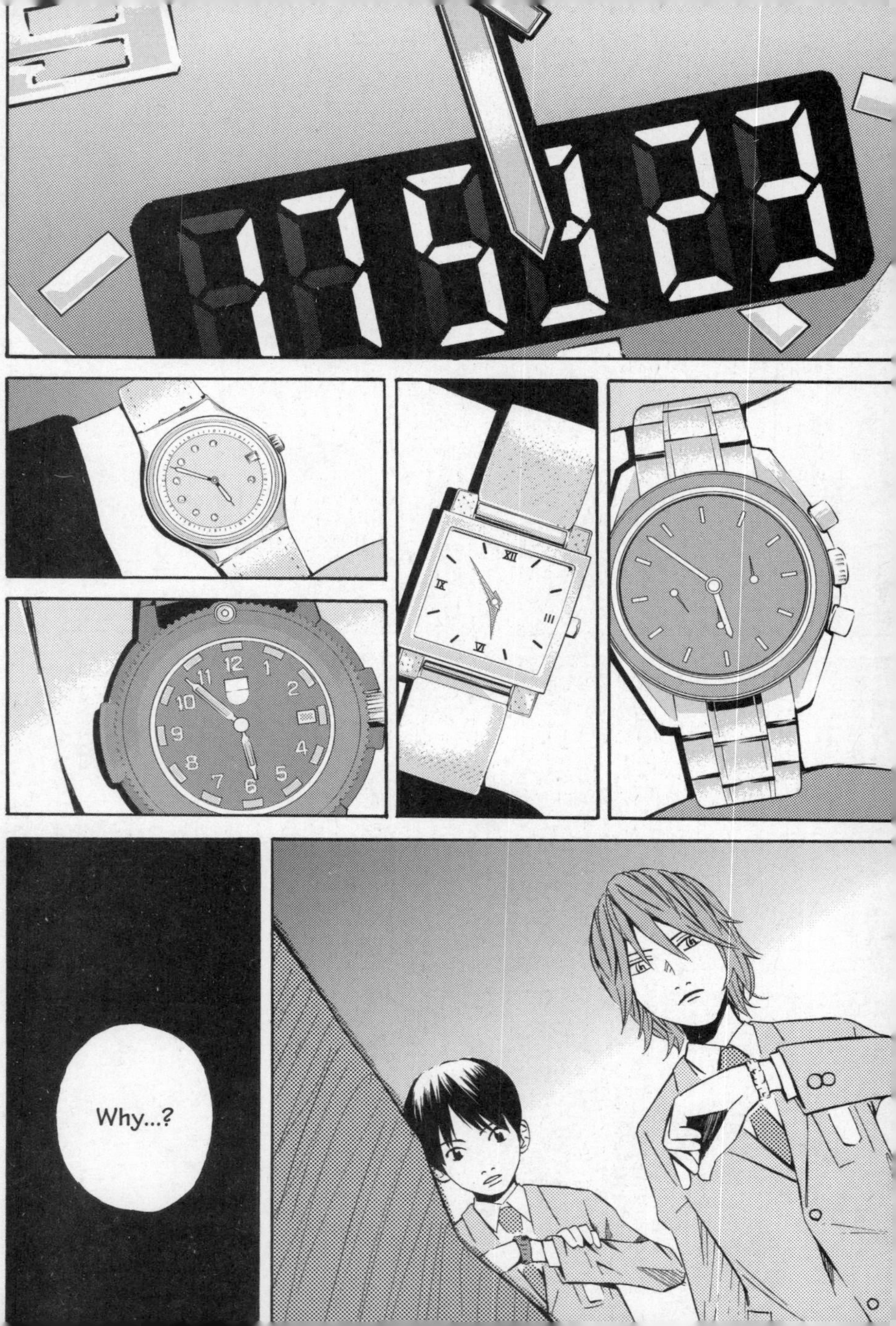
Why...?

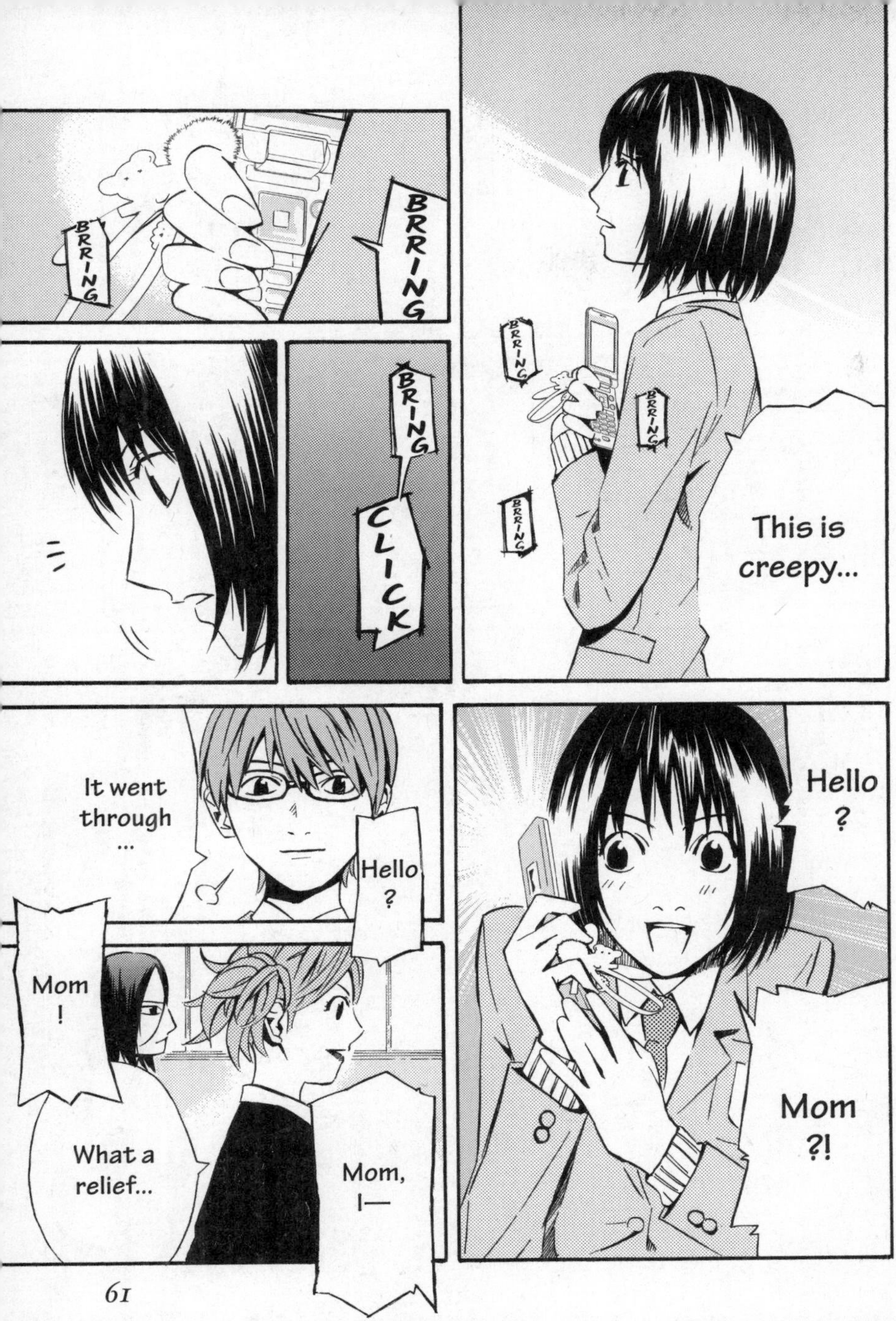
BRRING
BRRING
BRRING
This is creepy...
BRRING
BRRING
BRRING
CLICK
Hello?
Mom?!
It went through...
Hello?
Mom!
What a relief...
Mom, I—

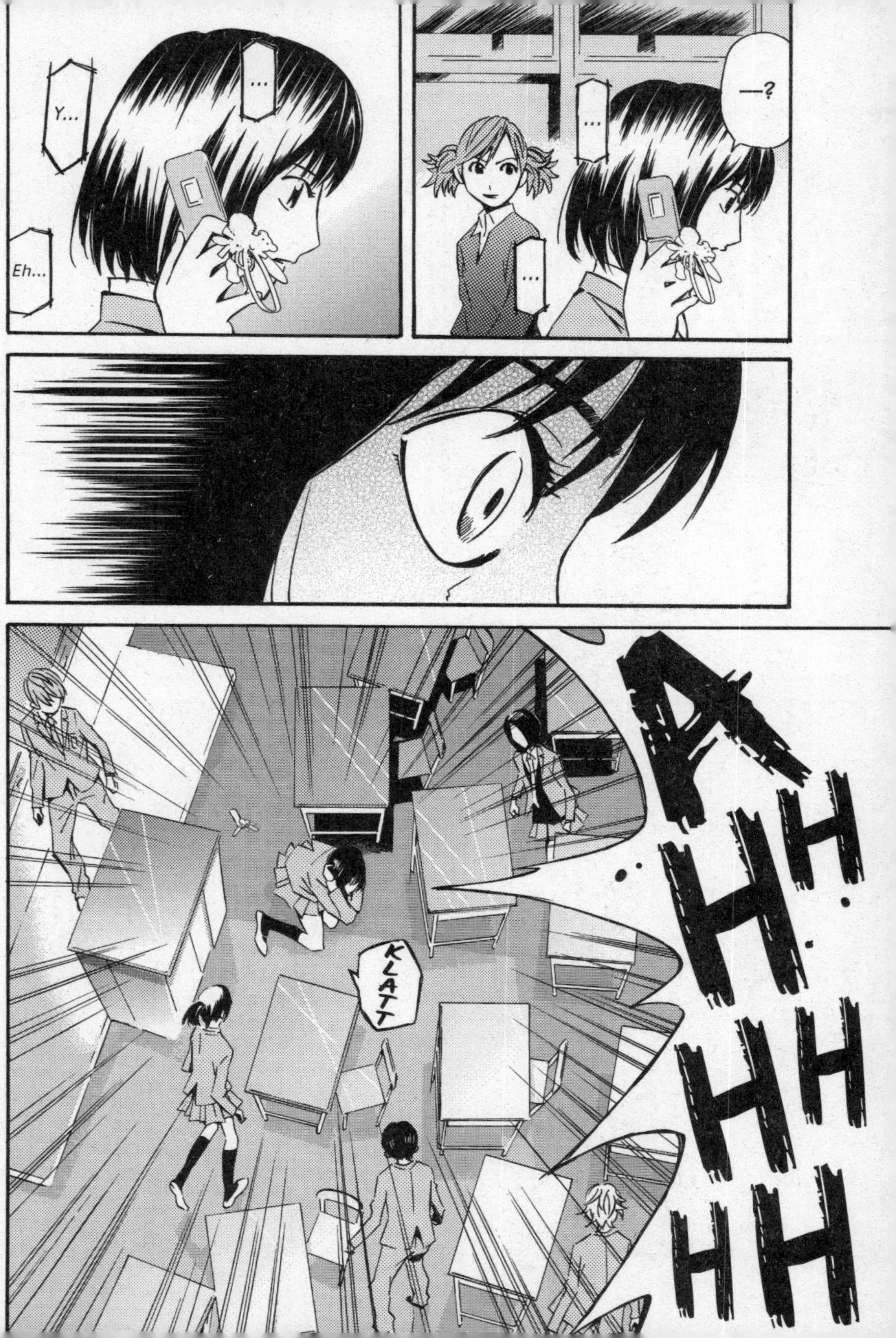
—?
...
...
...
Y...
Eh...
AHHHHHH
KLATT

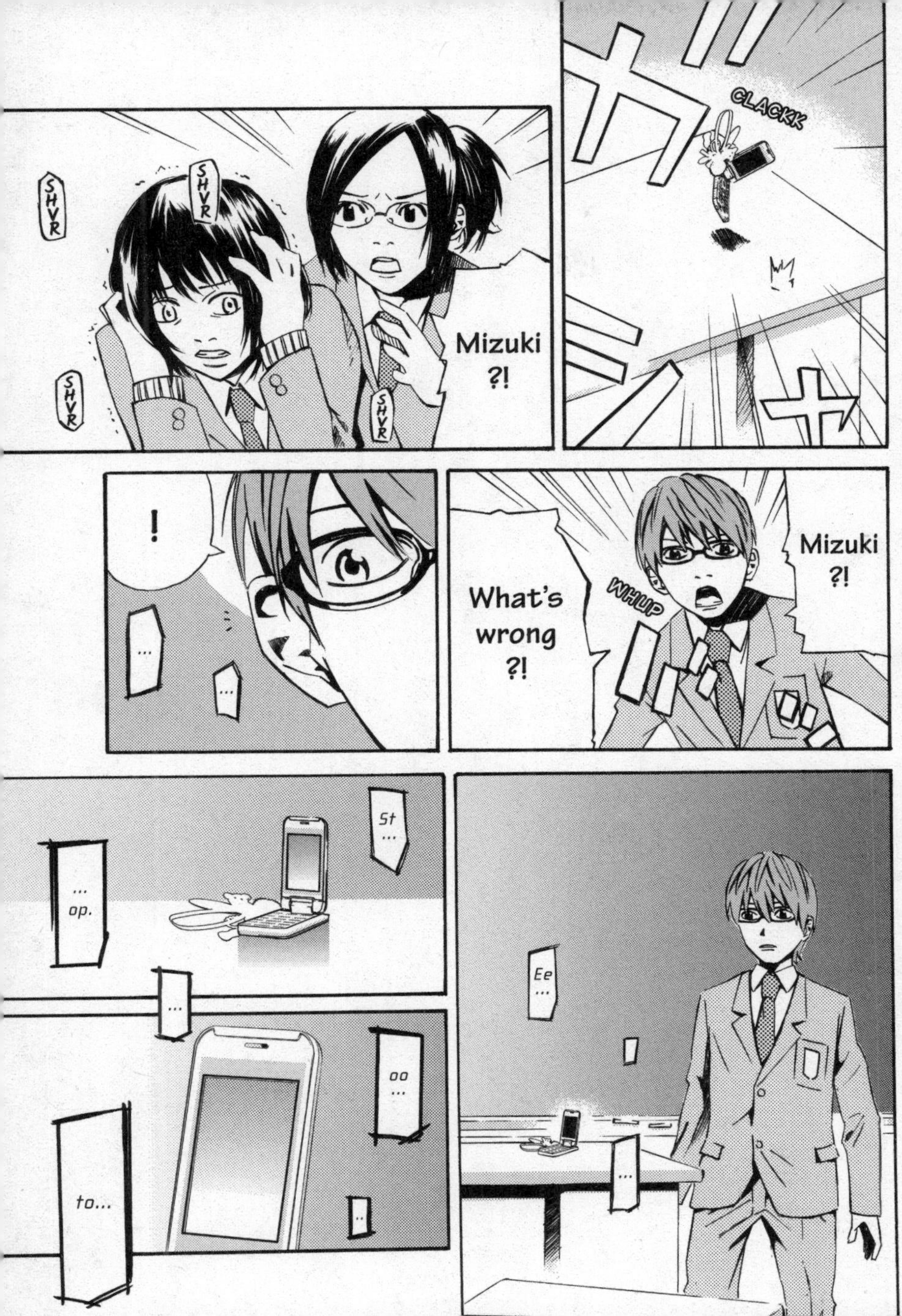

CLACKK
SHVR
SHVR
SHVR
Mizuki ?!
Mizuki ?!
WHUP
What's wrong ?!
!
...
...
Ee ...
...
St ...
... op.
...
oo ...
to...
..

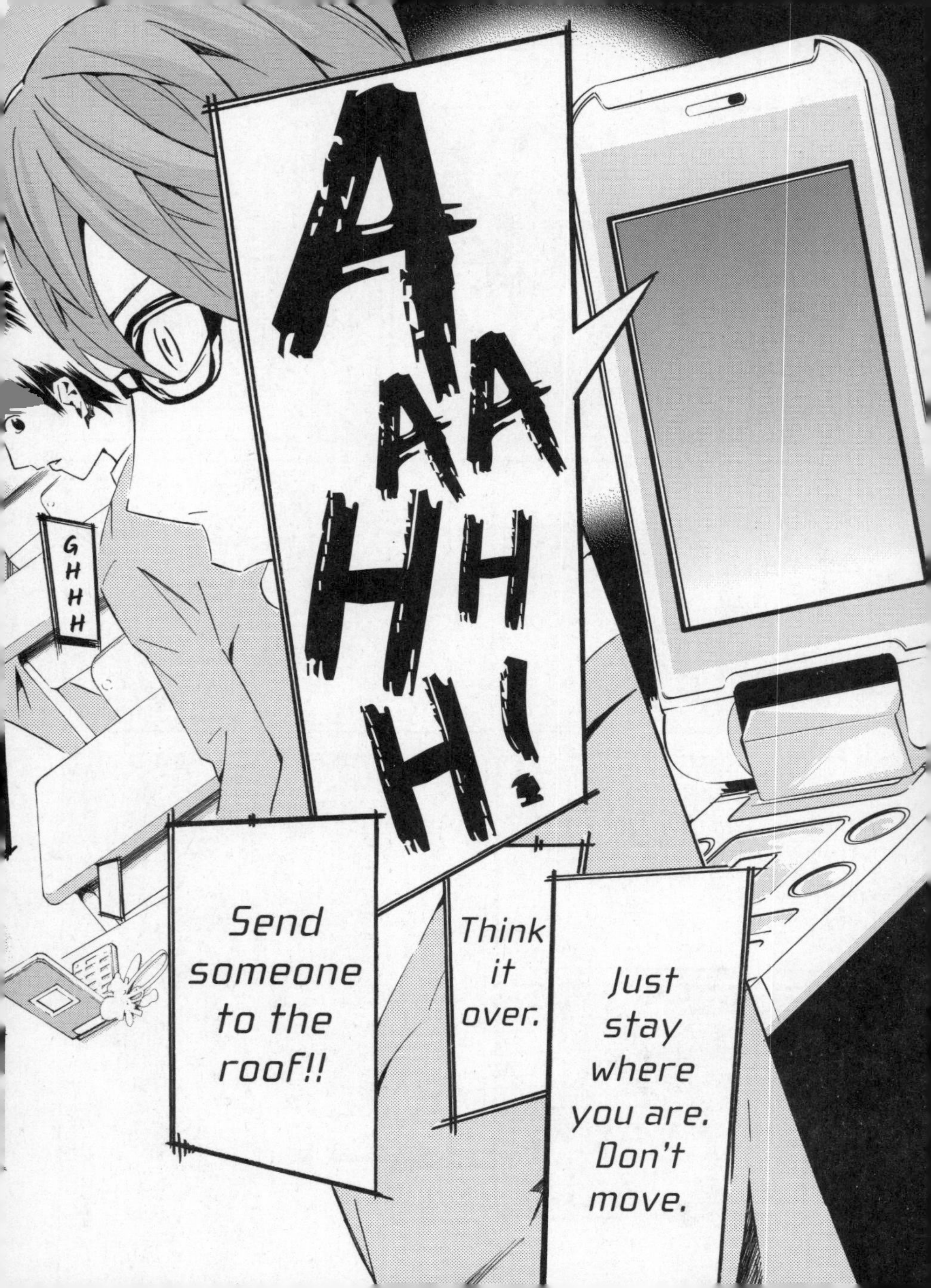
AAAHHHH!
GHHH
Just stay where you are. Don't move.
Think it over.
Send someone to the roof!!

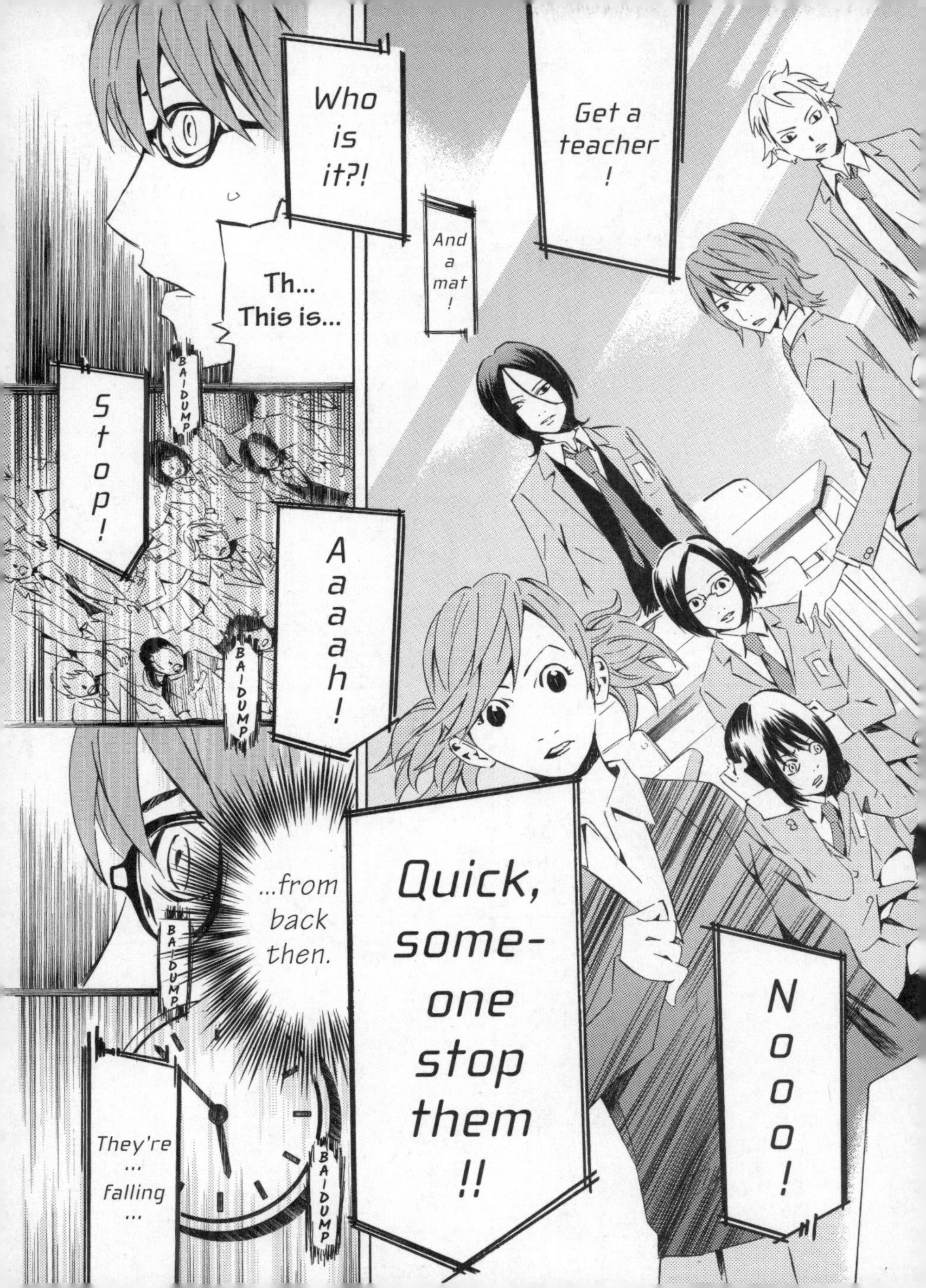

Get a teacher!
And a mat!
Who is it?!
Noooo!
Quick, someone stop them!!
Th... This is...
BAIDUMP
Stop!
Aaaah!
BAIDUMP
BAIDUMP
...from back then.
BAIDUMP
They're... falling...

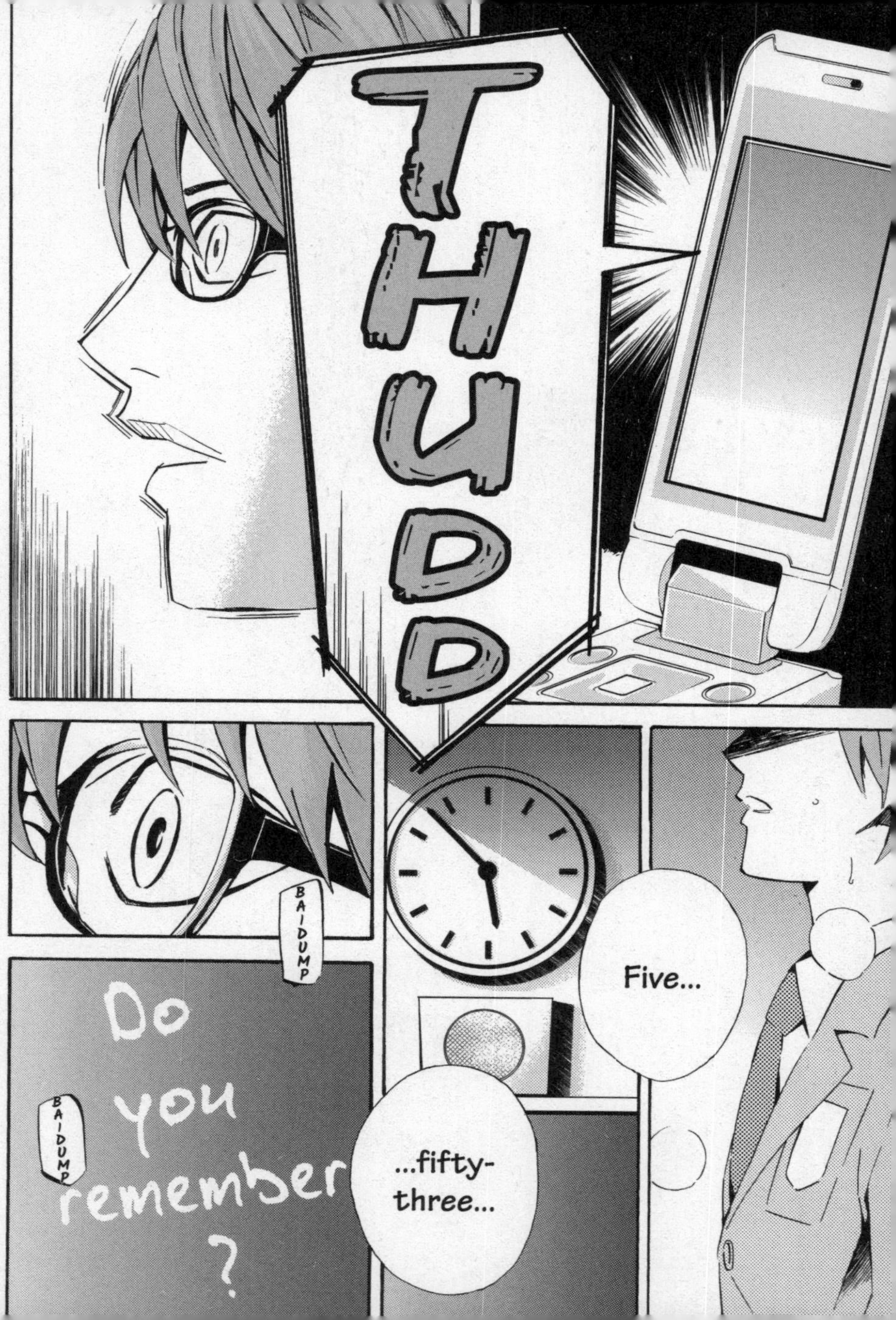
THUDD
Five...
...fifty-three...
BAIDUMP
BAIDUMP
Do you remember?

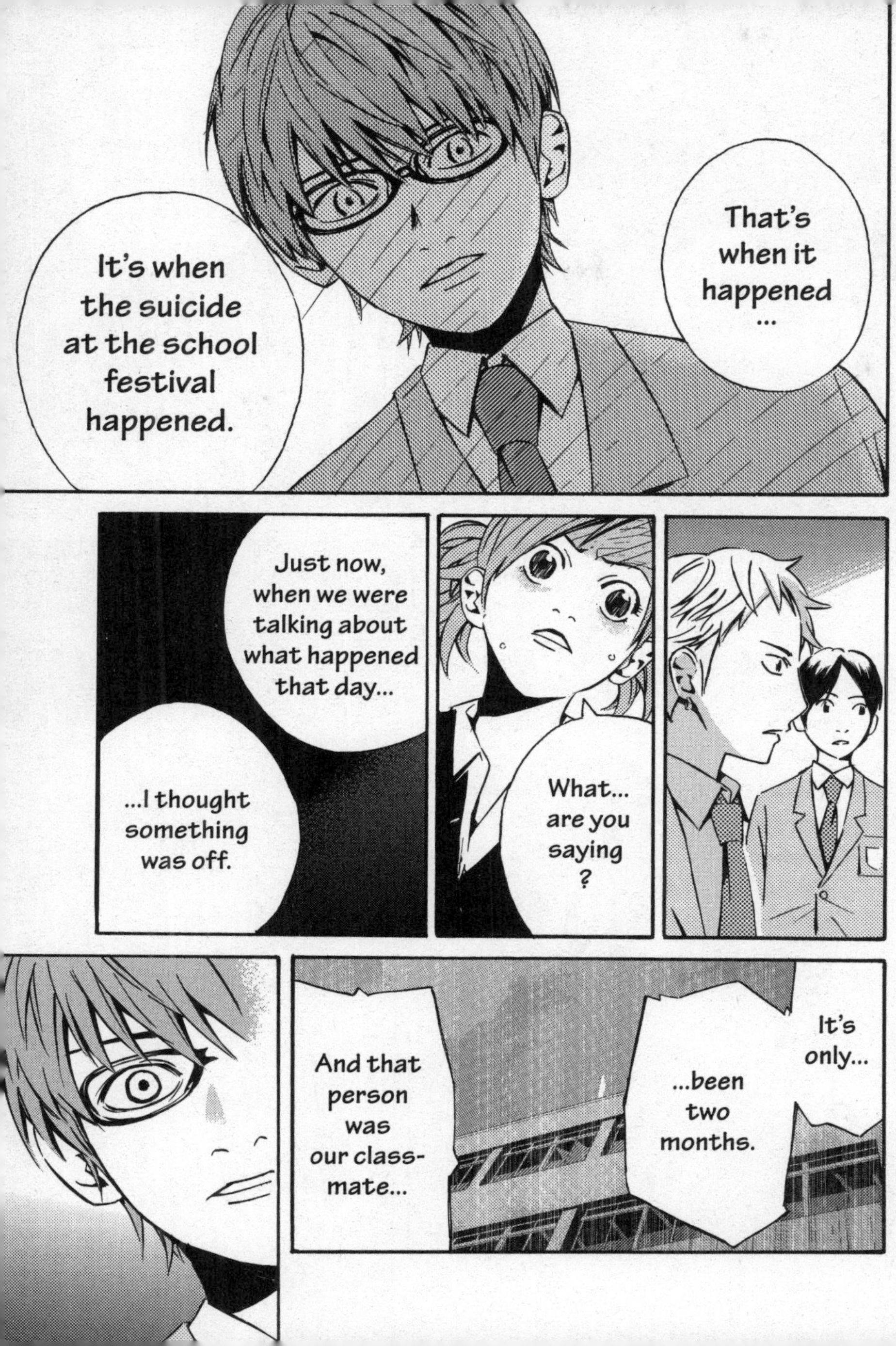
That's when it happened...
It's when the suicide at the school festival happened.
What... are you saying?
Just now, when we were talking about what happened that day...
...I thought something was off.
It's only...
...been two months.
And that person was our class-mate...

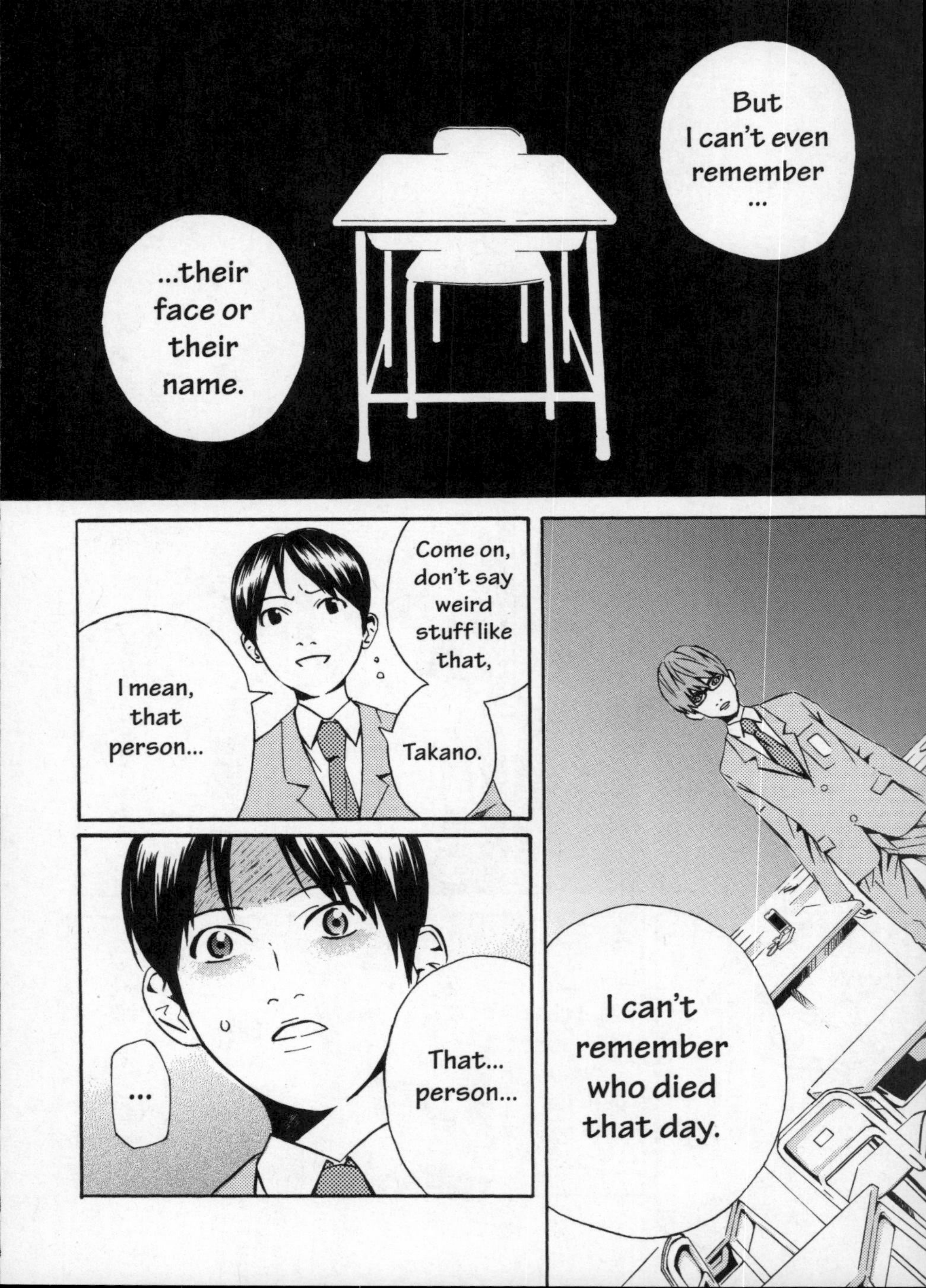
But I can't even remember ...
...their face or their name.
I can't remember who died that day.
Come on, don't say weird stuff like that,
Takano.
I mean, that person...
That... person...
...

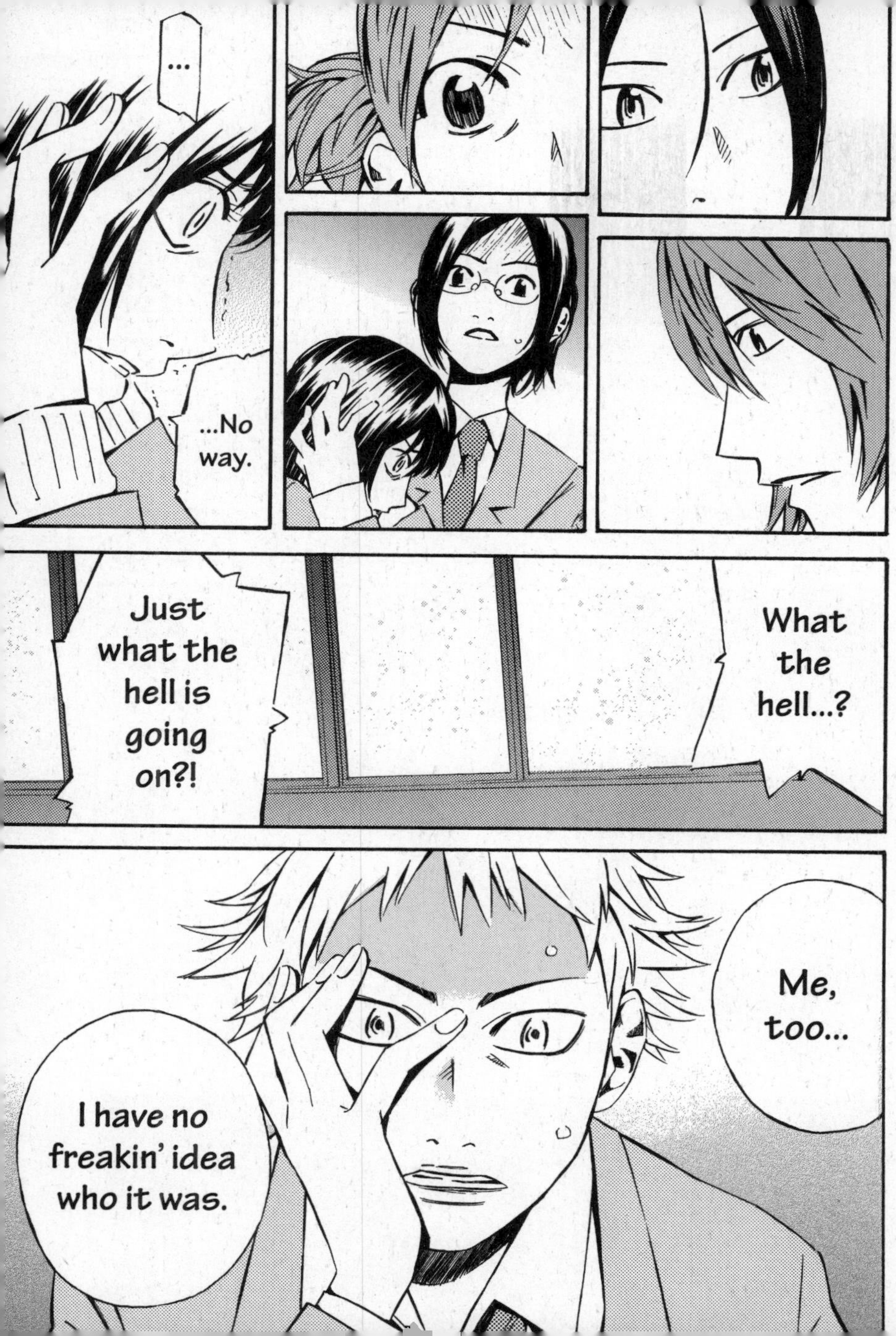
...
...No way.
What the hell...?
Just what the hell is going on?!
Me, too...
I have no freakin' idea who it was.

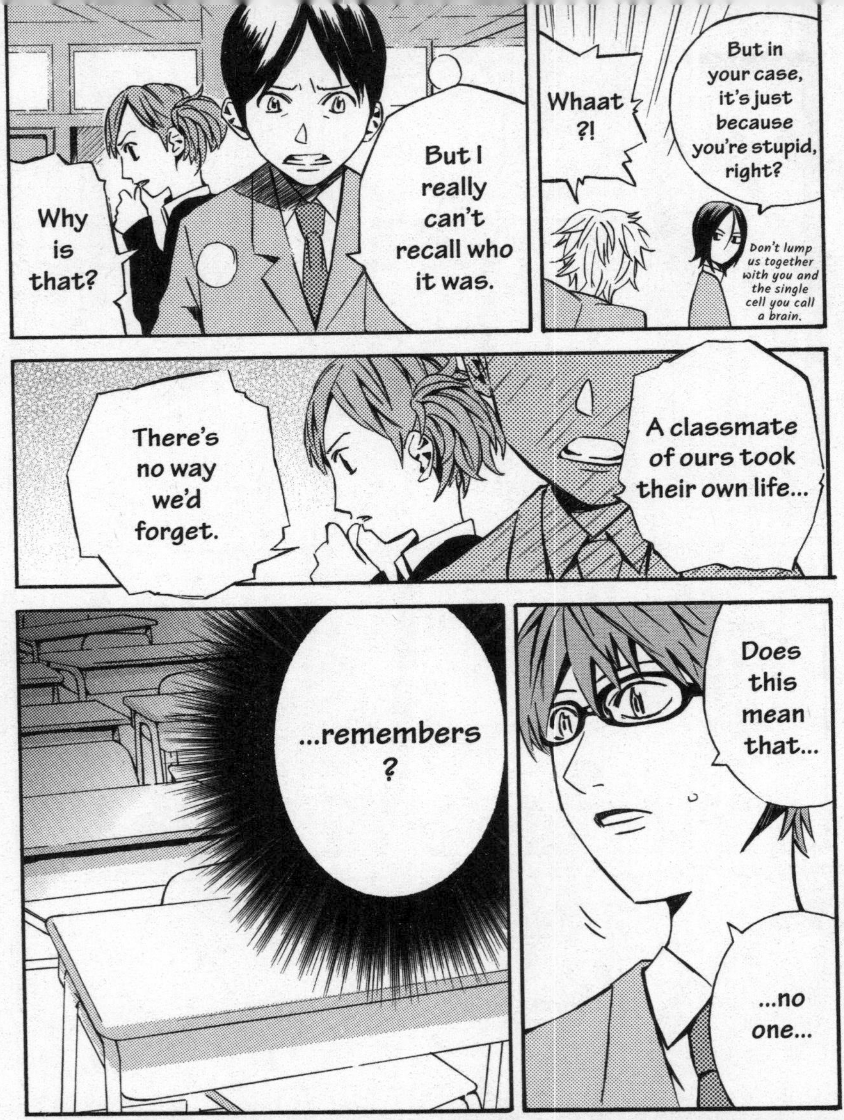
But in your case, it's just because you're stupid, right?
Whaat ?!
Don't lump us together with you and the single cell you call a brain.
But I really can't recall who it was.
Why is that?
A classmate of ours took their own life...
There's no way we'd forget.
Does this mean that...
...no one...
...remembers ?

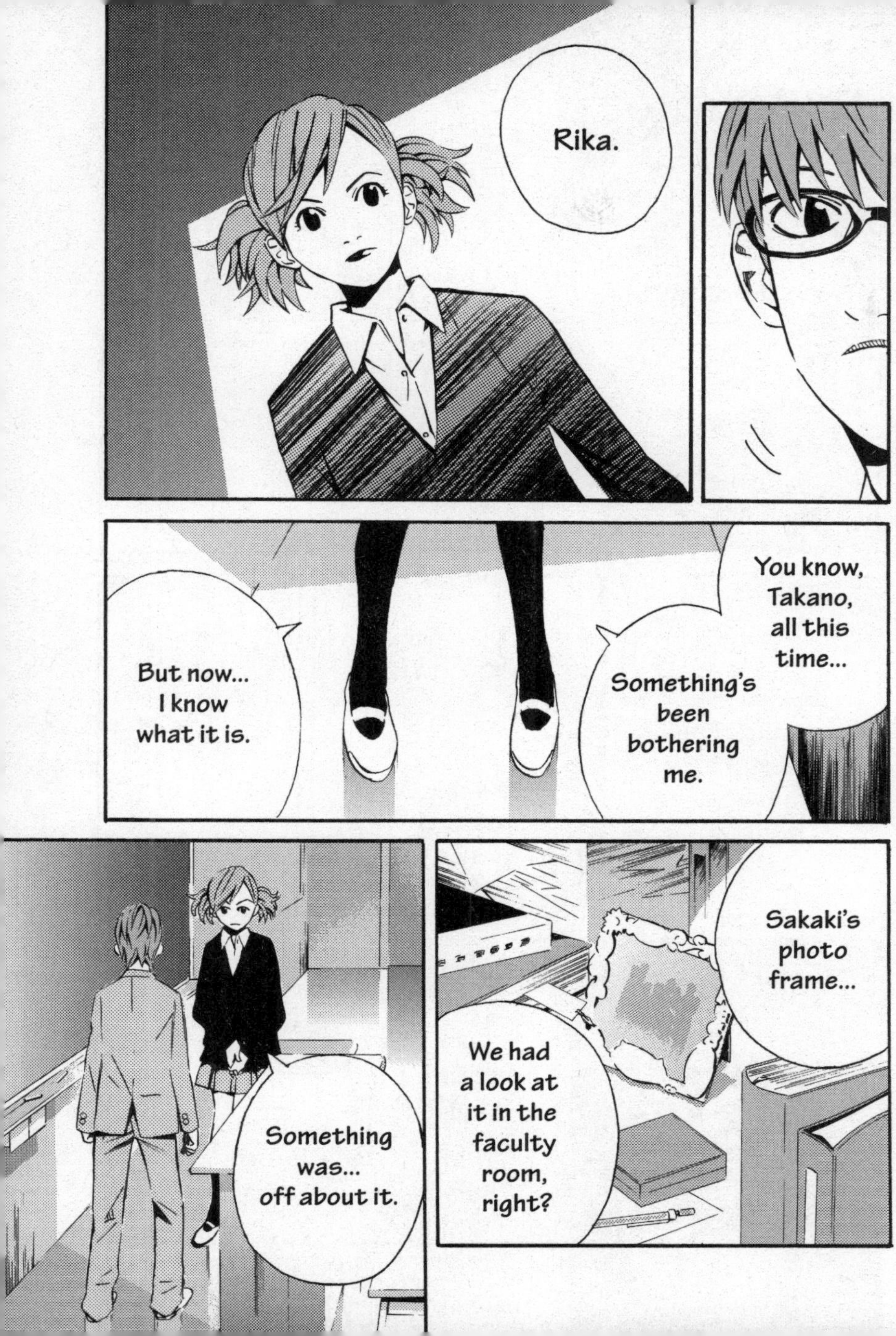
Rika.
You know, Takano, all this time...
Something's been bothering me.
But now... I know what it is.
Sakaki's photo frame...
We had a look at it in the faculty room, right?
Something was... off about it.

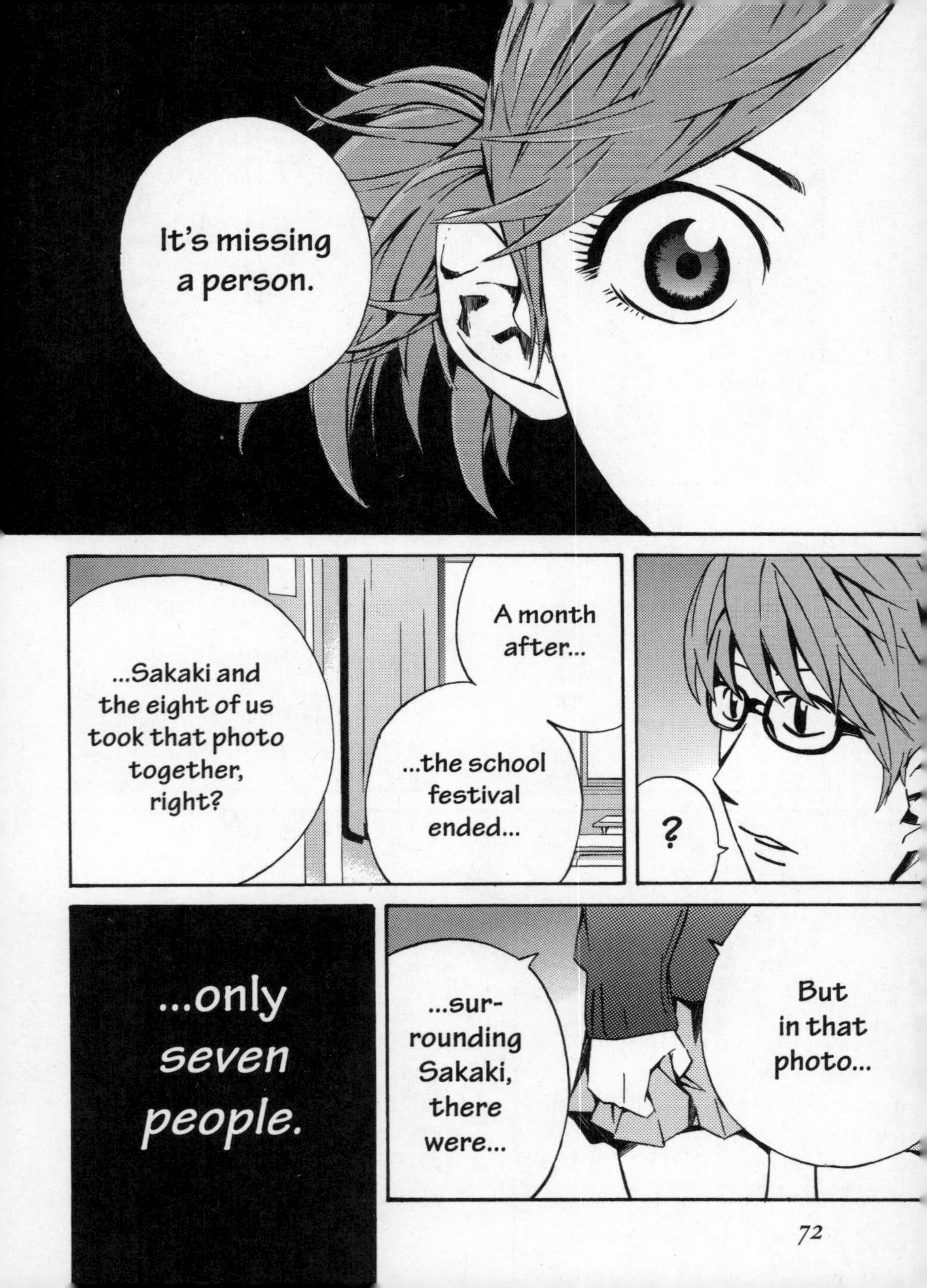
It's missing a person.
?
A month after...
...the school festival ended...
...Sakaki and the eight of us took that photo together, right?
But in that photo...
...sur-rounding Sakaki, there were...
...only seven people.

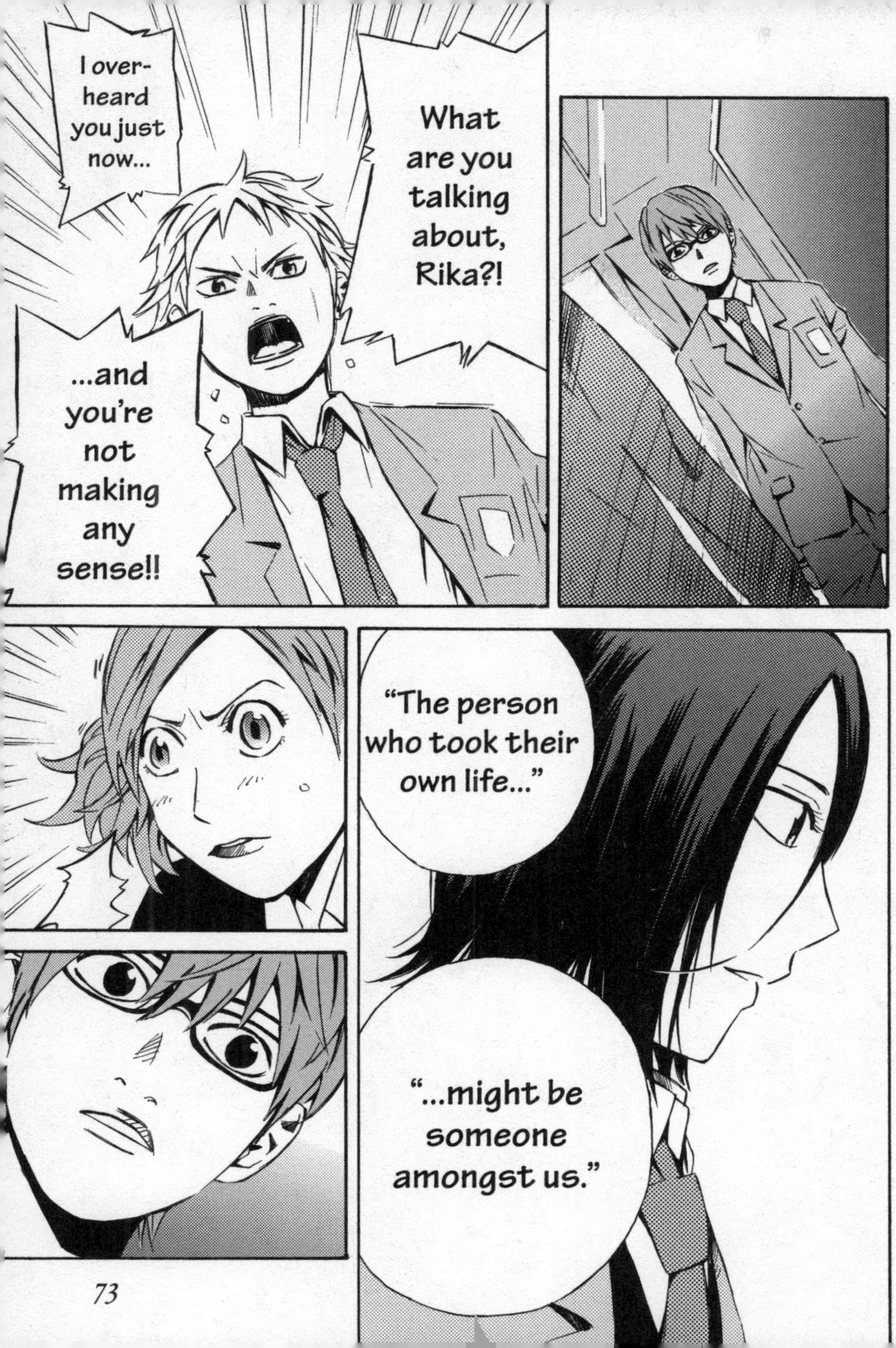
What are you talking about, Rika?!
I over-heard you just now...
...and you're not making any sense!!
"The person who took their own life..."
"...might be someone amongst us."

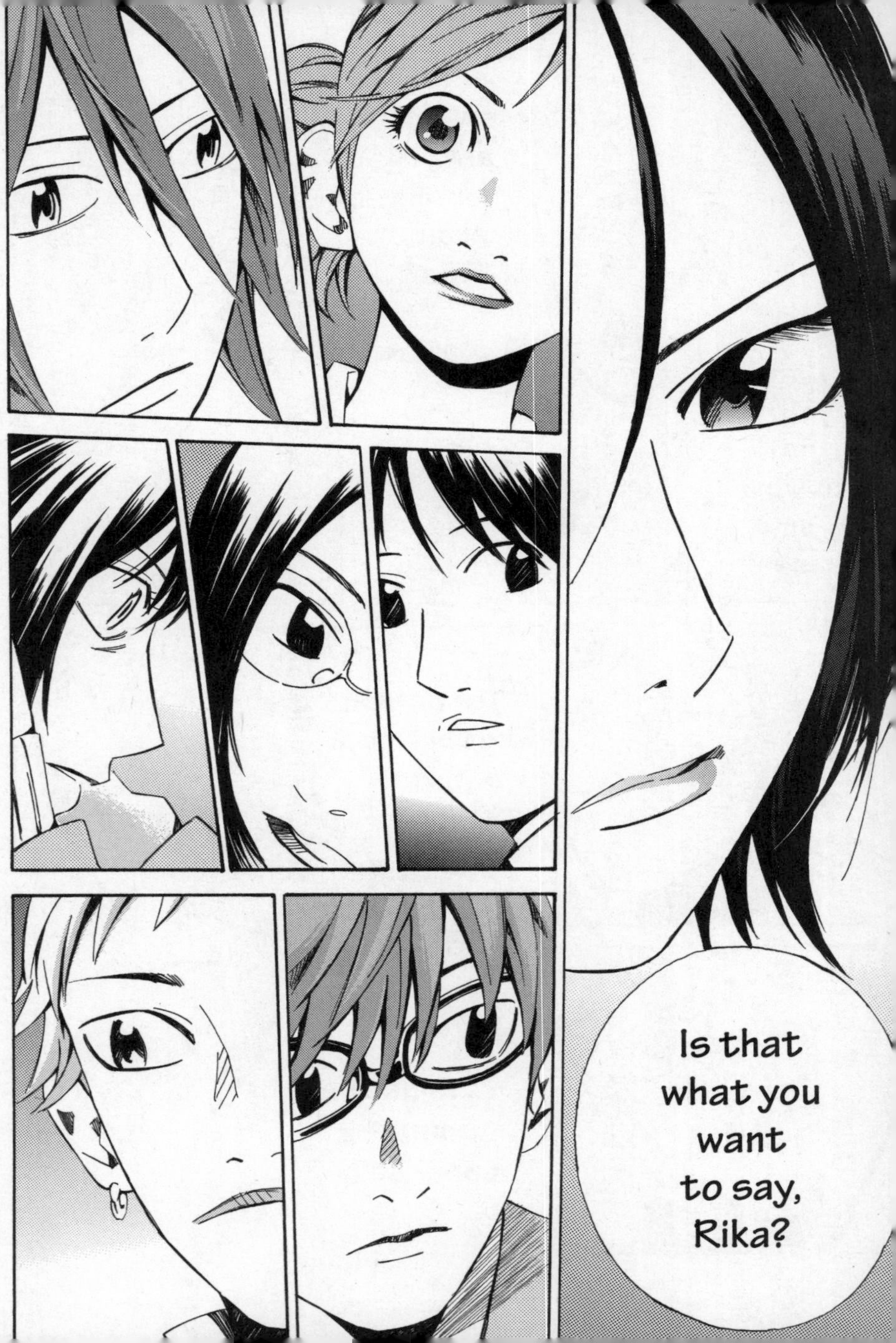
Is that what you want to say, Rika?

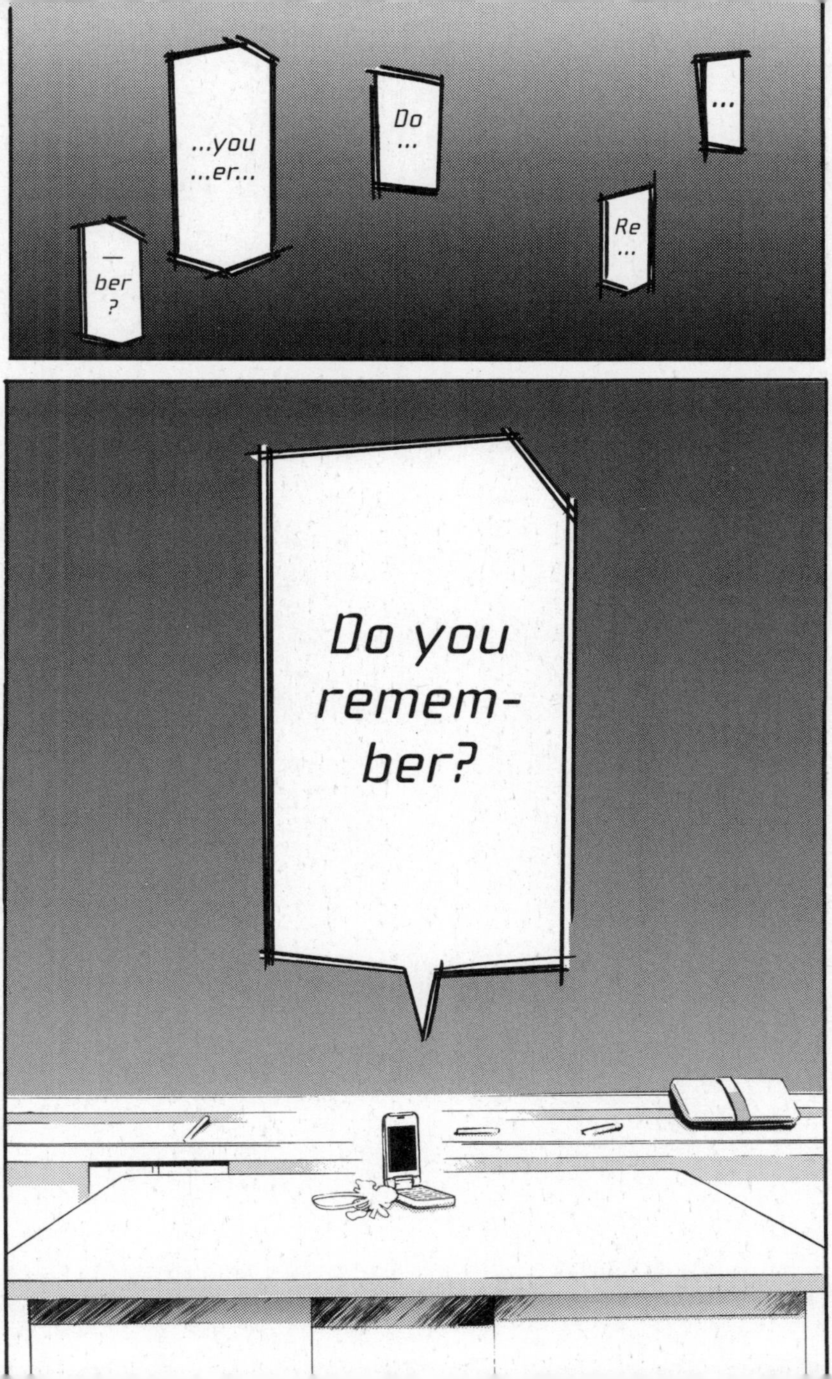
...
Re ...
Do ...
...you ...er...
— ber ?
Do you remem-ber?

A School
Frozen
in Time

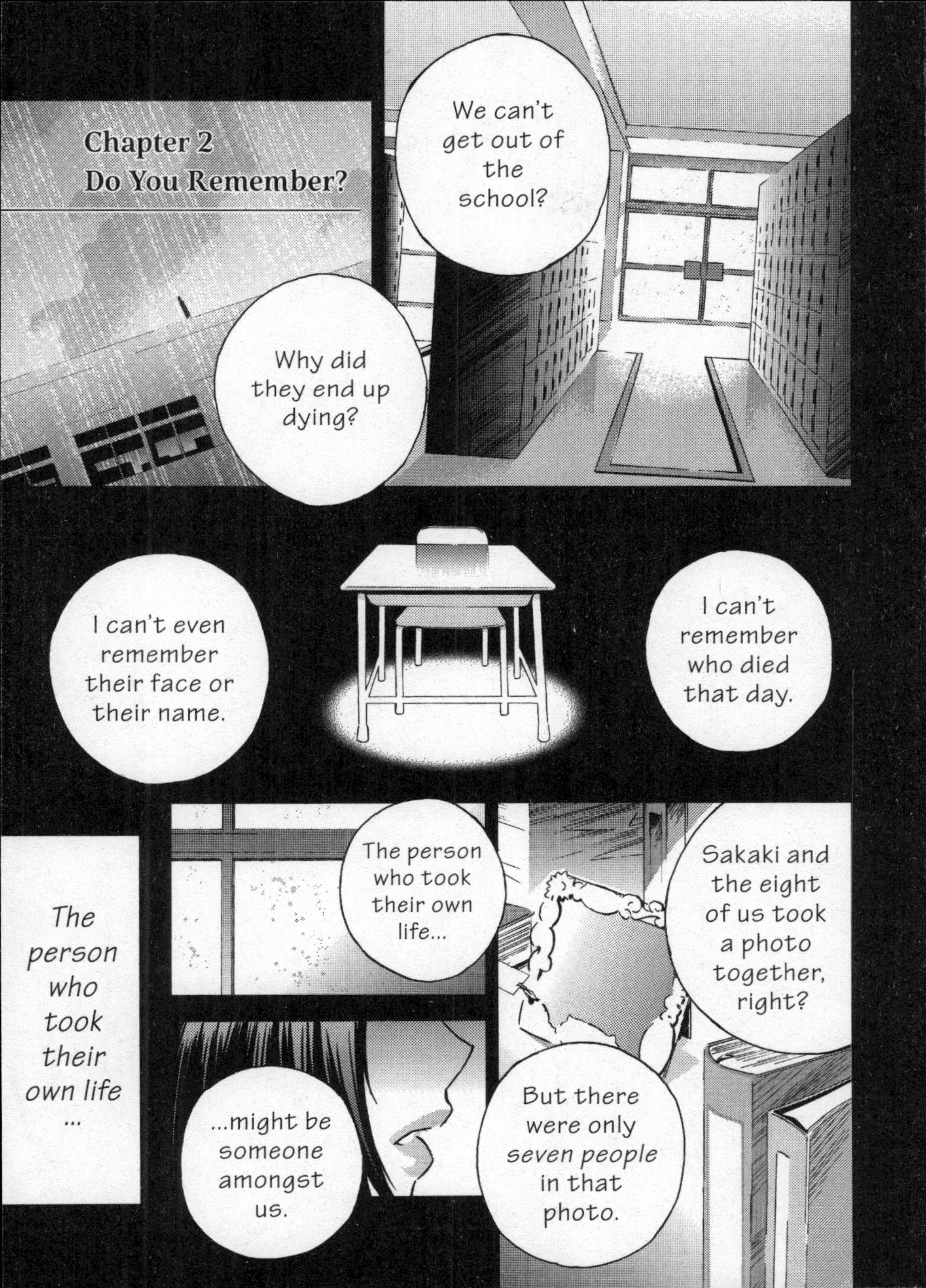
We can't get out of the school?
Why did they end up dying?
Chapter 2
Do You Remember?
I can't remember who died that day.
I can't even remember their face or their name.
Sakaki and the eight of us took a photo together, right?
But there were only seven people in that photo.
The person who took their own life...
...might be someone amongst us.
The person who took their own life ...

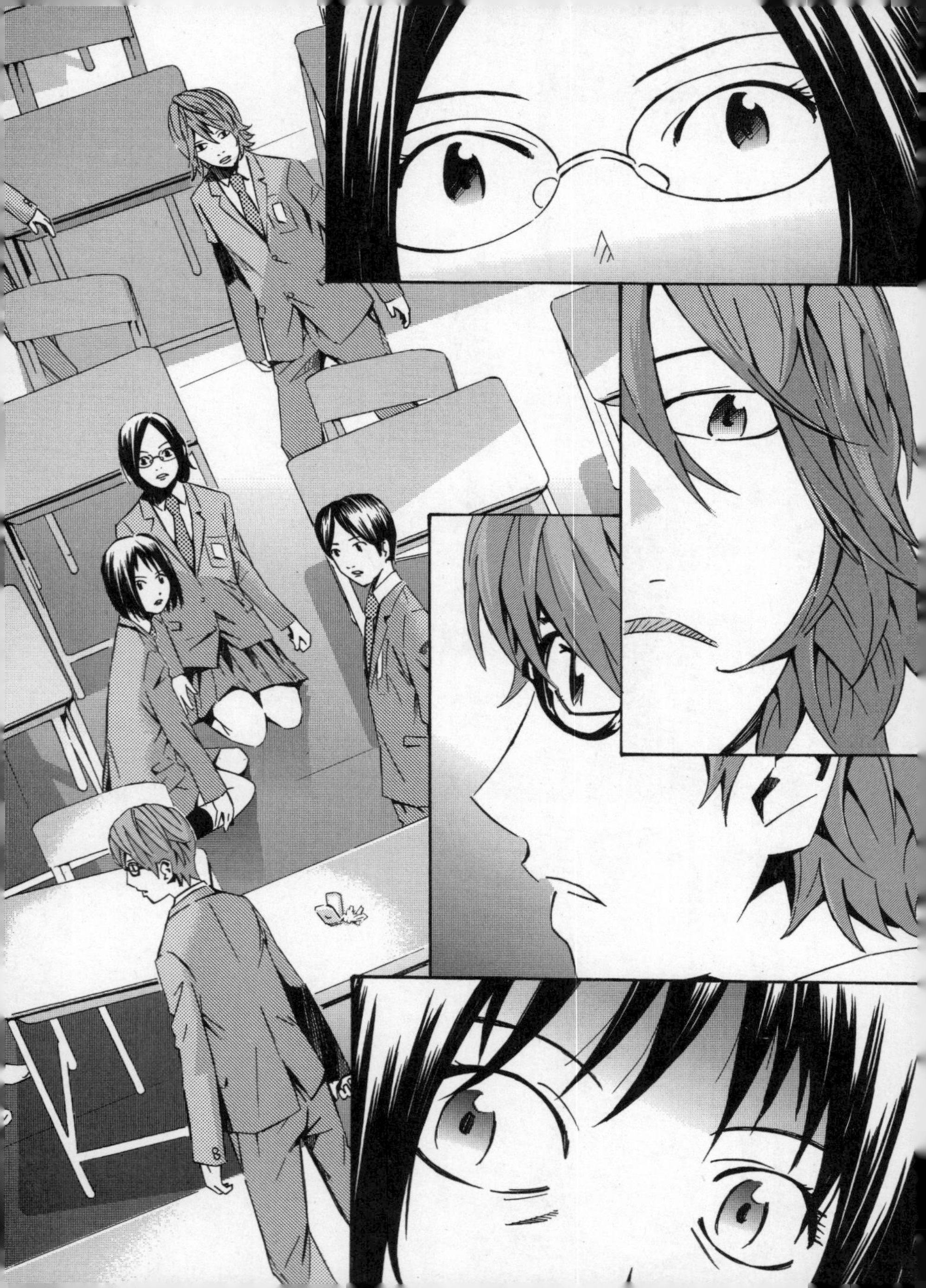

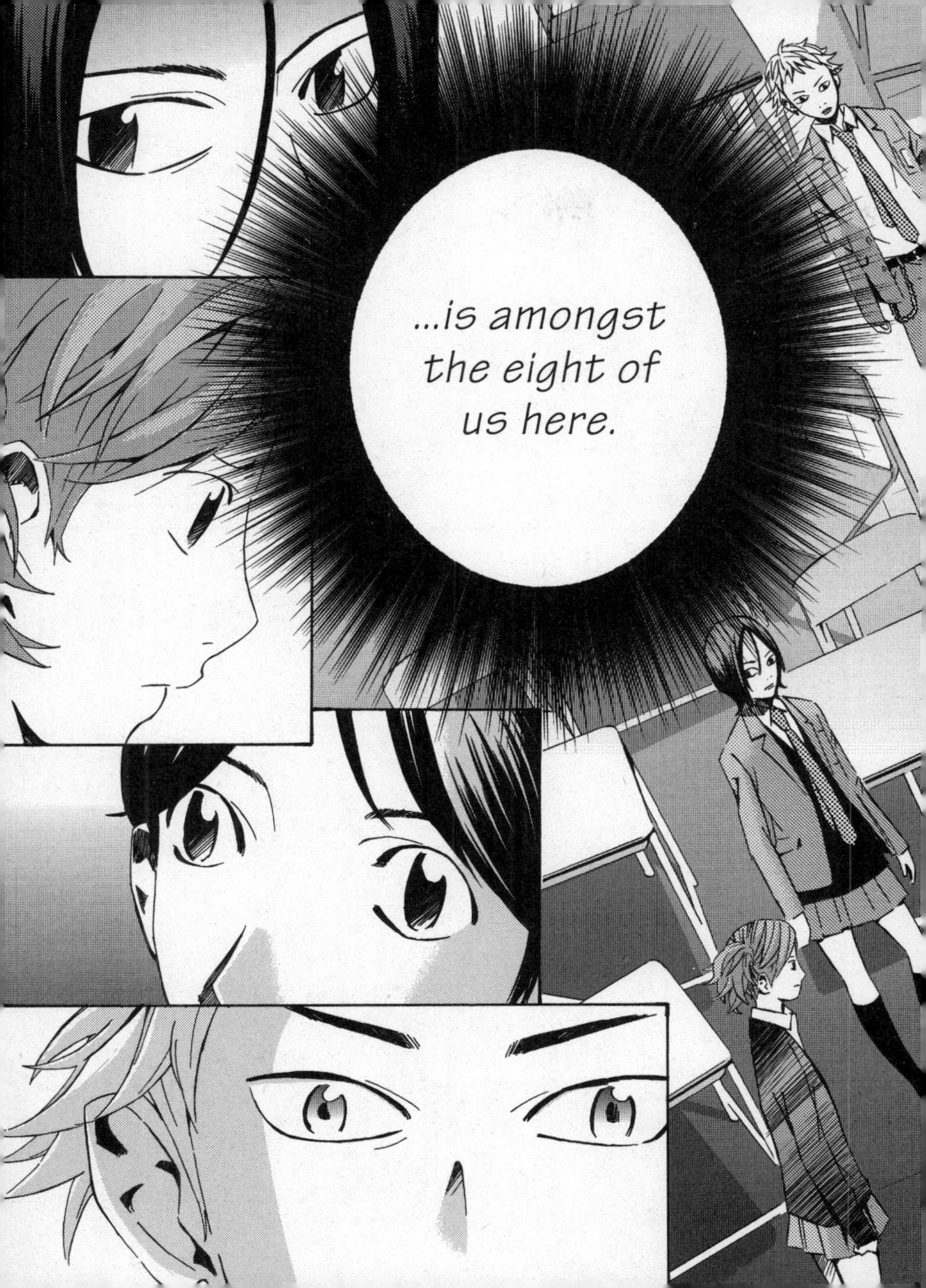
...is amongst the eight of us here.

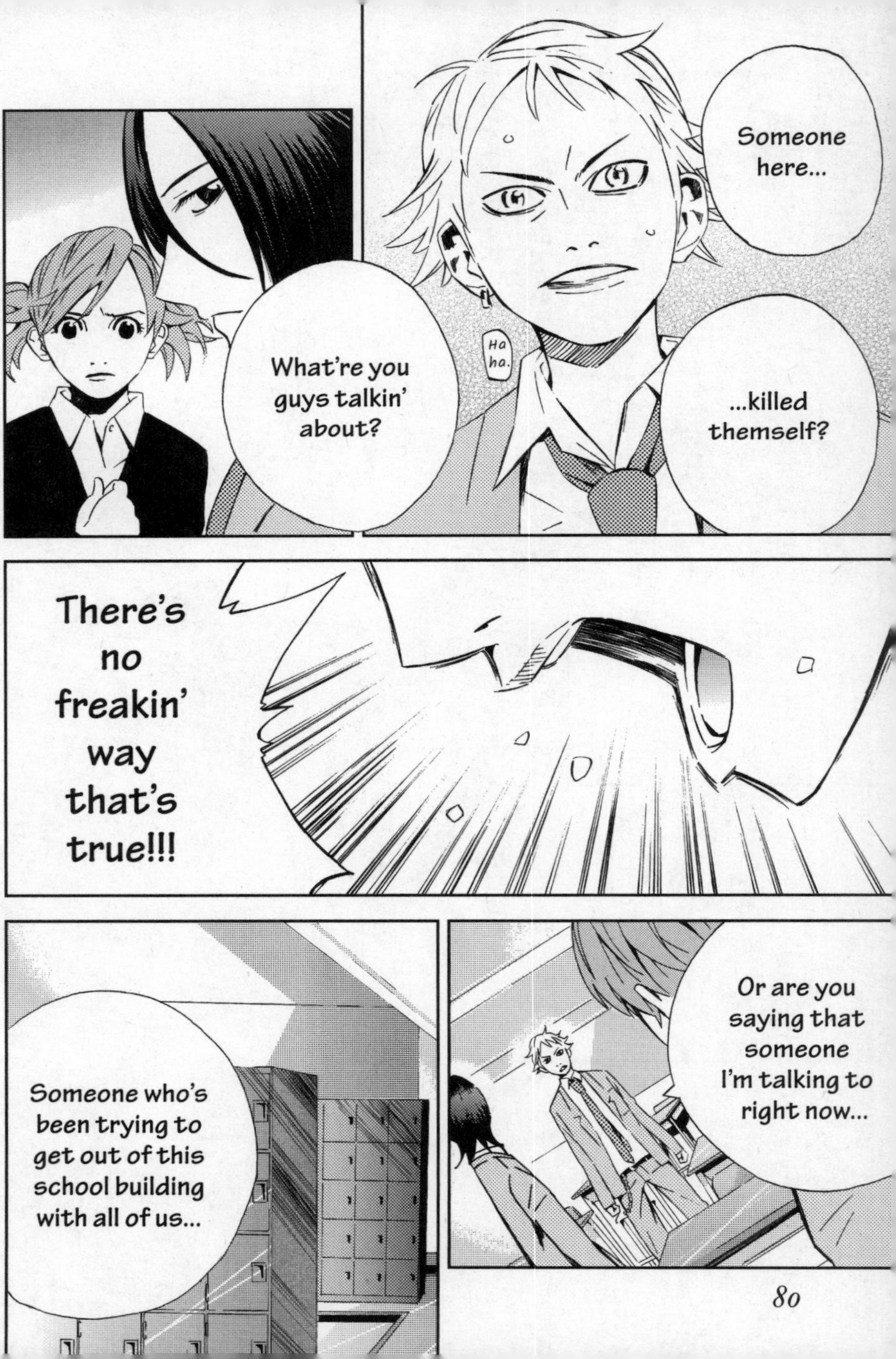
Someone here...
Ha ha.
...killed themself?
What're you guys talkin' about?
There's no freakin' way that's true!!!
Or are you saying that someone I'm talking to right now...
Someone who's been trying to get out of this school building with all of us...

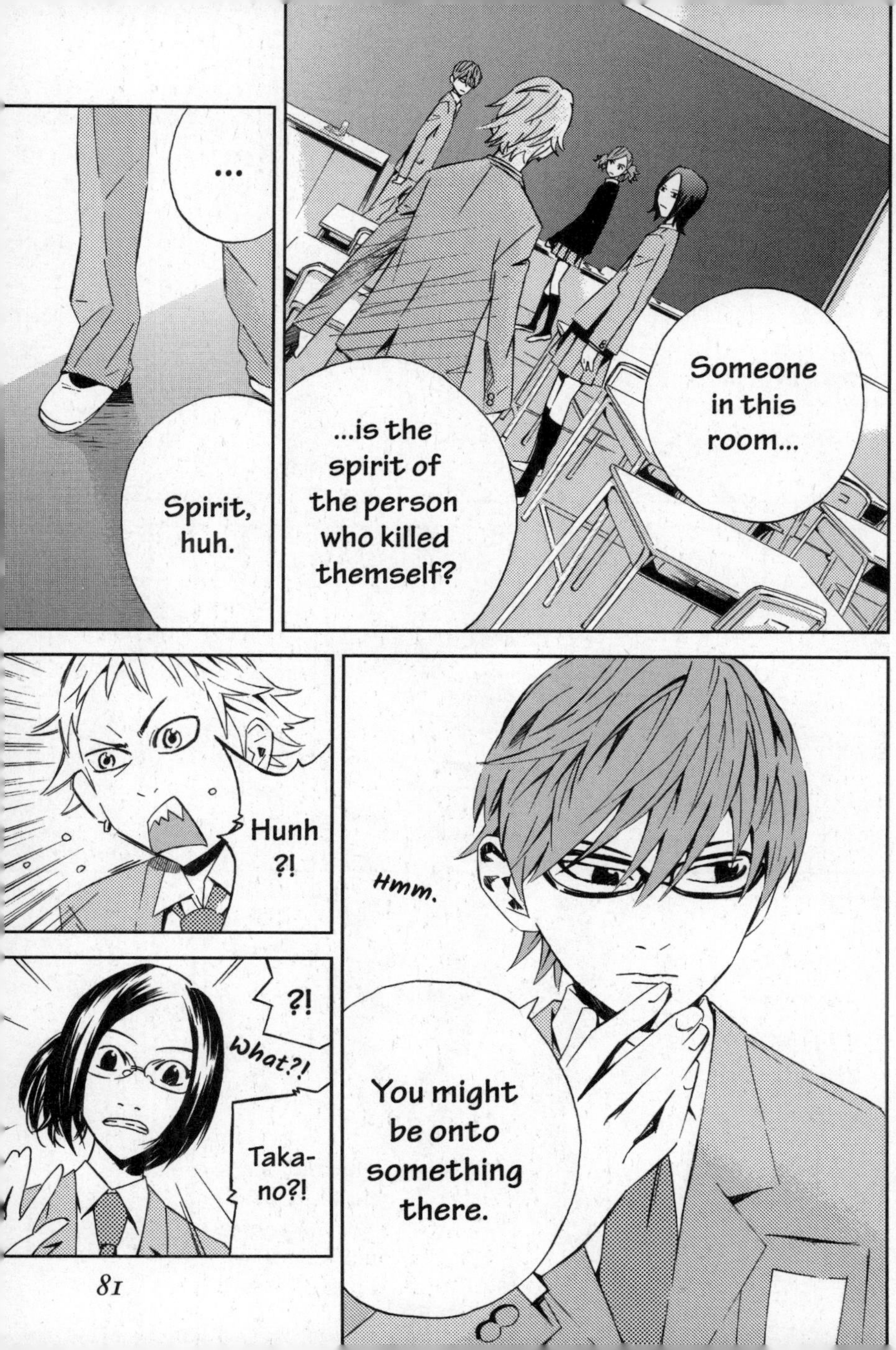
Someone in this room...
...is the spirit of the person who killed themself?
...
Spirit, huh.
Hmm.
You might be onto something there.
Hunh ?!
?!
What?!
Taka-no?!

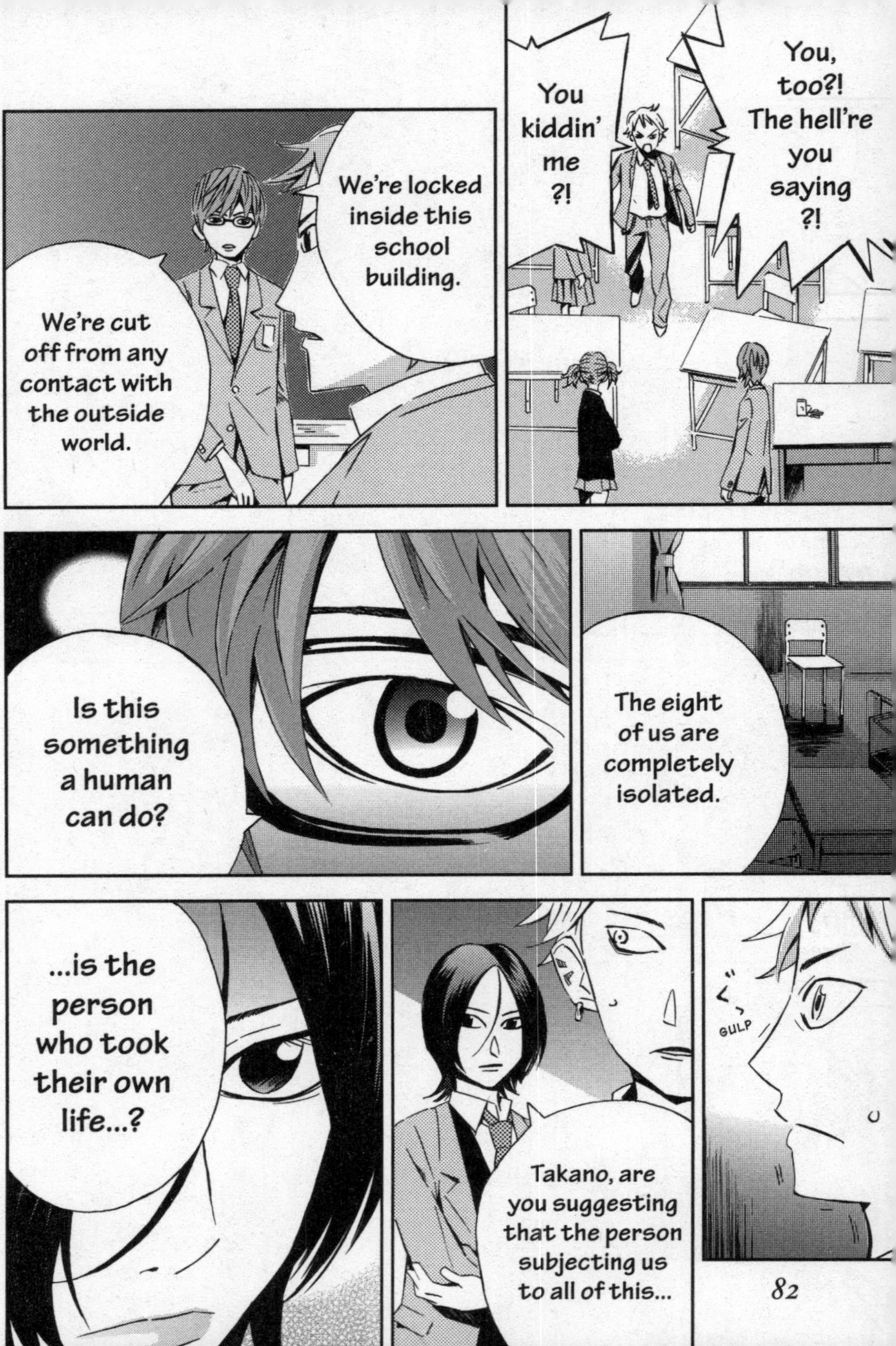
You, too?! The hell're you saying ?!
You kiddin' me ?!
We're locked inside this school building.
We're cut off from any contact with the outside world.
The eight of us are completely isolated.
Is this something a human can do?
GULP
Takano, are you suggesting that the person subjecting us to all of this...
...is the person who took their own life...?

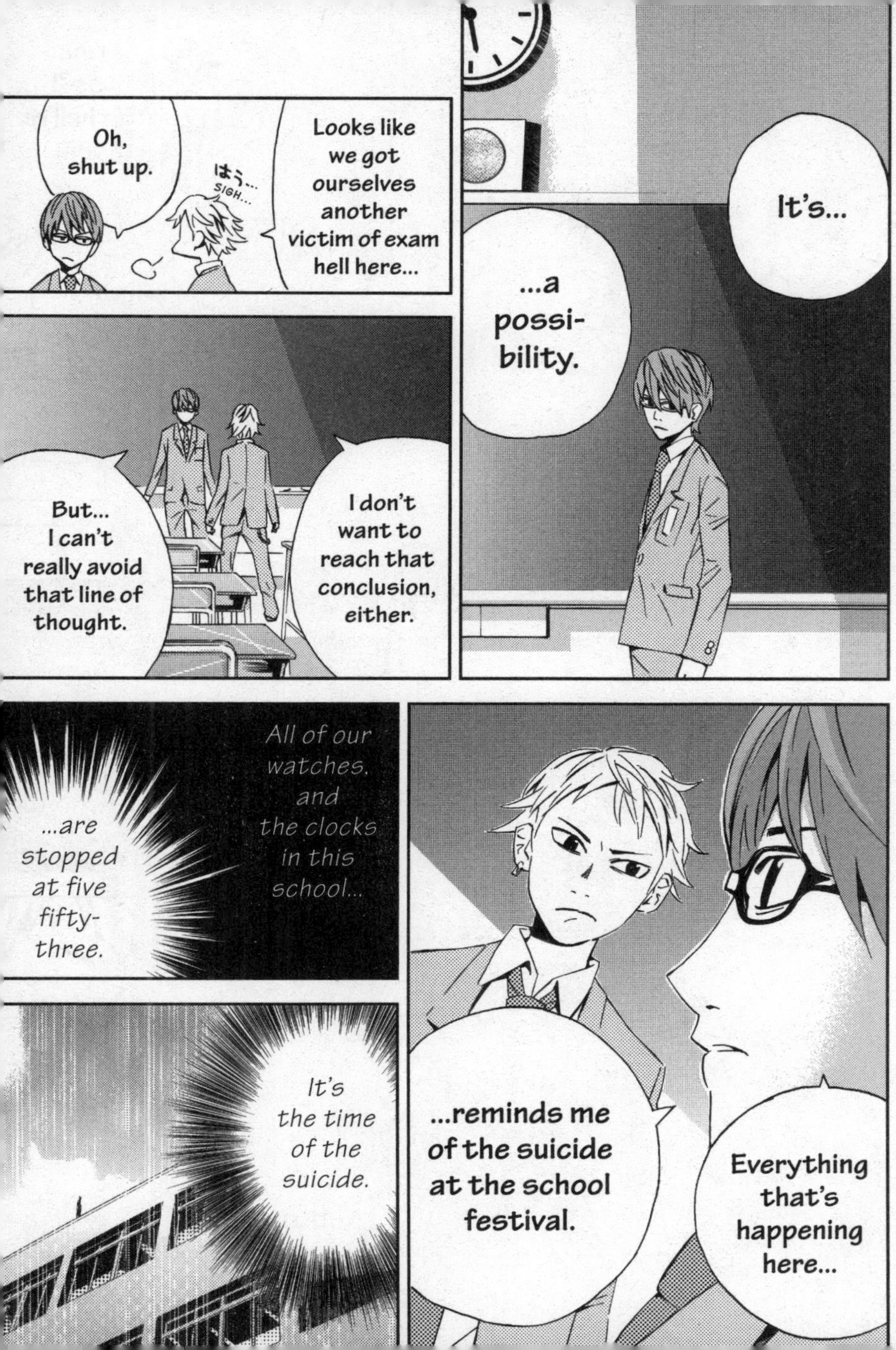
It's...
...a possibility.
Looks like we got ourselves another victim of exam hell here...
はぅ… SIGH...
Oh, shut up.
I don't want to reach that conclusion, either.
But... I can't really avoid that line of thought.
Everything that's happening here...
...reminds me of the suicide at the school festival.
All of our watches, and the clocks in this school...
...are stopped at five fifty-three.
It's the time of the suicide.

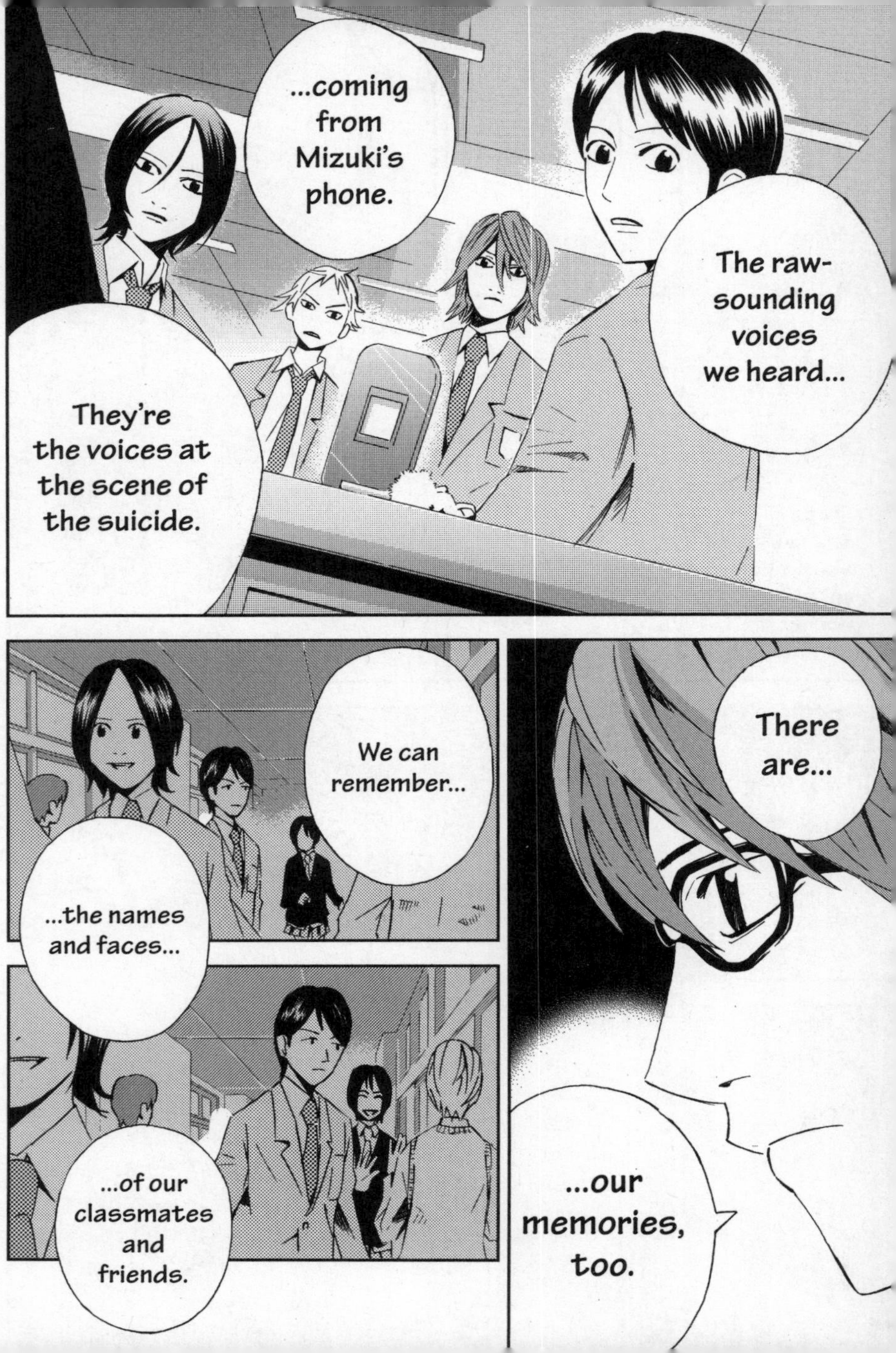
The raw-sounding voices we heard...
...coming from Mizuki's phone.
They're the voices at the scene of the suicide.
There are...
...our memories, too.
We can remember...
...the names and faces...
...of our classmates and friends.

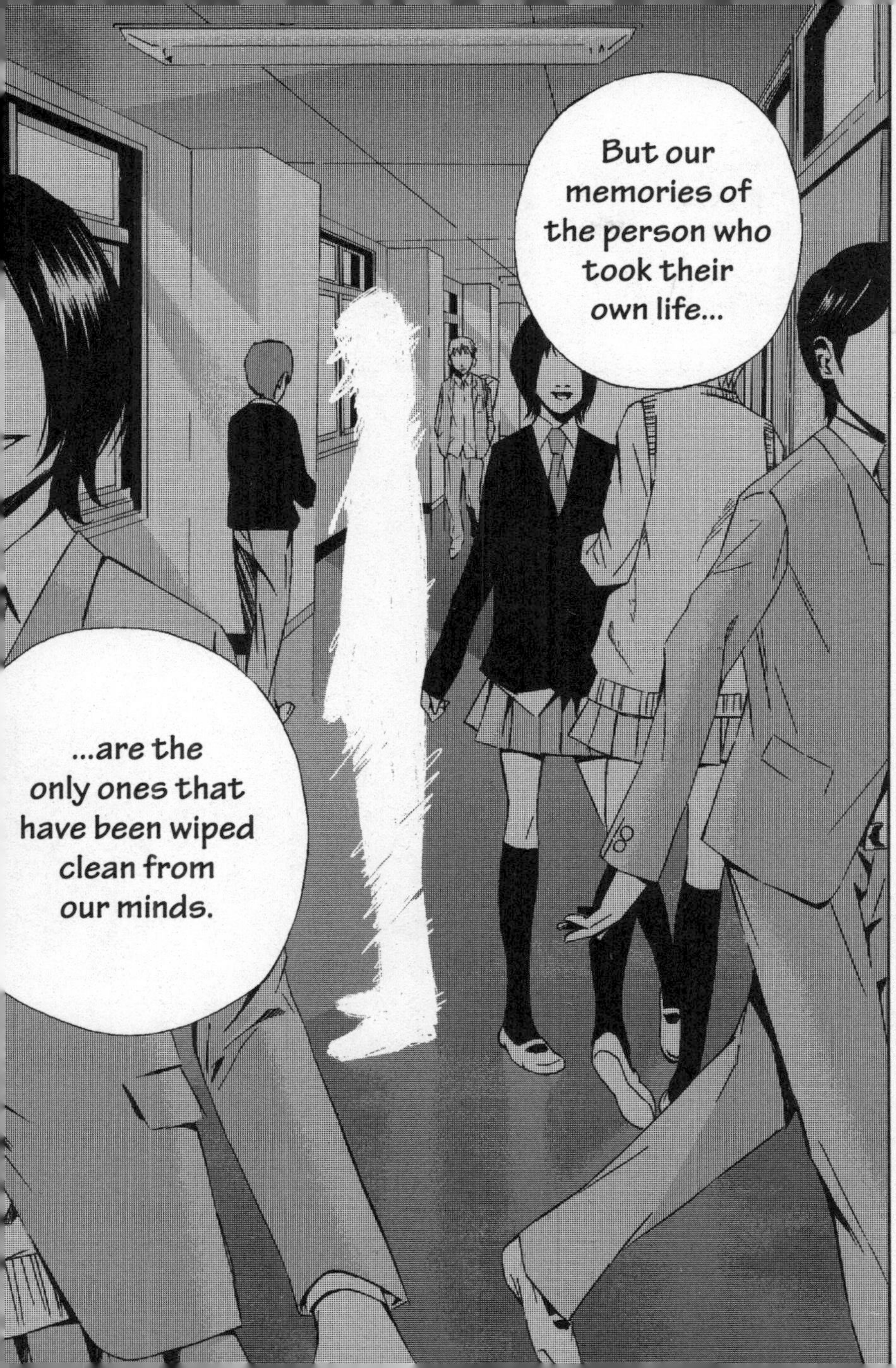
But our memories of the person who took their own life...
...are the only ones that have been wiped clean from our minds.

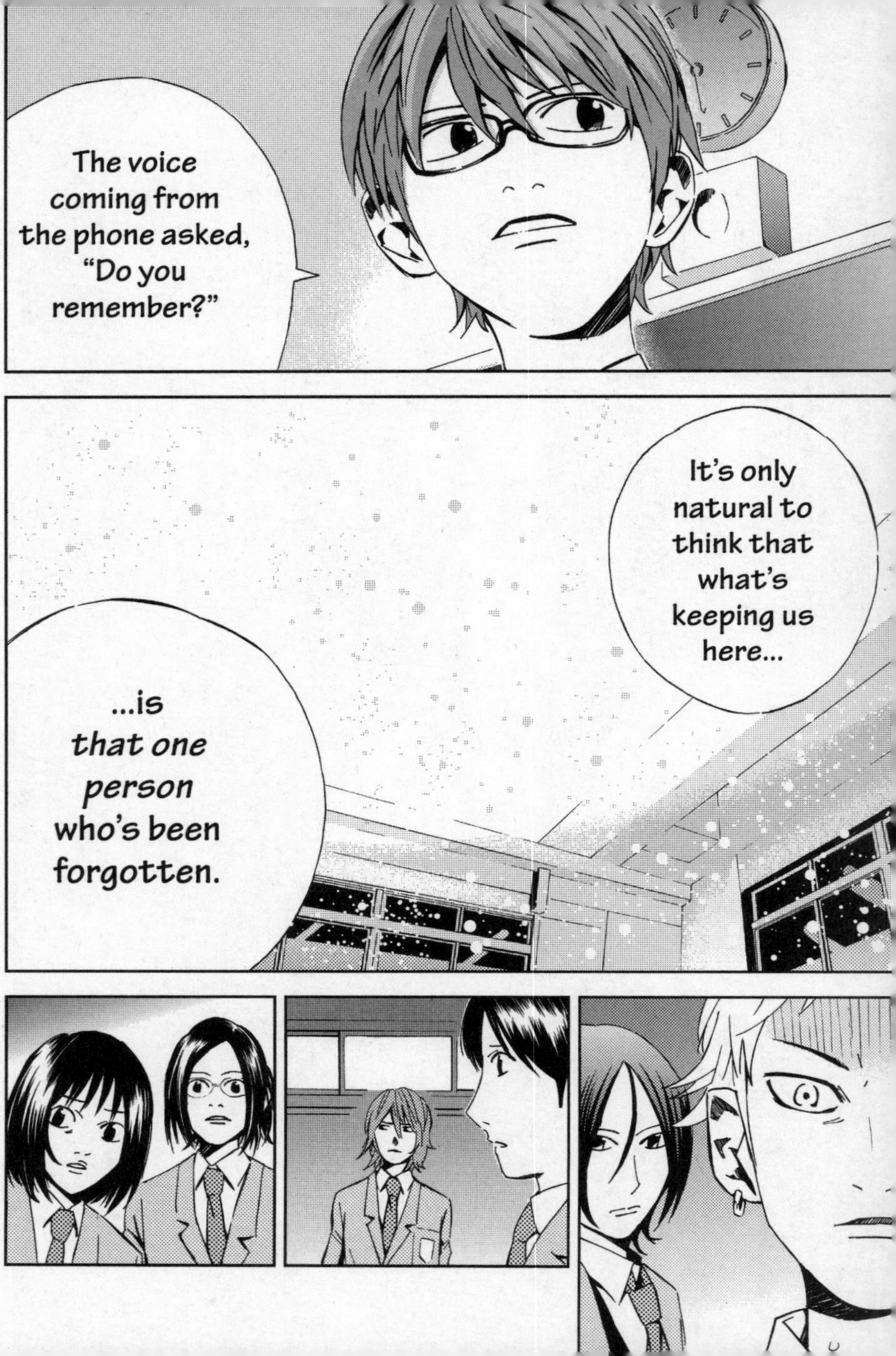
The voice coming from the phone asked, "Do you remember?"
It's only natural to think that what's keeping us here...
...is *that one person* who's been forgotten.

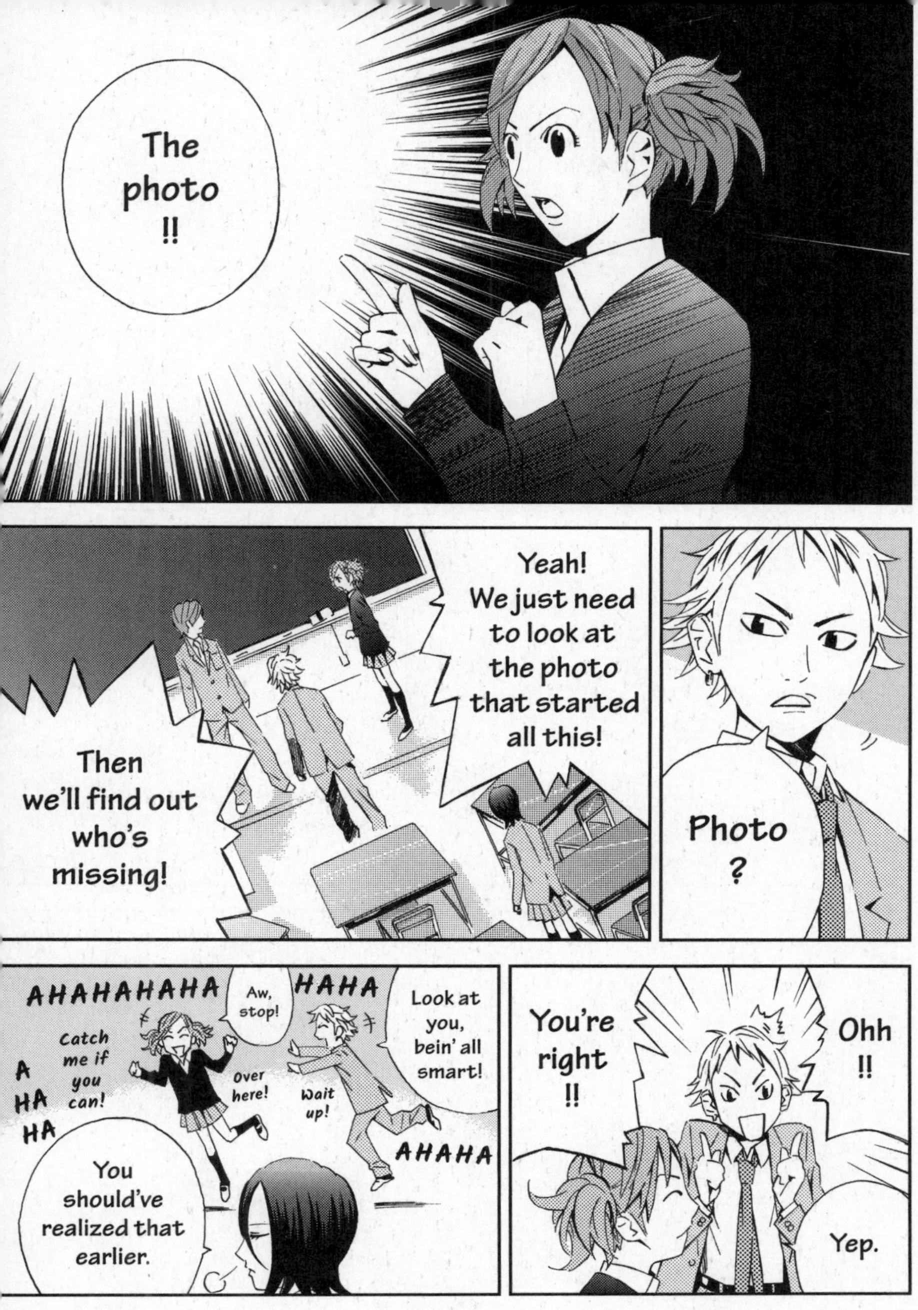
The photo !!
Photo ?
Yeah! We just need to look at the photo that started all this!
Then we'll find out who's missing!
Ohh !!
You're right !!
Yep.
Look at you, bein' all smart!
HAHA
Aw, stop!
AHAHAHAHA
Catch me if you can!
Over here!
Wait up!
A HA HA
AHAHA
You should've realized that earlier.

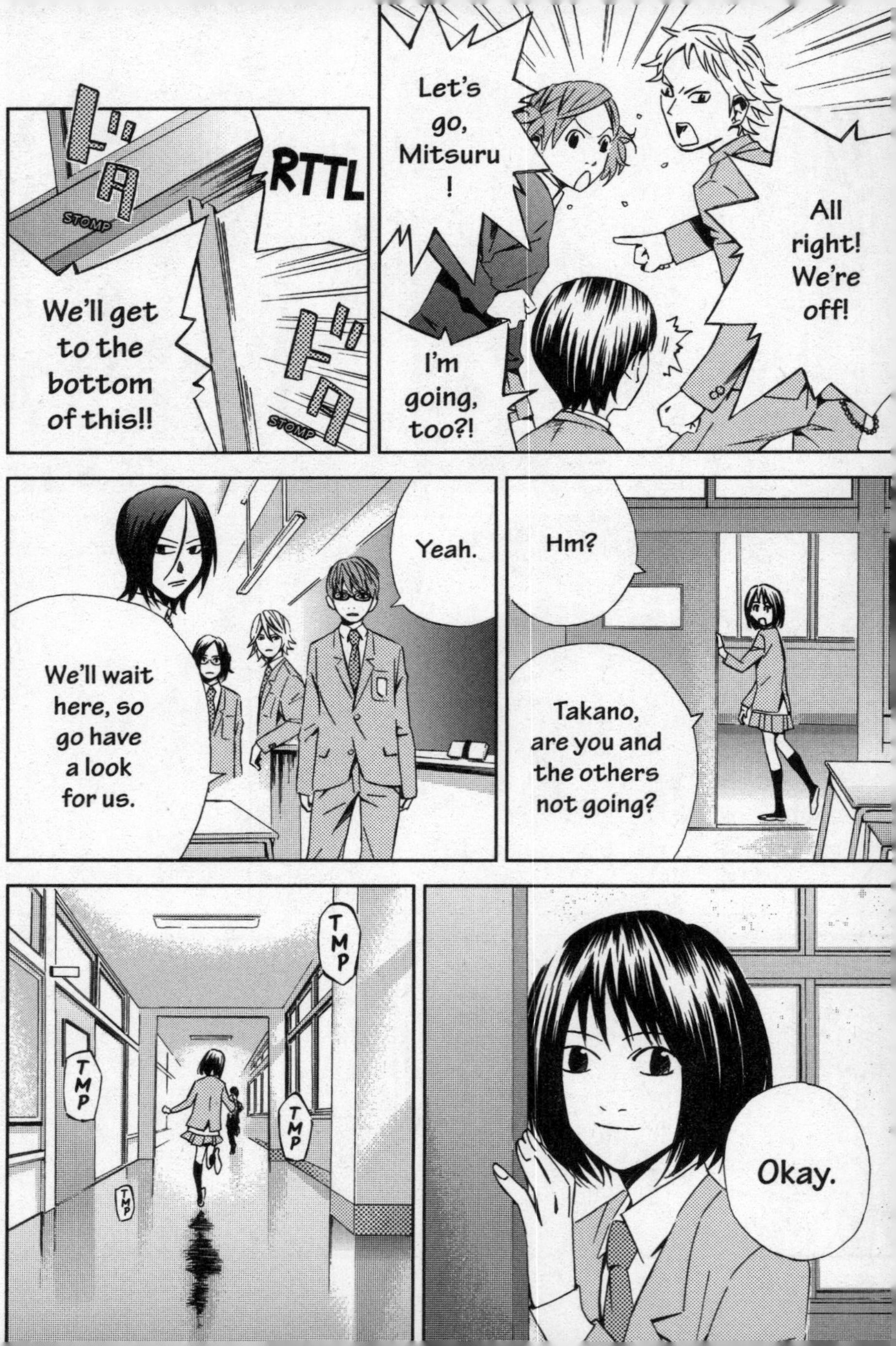
Let's go, Mitsuru!
All right! We're off!
I'm going, too?!
RTTL
STOMP
STOMP
We'll get to the bottom of this!!
Hm?
Takano, are you and the others not going?
Yeah.
We'll wait here, so go have a look for us.
Okay.
TMP
TMP
TMP
TMP

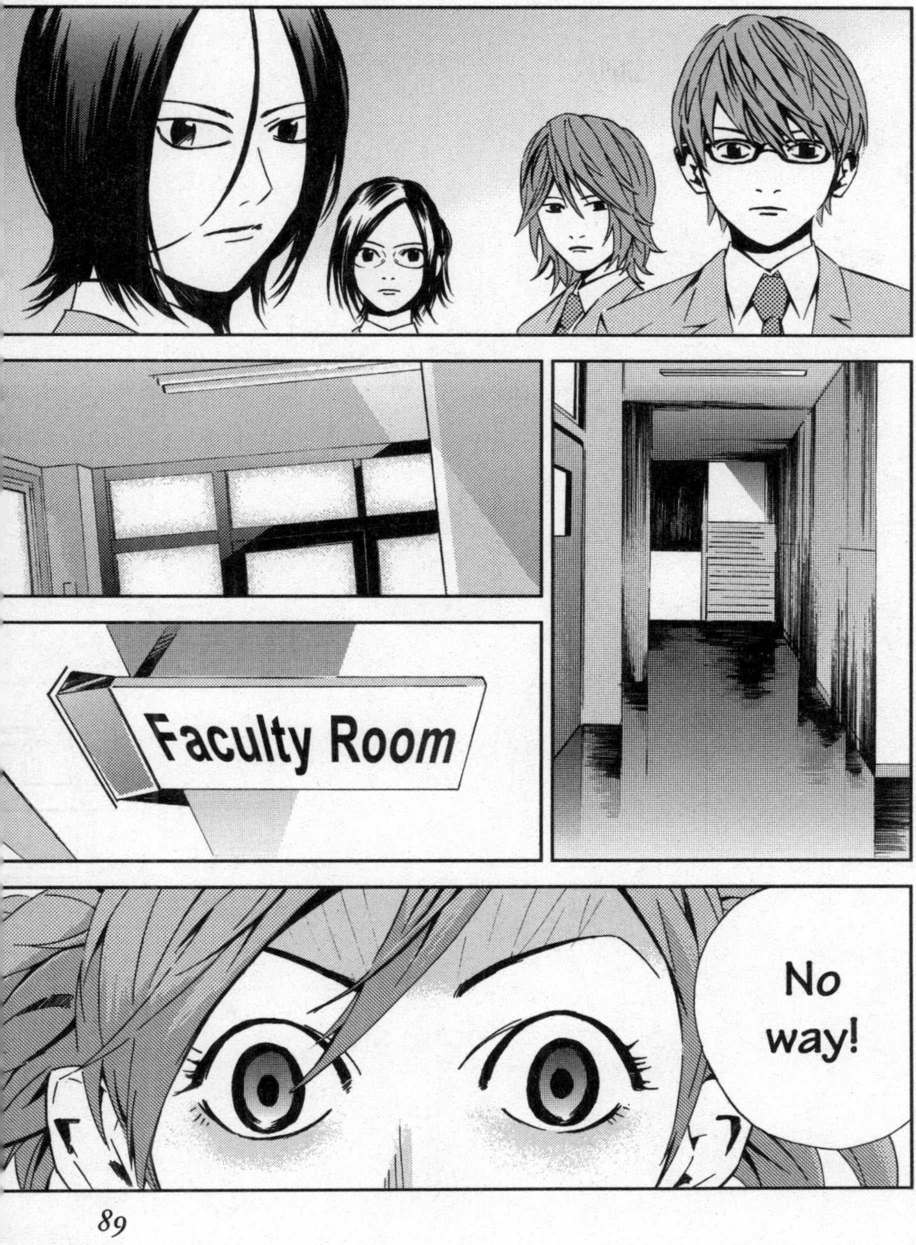
Faculty Room
No way!

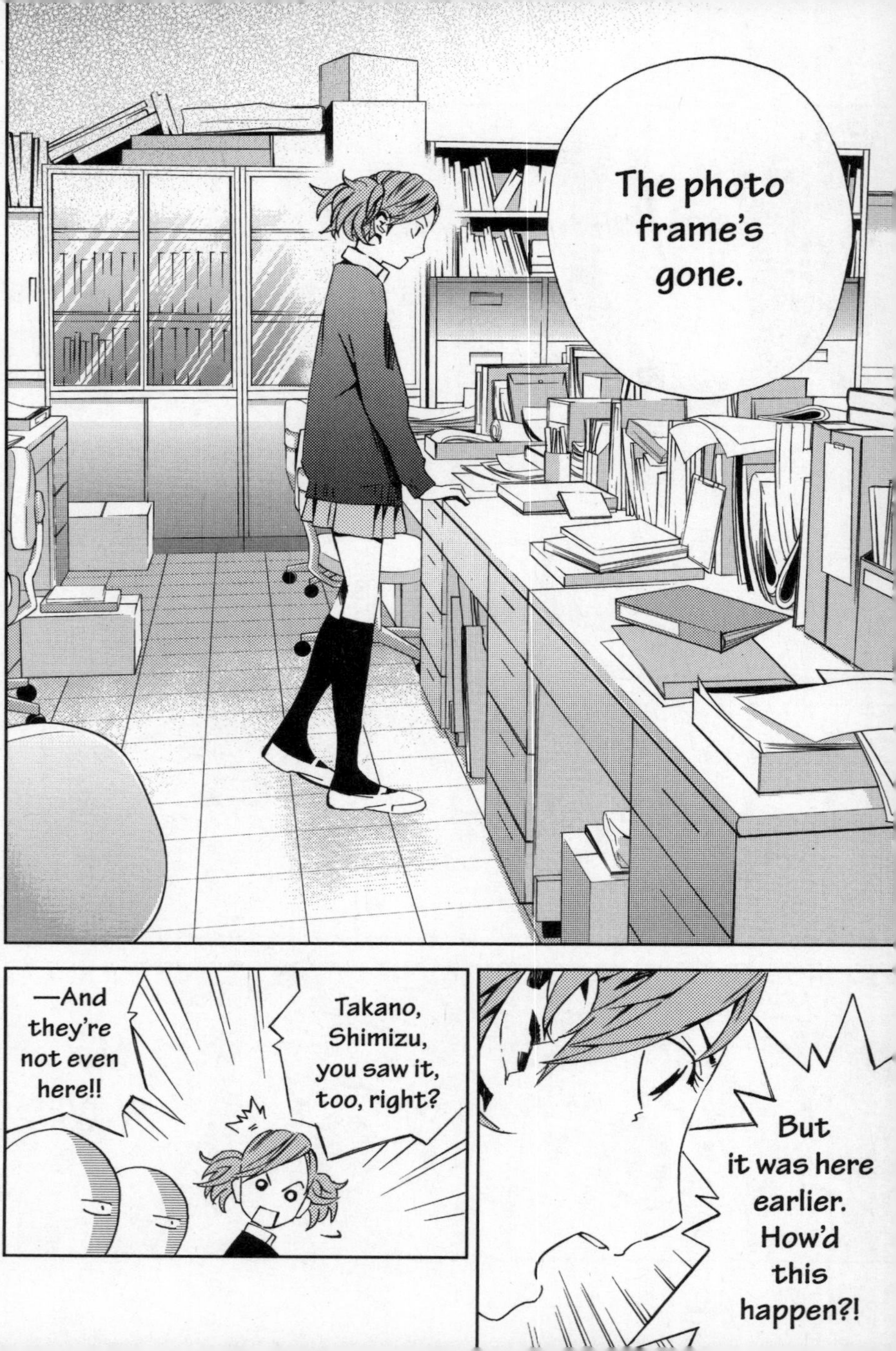
The photo frame's gone.
But it was here earlier. How'd this happen?!
Takano, Shimizu, you saw it, too, right?
—And they're not even here!!

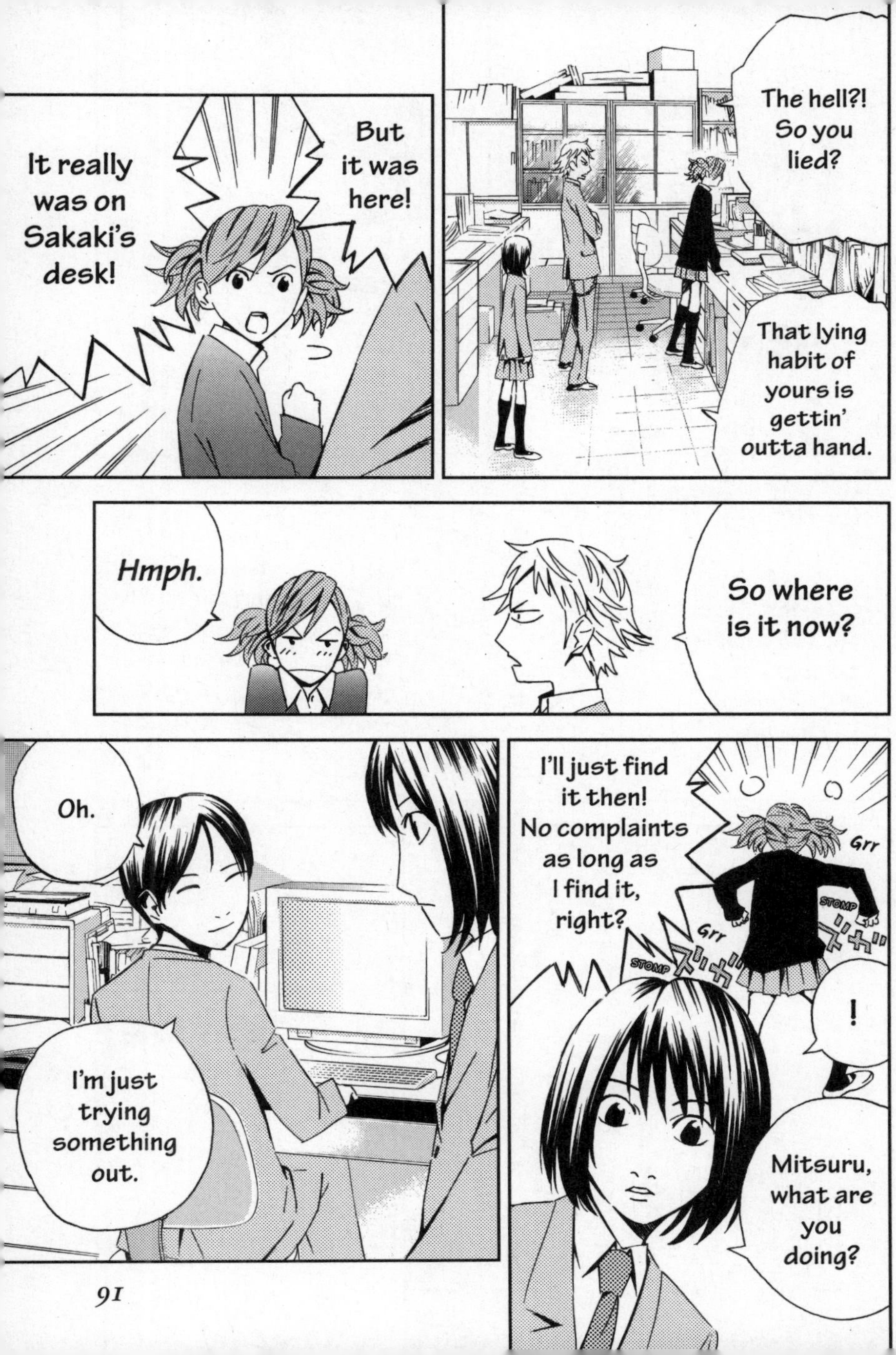
The hell?! So you lied?
That lying habit of yours is gettin' outta hand.
But it was here!
It really was on Sakaki's desk!
So where is it now?
Hmph.
I'll just find it then! No complaints as long as I find it, right?
Grr
STOMP
Grr
STOMP
!
Mitsuru, what are you doing?
Oh.
I'm just trying something out.

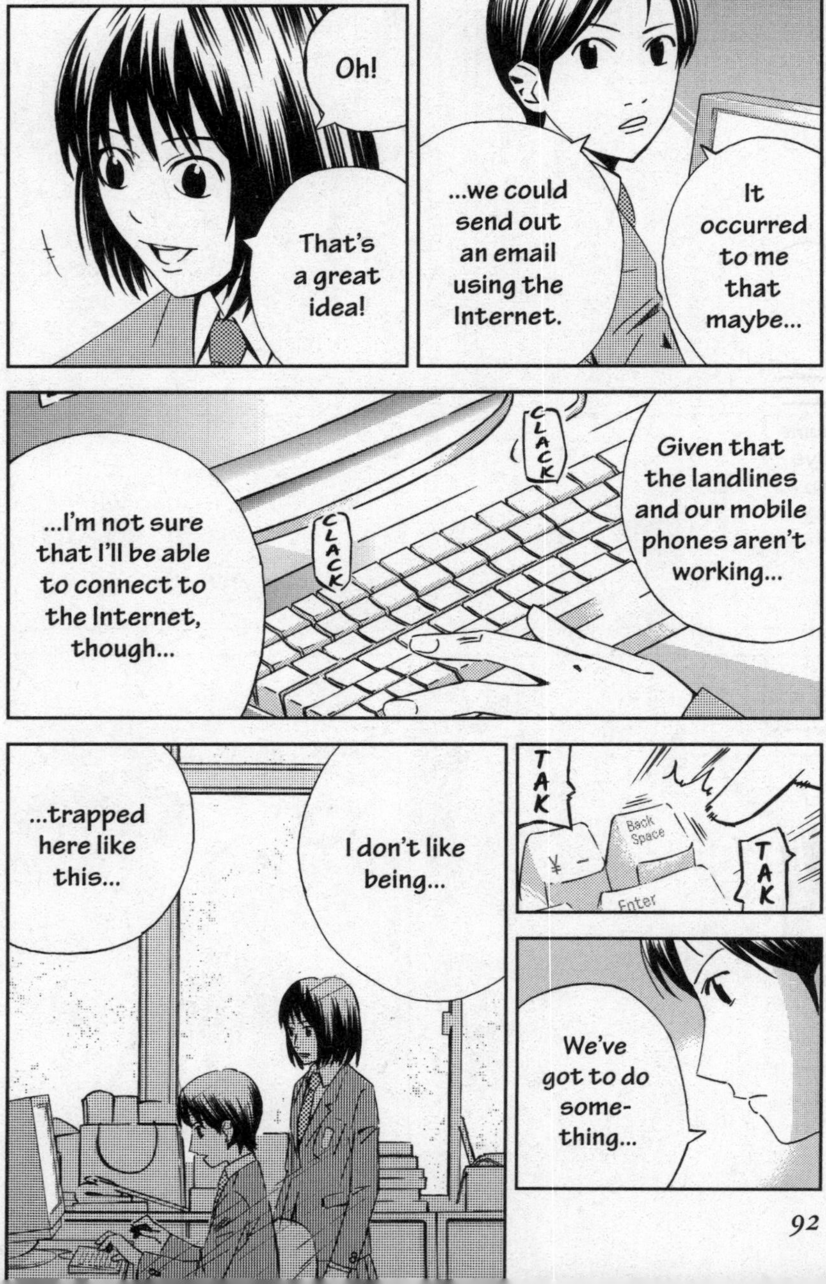
It occurred to me that maybe...
...we could send out an email using the Internet.
Oh!
That's a great idea!
Given that the landlines and our mobile phones aren't working...
CLACK
CLACK
...I'm not sure that I'll be able to connect to the Internet, though...
TAK
TAK
Back Space
Enter
We've got to do some-thing...
I don't like being...
...trapped here like this...

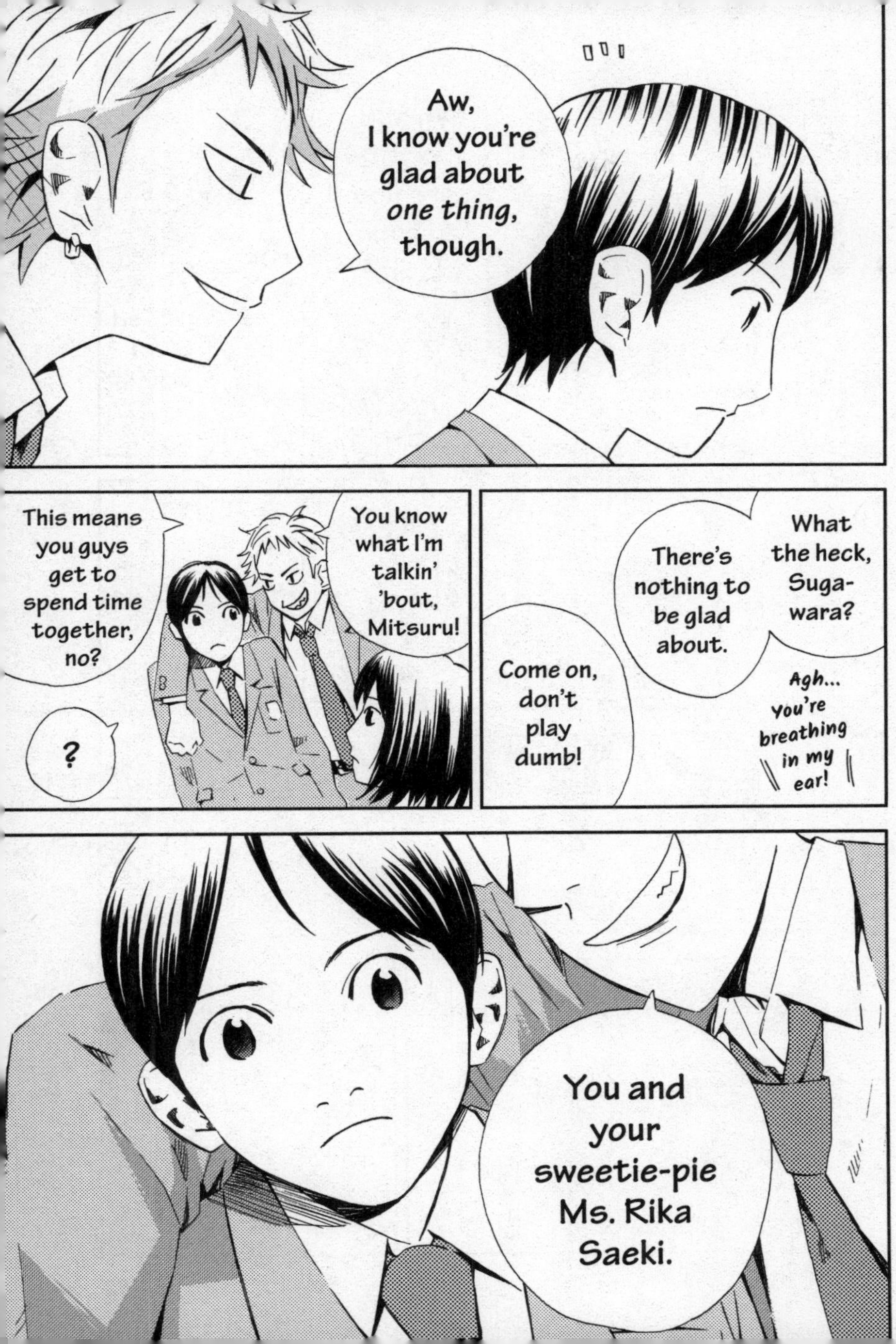
Aw, I know you're glad about *one thing,* though.
What the heck, Suga-wara?
There's nothing to be glad about.
Agh... You're breathing in my ear!
Come on, don't play dumb!
You know what I'm talkin' 'bout, Mitsuru!
This means you guys get to spend time together, no?
?
You and your sweetie-pie Ms. Rika Saeki.

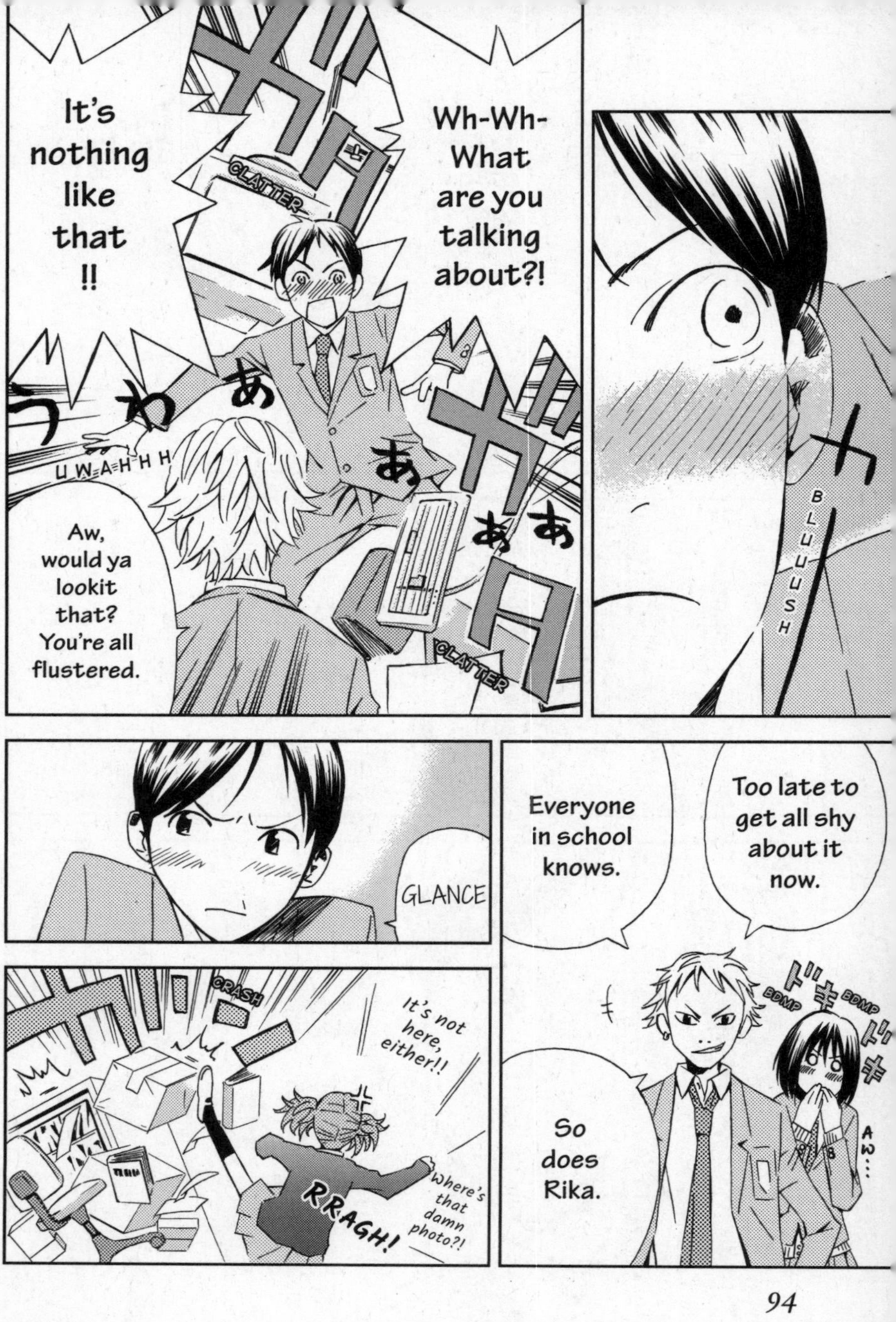
BLUUUSH
Wh-Wh-What are you talking about?!
CLATTER
It's nothing like that!!
UWAHHH
CLATTER
Aw, would ya lookit that? You're all flustered.
Too late to get all shy about it now.
Everyone in school knows.
BDMP BDMP
So does Rika.
AW...
GLANCE
CRASH
It's not here, either!!
RRAGH!
Where's that damn photo?!

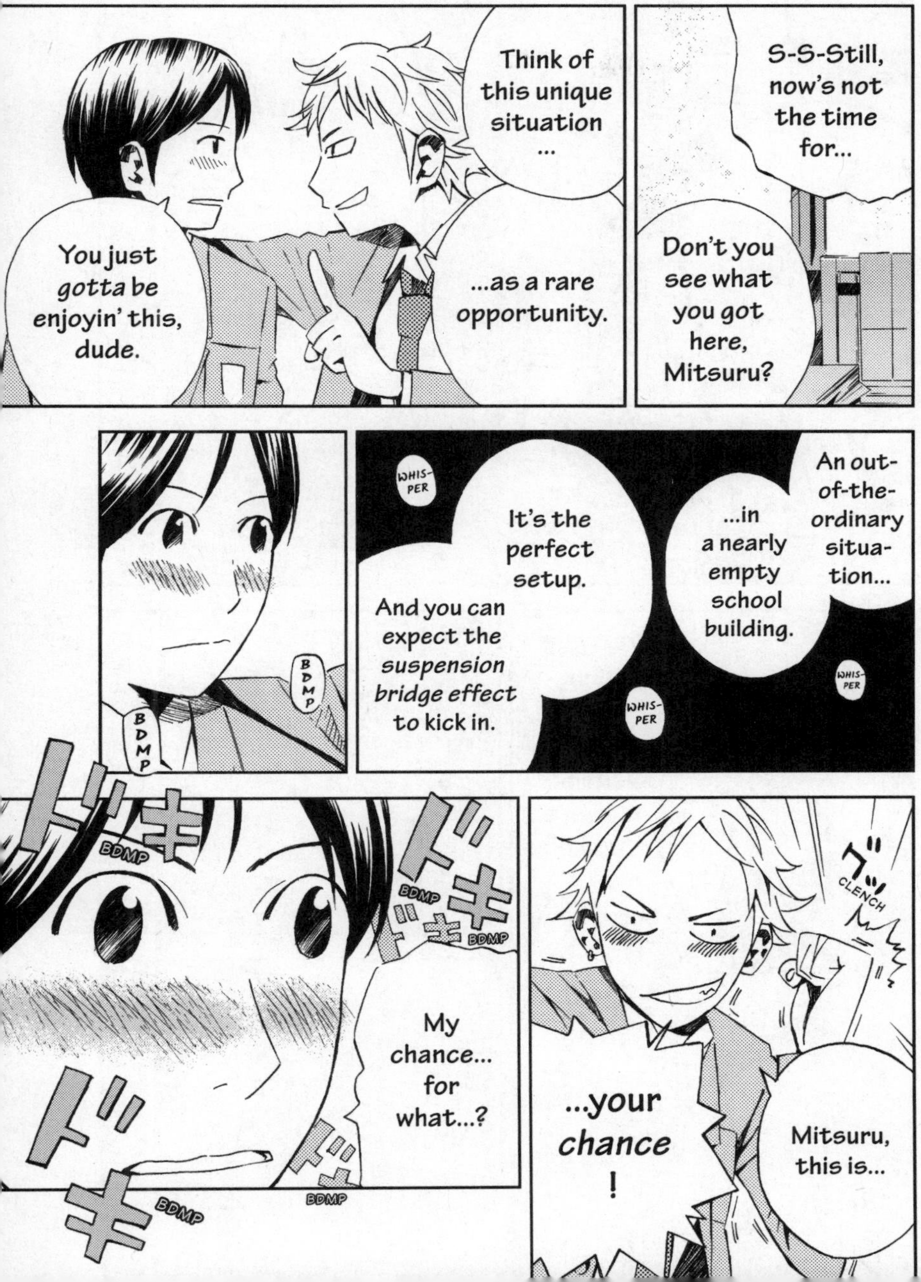
S-S-Still, now's not the time for...
Don't you see what you got here, Mitsuru?
Think of this unique situation ...
...as a rare opportunity.
You just gotta be enjoyin' this, dude.
An out-of-the-ordinary situation...
...in a nearly empty school building.
WHISPER
WHISPER
It's the perfect setup.
And you can expect the suspension bridge effect to kick in.
WHISPER
BDMP
BDMP
CLENCH
Mitsuru, this is...
...your chance!
BDMP
BDMP
BDMP
My chance... for what...?
BDMP
BDMP

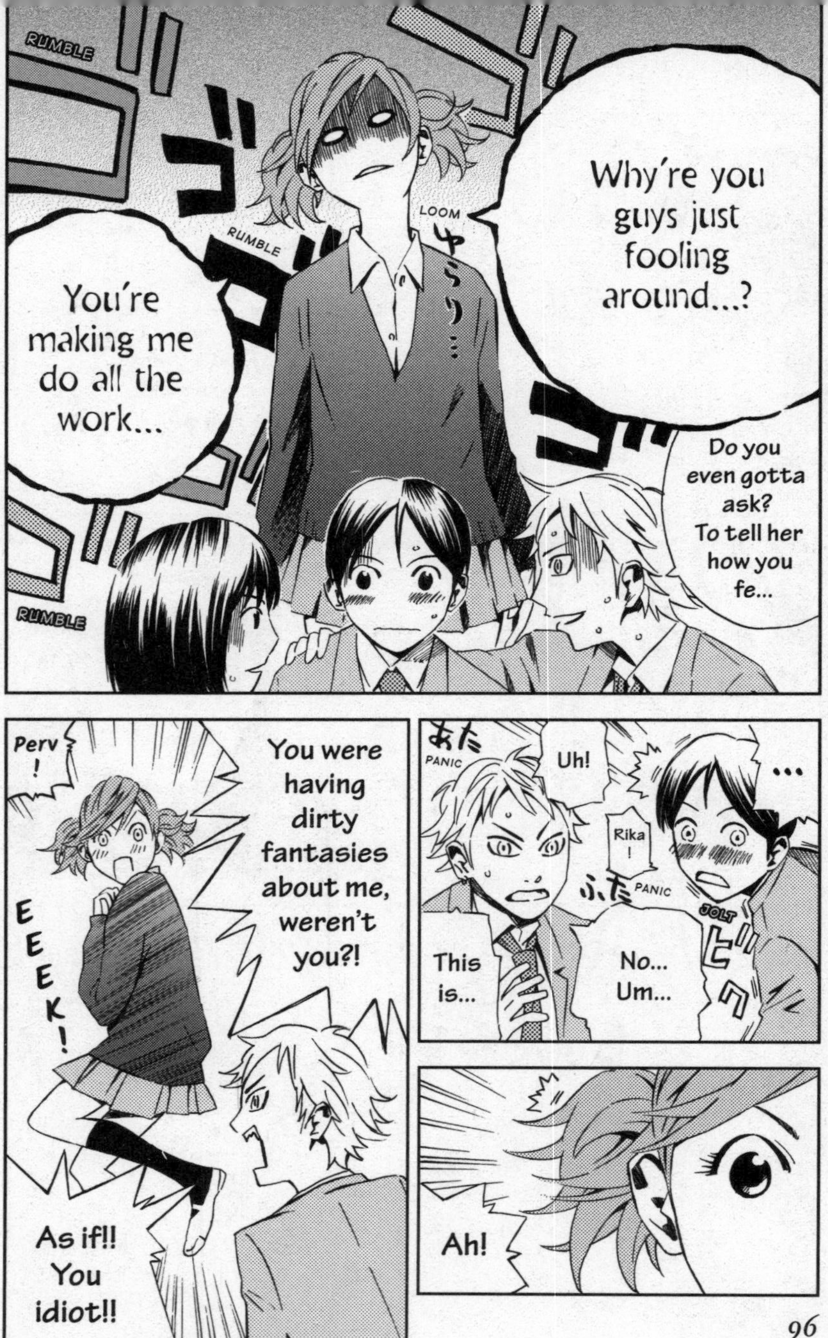
Why're you guys just fooling around...?
LOOM
RUMBLE
RUMBLE
You're making me do all the work...
Do you even gotta ask? To tell her how you fe...
RUMBLE
...
Uh!
PANIC
Rika!
PANIC
JOLT
No... Um...
This is...
Ah!
You were having dirty fantasies about me, weren't you?!
Perv!
EEEK!
As if!! You idiot!!

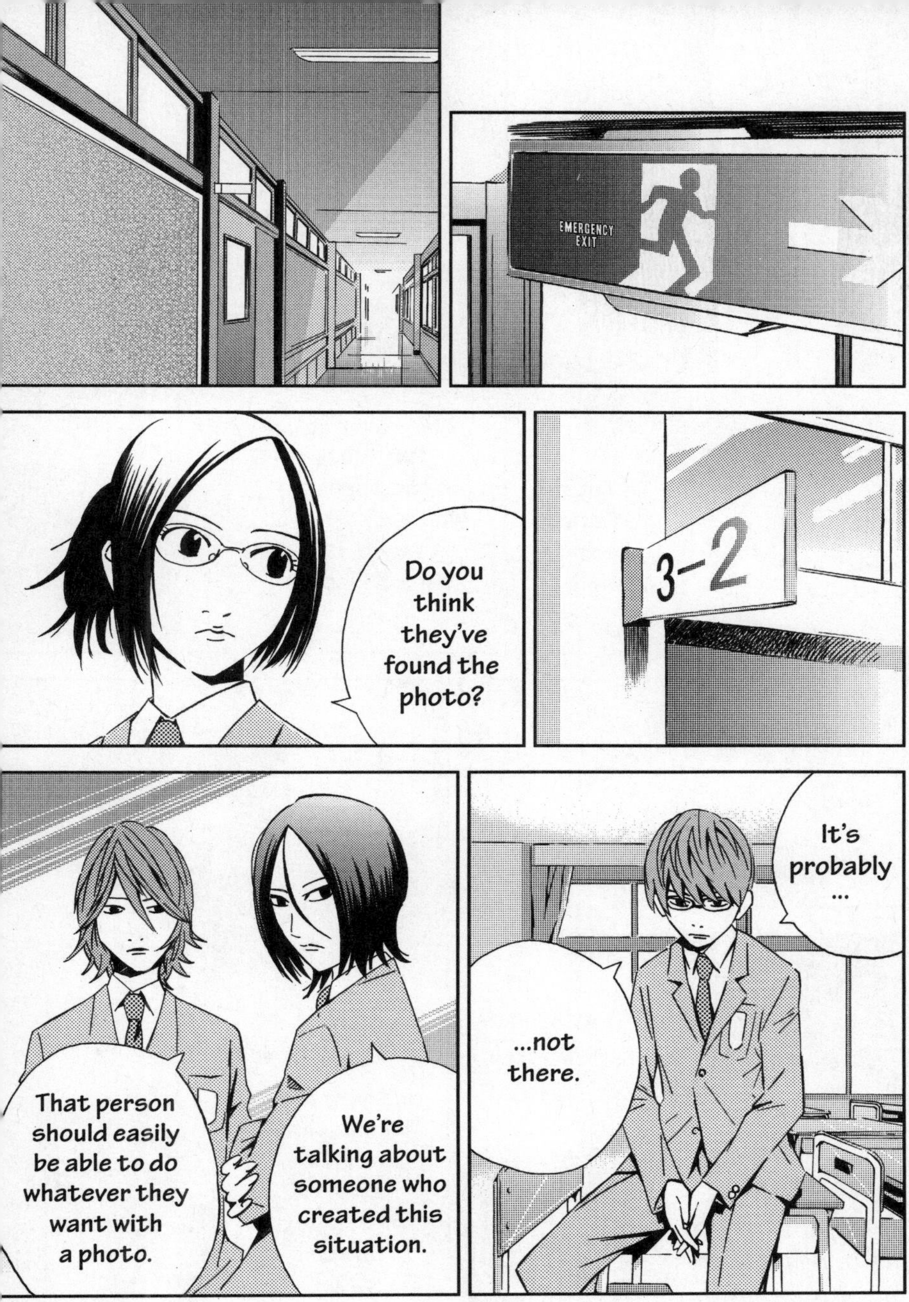
EMERGENCY EXIT
3–2
Do you think they've found the photo?
It's probably ...
...not there.
We're talking about someone who created this situation.
That person should easily be able to do whatever they want with a photo.

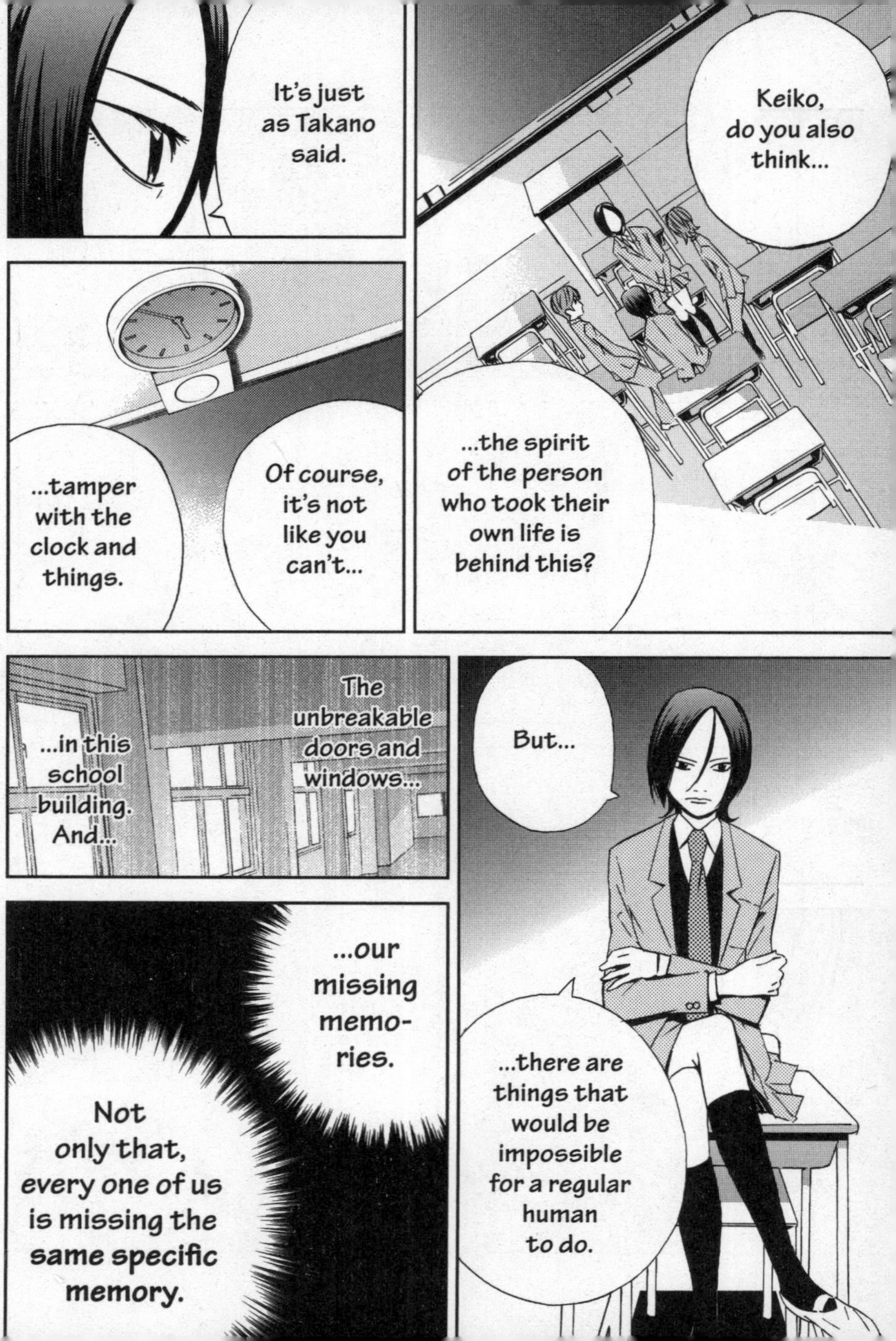
Keiko, do you also think...
...the spirit of the person who took their own life is behind this?
It's just as Takano said.
Of course, it's not like you can't...
...tamper with the clock and things.
But...
...there are things that would be impossible for a regular human to do.
The unbreakable doors and windows...
...in this school building. And...
...our missing memories.
Not only that, every one of us is missing the same specific memory.

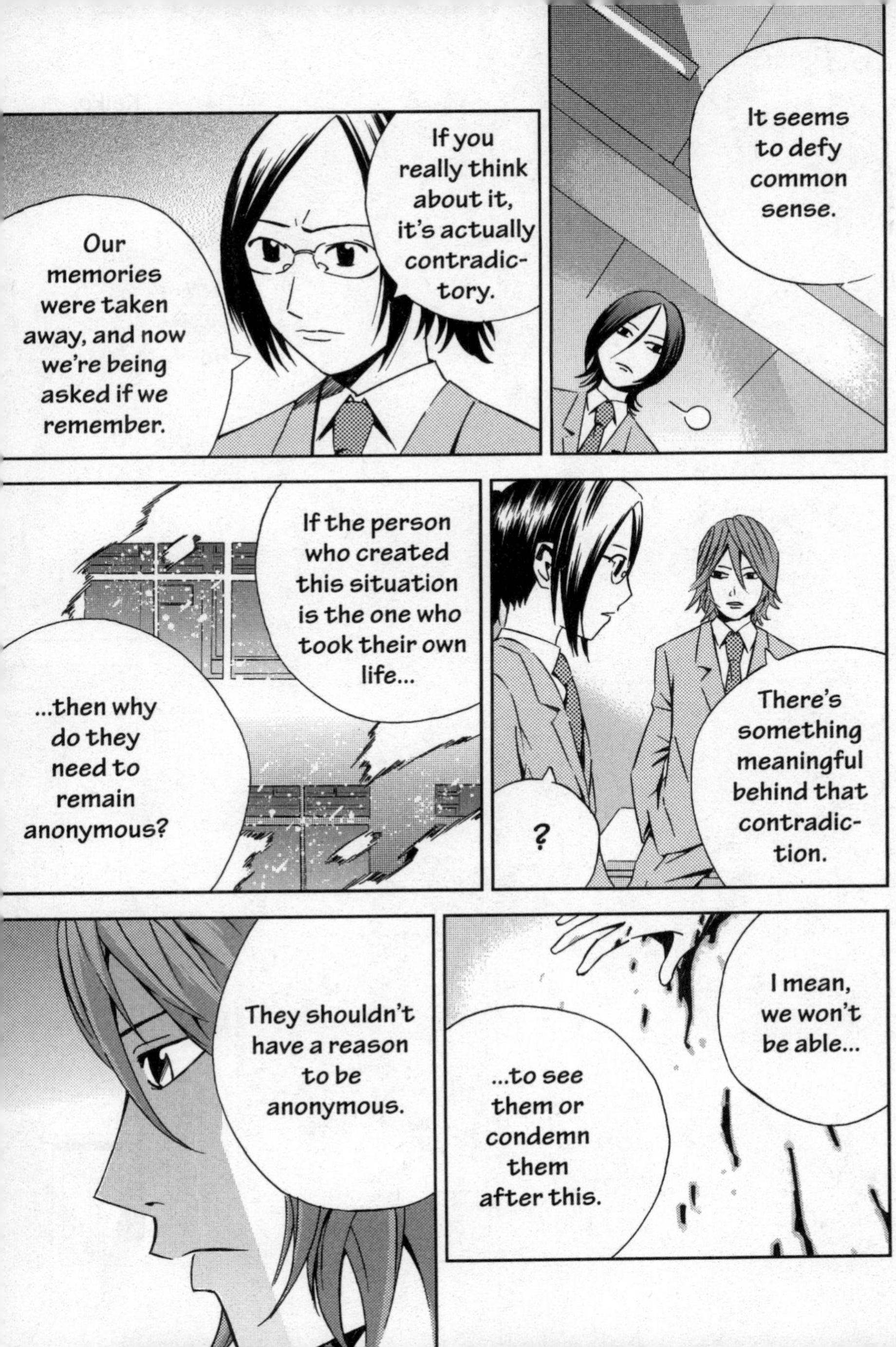
It seems to defy common sense.
If you really think about it, it's actually contradictory.
Our memories were taken away, and now we're being asked if we remember.
There's something meaningful behind that contradiction.
?
If the person who created this situation is the one who took their own life...
...then why do they need to remain anonymous?
I mean, we won't be able...
...to see them or condemn them after this.
They shouldn't have a reason to be anonymous.

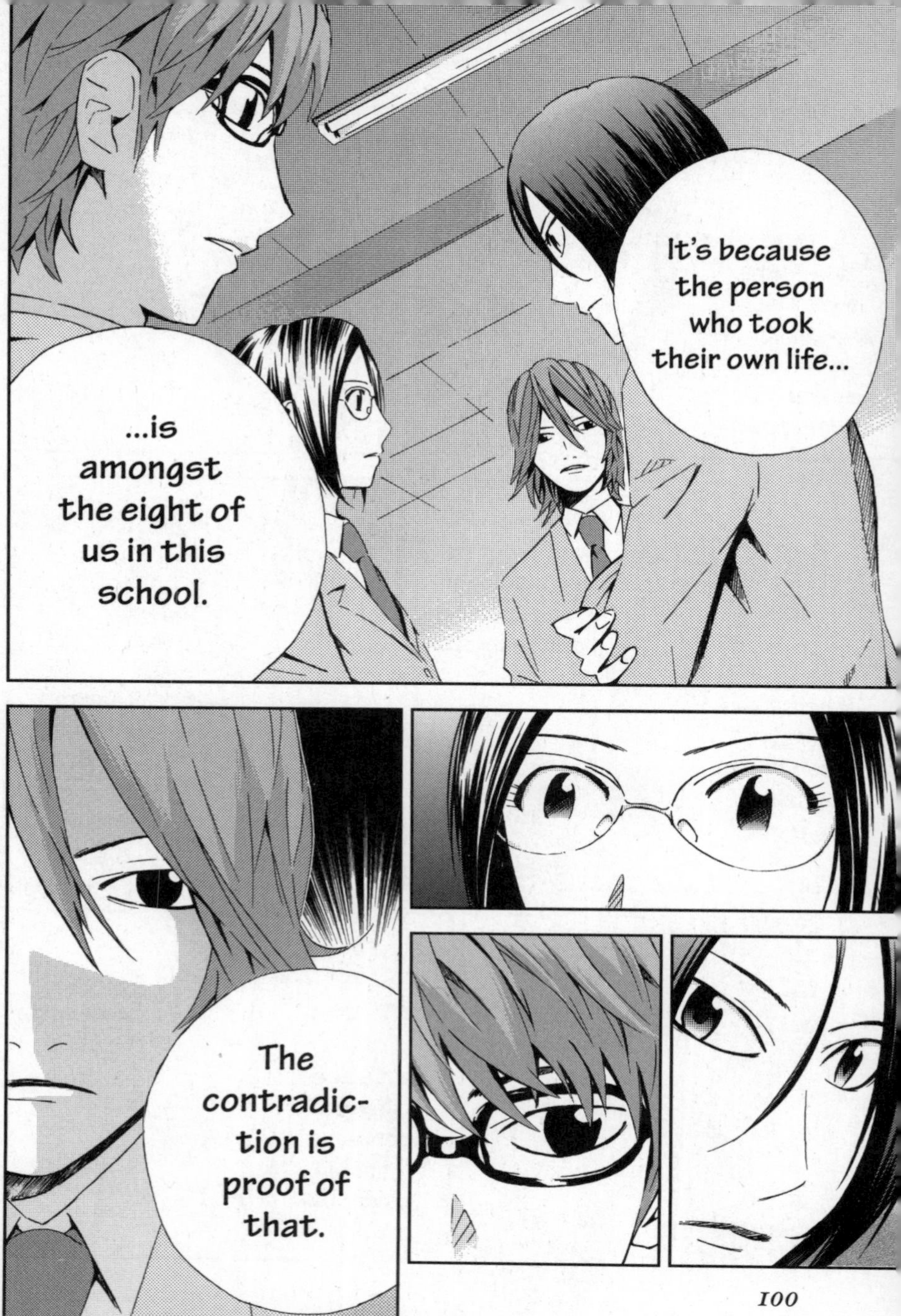
It's because the person who took their own life...
...is amongst the eight of us in this school.
The contradiction is proof of that.

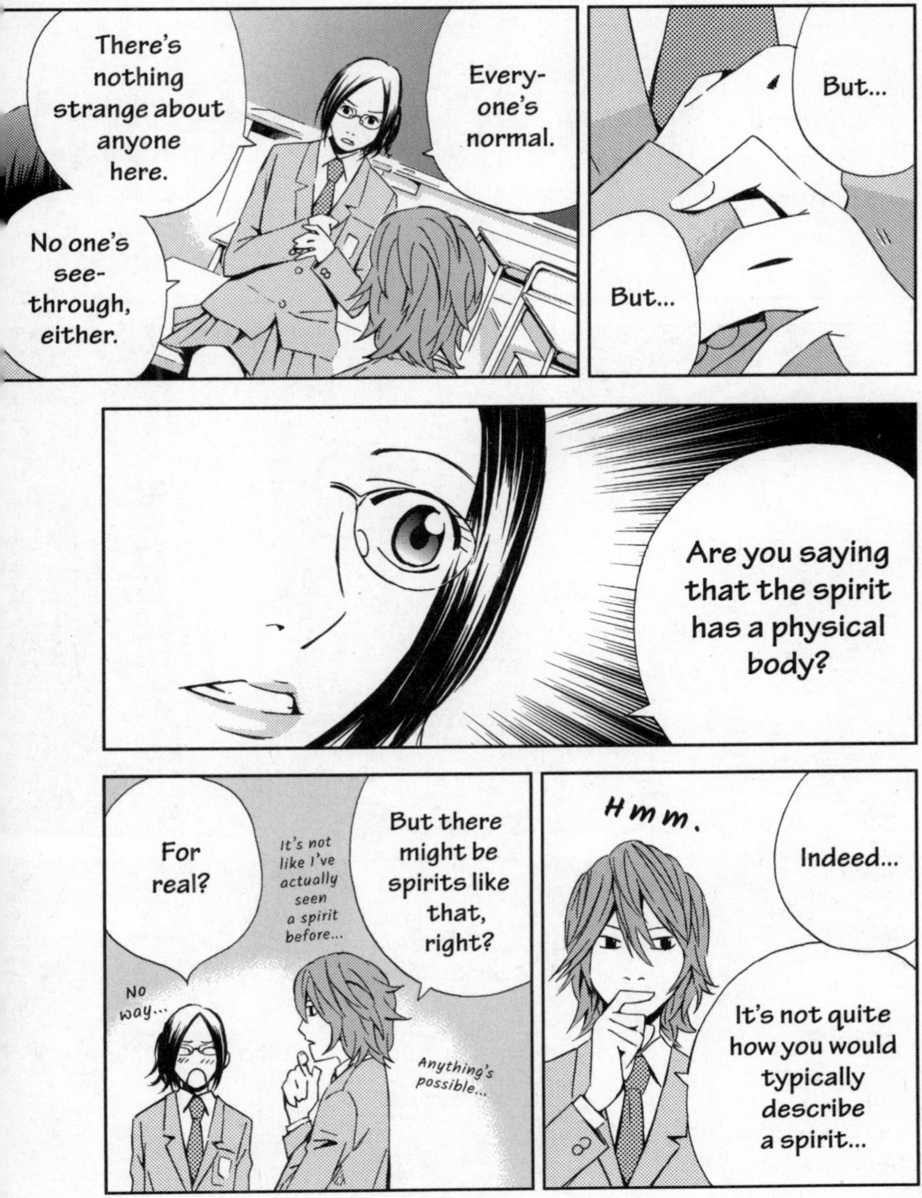
But...
But...
Every-one's normal.
There's nothing strange about anyone here.
No one's see-through, either.
Are you saying that the spirit has a physical body?
Hmm.
Indeed...
It's not quite how you would typically describe a spirit...
But there might be spirits like that, right?
It's not like I've actually seen a spirit before...
For real?
Anything's possible...
No way...

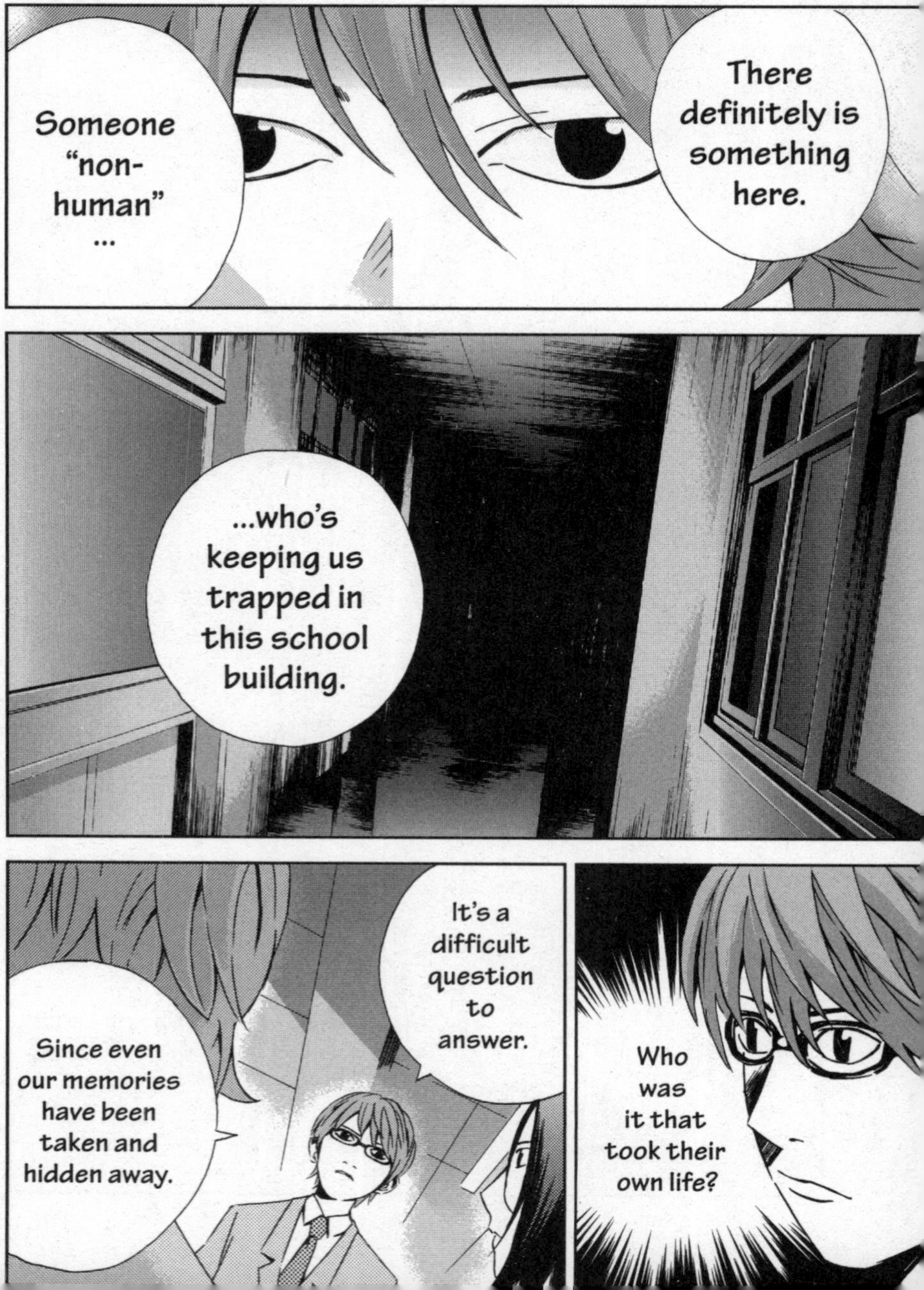
There definitely is something here.
Someone "non-human" ...
...who's keeping us trapped in this school building.
Who was it that took their own life?
It's a difficult question to answer.
Since even our memories have been taken and hidden away.

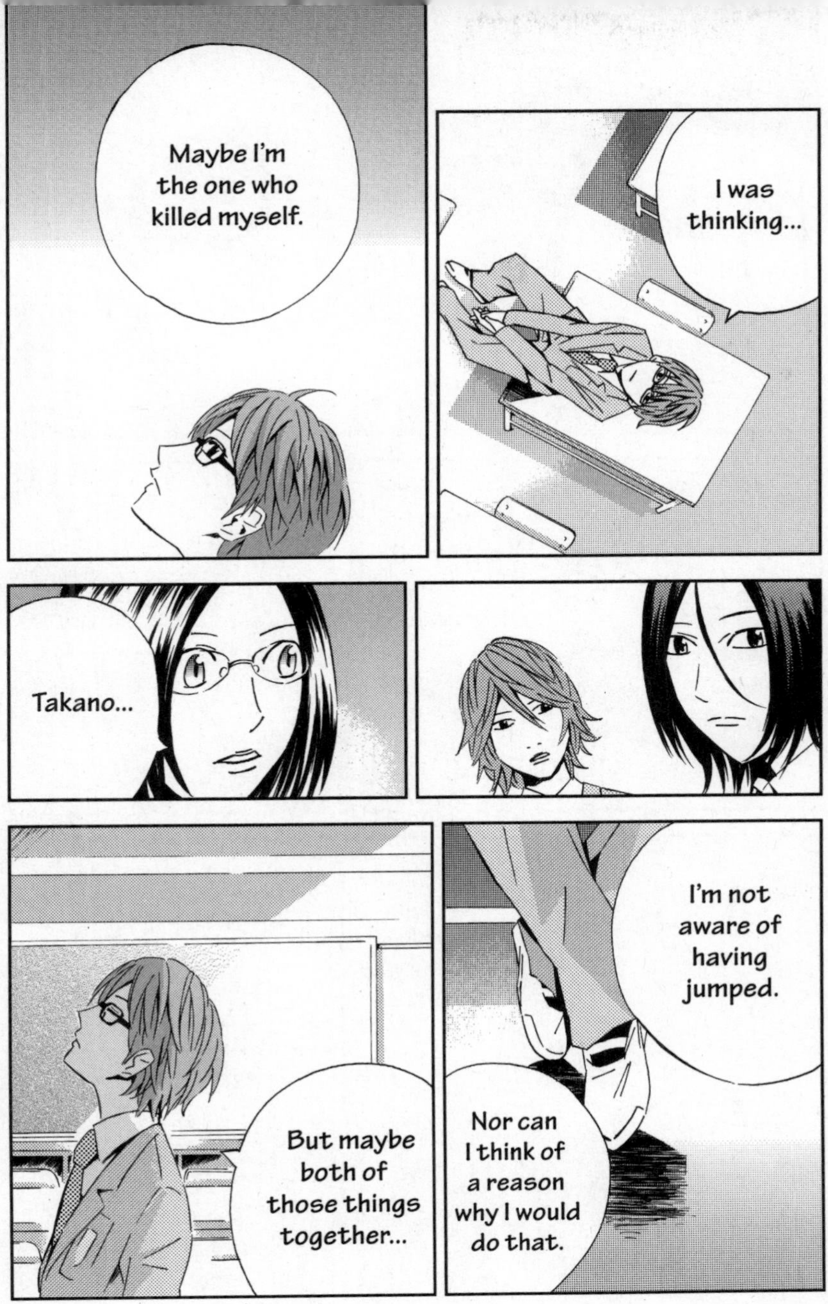
I was thinking...
Maybe I'm the one who killed myself.
Takano...
I'm not aware of having jumped.
Nor can I think of a reason why I would do that.
But maybe both of those things together...

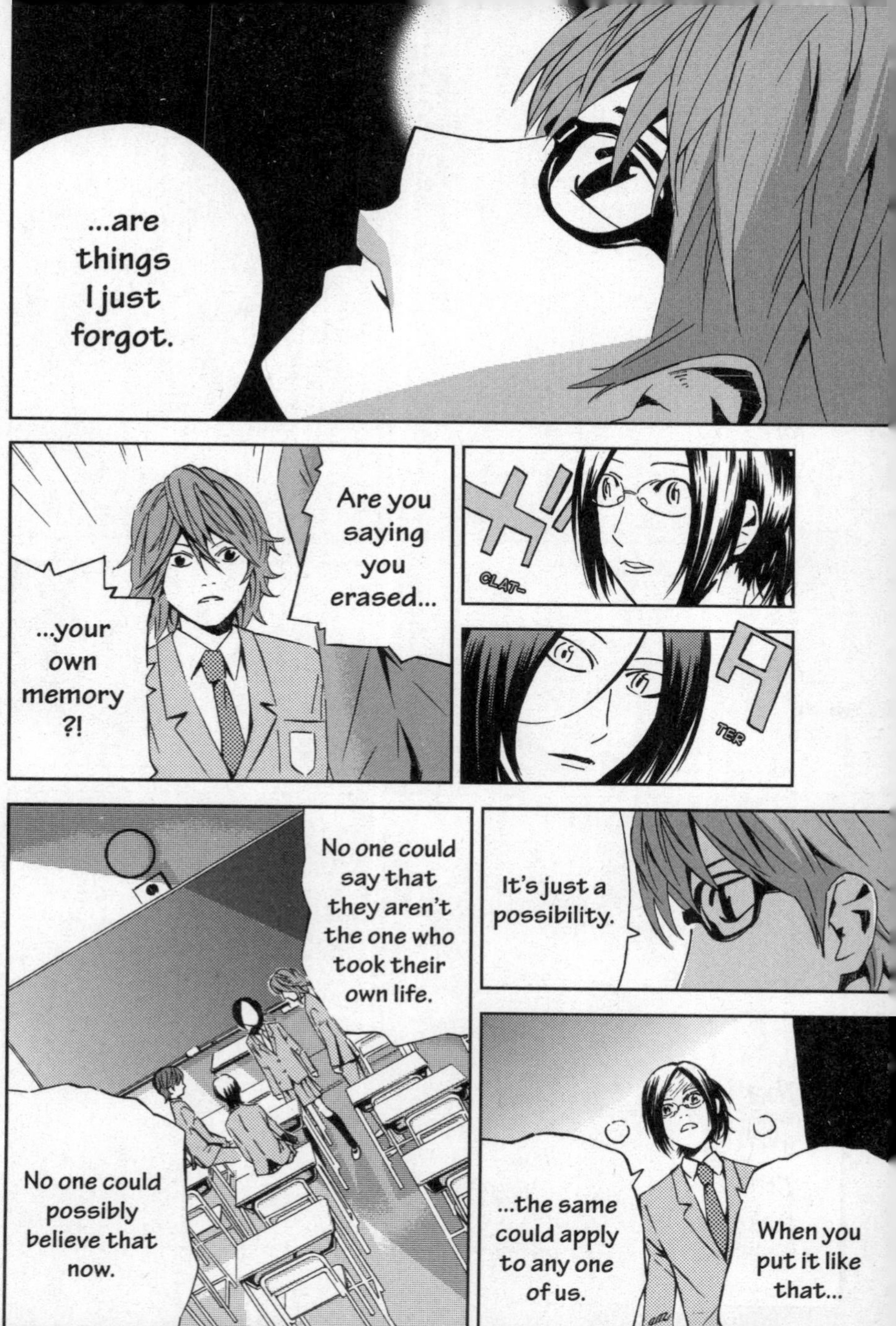
...are things I just forgot.
CLAT-
TER
Are you saying you erased...
...your own memory?!
It's just a possibility.
When you put it like that...
...the same could apply to any one of us.
No one could say that they aren't the one who took their own life.
No one could possibly believe that now.

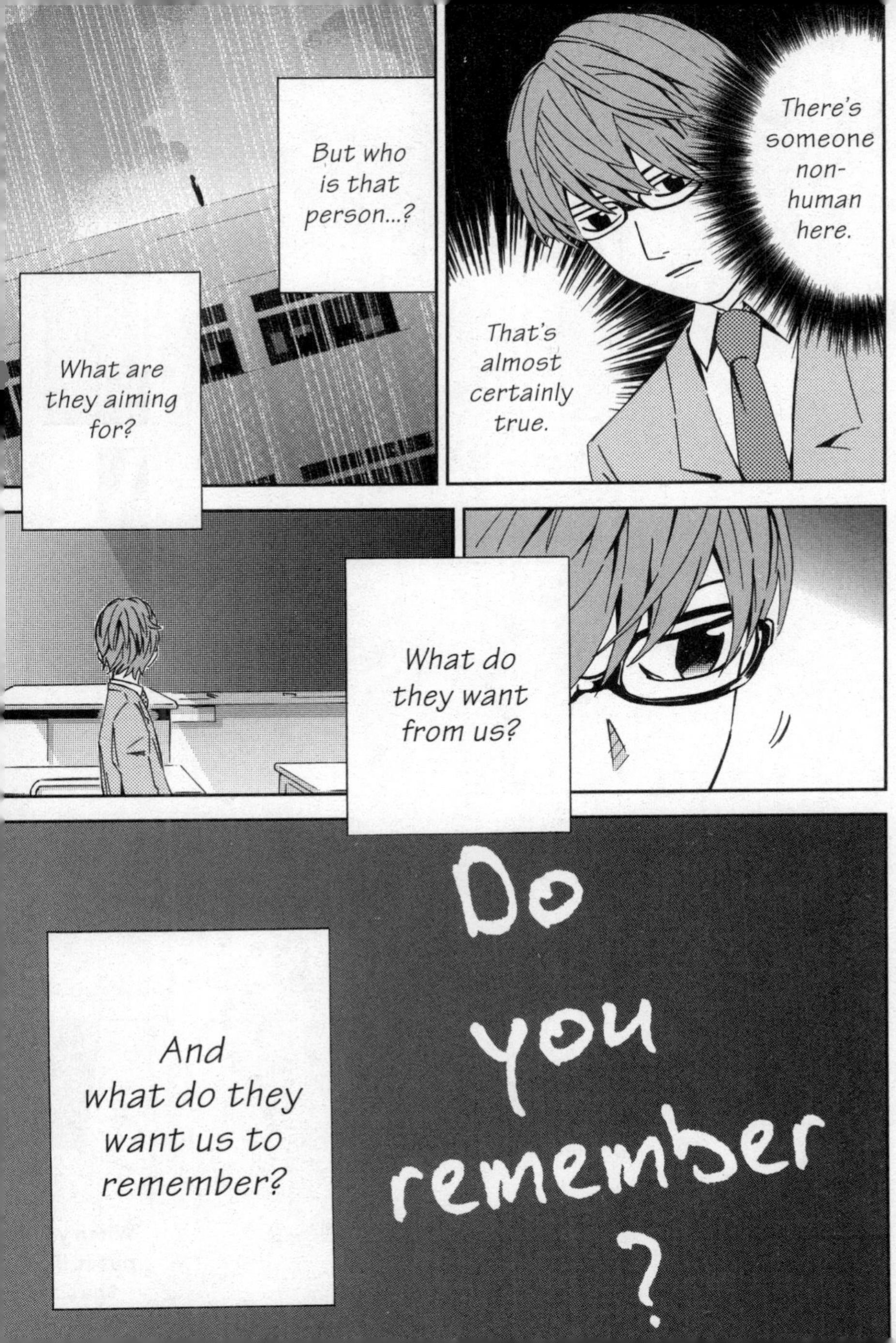
There's someone non-human here.
That's almost certainly true.
But who is that person...?
What are they aiming for?
What do they want from us?
Do you remember?
And what do they want us to remember?

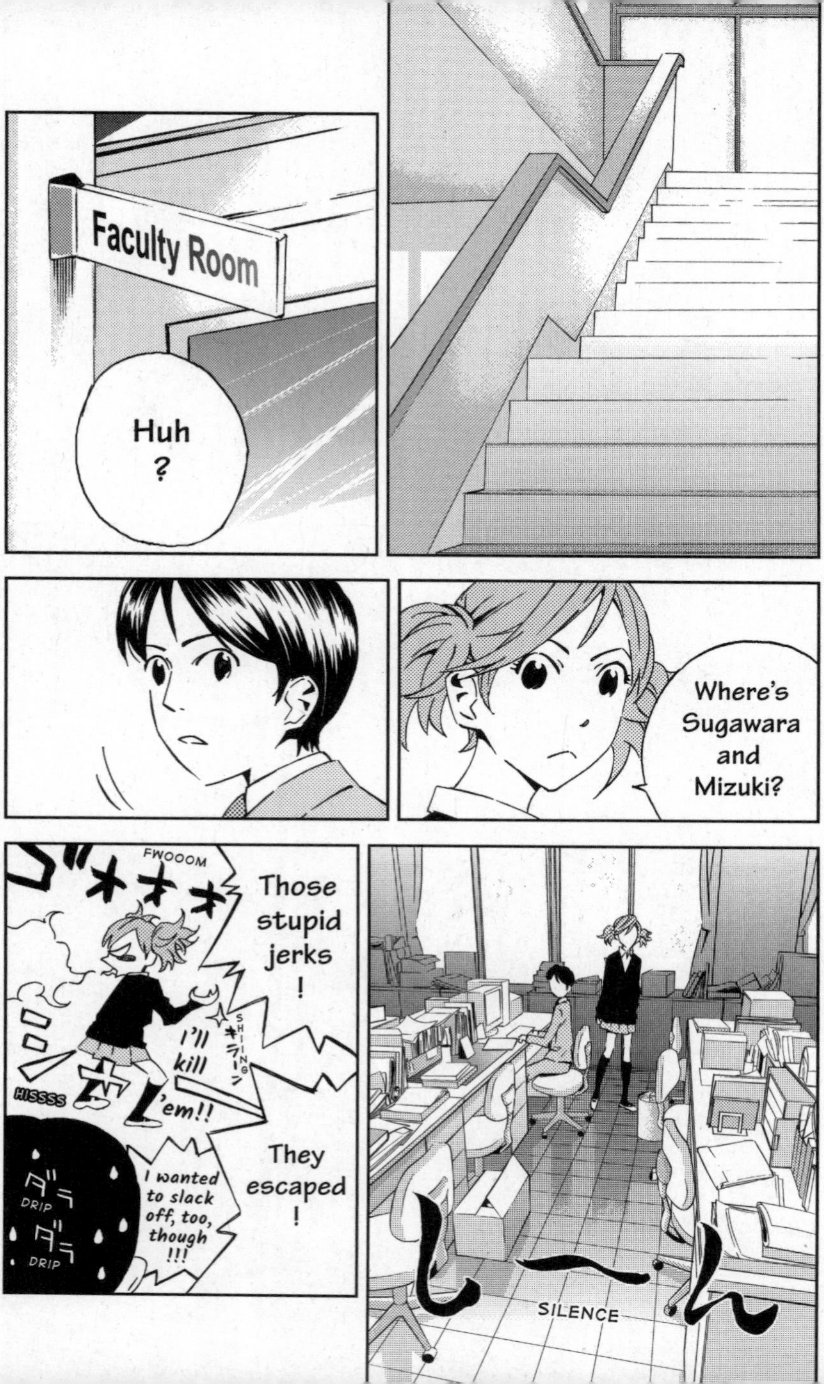
Faculty Room
Huh?
Where's Sugawara and Mizuki?
しーん
SILENCE
ゴオオオ
FWOOOM
Those stupid jerks!
キラーン
SHIING
I'll kill 'em!!
HISSSS
They escaped!
I wanted to slack off, too, though!!!
ダラダラ
DRIP DRIP

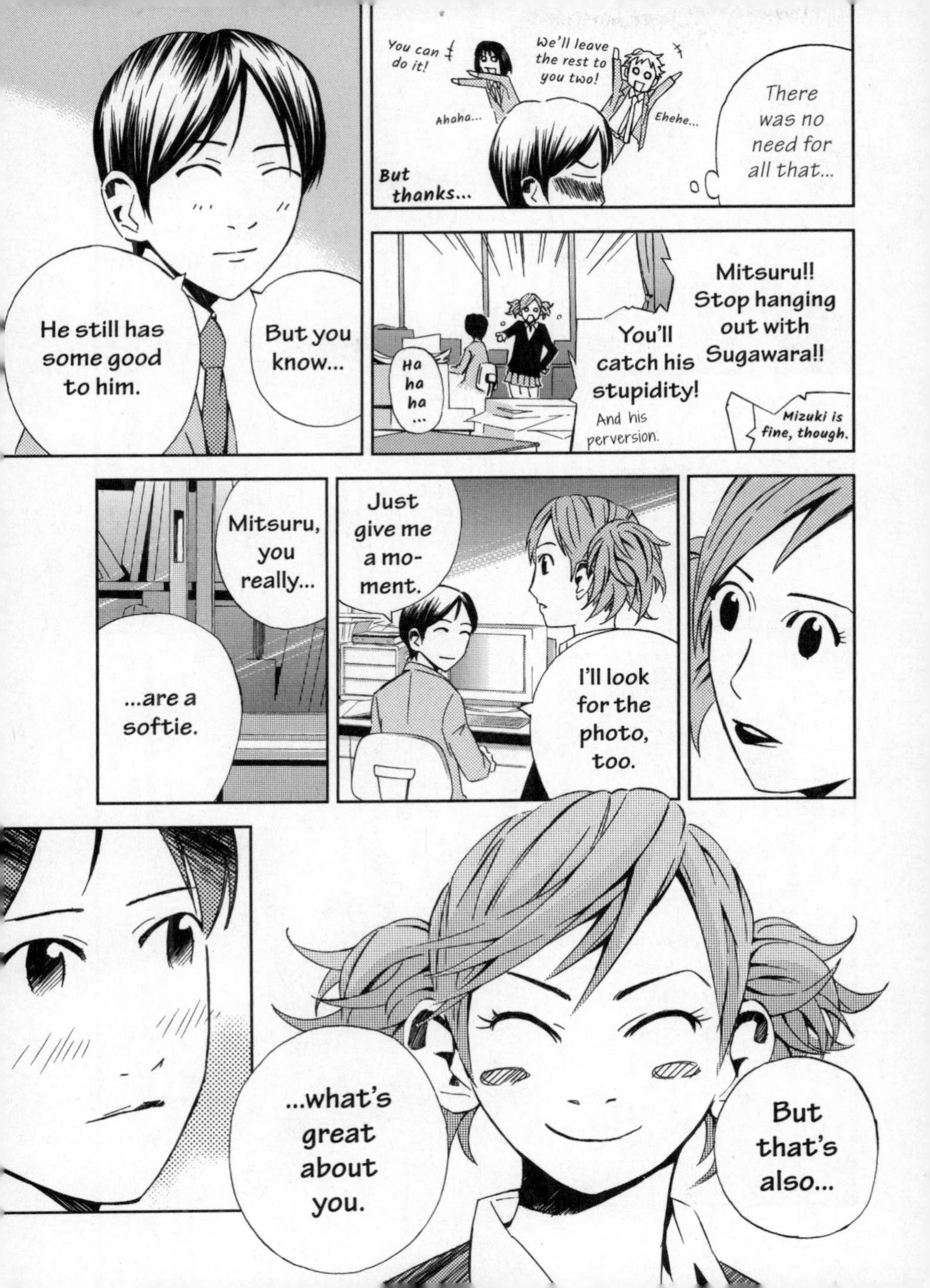
There was no need for all that...
We'll leave the rest to you two!
Ehehe...
You can do it!
Ahaha...
But thanks...
Mitsuru!! Stop hanging out with Sugawara!!
Mizuki is fine, though.
You'll catch his stupidity!
And his perversion.
Ha ha ha...
But you know...
He still has some good to him.
Just give me a moment.
I'll look for the photo, too.
Mitsuru, you really...
...are a softie.
But that's also...
...what's great about you.

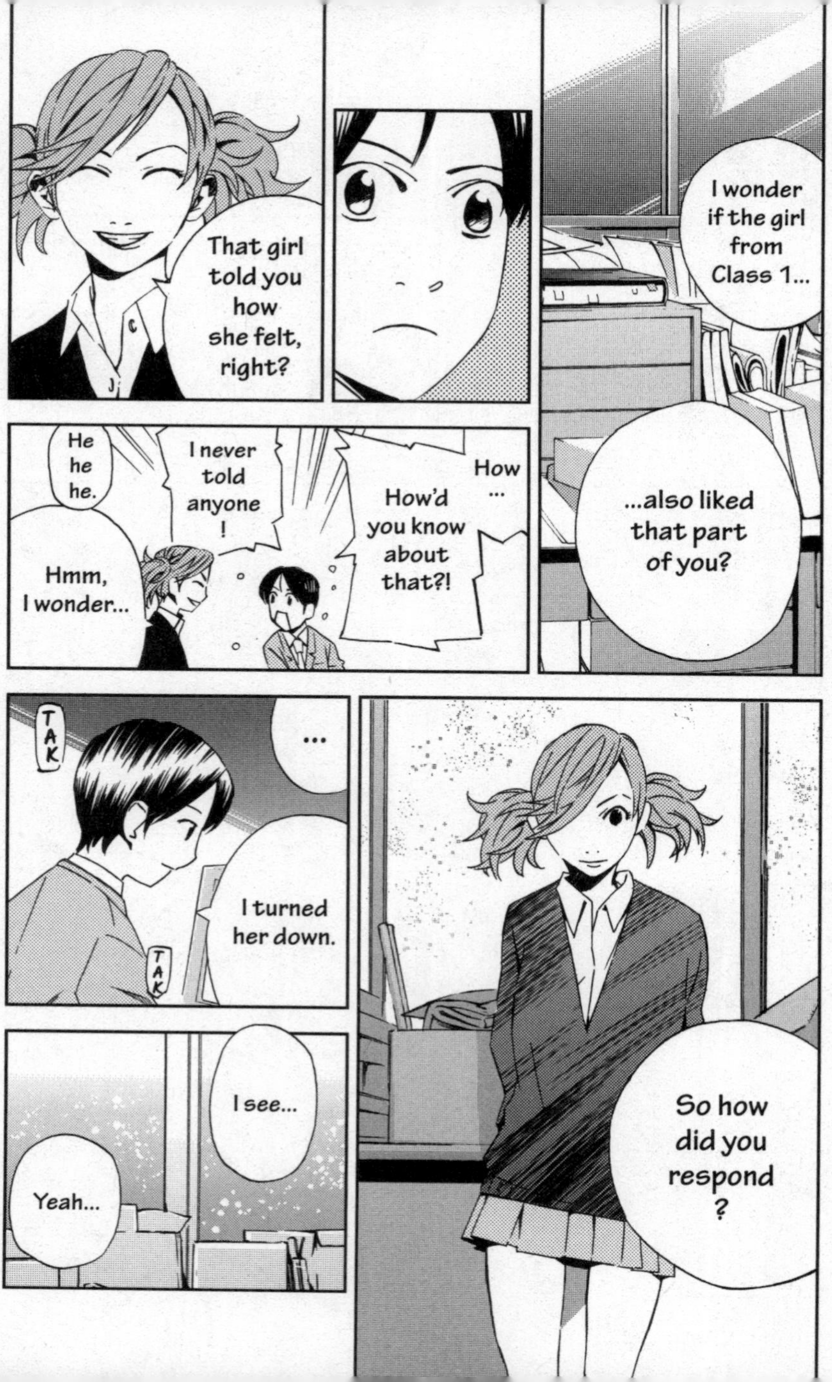

I wonder if the girl from Class 1...
...also liked that part of you?
That girl told you how she felt, right?
How...
How'd you know about that?!
I never told anyone!
He he he.
Hmm, I wonder...
So how did you respond?
TAK
...
I turned her down.
TAK
I see...
Yeah...

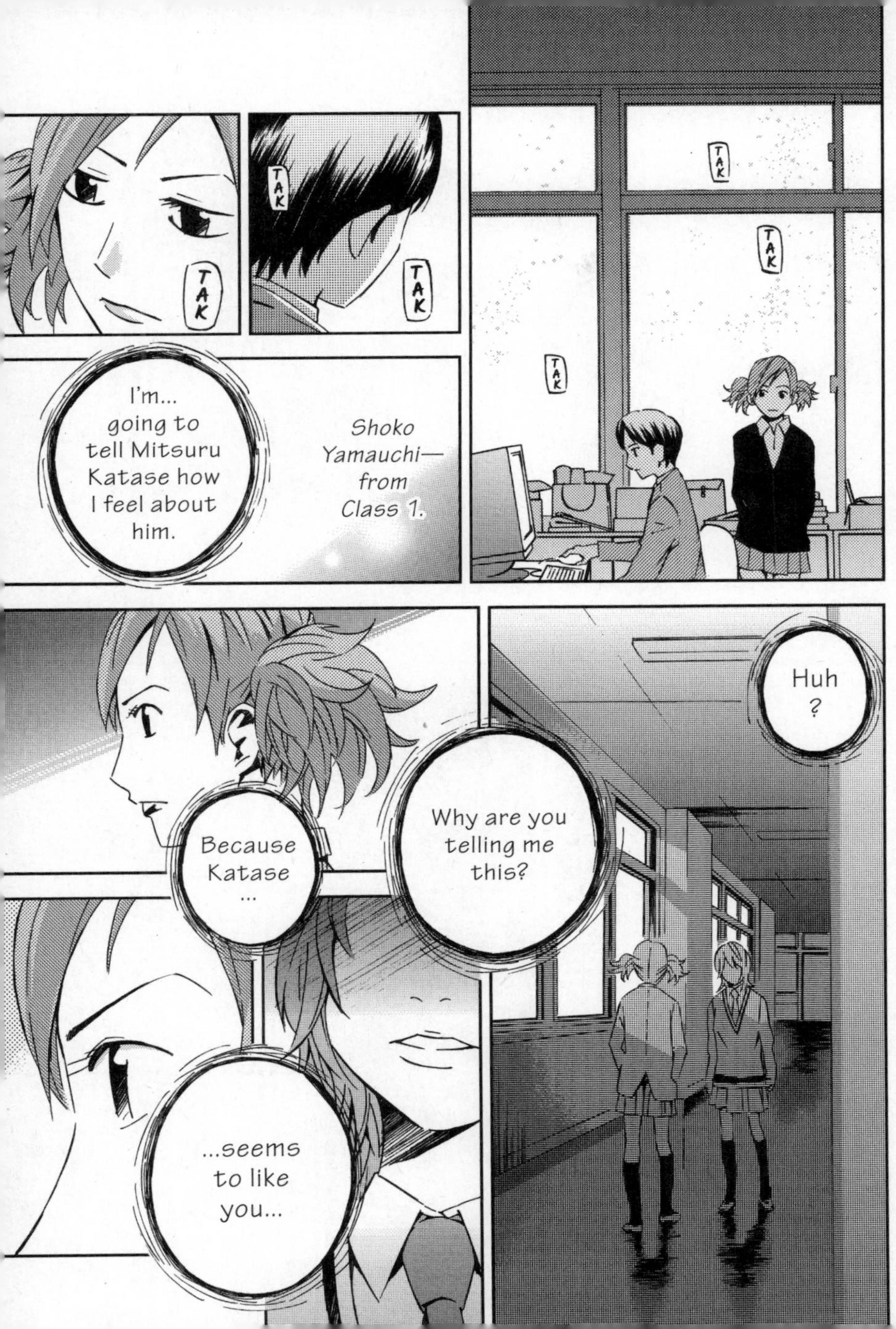
TAK
TAK
TAK
TAK
TAK
TAK
Shoko Yamauchi—from Class 1.
I'm... going to tell Mitsuru Katase how I feel about him.
Huh?
Why are you telling me this?
Because Katase...
...seems to like you...

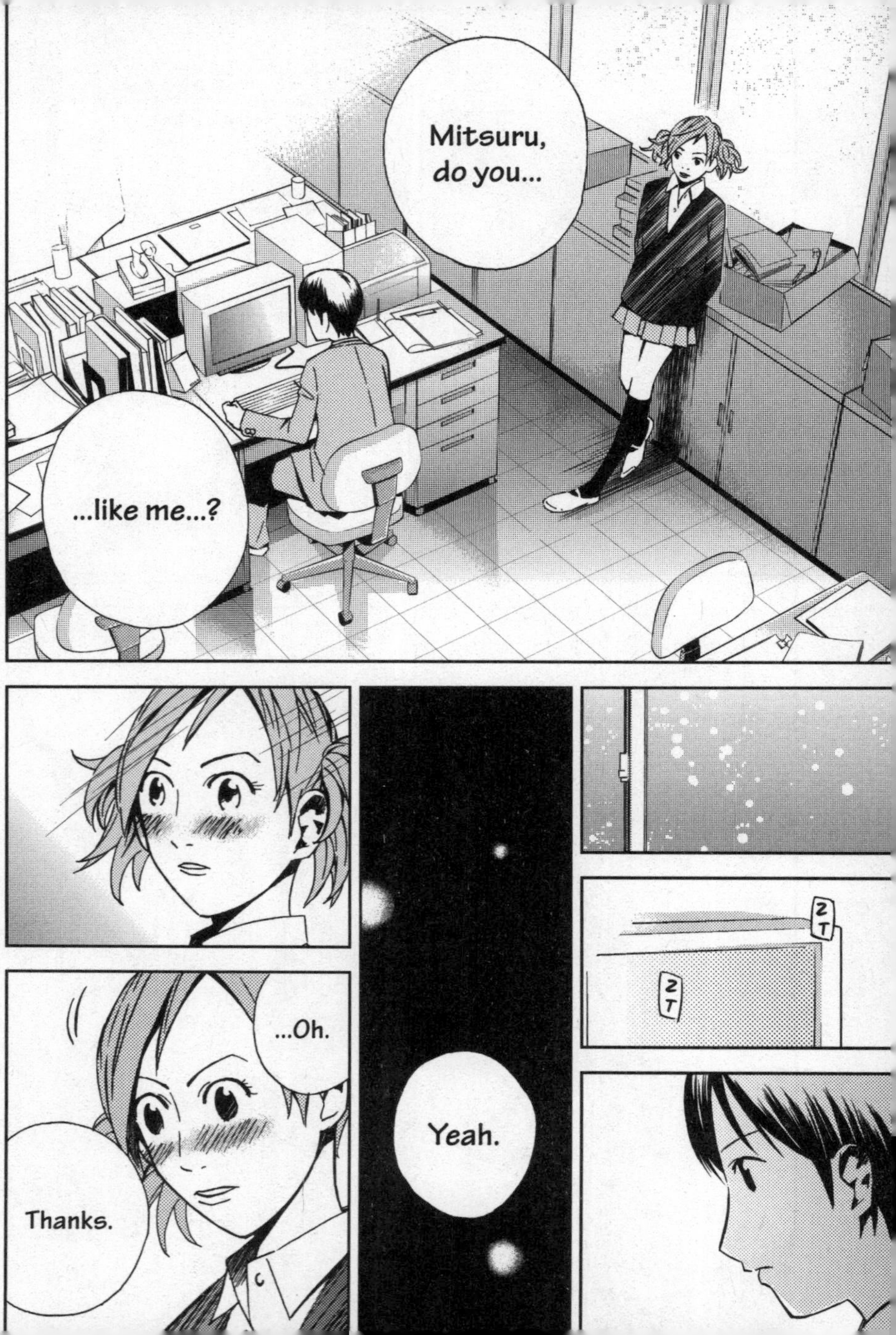
Mitsuru, do you...
...like me...?
ZT
ZT
Yeah.
...Oh.
Thanks.

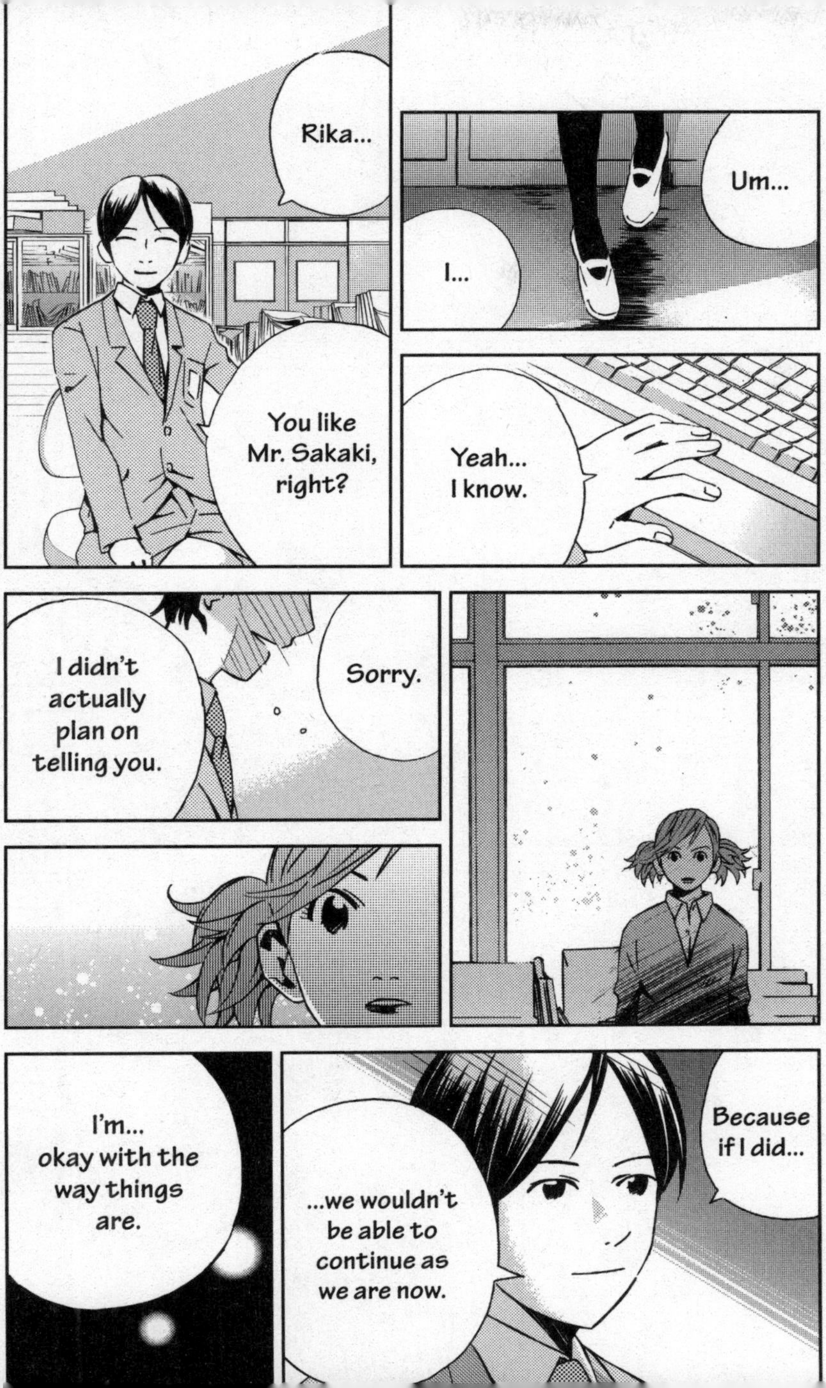
Um...
I...
Yeah... I know.
Rika...
You like Mr. Sakaki, right?
Sorry.
I didn't actually plan on telling you.
Because if I did...
...we wouldn't be able to continue as we are now.
I'm... okay with the way things are.

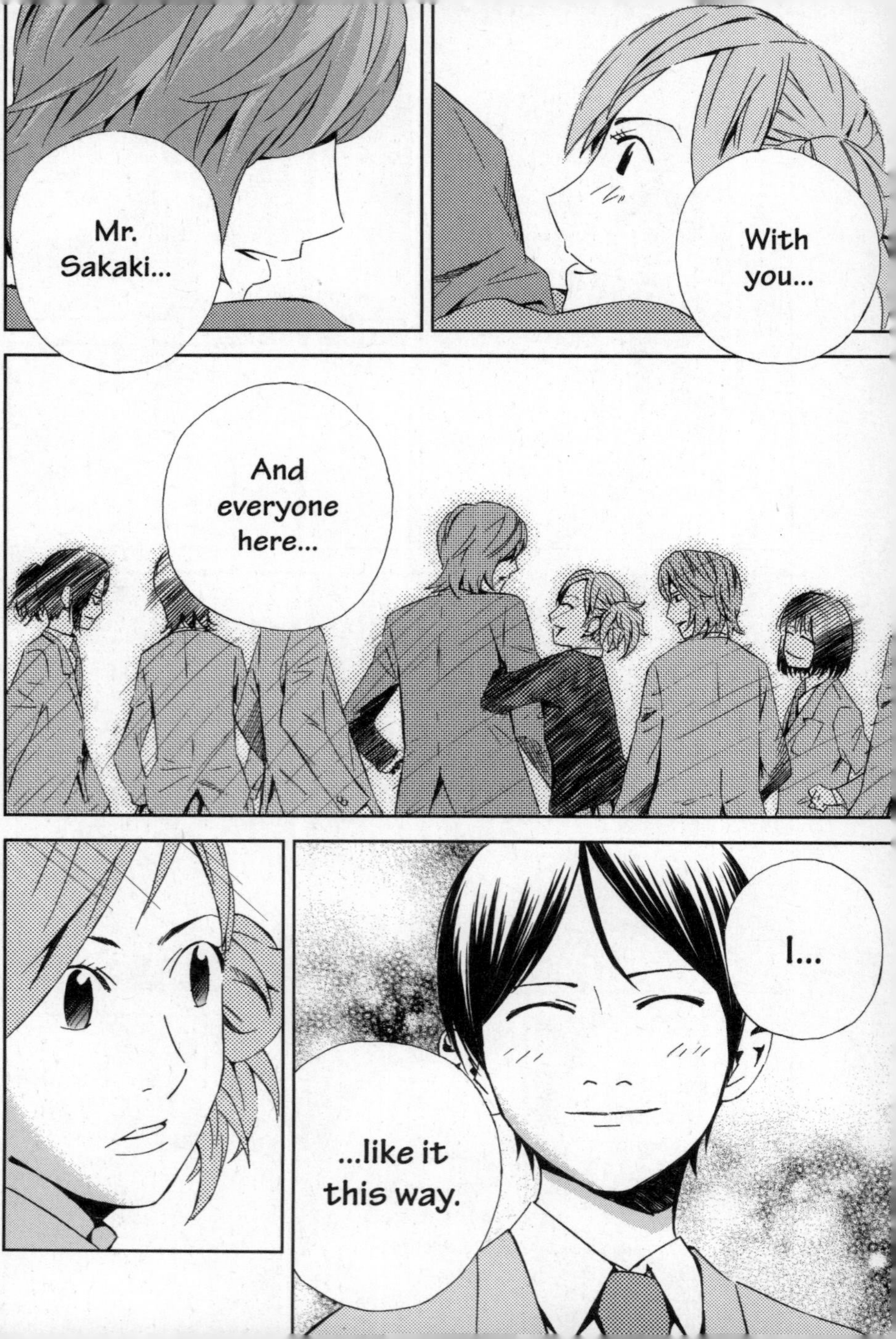
With you...
Mr. Sakaki...
And everyone here...
I...
...like it this way.

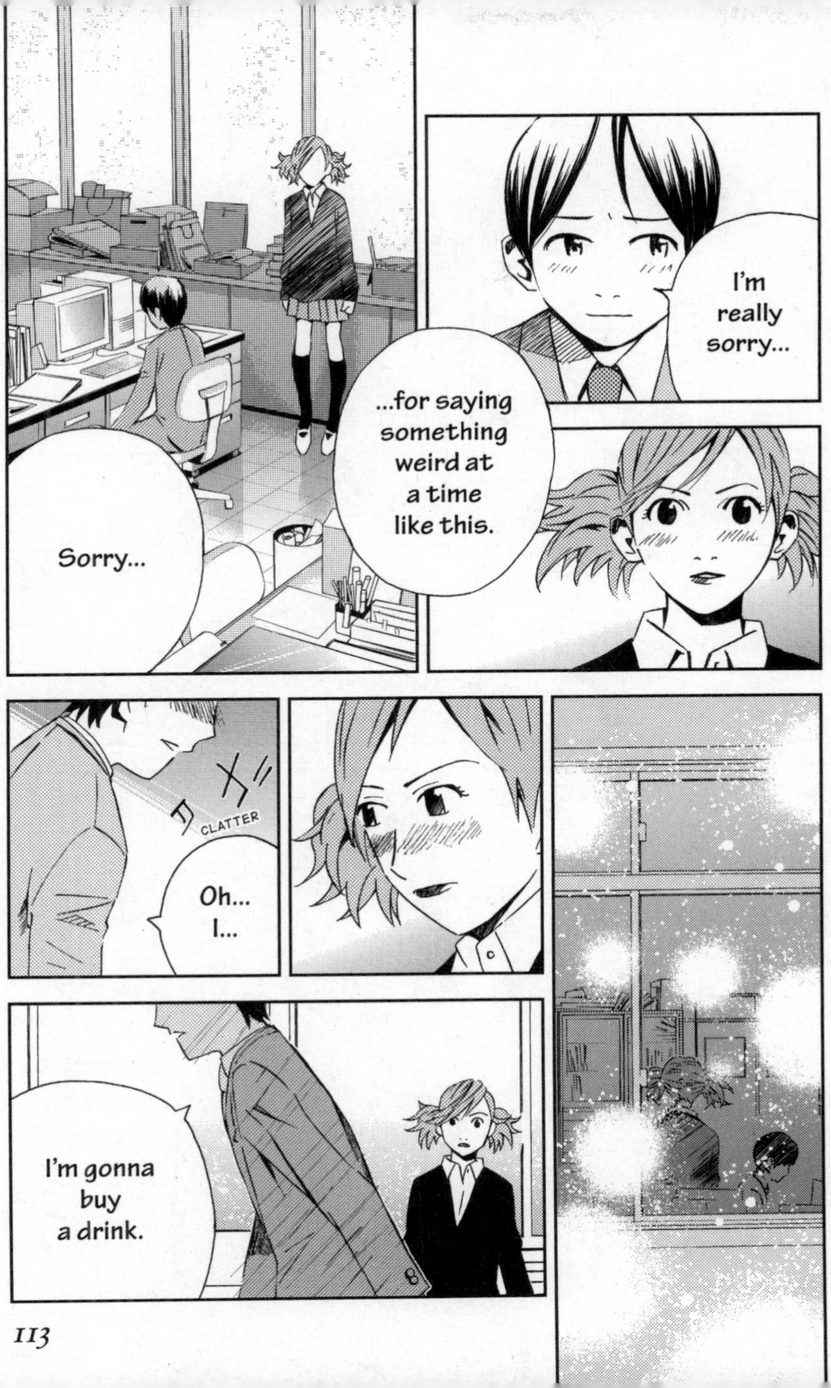
I'm really sorry...
...for saying something weird at a time like this.
Sorry...
CLATTER
Oh... I...
I'm gonna buy a drink.

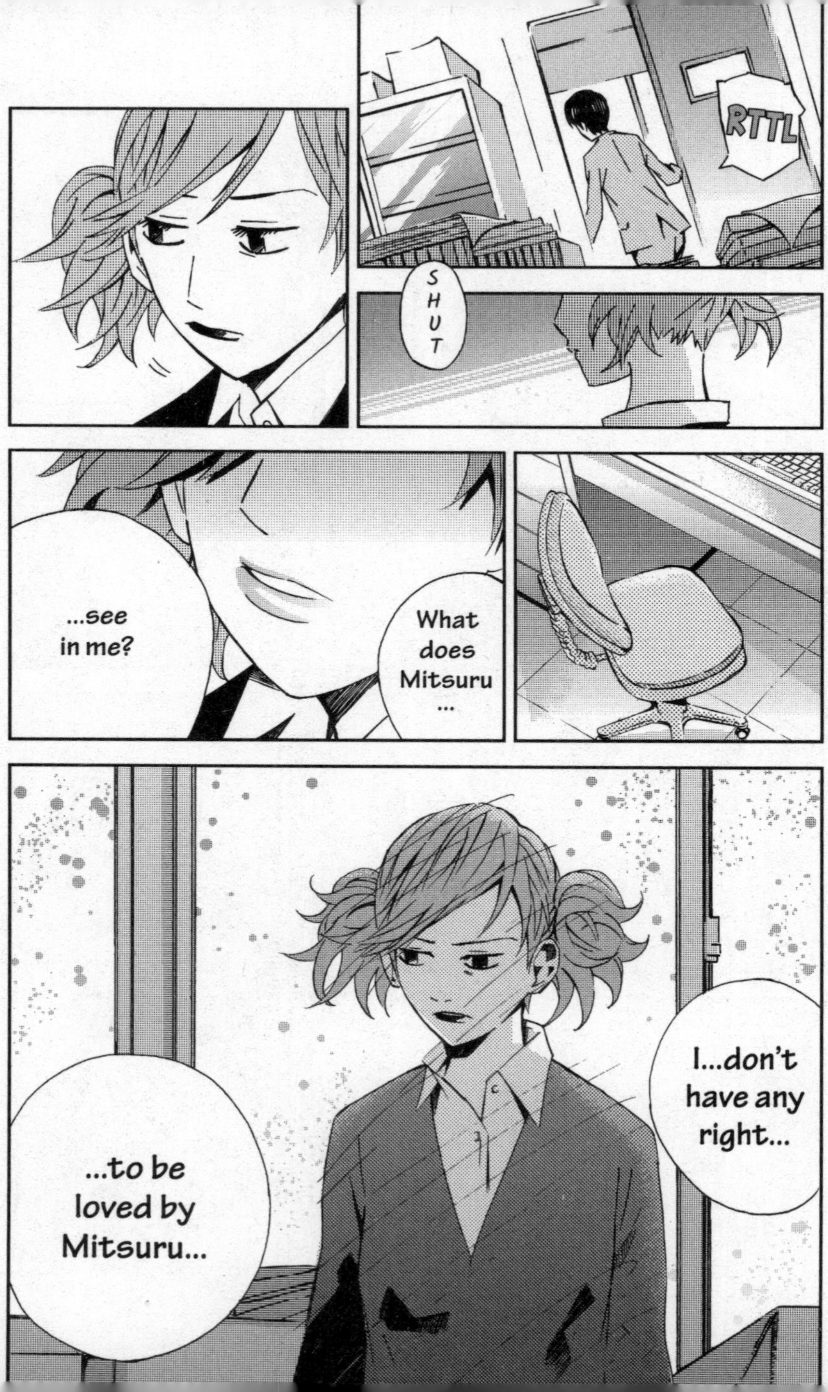
RTTL
SHUT
What does Mitsuru...
...see in me?
I...don't have any right...
...to be loved by Mitsuru...

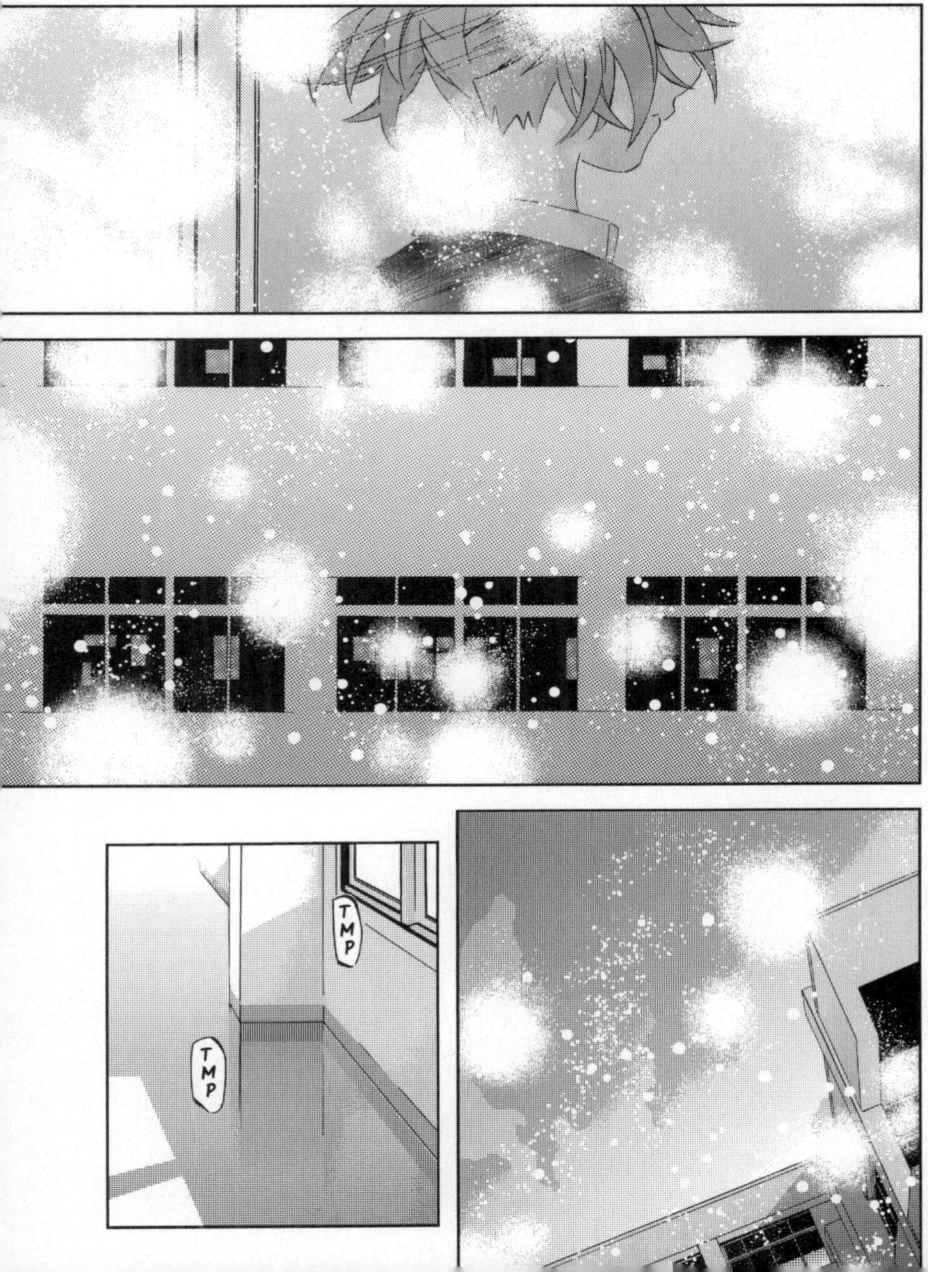
TMP
TMP

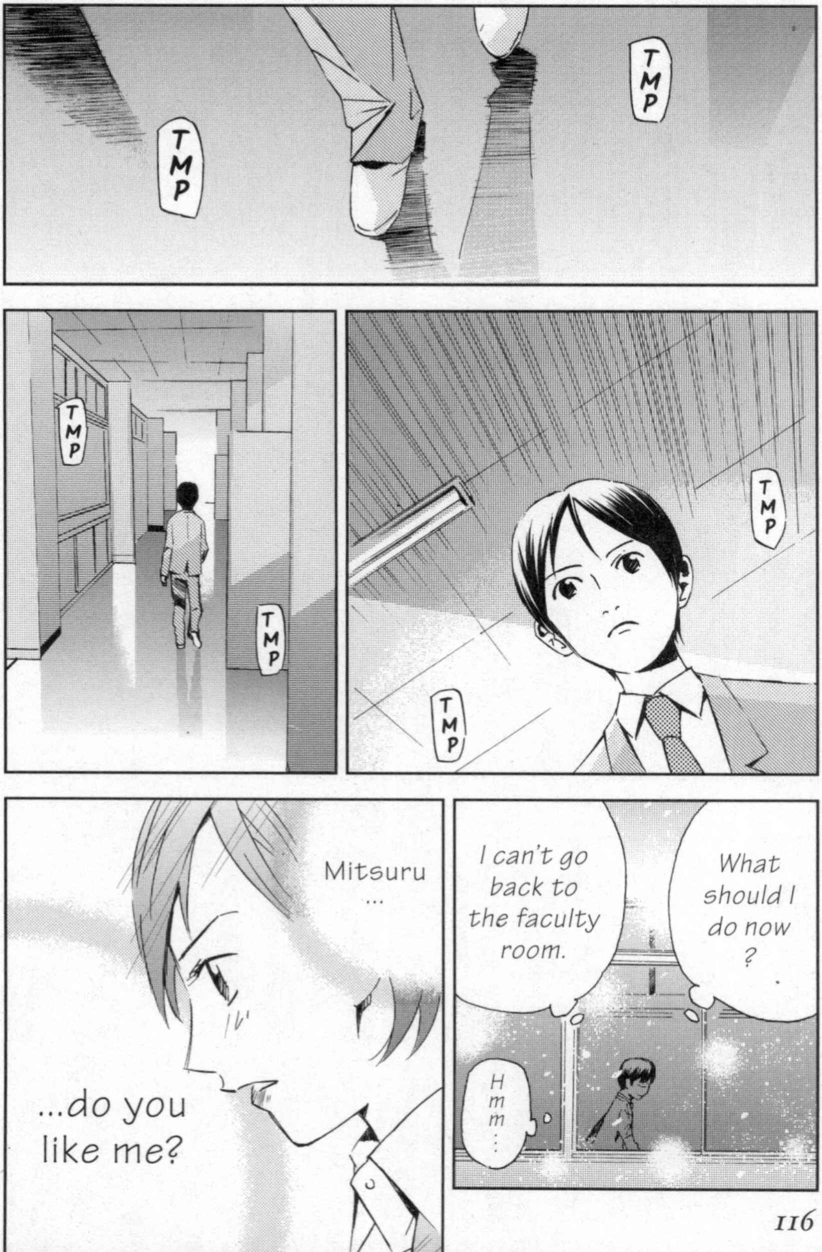
TMP
TMP
TMP
TMP
TMP
TMP
What should I do now?
I can't go back to the faculty room.
Hmm...
Mitsuru...
...do you like me?

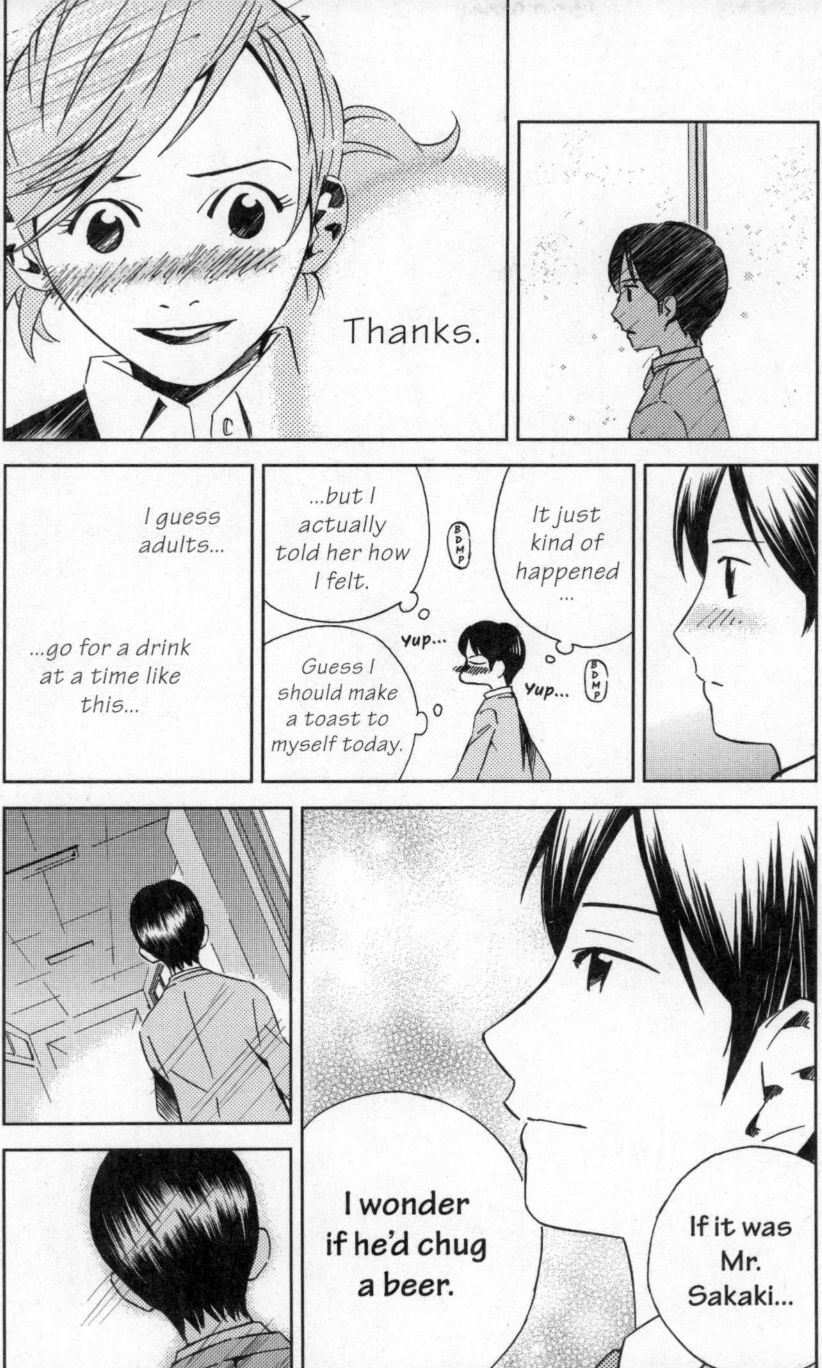
Thanks.
It just kind of happened ...
BDMP
Yup...
...but I actually told her how I felt.
BDMP
Yup...
Guess I should make a toast to myself today.
I guess adults...
...go for a drink at a time like this...
If it was Mr. Sakaki...
I wonder if he'd chug a beer.

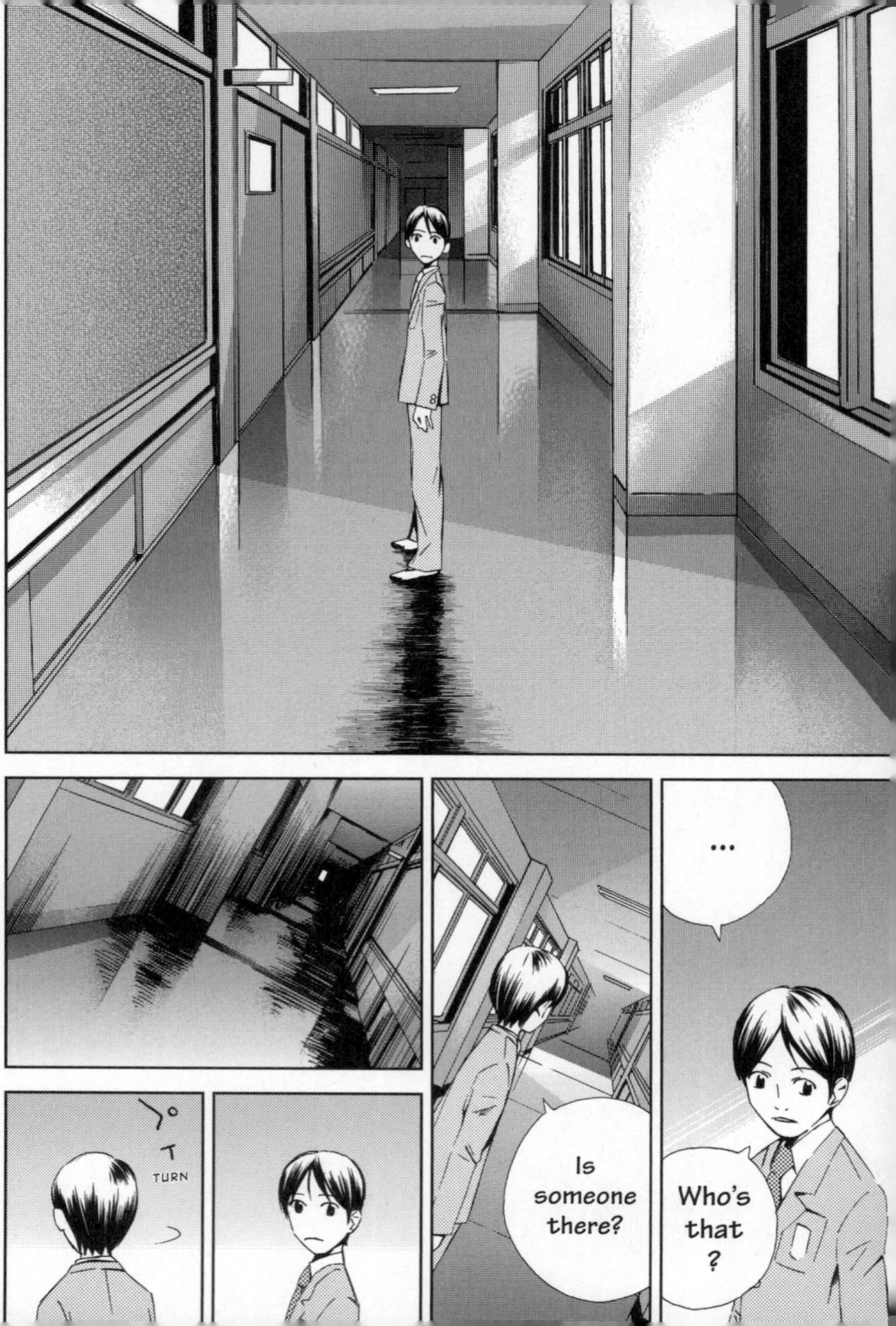
...
Who's that?
Is someone there?
TURN

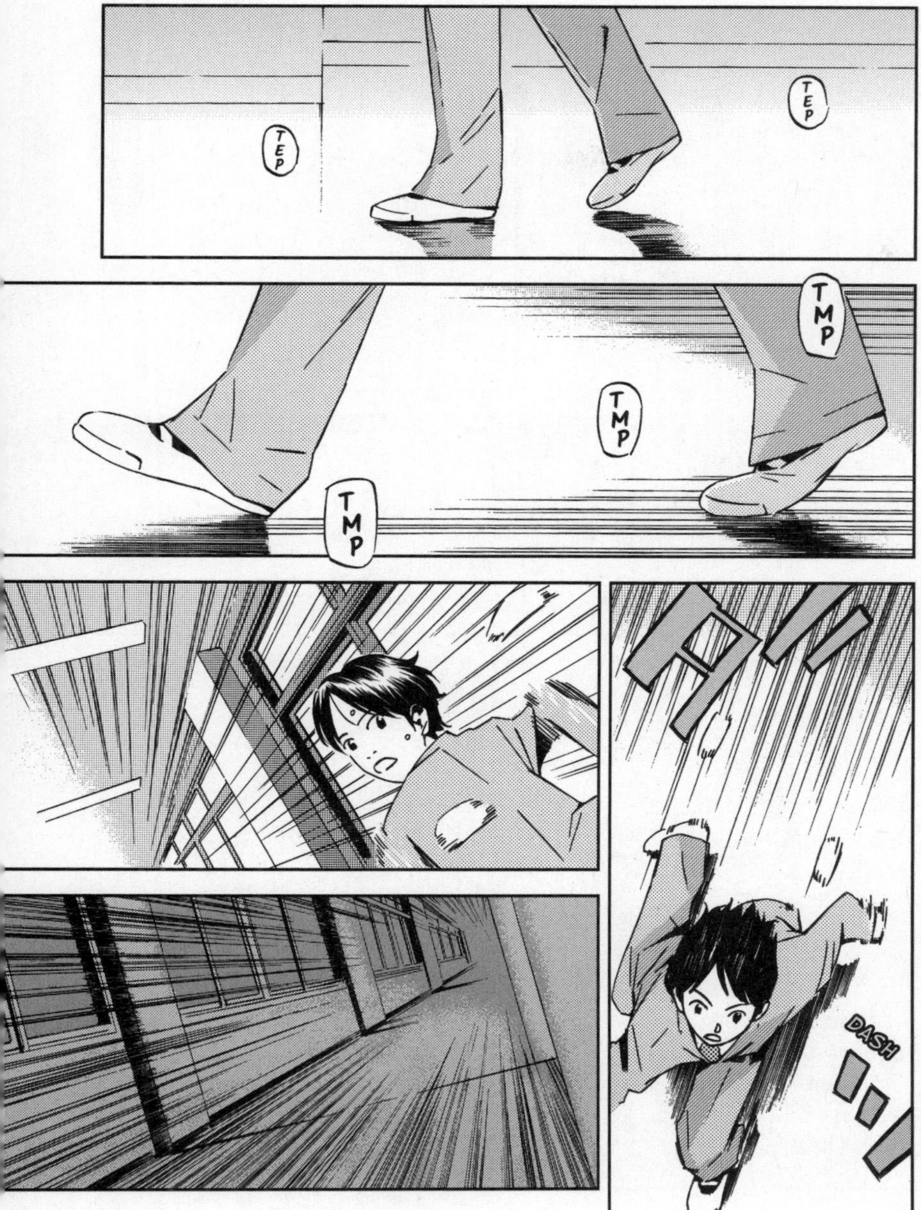
TEP
TEP
TMP
TMP
TMP
DASH

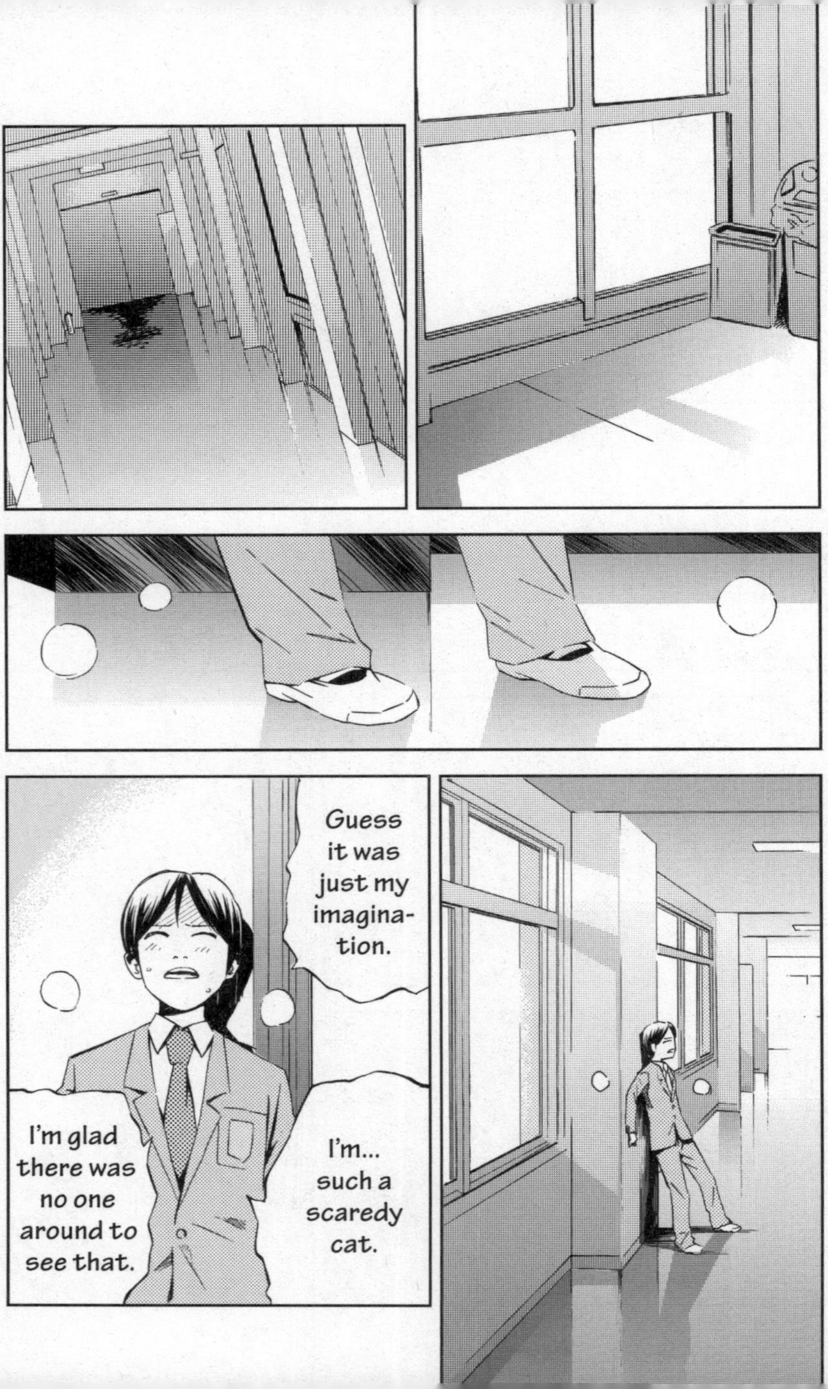
Guess it was just my imagina-tion.
I'm... such a scaredy cat.
I'm glad there was no one around to see that.

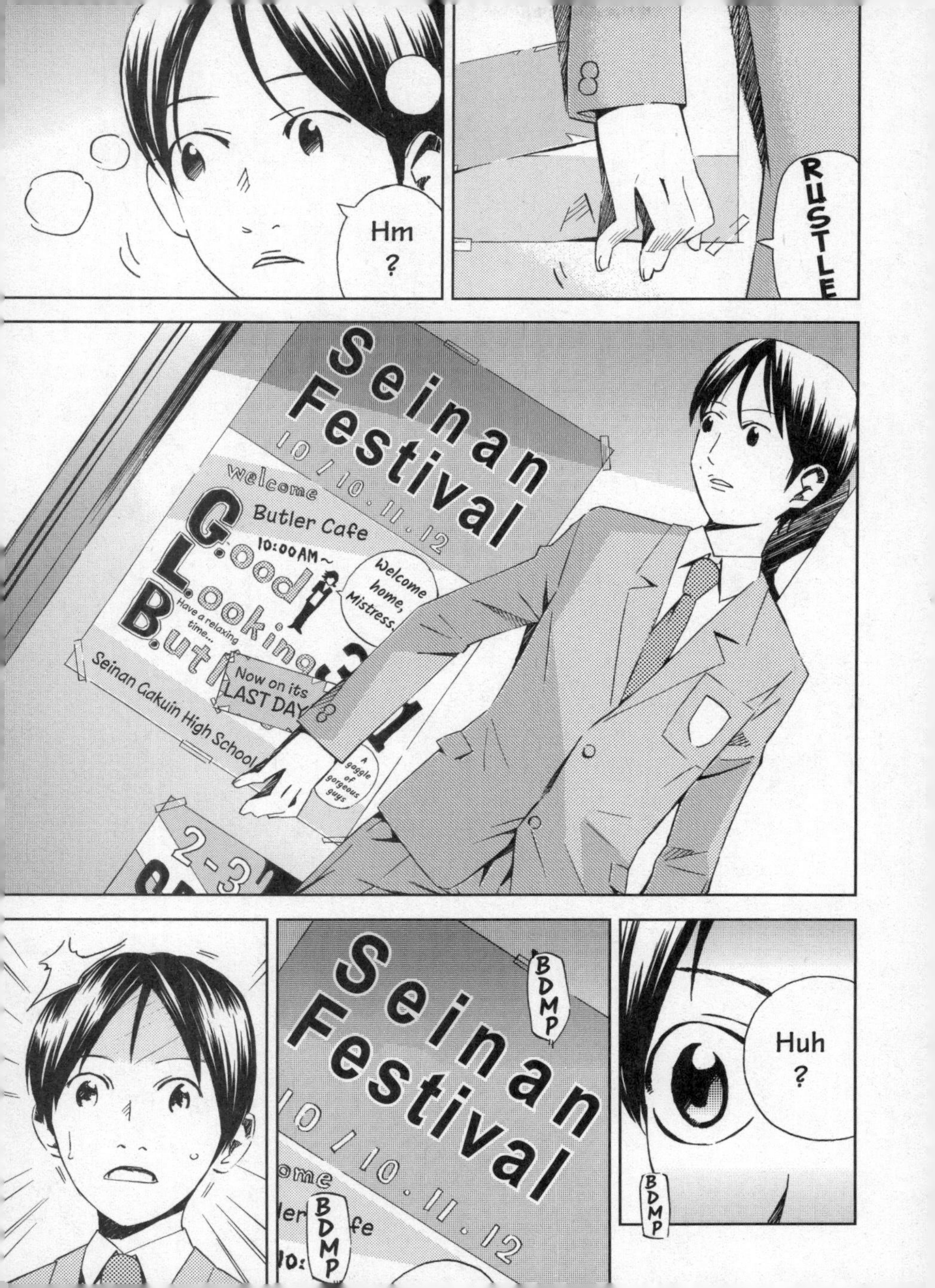
RUSTLE
Hm ?
Seinan Festival
10/10.11.12
welcome
Butler Cafe
10:00AM~
G.ood L.ooking
Have a relaxing time...
Welcome home, Mistress.
Now on its LAST DAY
Seinan Gakuin High School
A gaggle of gorgeous guys
2-3
Huh ?
BDMP
BDMP
Seinan Festival
10/10.11.12
BDMP

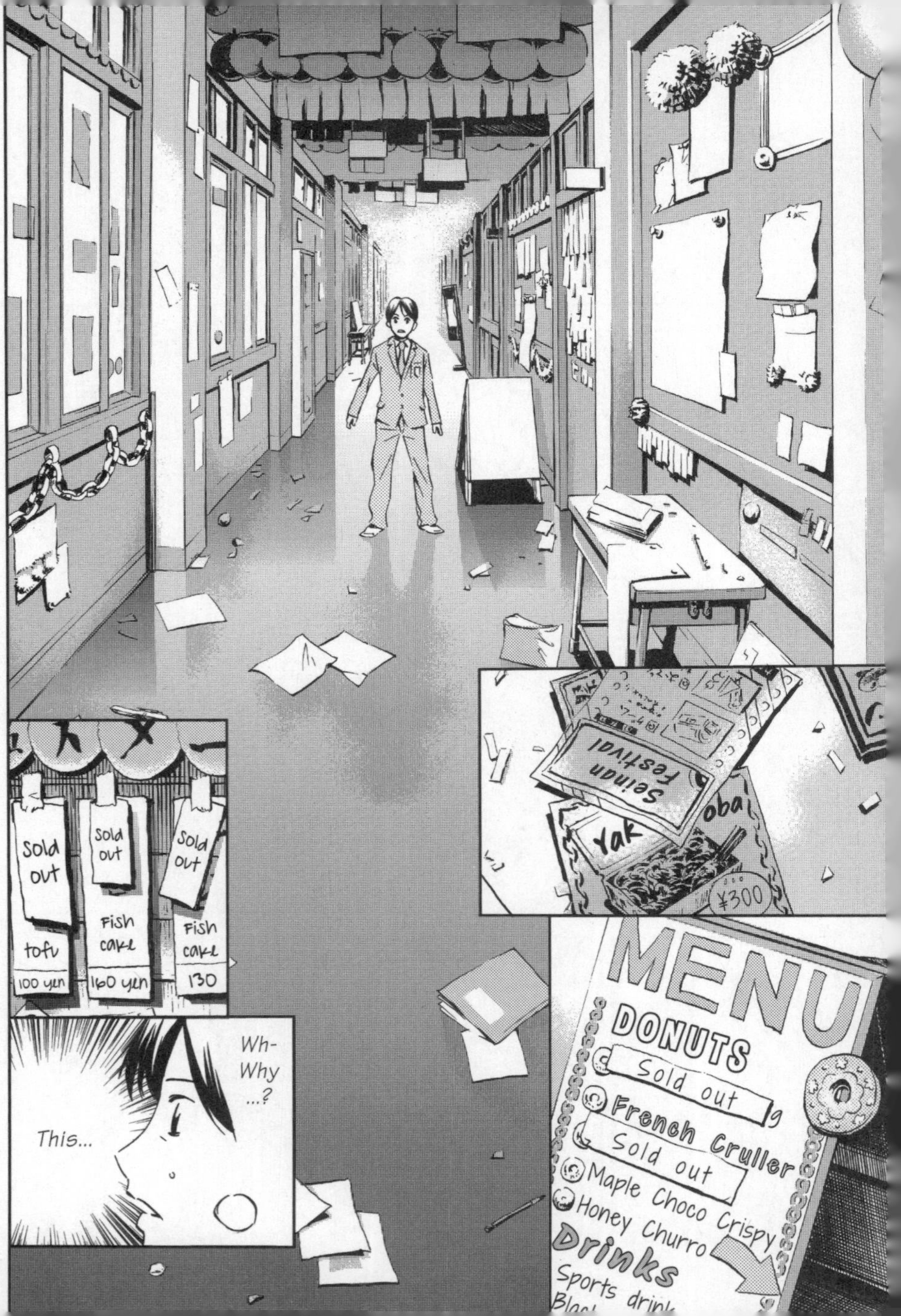
Seinan Festival
Yak
oba
¥300
Sold out
tofu
100 yen
Sold out
Fish cake
160 yen
Sold out
Fish cake
130
MENU
DONUTS
Sold out
French Cruller
Sold out
Maple Choco Crispy
Honey Churro
Drinks
Sports drink
Wh- Why ...?
This...

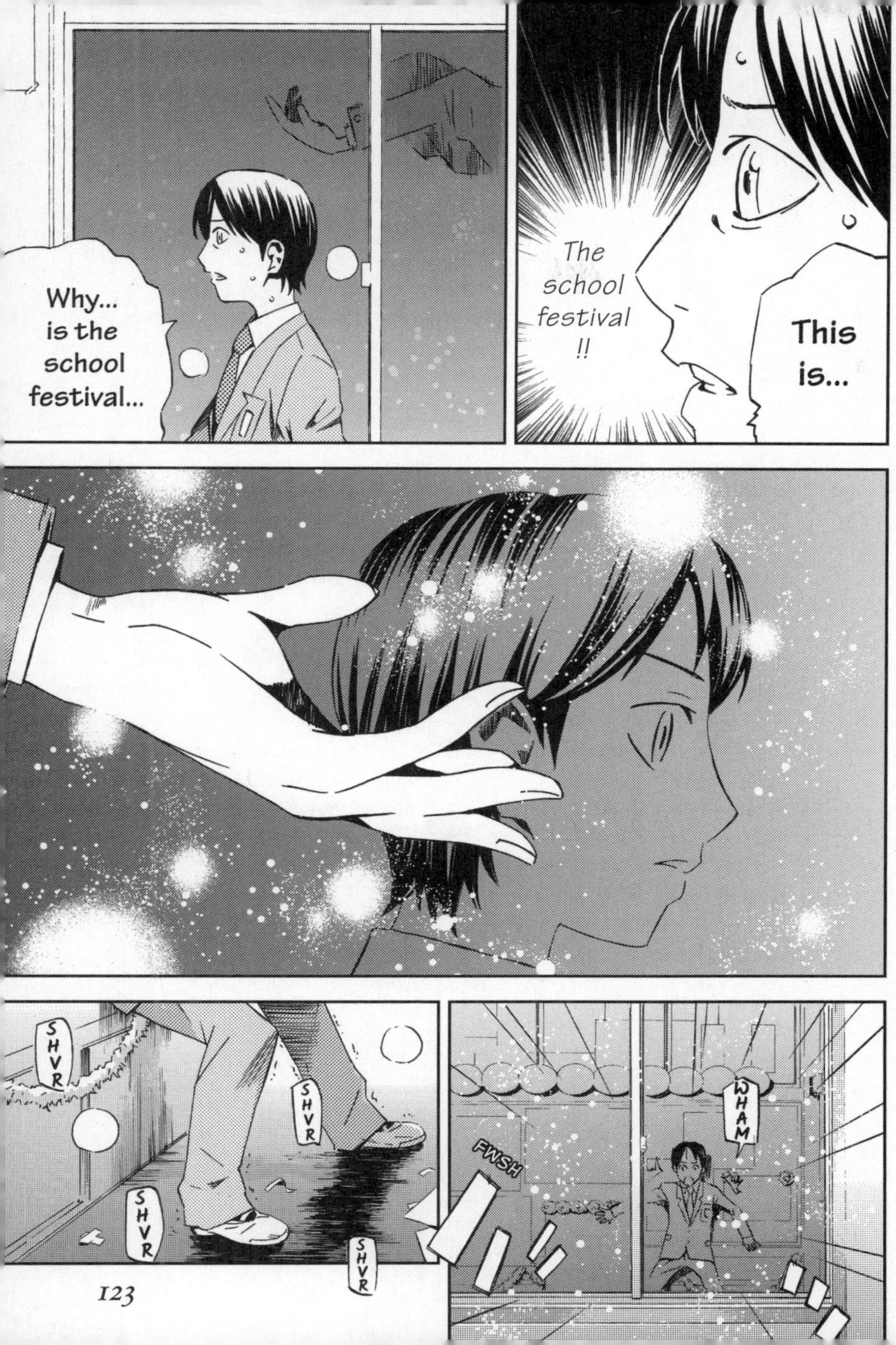
This is...
The school festival !!
Why... is the school festival...
WHAM
FWSH
SHVR
SHVR
SHVR
SHVR

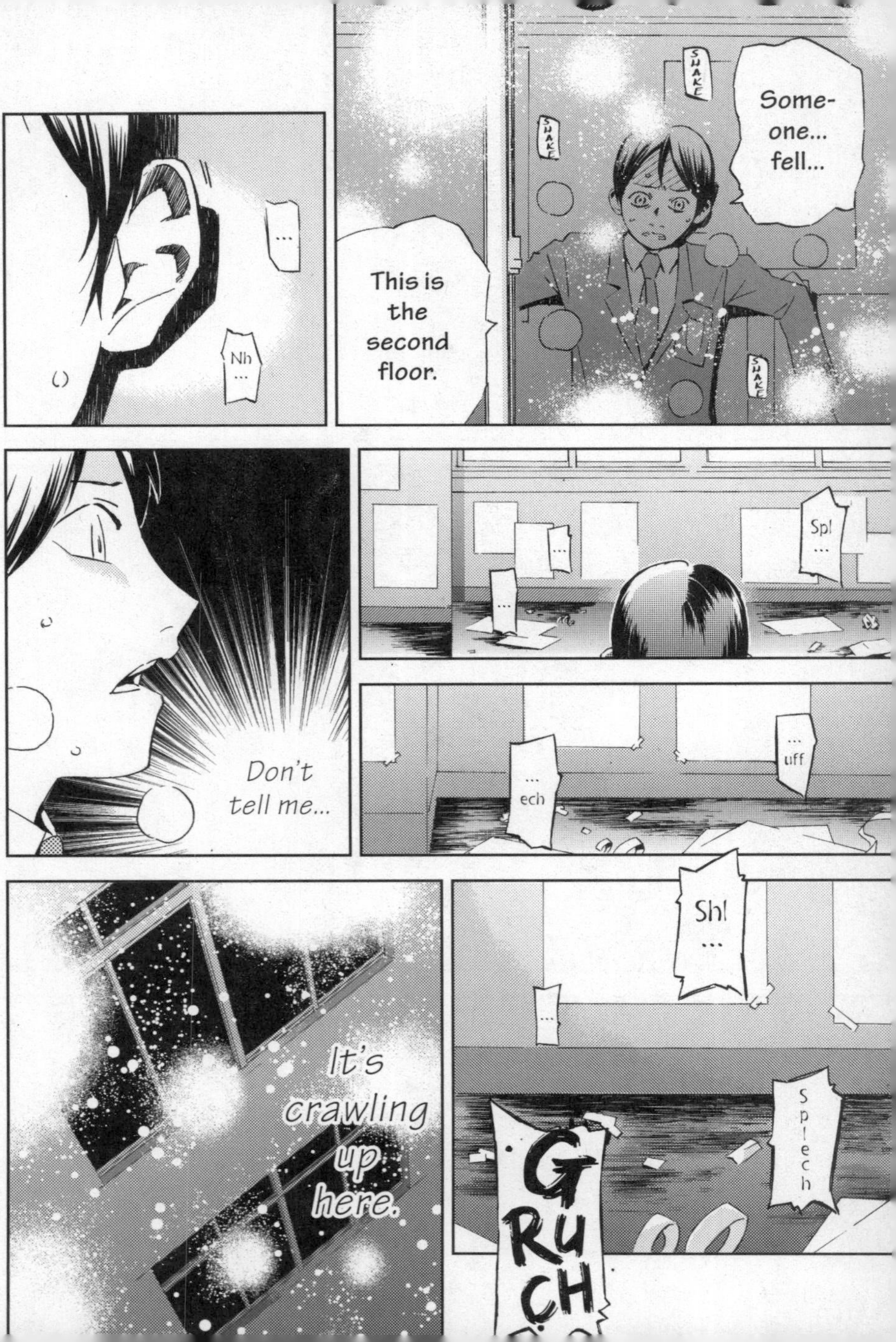
SHAKE
SHAKE
Some-one... fell...
SHAKE
This is the second floor.
...
Nh...
Spl...
...
...
... uff
... ech
Don't tell me...
Shl...
...
Splech
GRUCH
It's crawling up here.

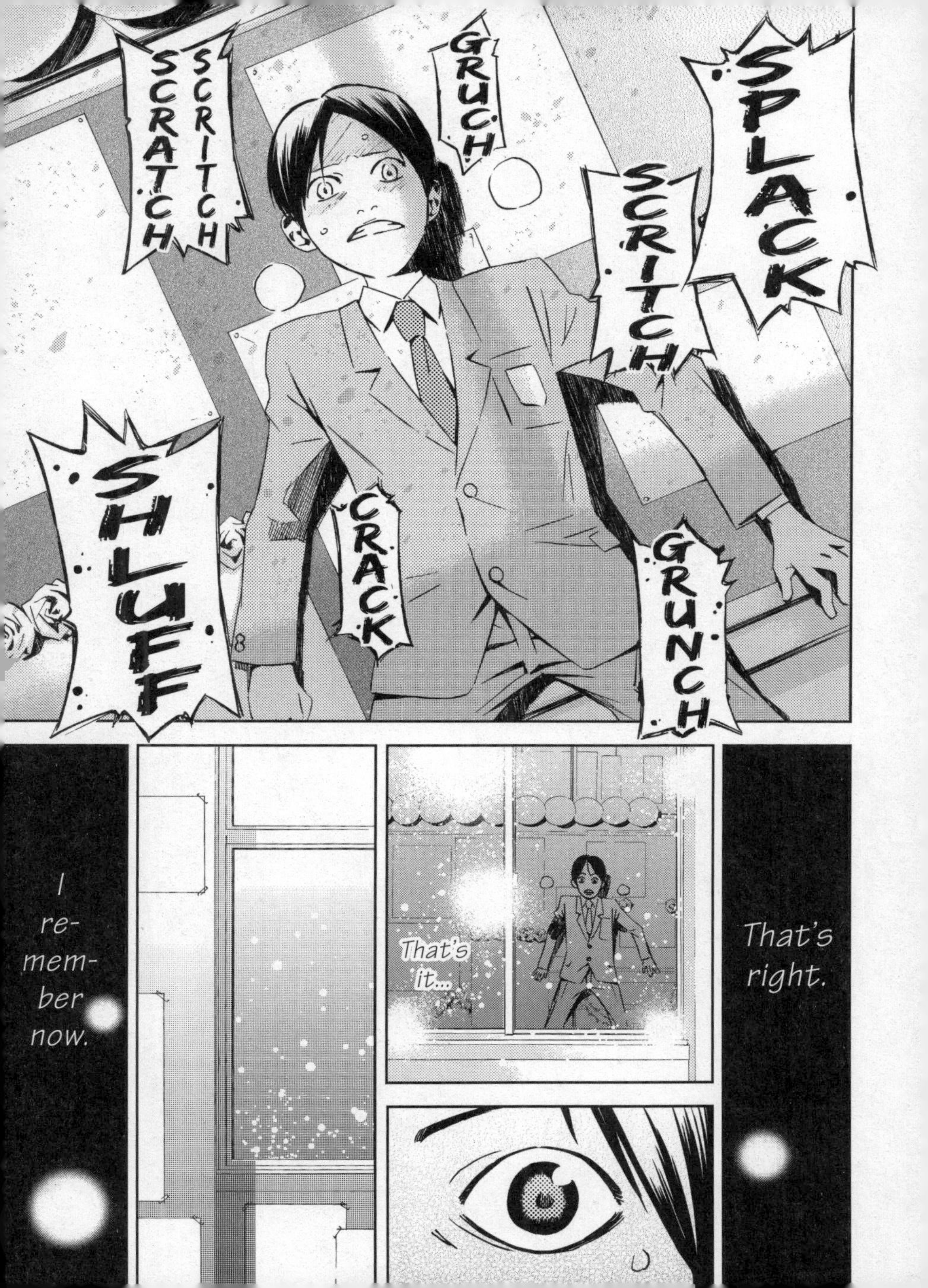
SPLACK
SCRITCH
GRUCH
SCRITCH
SCRATCH
GRUNCH
CRACK
SHLUFF
That's right.
That's it...
I remember now.

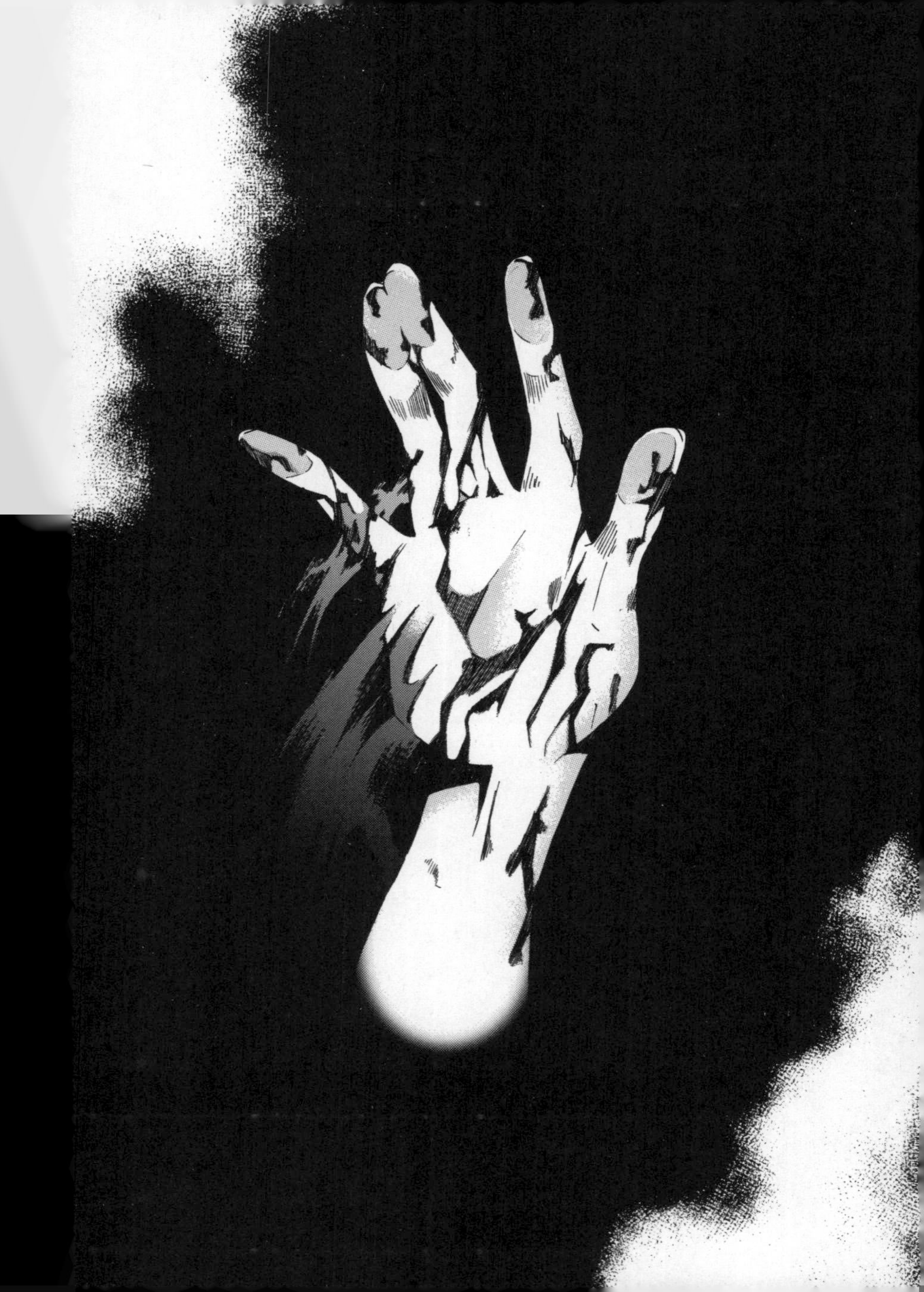

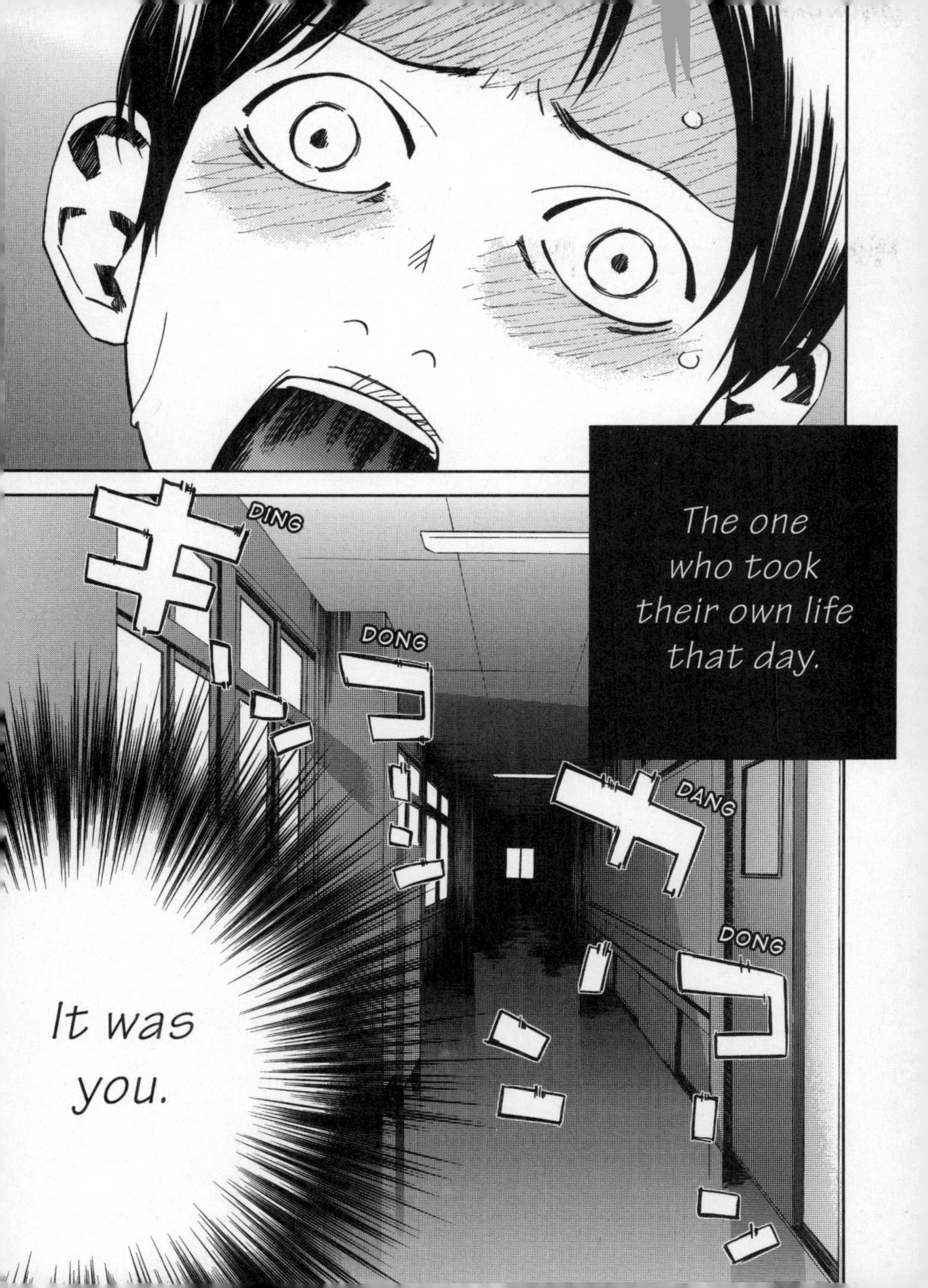
The one who took their own life that day.
DING
DONG
DANG
DONG
It was you.

A School
Frozen
in Time

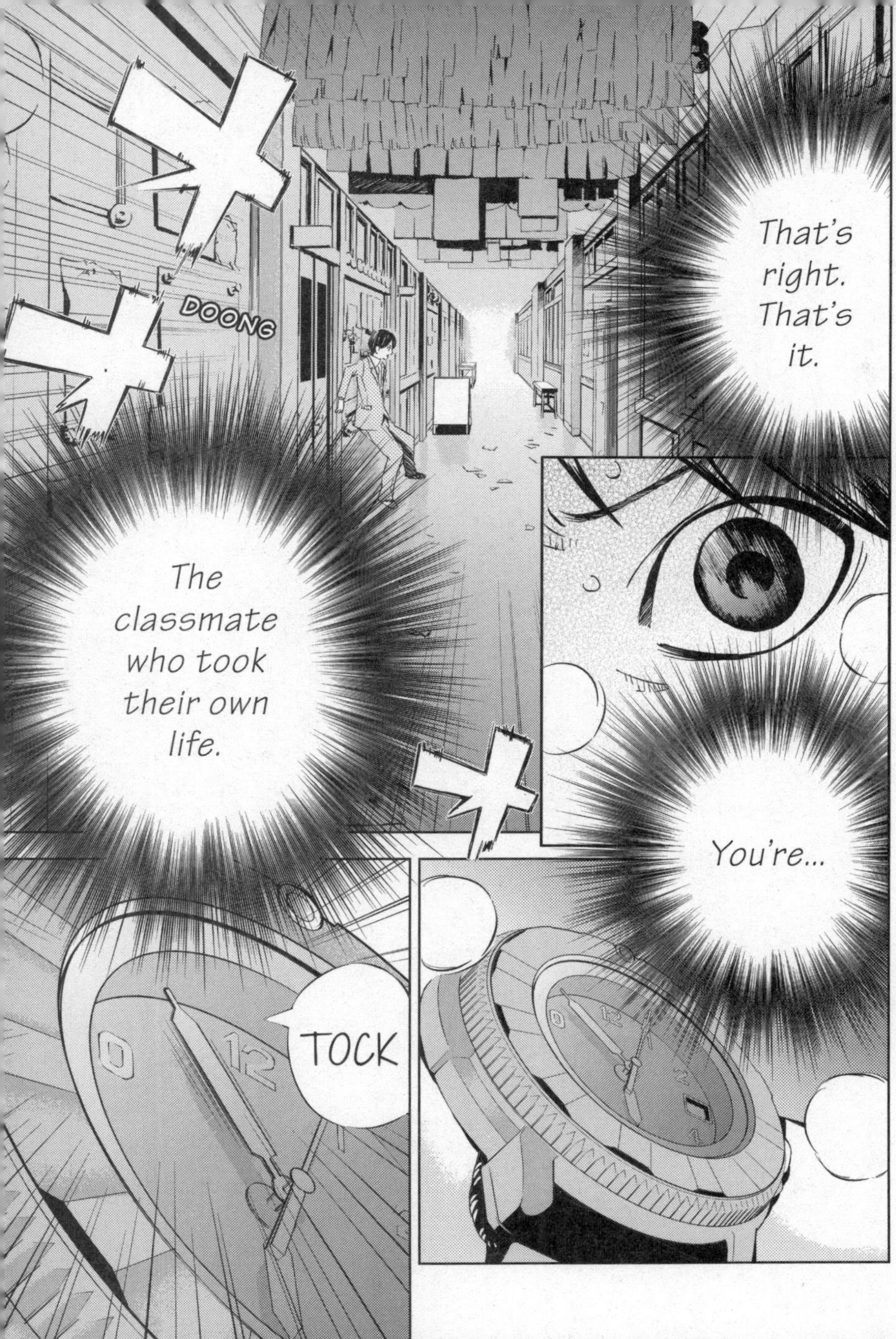
That's right. That's it.
DOONG
The classmate who took their own life.
You're...
TOCK

Chapter 3
Chime

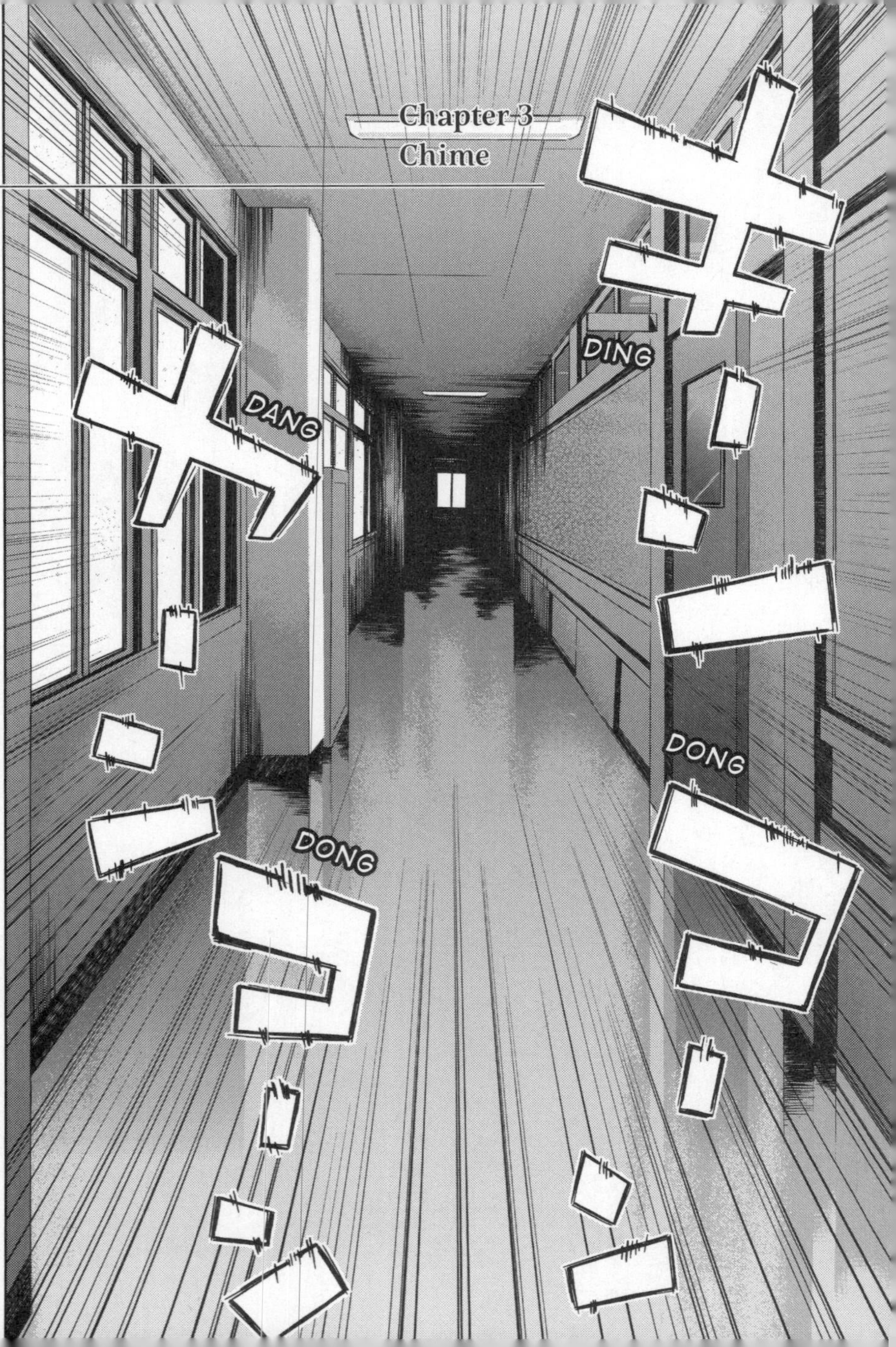
DING
DANG
DONG
DONG

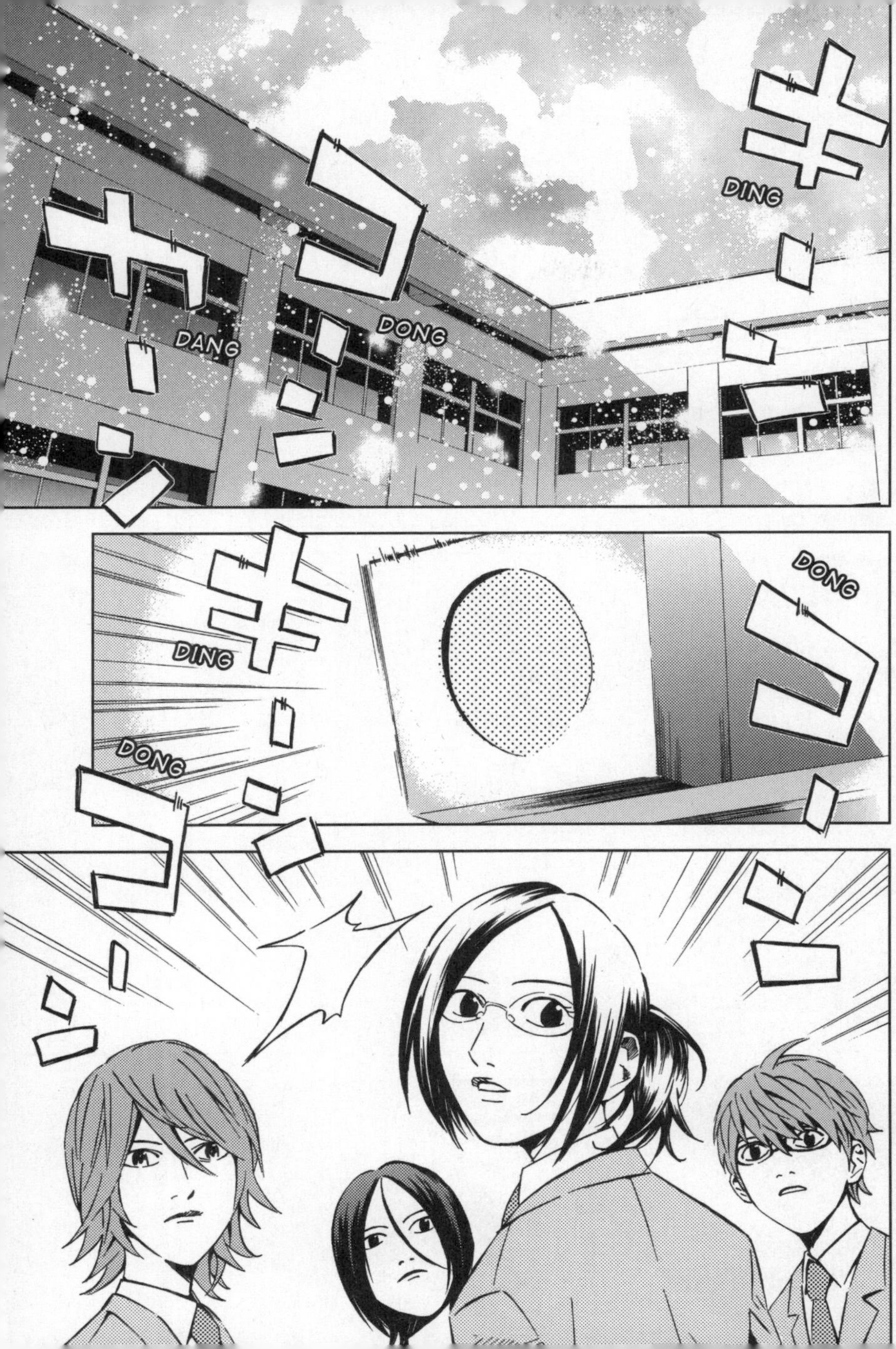
DING
DONG
DANG
DONG
DING
DONG

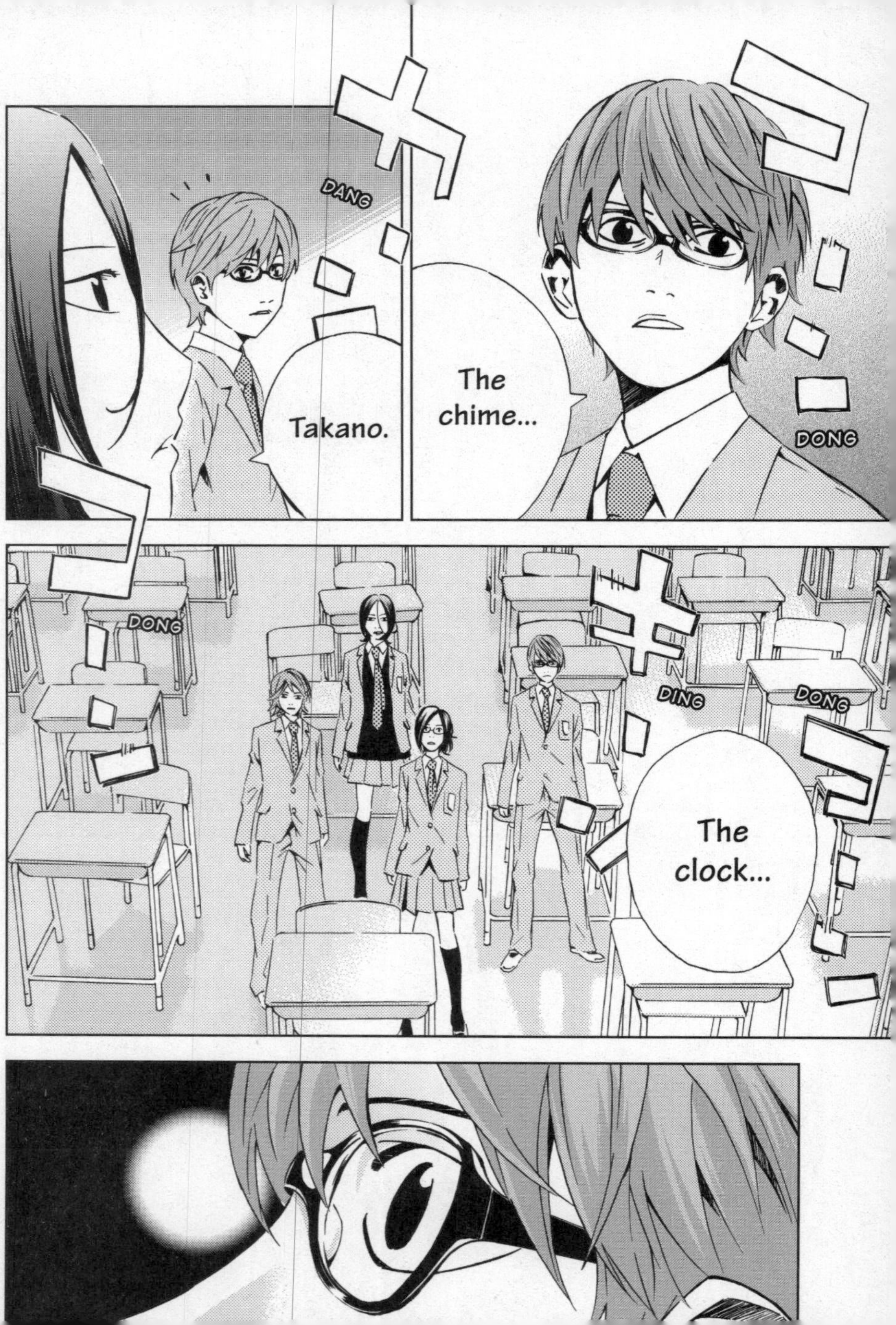
DONG
The chime...
DANG
Takano.
DONG
DING
The clock...
DONG

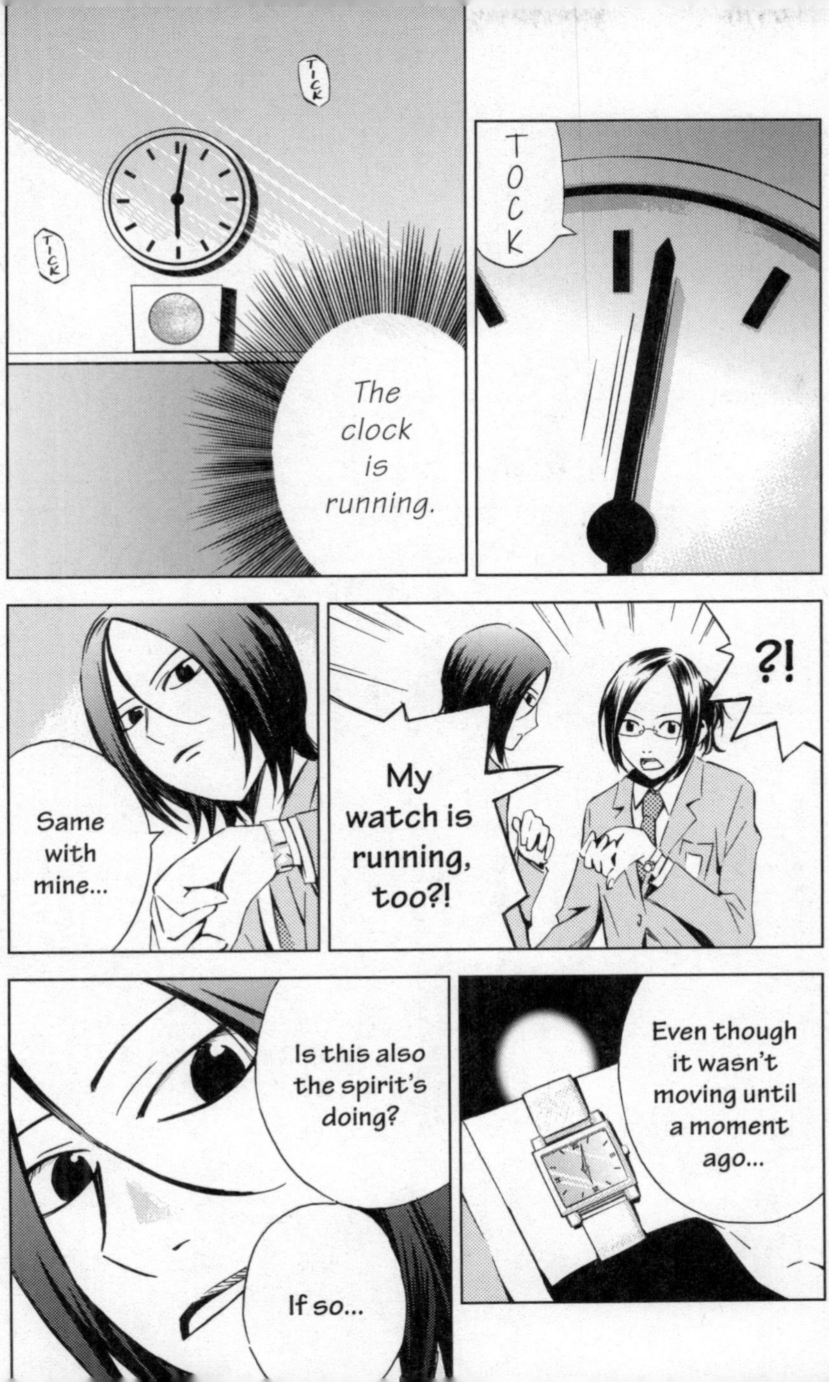
TOCK
TICK
TICK
The clock is running.
?!
My watch is running, too?!
Same with mine...
Even though it wasn't moving until a moment ago...
Is this also the spirit's doing?
If so...

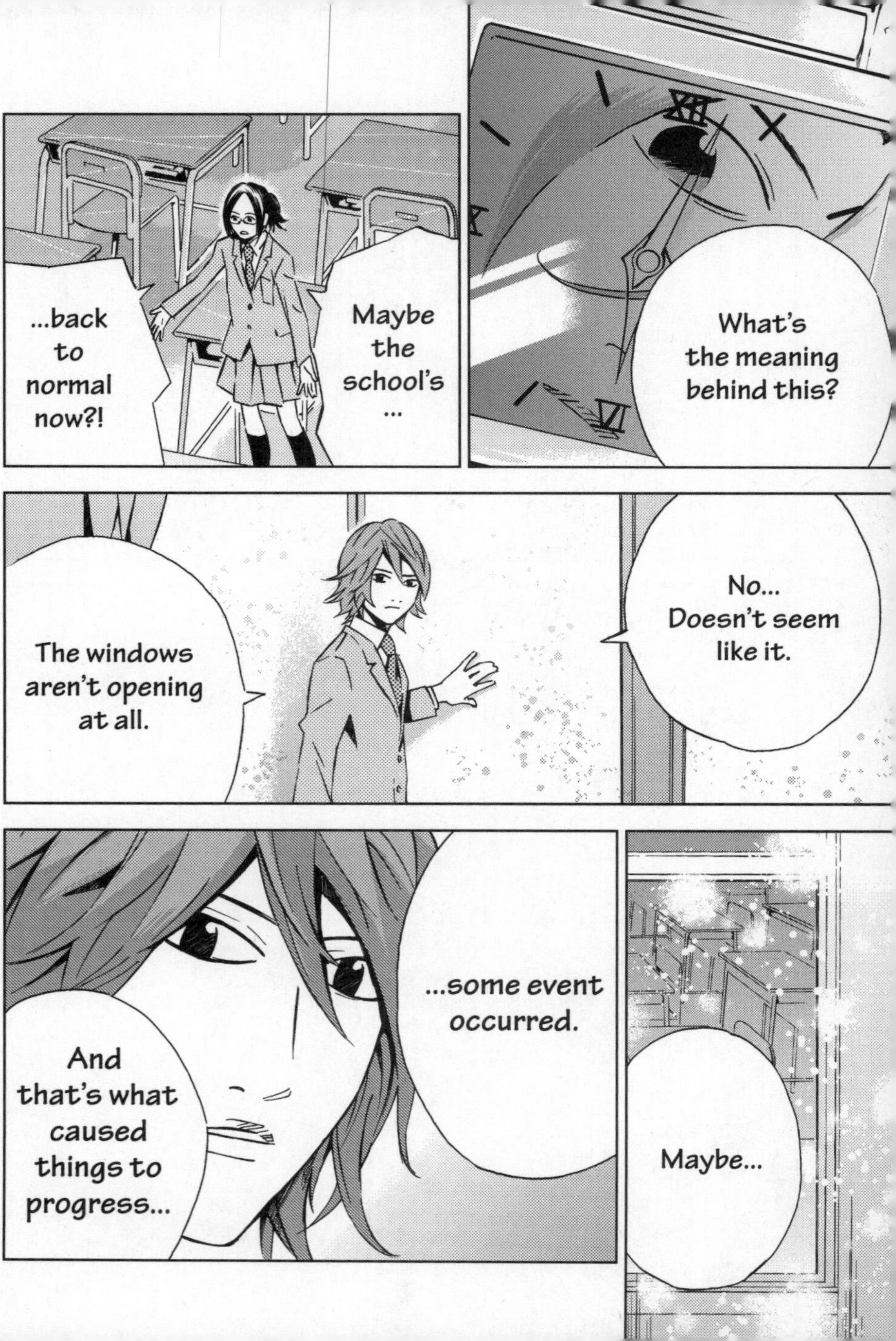
What's the meaning behind this?
Maybe the school's ...
...back to normal now?!
No... Doesn't seem like it.
The windows aren't opening at all.
Maybe...
...some event occurred.
And that's what caused things to progress...

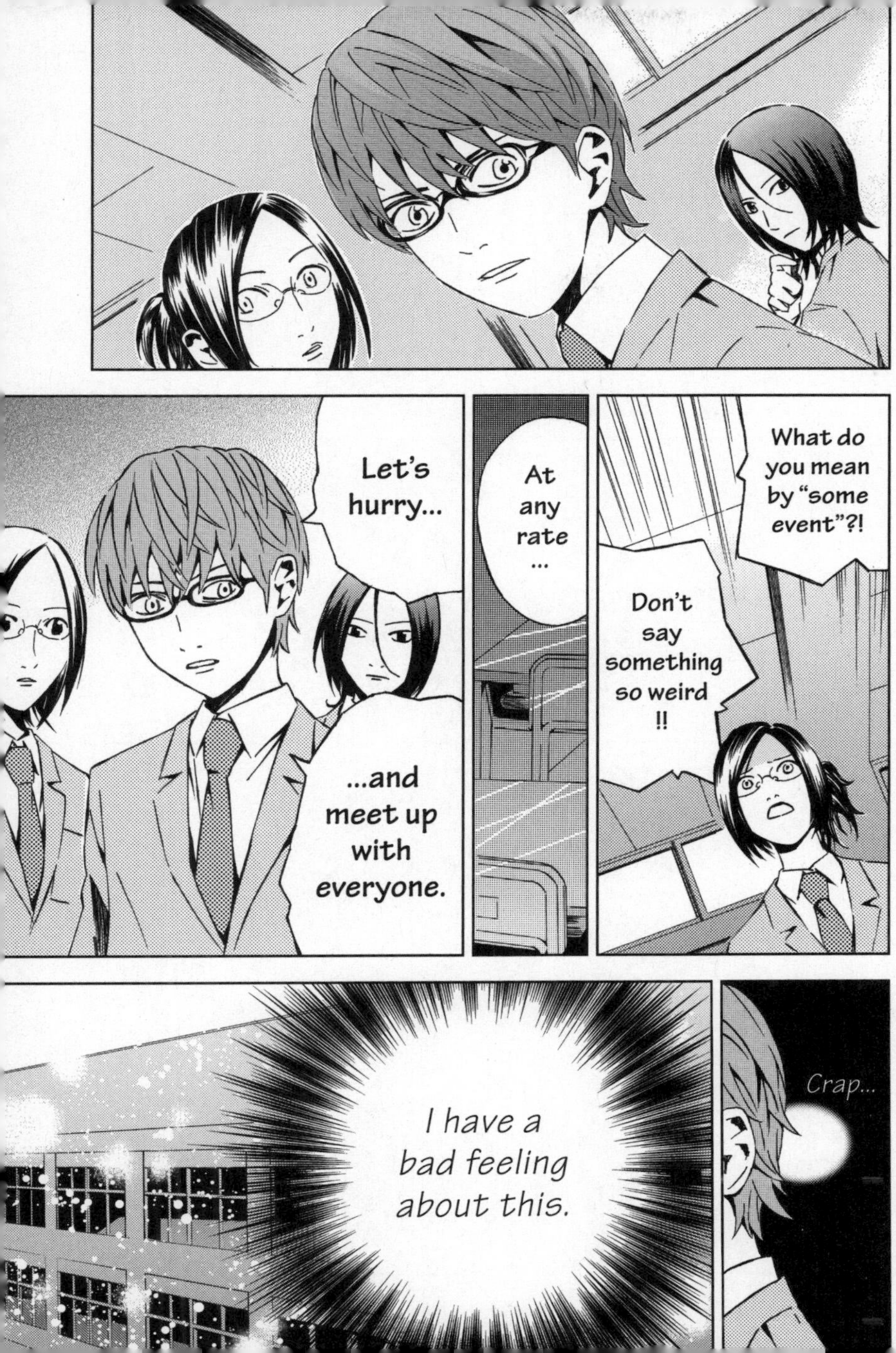
What do you mean by “some event”?!
Don’t say something so weird!!
At any rate...
Let’s hurry...
...and meet up with everyone.
Crap...
I have a bad feeling about this.

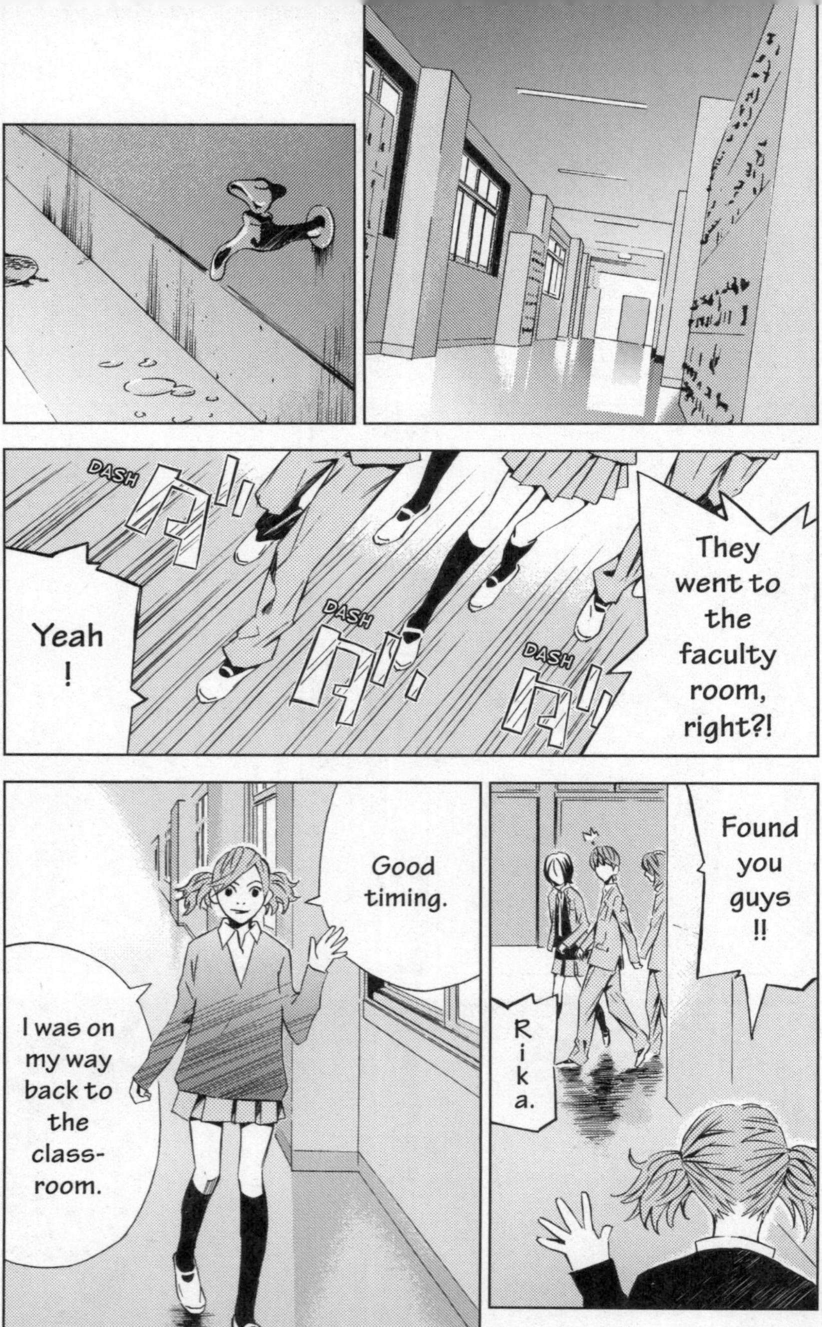
They went to the faculty room, right?!
DASH
DASH
DASH
Yeah!
Found you guys!!
Rika.
Good timing.
I was on my way back to the classroom.

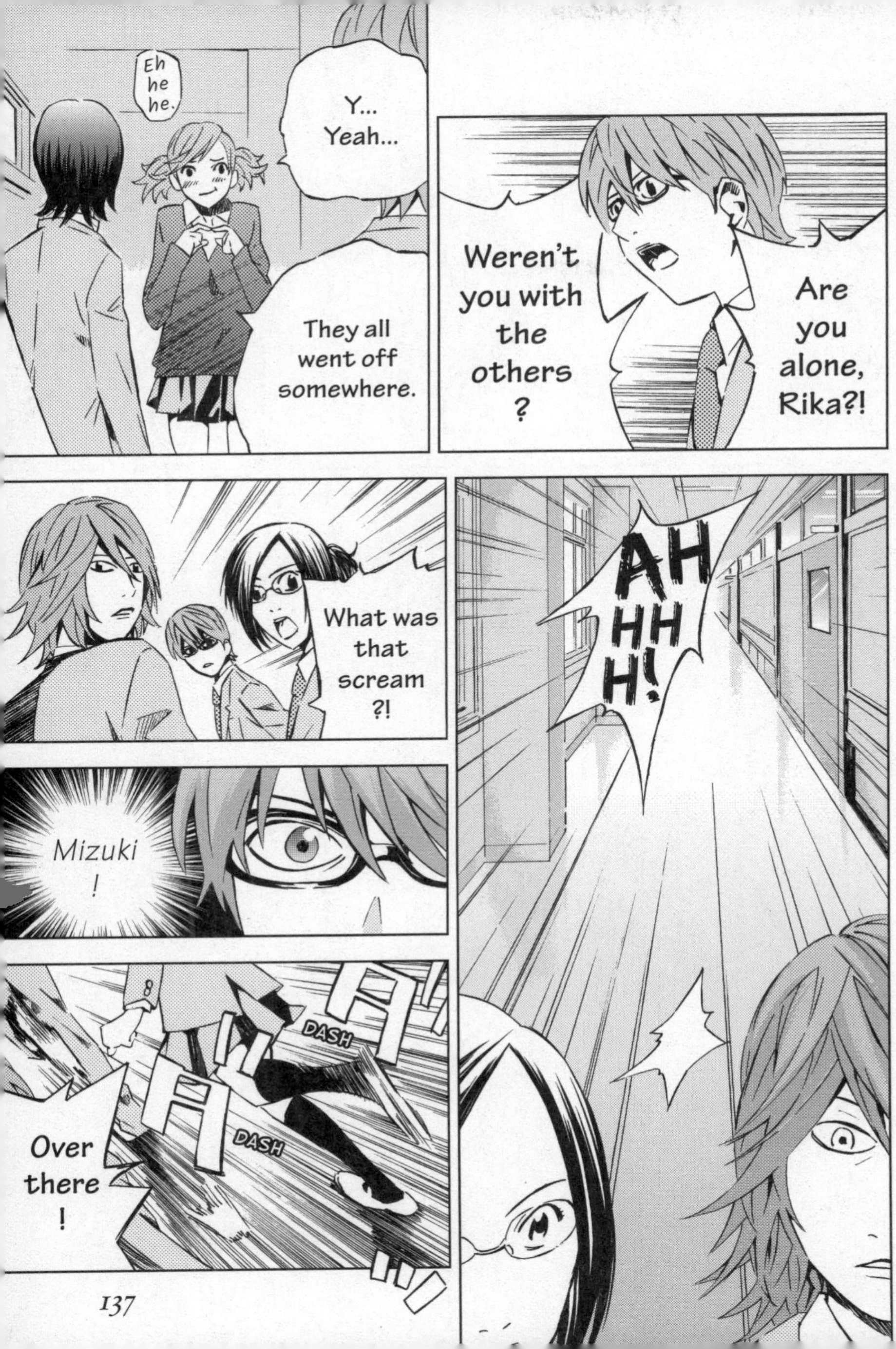
Are you alone, Rika?!
Weren't you with the others?
Y... Yeah...
They all went off somewhere.
Eh he he.
AHHHHH!
What was that scream?!
Mizuki!
DASH
DASH
Over there!

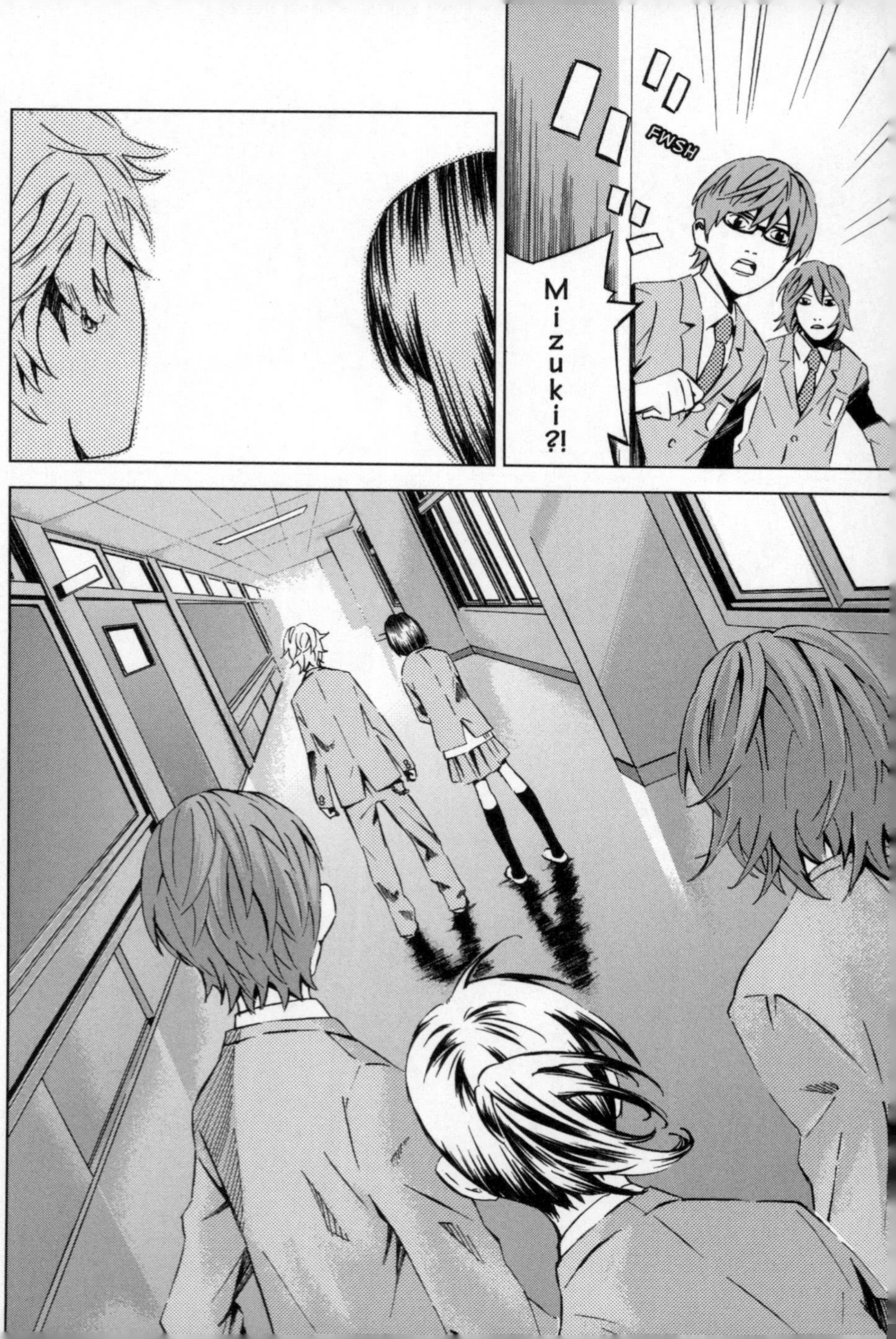
FWSH
Mizuki?!

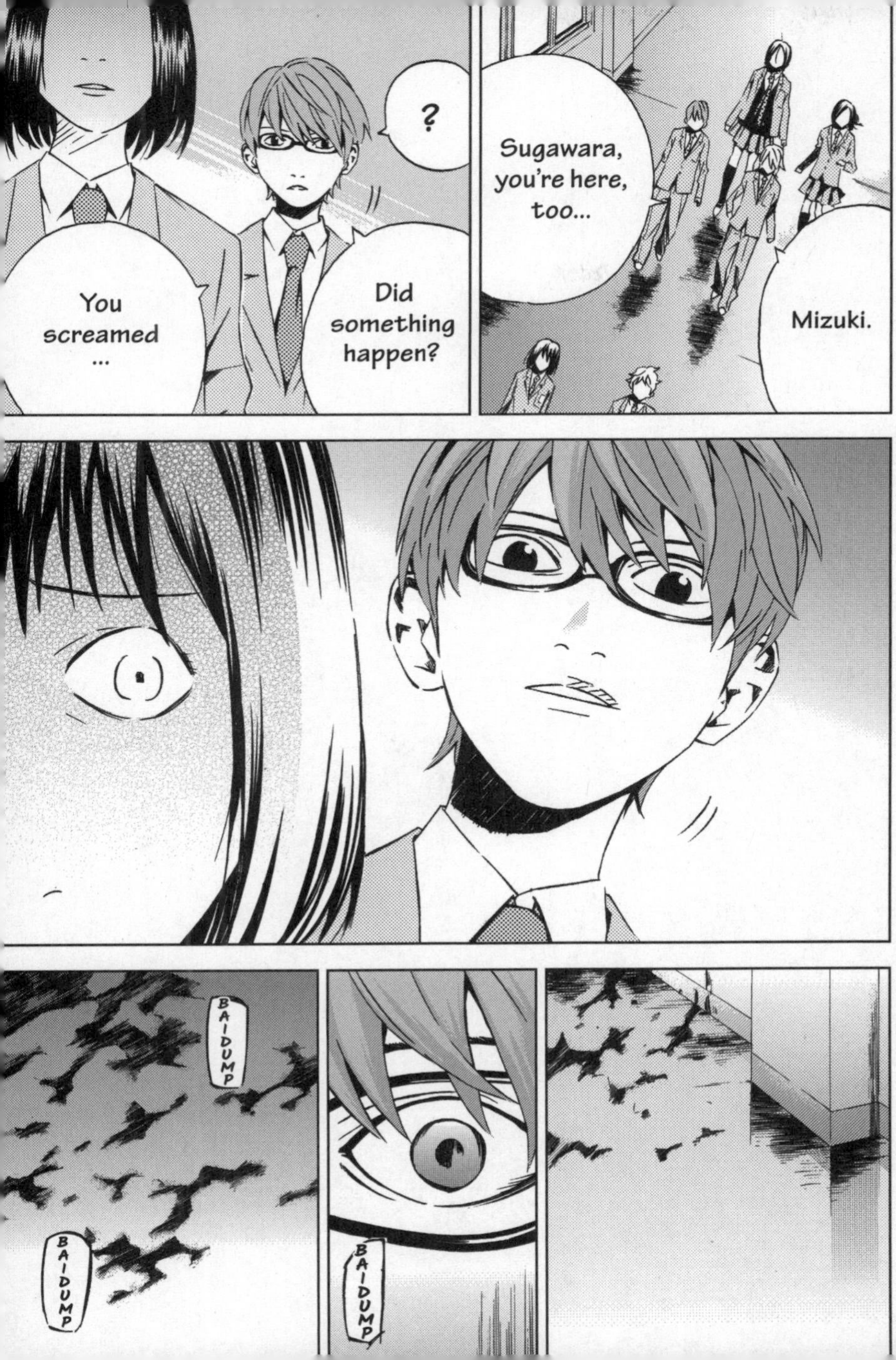
Mizuki.
Sugawara, you're here, too...
?
Did something happen?
You screamed ...
BAIDUMP
BAIDUMP
BAIDUMP

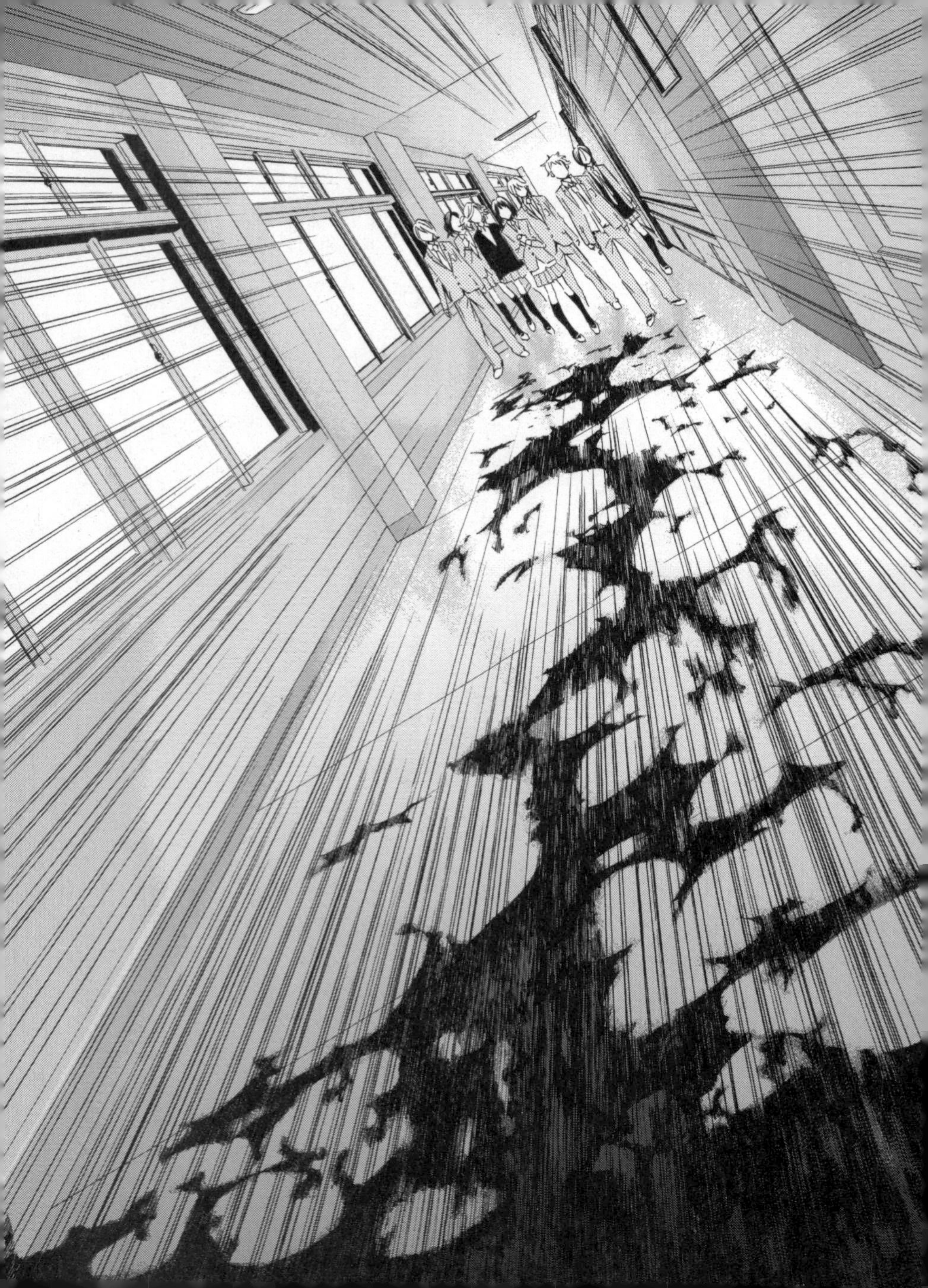

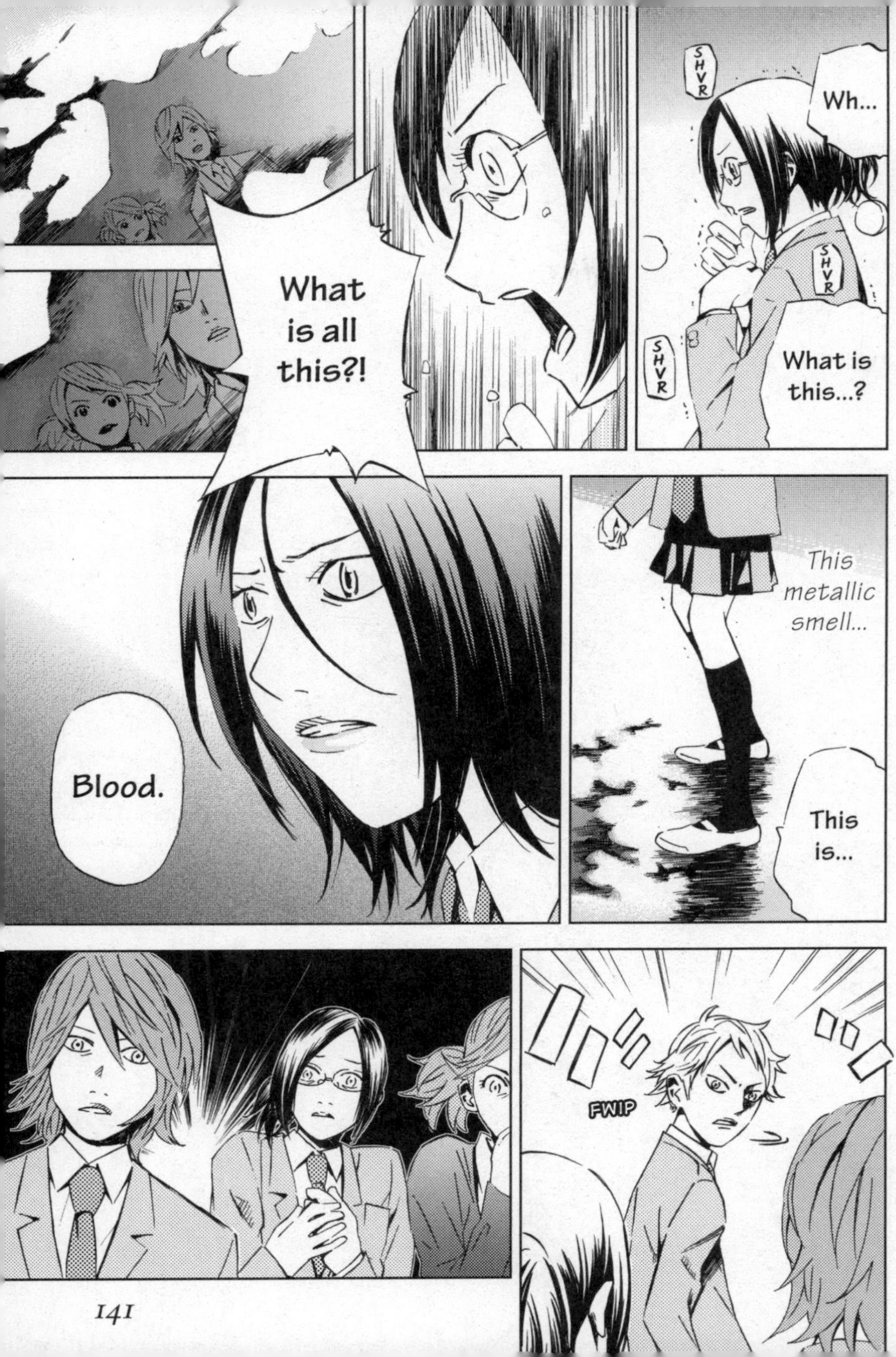
SHVR
Wh...
SHVR
SHVR
What is this...?
What is all this?!
This metallic smell...
This is...
Blood.
FWIP

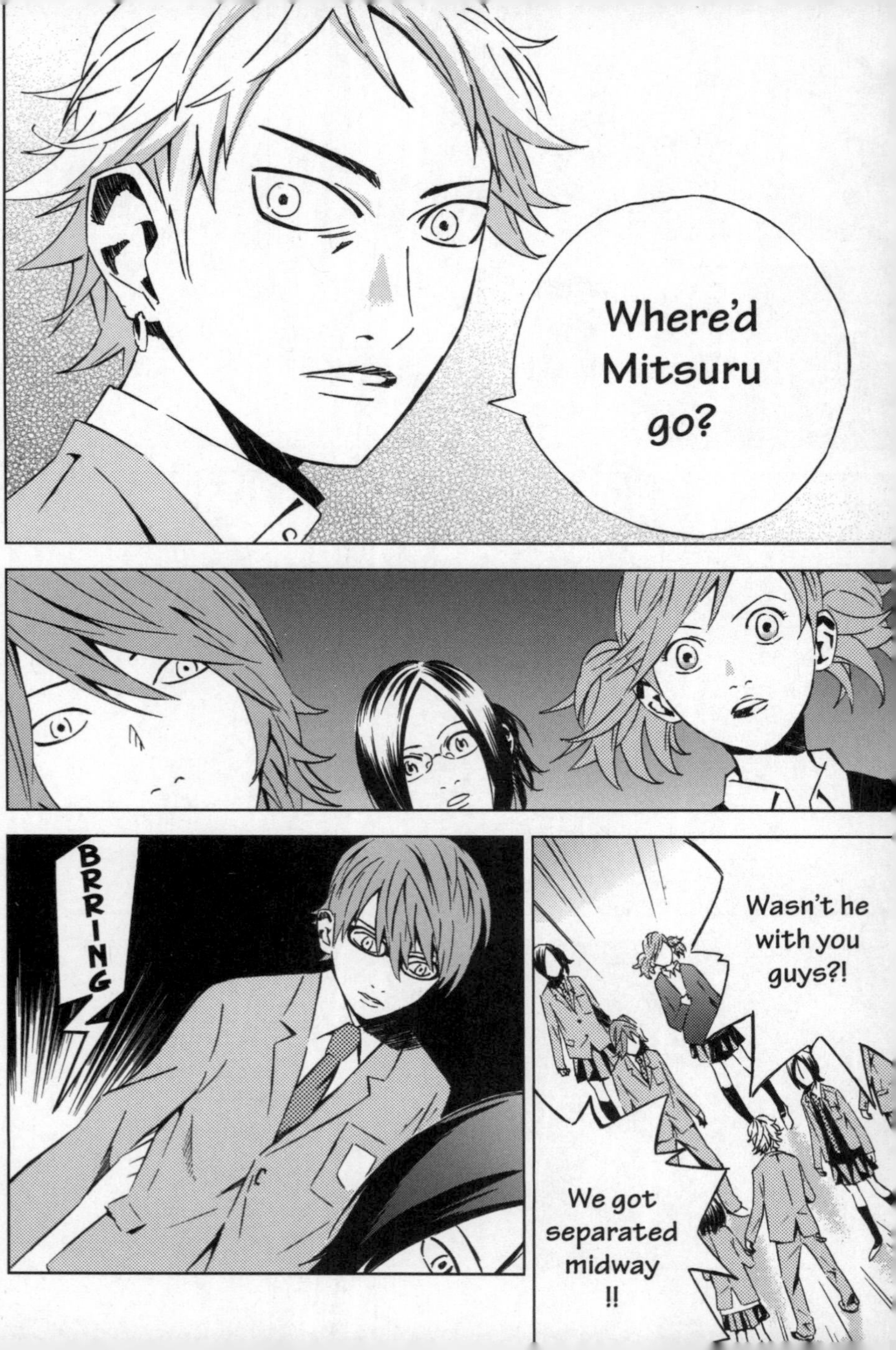
Where'd Mitsuru go?
Wasn't he with you guys?!
We got separated midway !!
BRRING

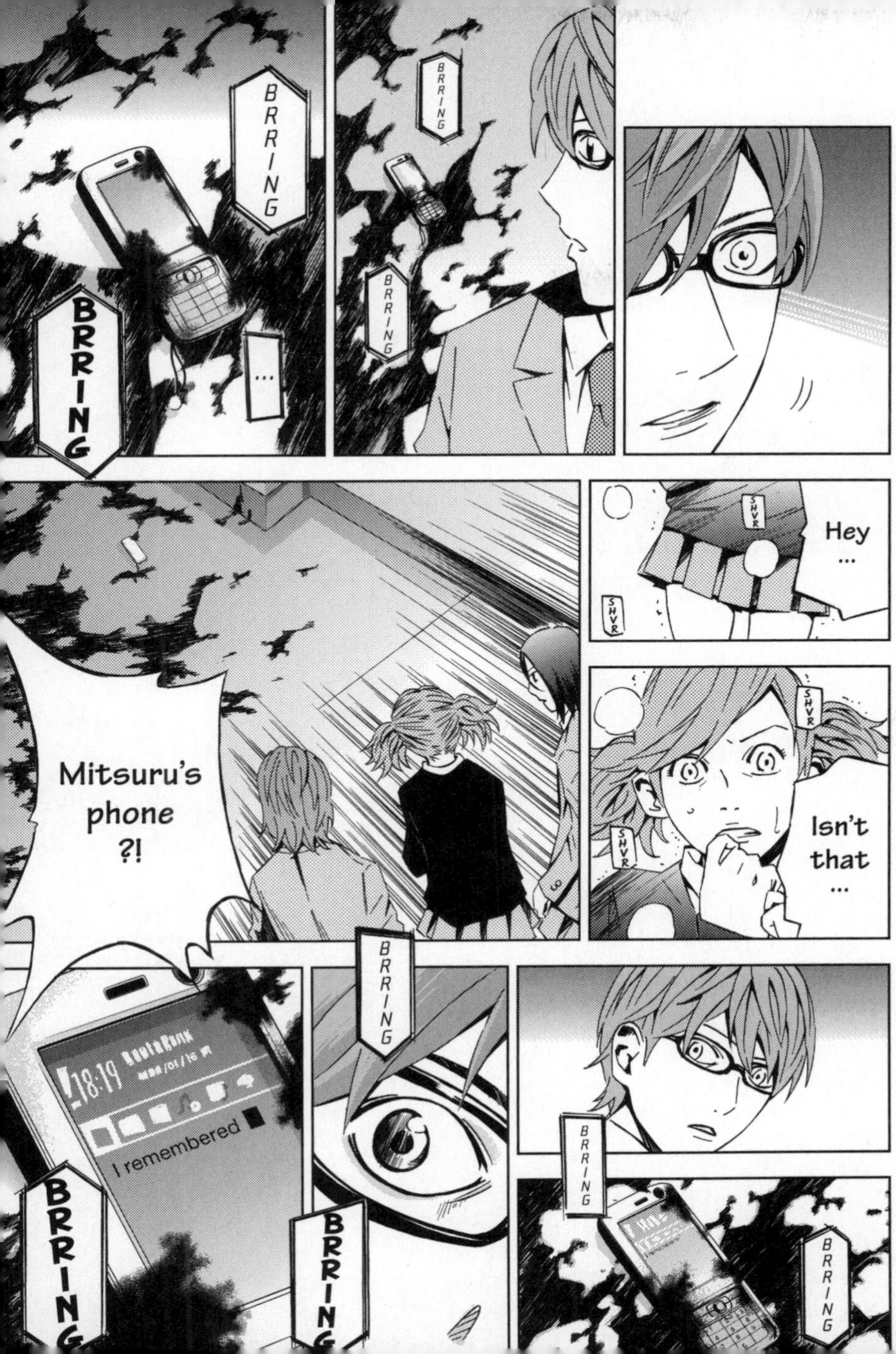
BRRING
BRRING
BRRING
BRRING
...
SHVR
SHVR
Hey ...
SHVR
SHVR
Isn't that ...
Mitsuru's phone ?!
BRRING
BRRING
BRRING
BRRING
BRRING
18:19
I remembered
BRRING

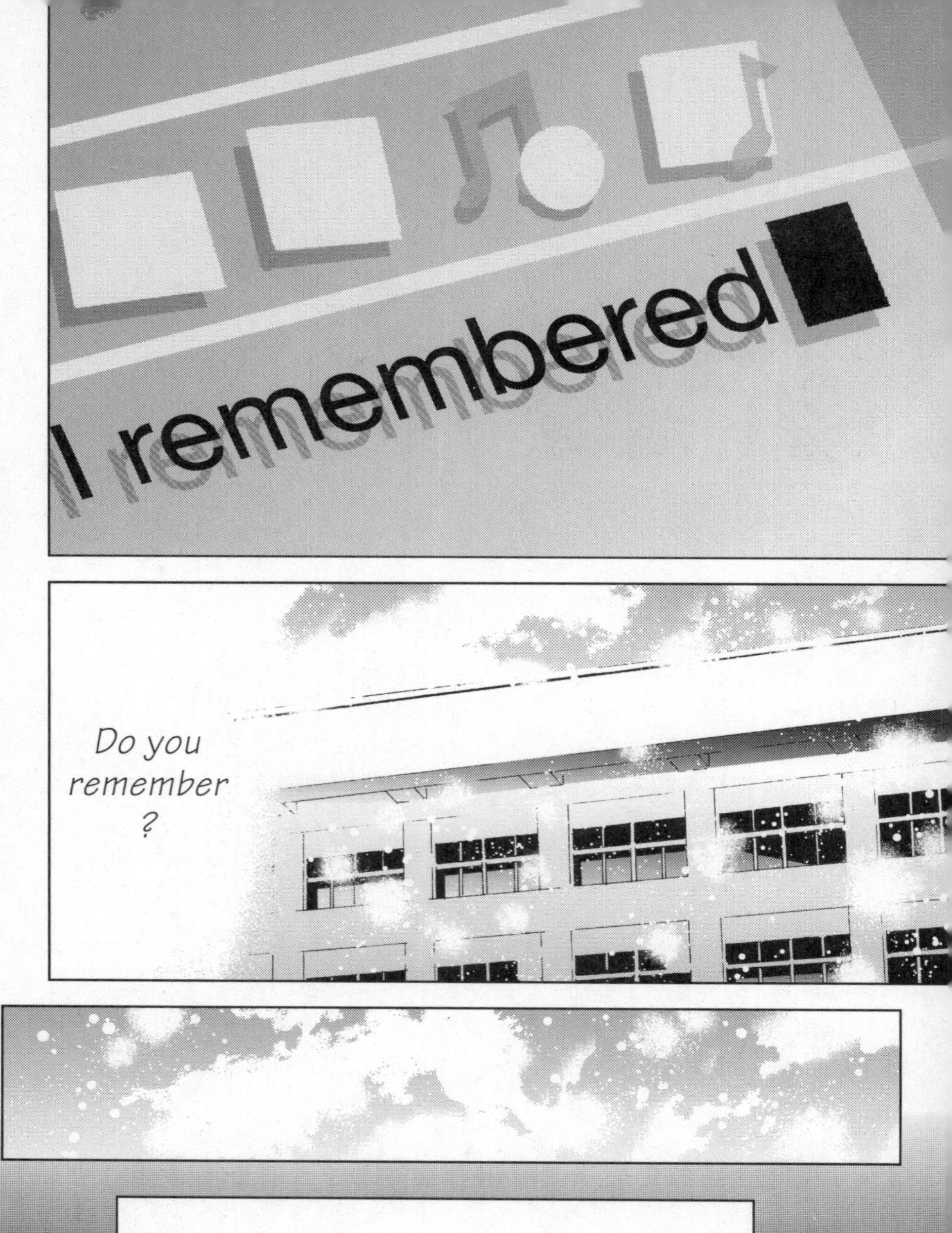
I remembered
Do you remember ?

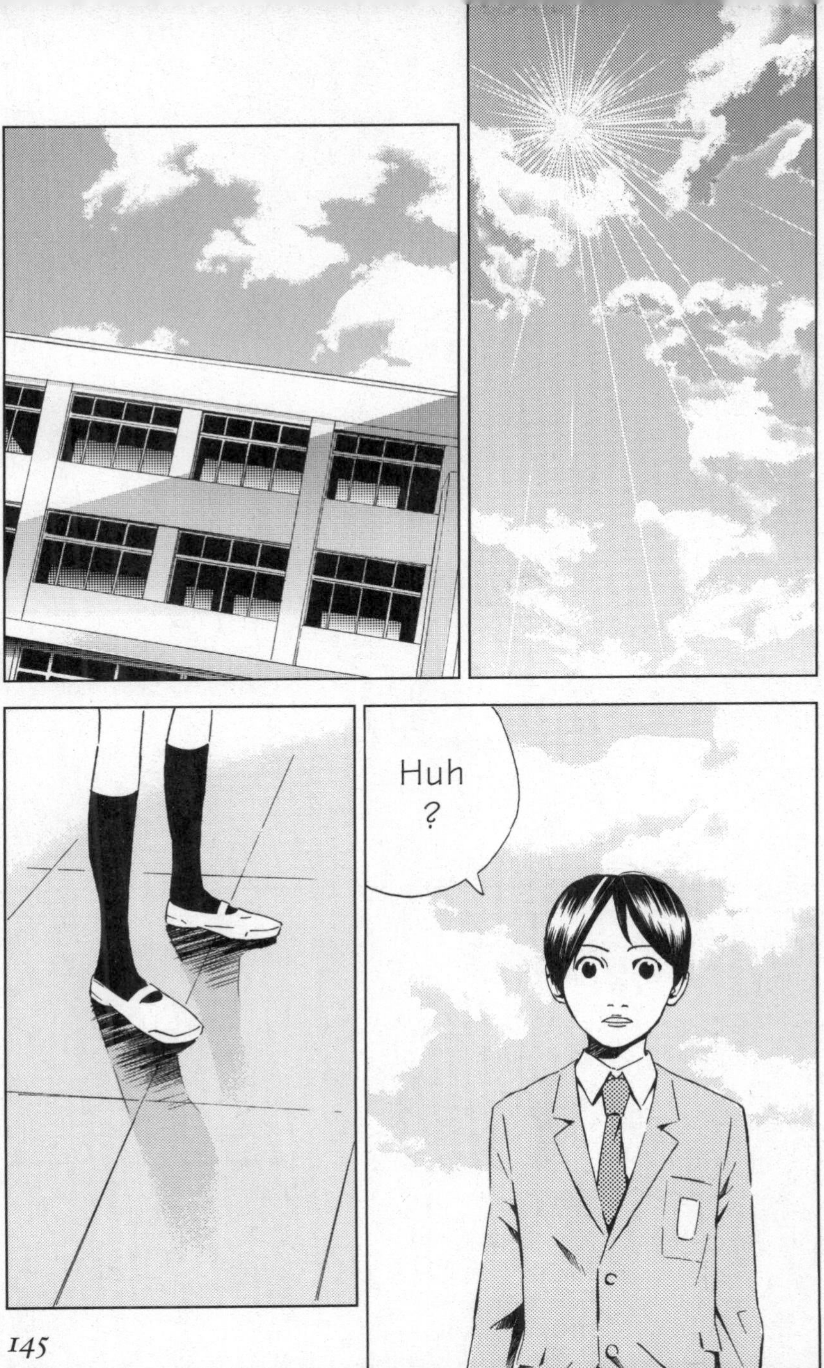
Huh
?

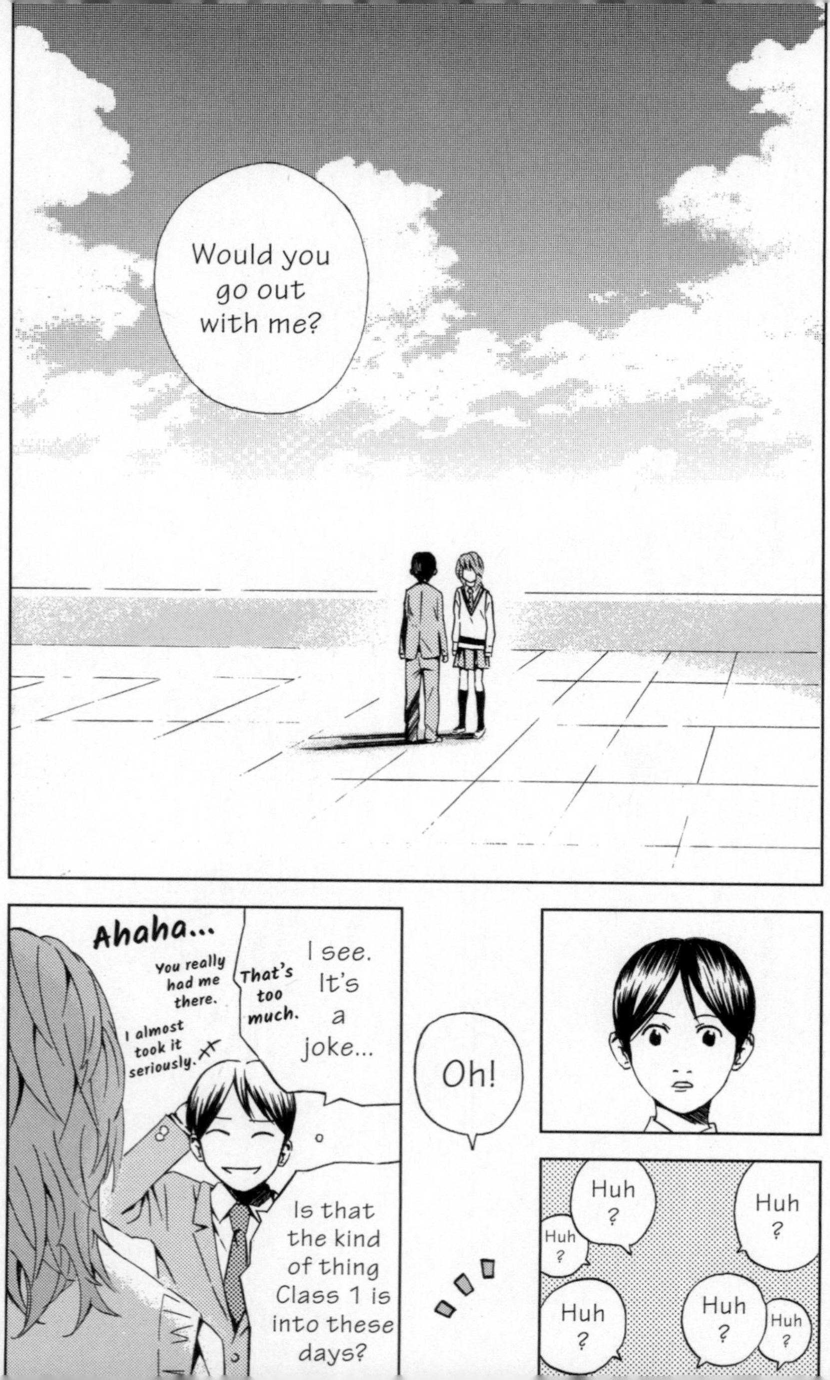

Would you go out with me?
Huh?
Huh?
Huh?
Huh?
Huh?
Huh?
Oh!
I see. It's a joke...
That's too much.
You really had me there.
I almost took it seriously.
Ahaha...
Is that the kind of thing Class 1 is into these days?

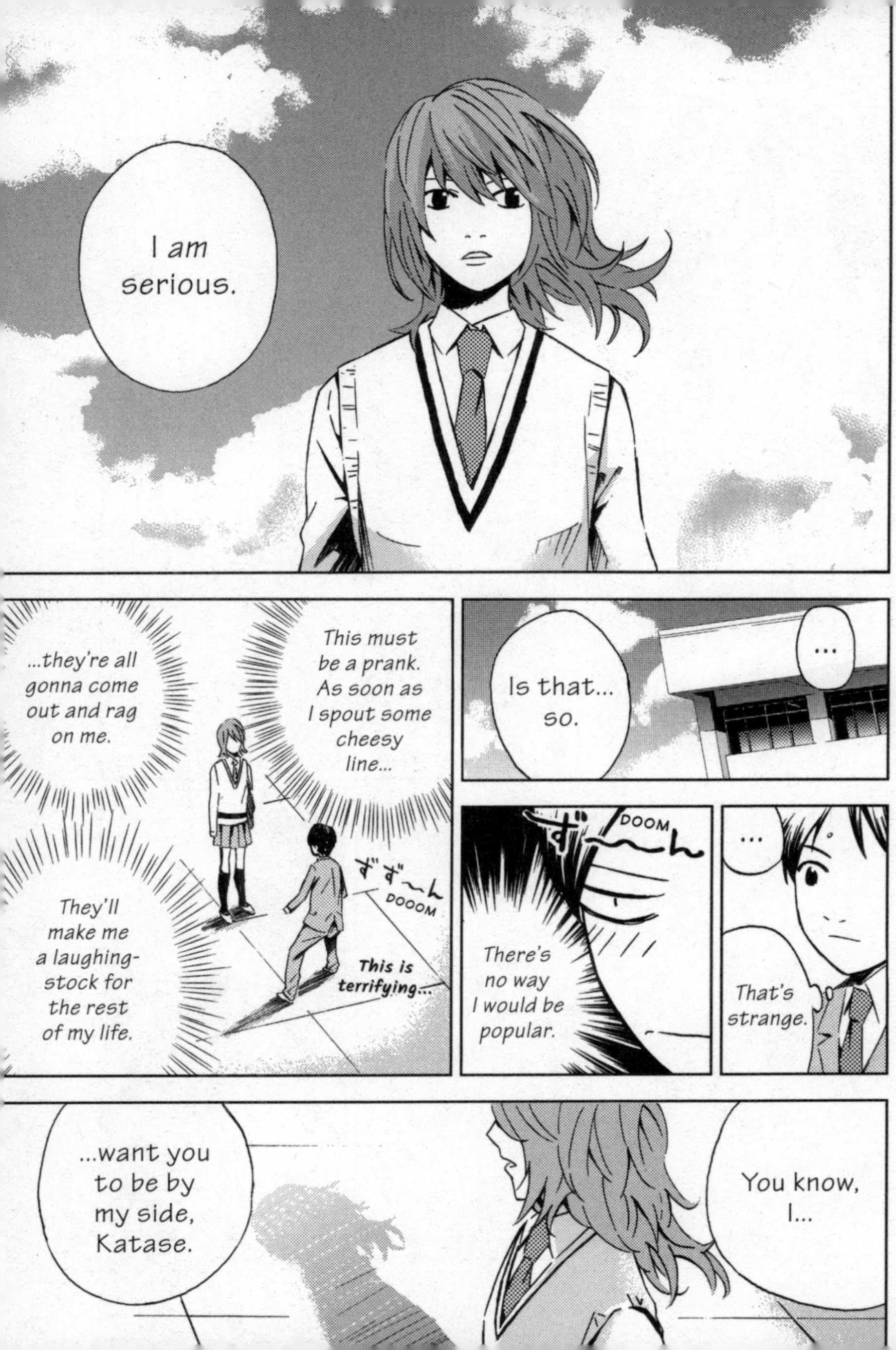

I am serious.
...
Is that... so.
...
That's strange.
ず〜ん
DOOM
There's no way I would be popular.
This must be a prank. As soon as I spout some cheesy line...
...they're all gonna come out and rag on me.
ずず〜ん
DOOOM
This is terrifying...
They'll make me a laughing-stock for the rest of my life.
You know, I...
...want you to be by my side, Katase.

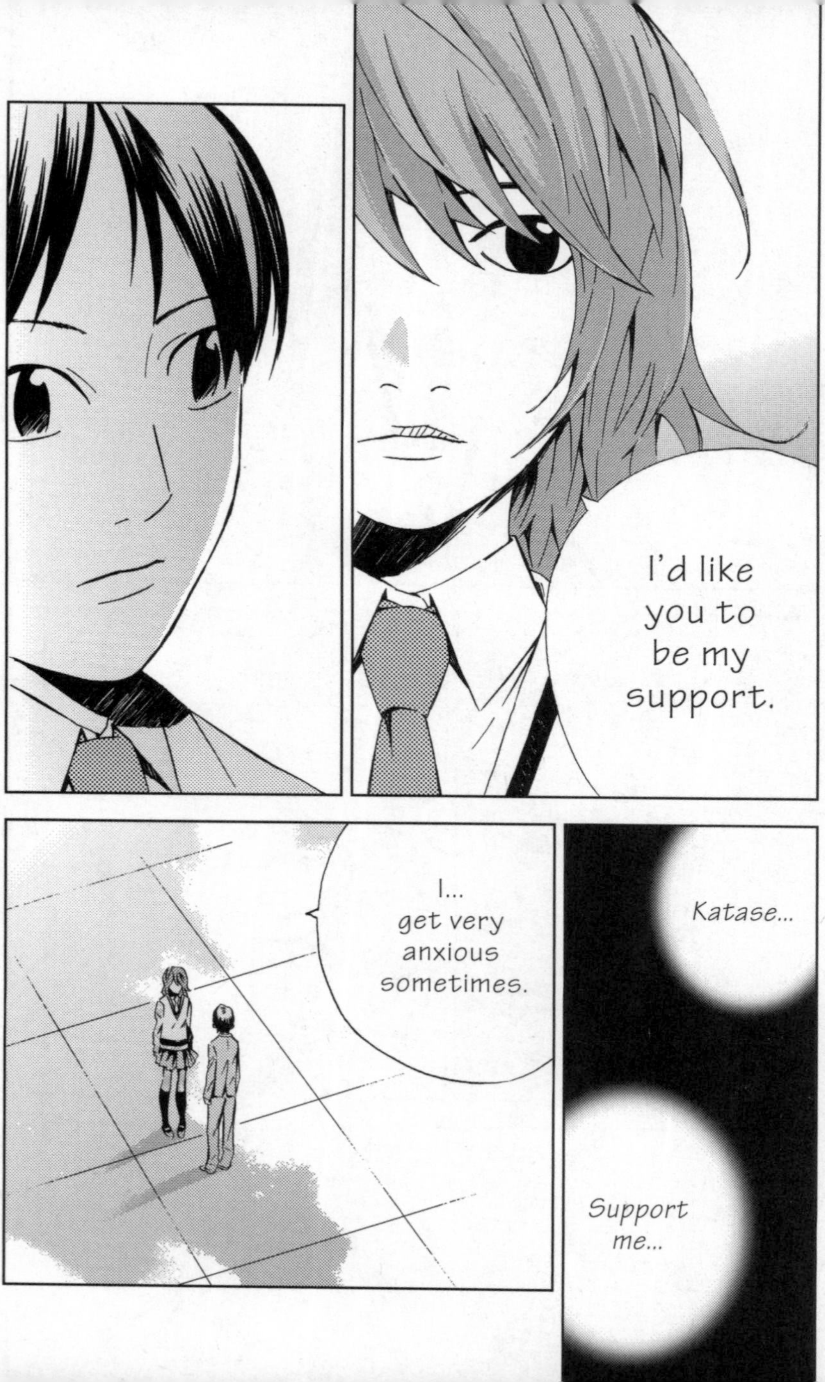
I'd like you to be my support.
Katase...
Support me...
I... get very anxious sometimes.

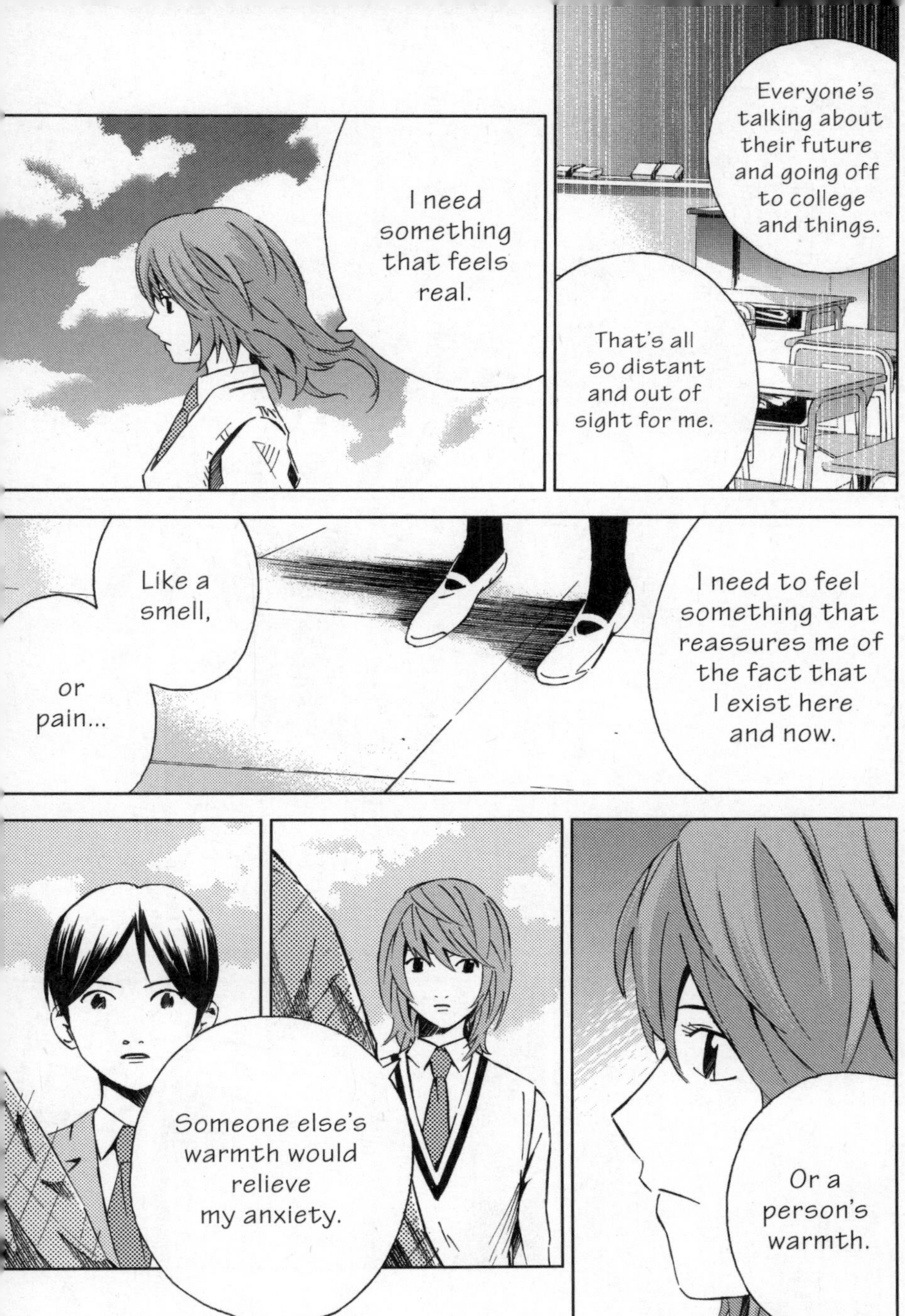
Everyone's talking about their future and going off to college and things.
That's all so distant and out of sight for me.
I need something that feels real.
I need to feel something that reassures me of the fact that I exist here and now.
Like a smell,
or pain...
Or a person's warmth.
Someone else's warmth would relieve my anxiety.

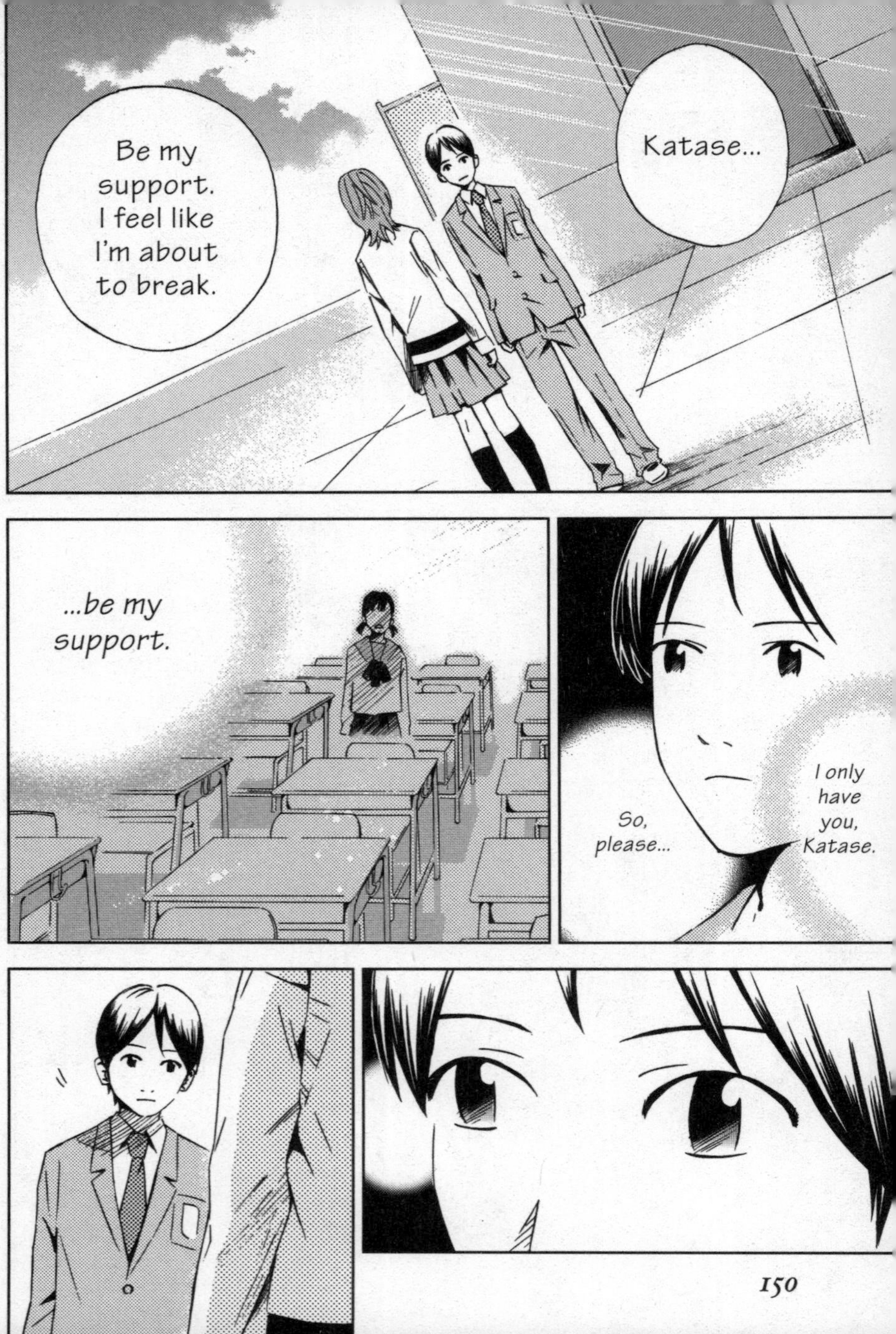
Katase...
Be my support. I feel like I'm about to break.
I only have you, Katase.
So, please...
...be my support.

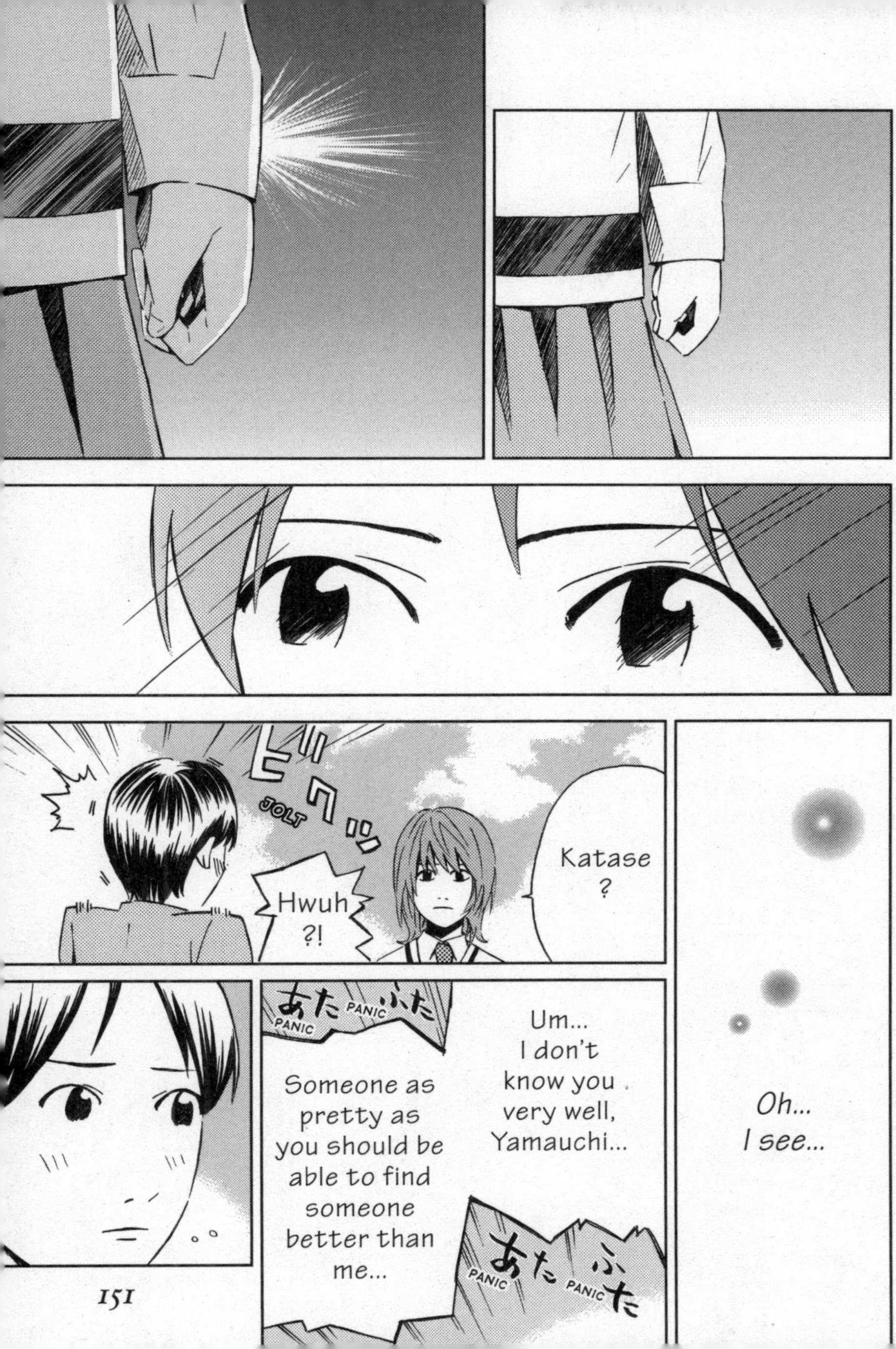
Oh... I see...
Katase ?
ビクッ
JOLT
Hwuh ?!
あたふた
PANIC PANIC
Um... I don't know you very well, Yamauchi...
Someone as pretty as you should be able to find someone better than me...
あたふた
PANIC PANIC

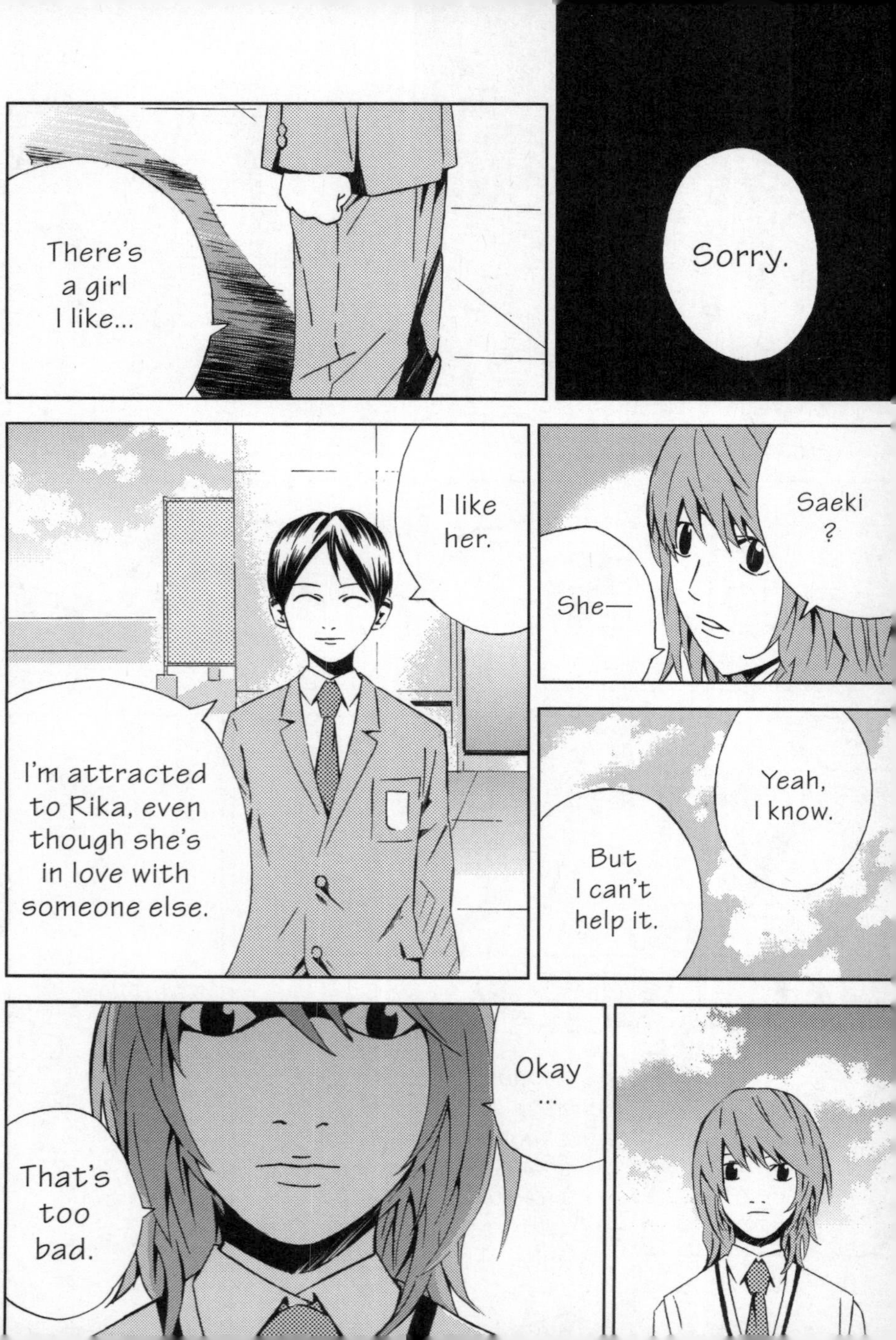
Sorry.
There's a girl I like...
Saeki ?
She—
Yeah, I know.
But I can't help it.
I like her.
I'm attracted to Rika, even though she's in love with someone else.
Okay ...
That's too bad.

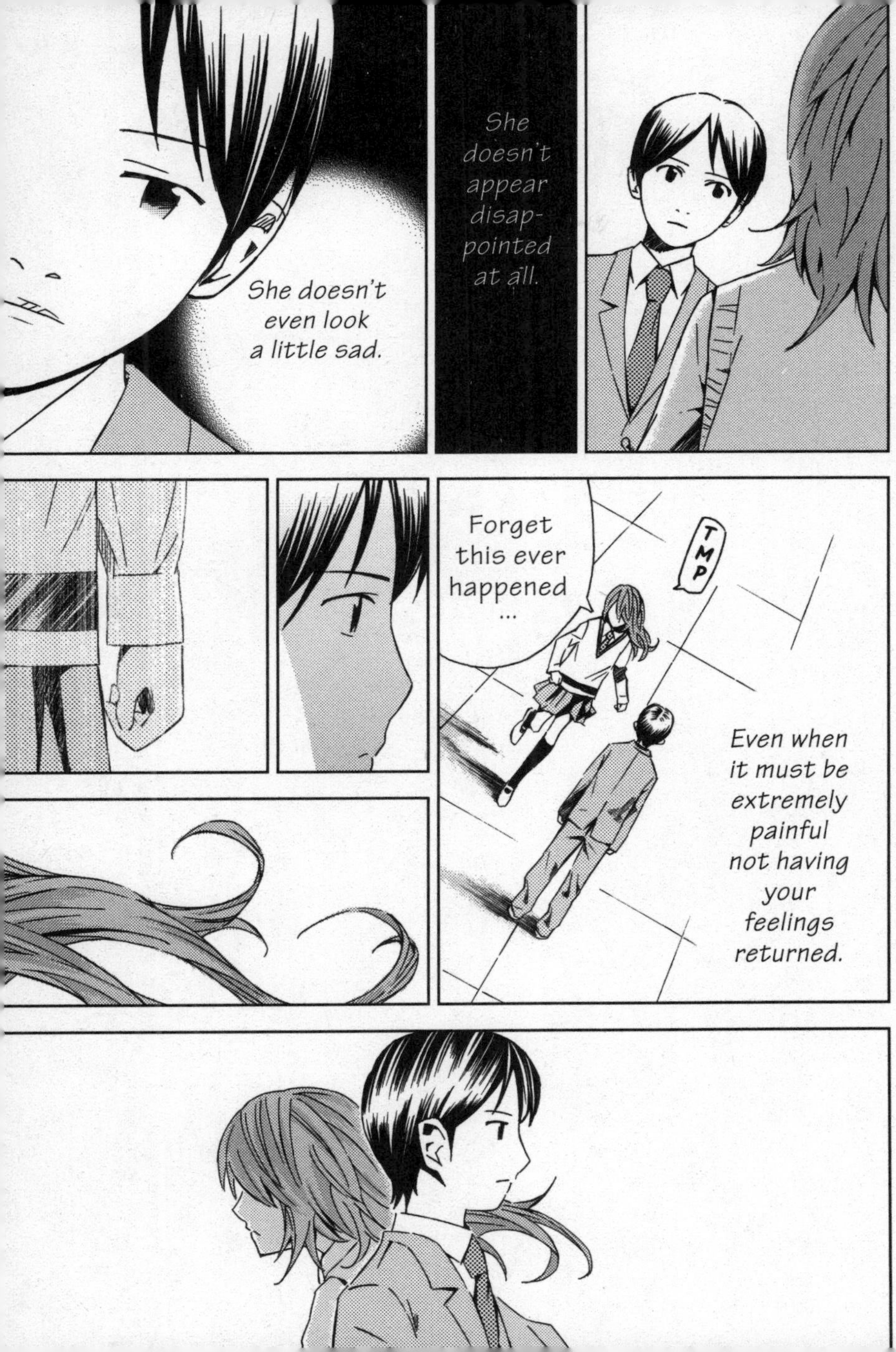
She doesn't appear disappointed at all.
She doesn't even look a little sad.
Forget this ever happened ...
TMP
Even when it must be extremely painful not having your feelings returned.

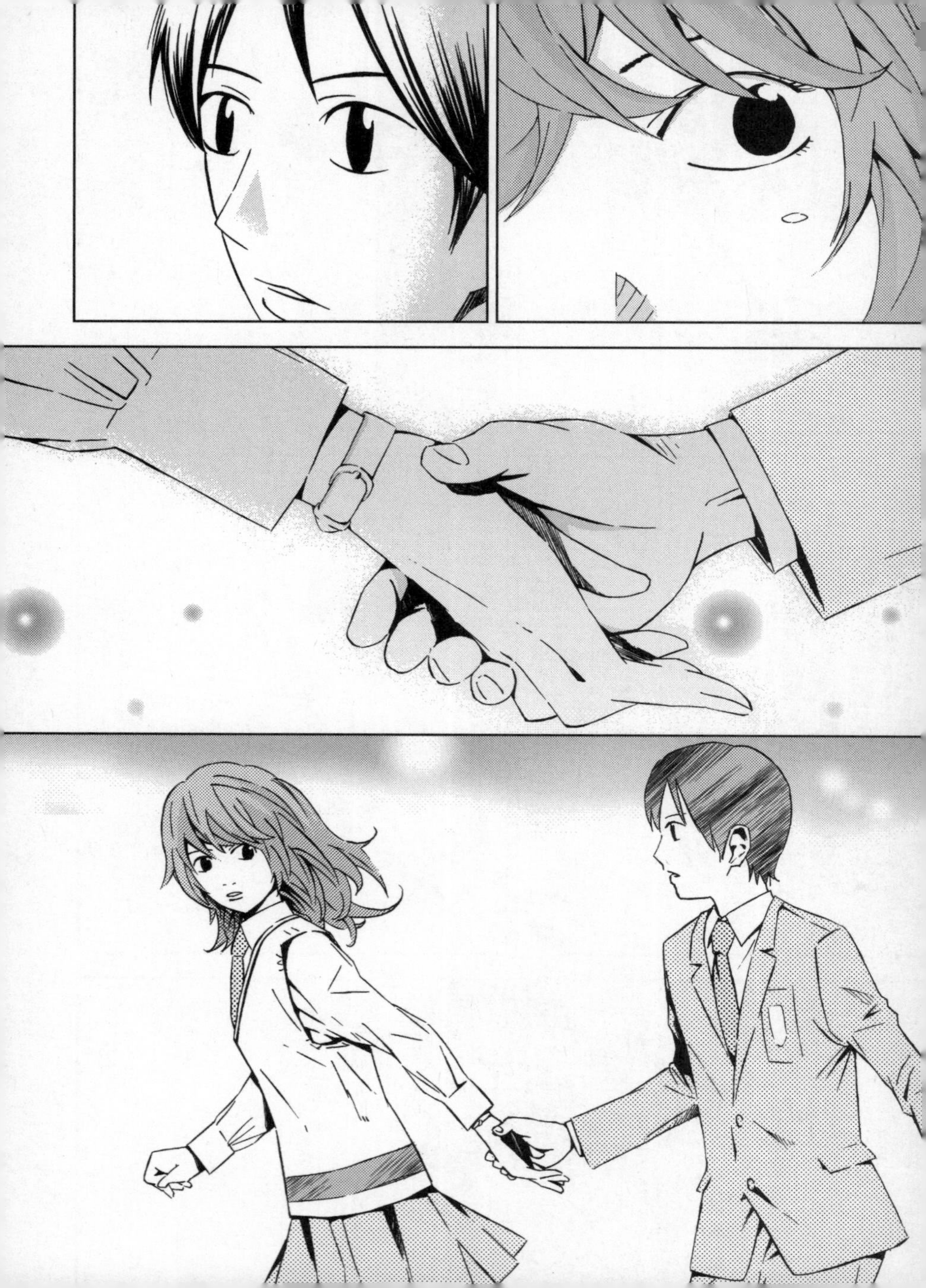

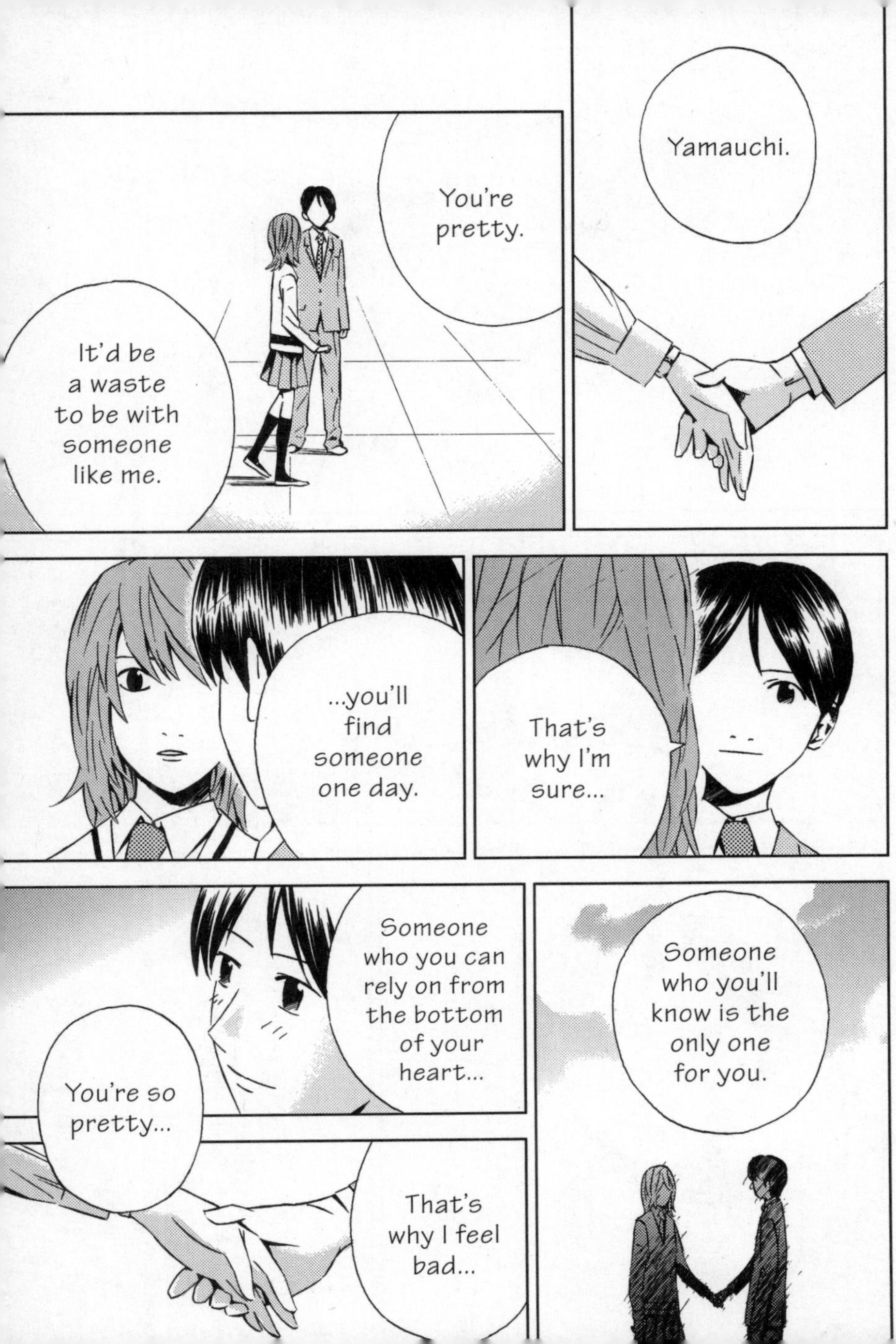
Yamauchi.
You're pretty.
It'd be a waste to be with someone like me.
That's why I'm sure...
...you'll find someone one day.
Someone who you'll know is the only one for you.
Someone who you can rely on from the bottom of your heart...
You're so pretty...
That's why I feel bad...

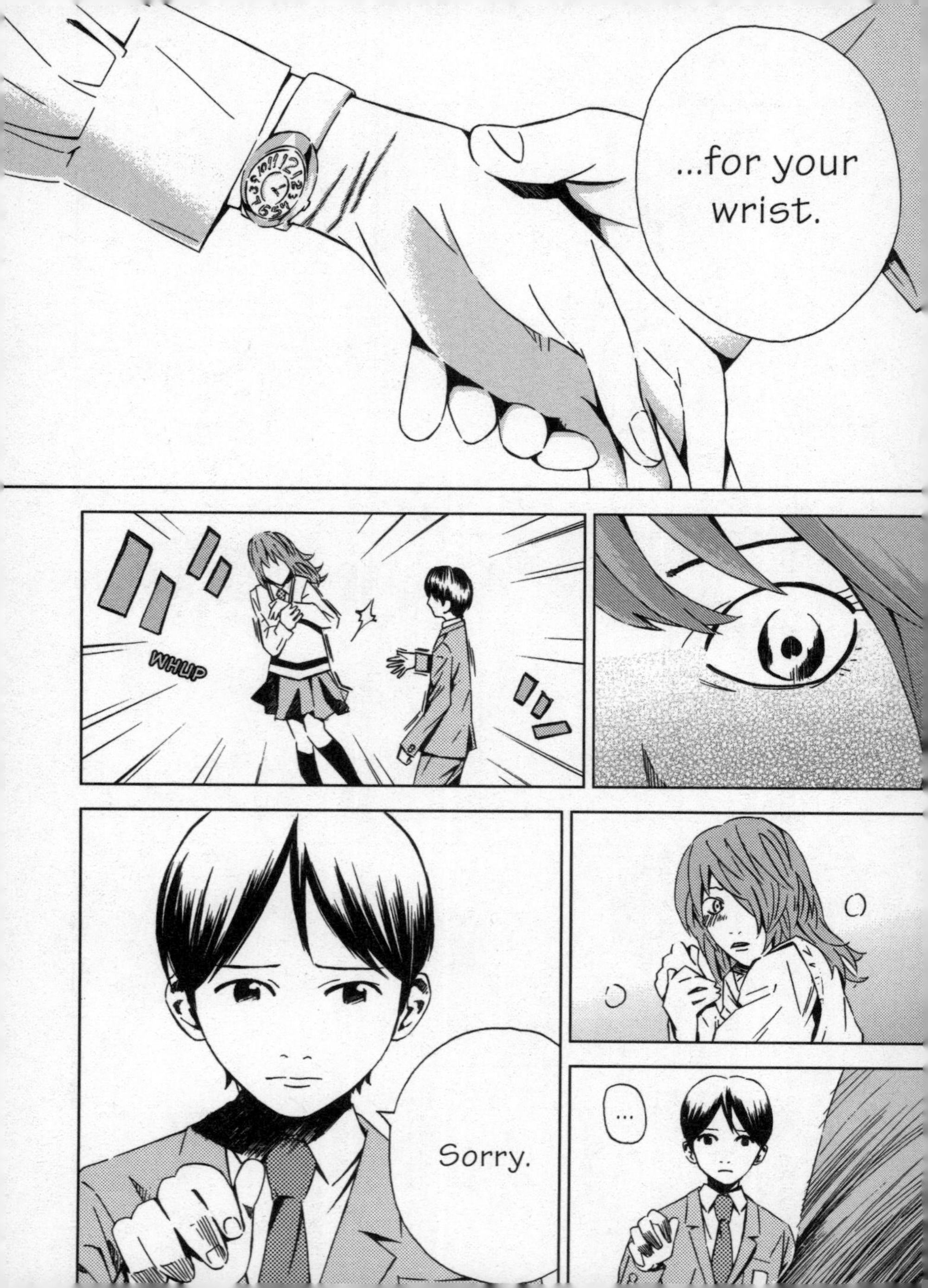
...for your wrist.
WHUP
...
Sorry.

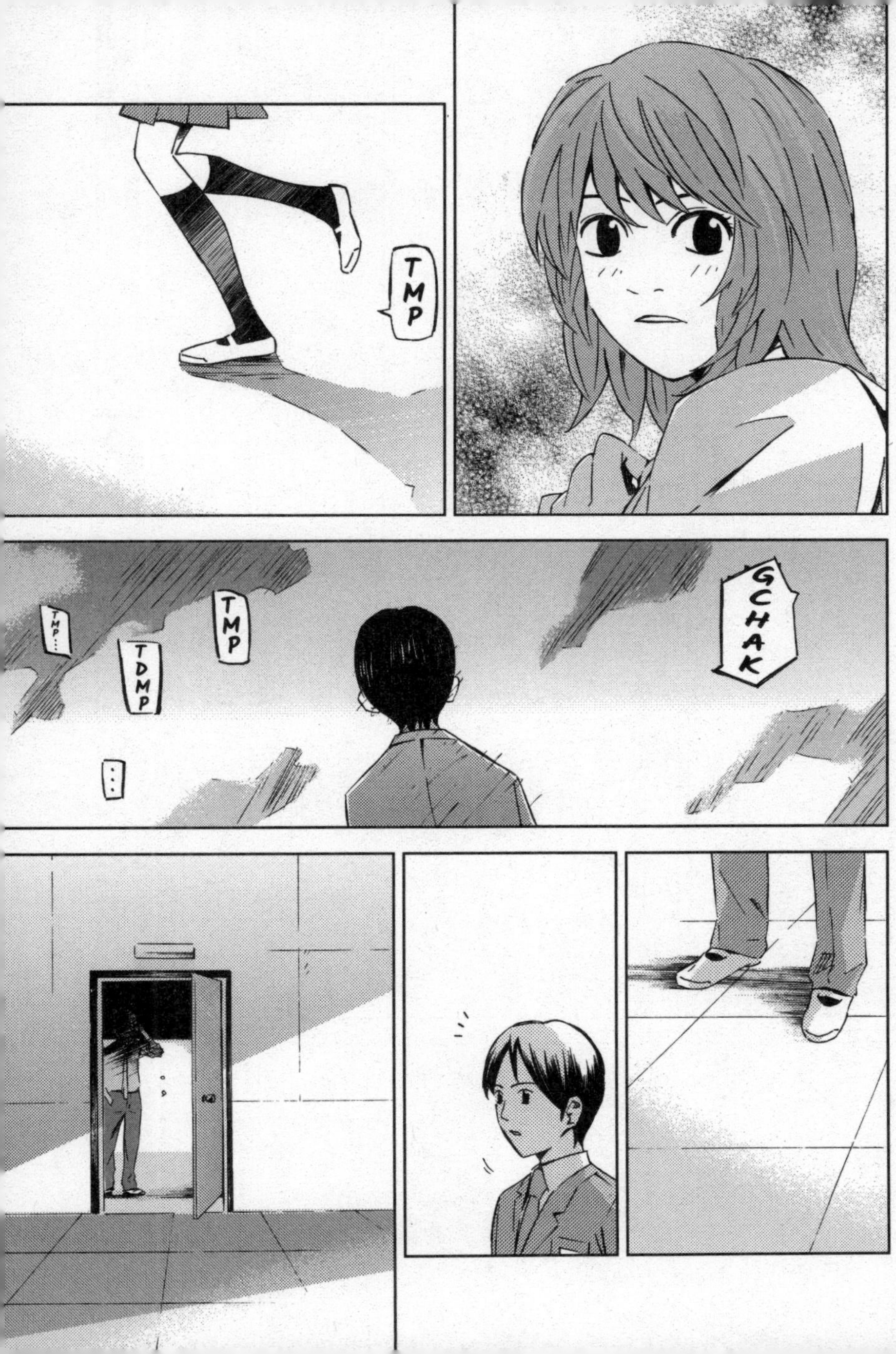
TMP
GCHAK
TMP
TDMP
TMP...
...

H-Hey, Katase!

What a coincidence! Aha... hahaha.

Mr.... Sakaki.

I wasn't tryin' to eavesdrop.

I came out here for a smoke...

Haha ...

Ha.

...

Sorry.

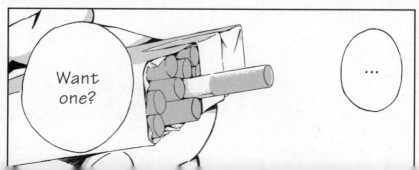

Want one?

...

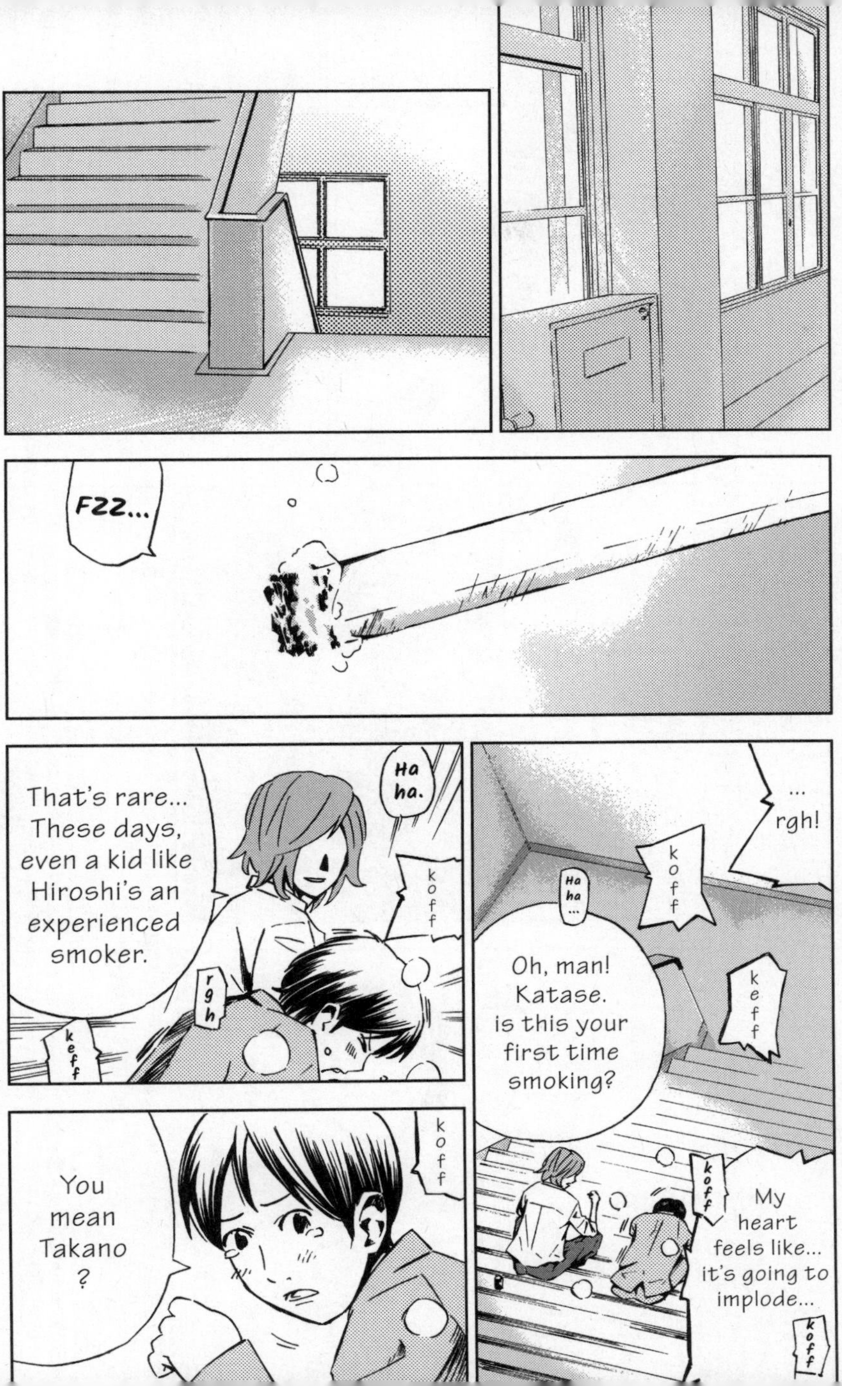

FZZ...
... rgh!
koff
Ha ha ...
Oh, man! Katase. is this your first time smoking?
keff
koff
My heart feels like... it's going to implode...
koff
Ha ha.
That's rare... These days, even a kid like Hiroshi's an experienced smoker.
koff
rgh
keff
koff
You mean Takano ?

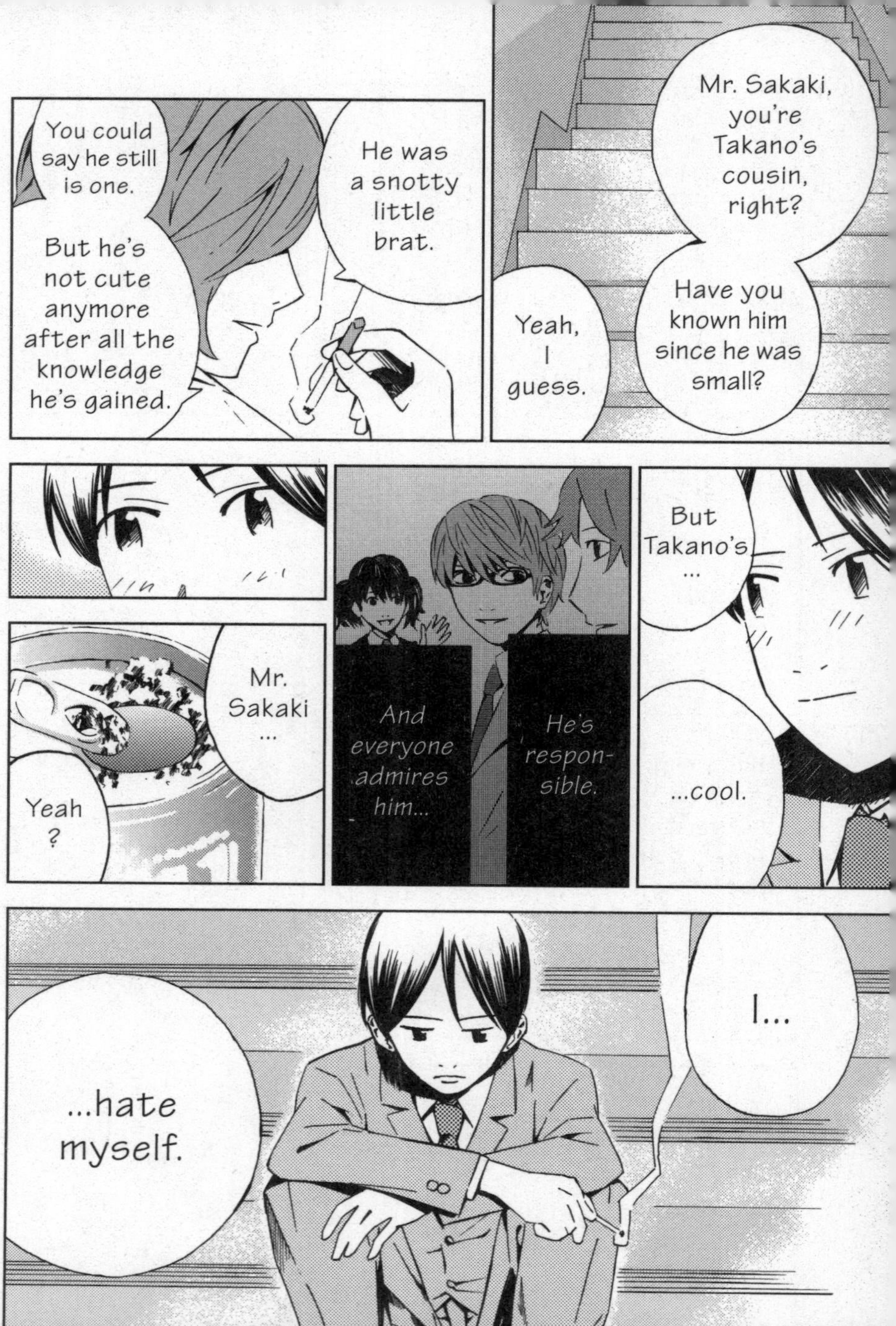
Mr. Sakaki, you're Takano's cousin, right?
Have you known him since he was small?
Yeah, I guess.
He was a snotty little brat.
You could say he still is one.
But he's not cute anymore after all the knowledge he's gained.
But Takano's...
...cool.
He's respon-sible.
And everyone admires him...
Mr. Sakaki...
Yeah?
I...
...hate myself.

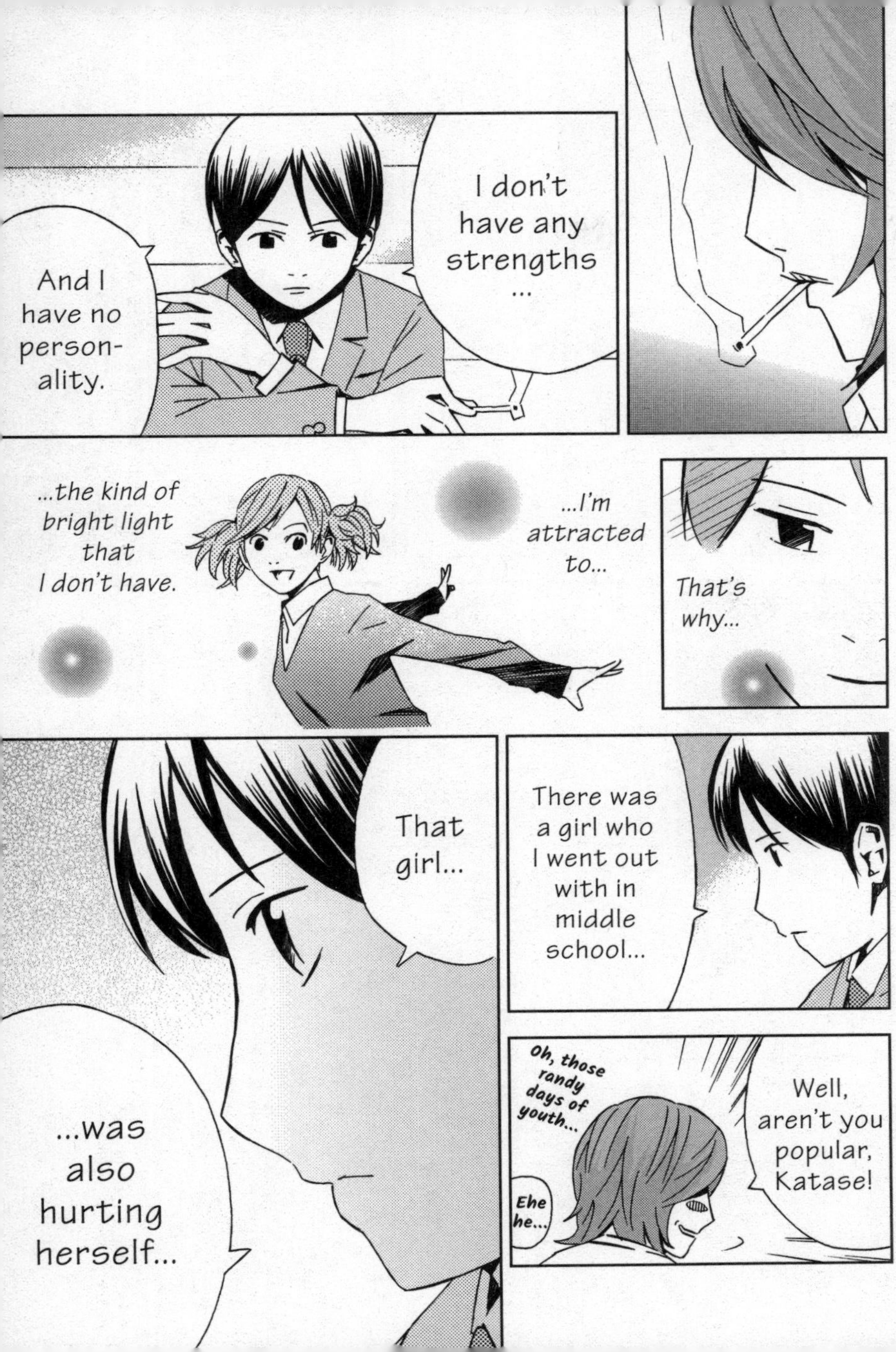
I don't have any strengths ...
And I have no personality.
That's why...
...I'm attracted to...
...the kind of bright light that I don't have.
There was a girl who I went out with in middle school...
Well, aren't you popular, Katase!
Oh, those randy days of youth...
Ehe he...
That girl...
...was also hurting herself...

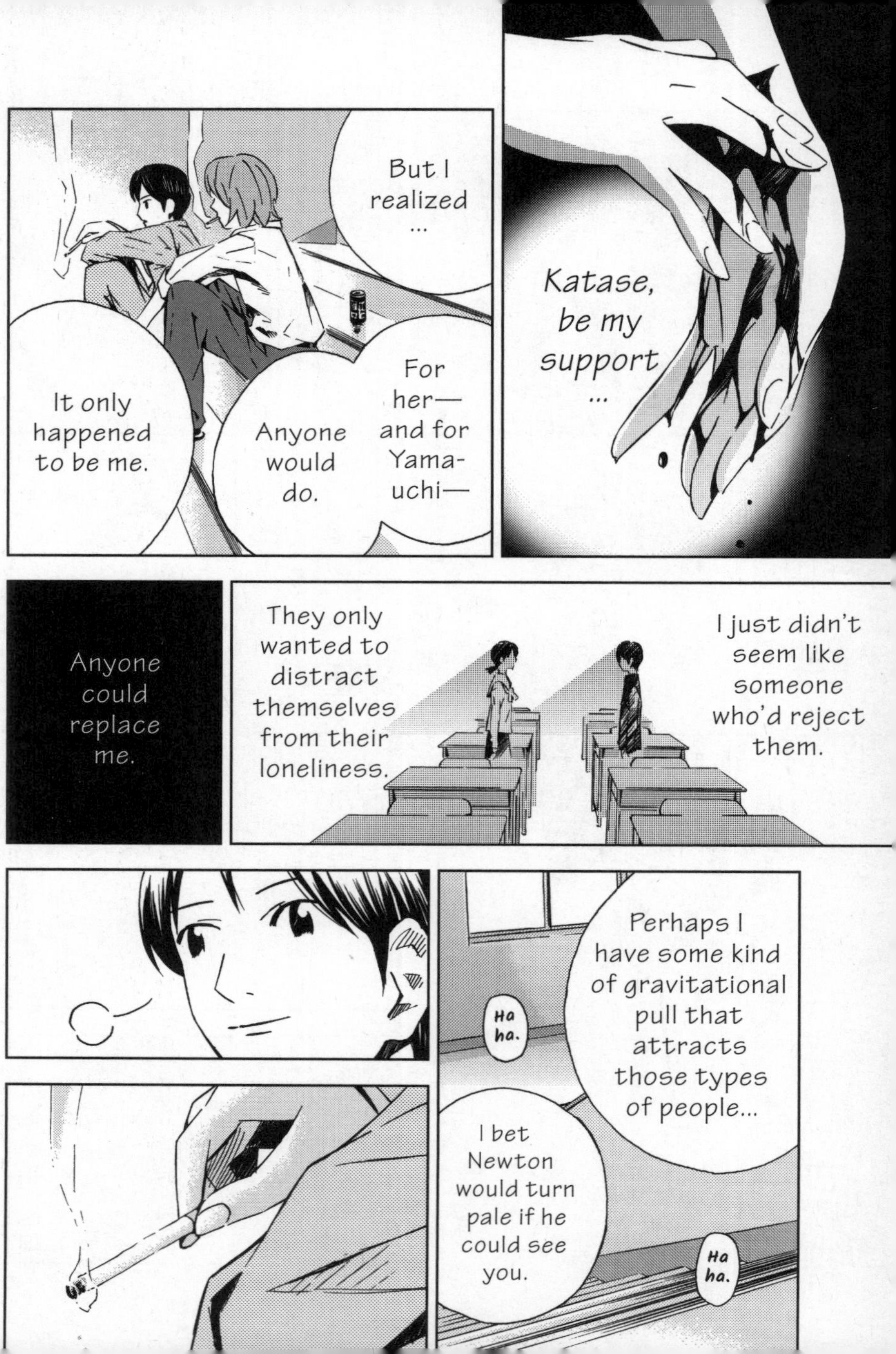
Katase, be my support ...
But I realized ...
For her— and for Yama-uchi—
Anyone would do.
It only happened to be me.
I just didn't seem like someone who'd reject them.
They only wanted to distract themselves from their loneliness.
Anyone could replace me.
Perhaps I have some kind of gravitational pull that attracts those types of people...
Ha ha.
I bet Newton would turn pale if he could see you.
Ha ha.

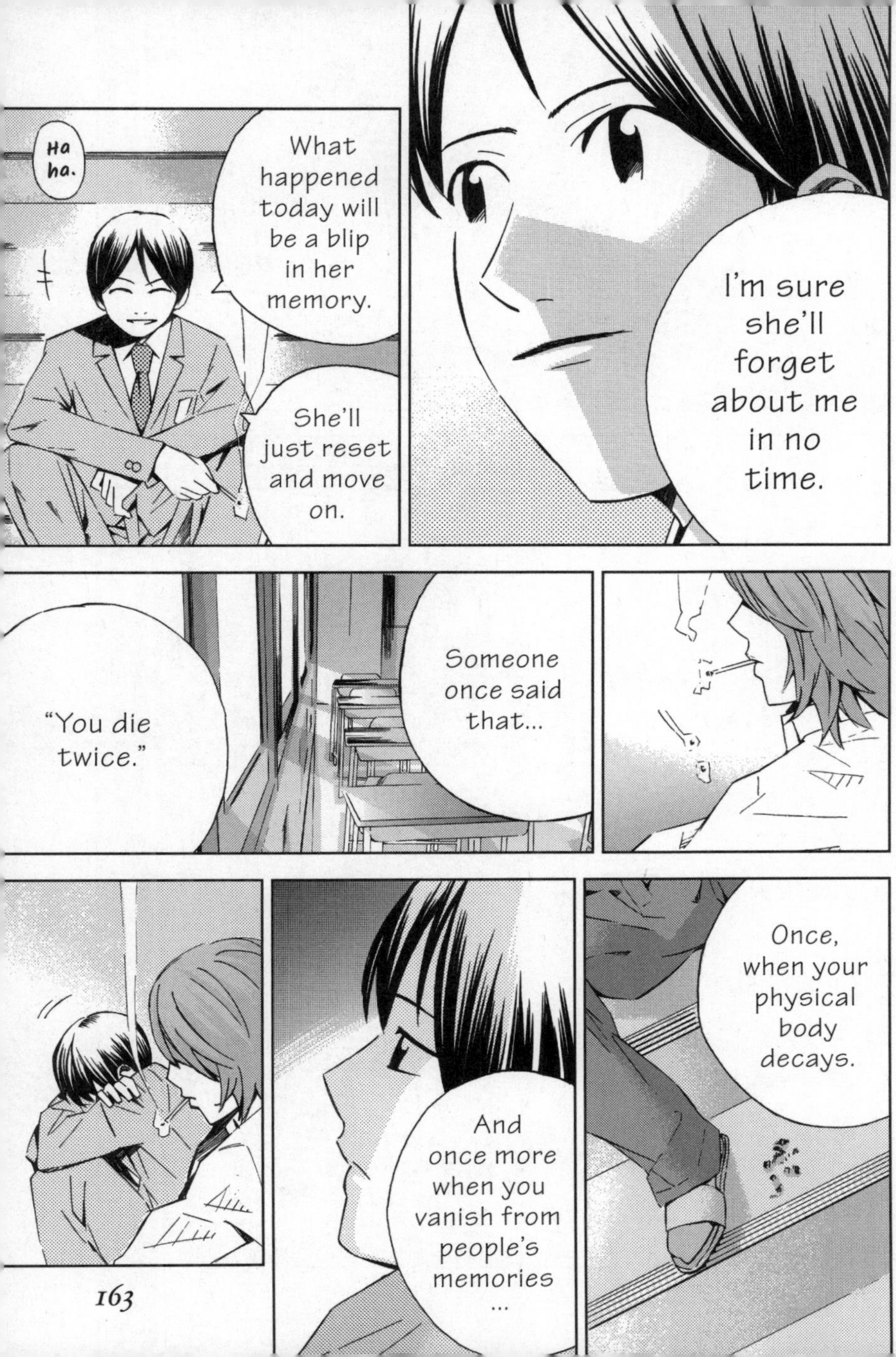
I'm sure she'll forget about me in no time.
What happened today will be a blip in her memory.
Ha ha.
She'll just reset and move on.
Someone once said that...
"You die twice."
Once, when your physical body decays.
And once more when you vanish from people's memories ...

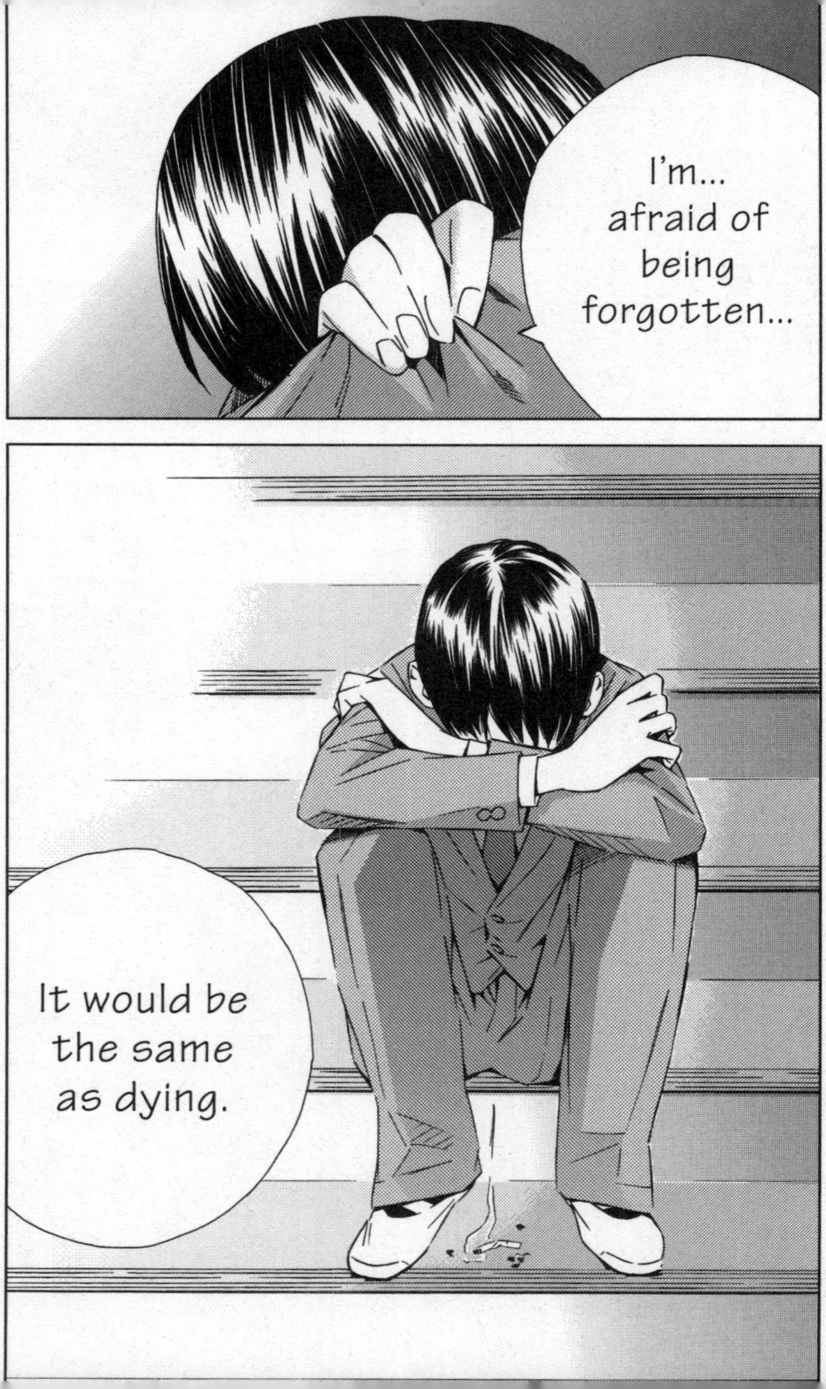
I'm... afraid of being forgotten...
It would be the same as dying.

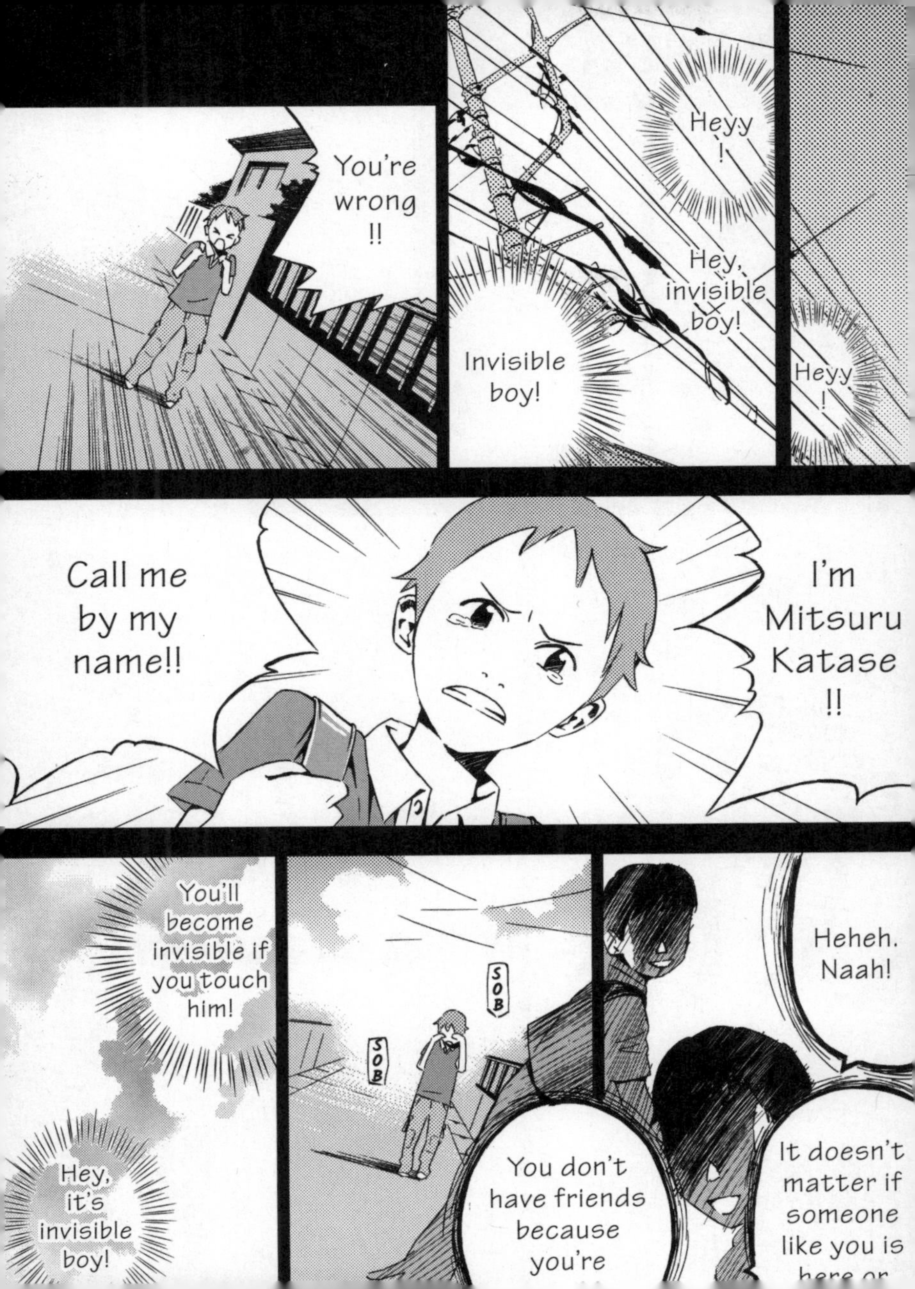

Heyy!
Heyy!
Hey, invisible boy!
Invisible boy!
You're wrong!!
I'm Mitsuru Katase!!
Call me by my name!!
Heheh. Naah!
It doesn't matter if someone like you is
You don't have friends because you're
SOB
SOB
You'll become invisible if you touch him!
Hey, it's invisible boy!

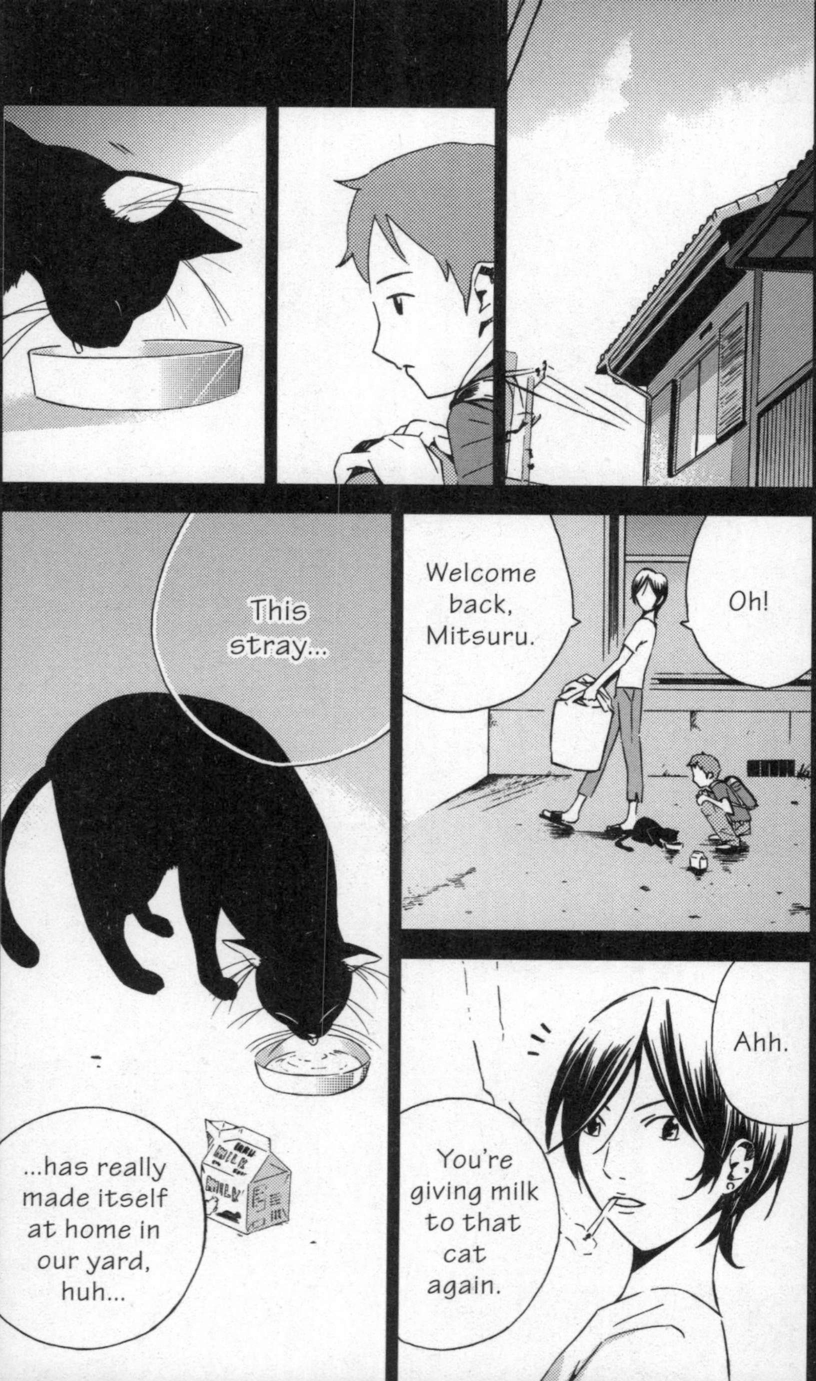
Oh!
Welcome back, Mitsuru.
Ahh.
You're giving milk to that cat again.
This stray...
...has really made itself at home in our yard, huh...

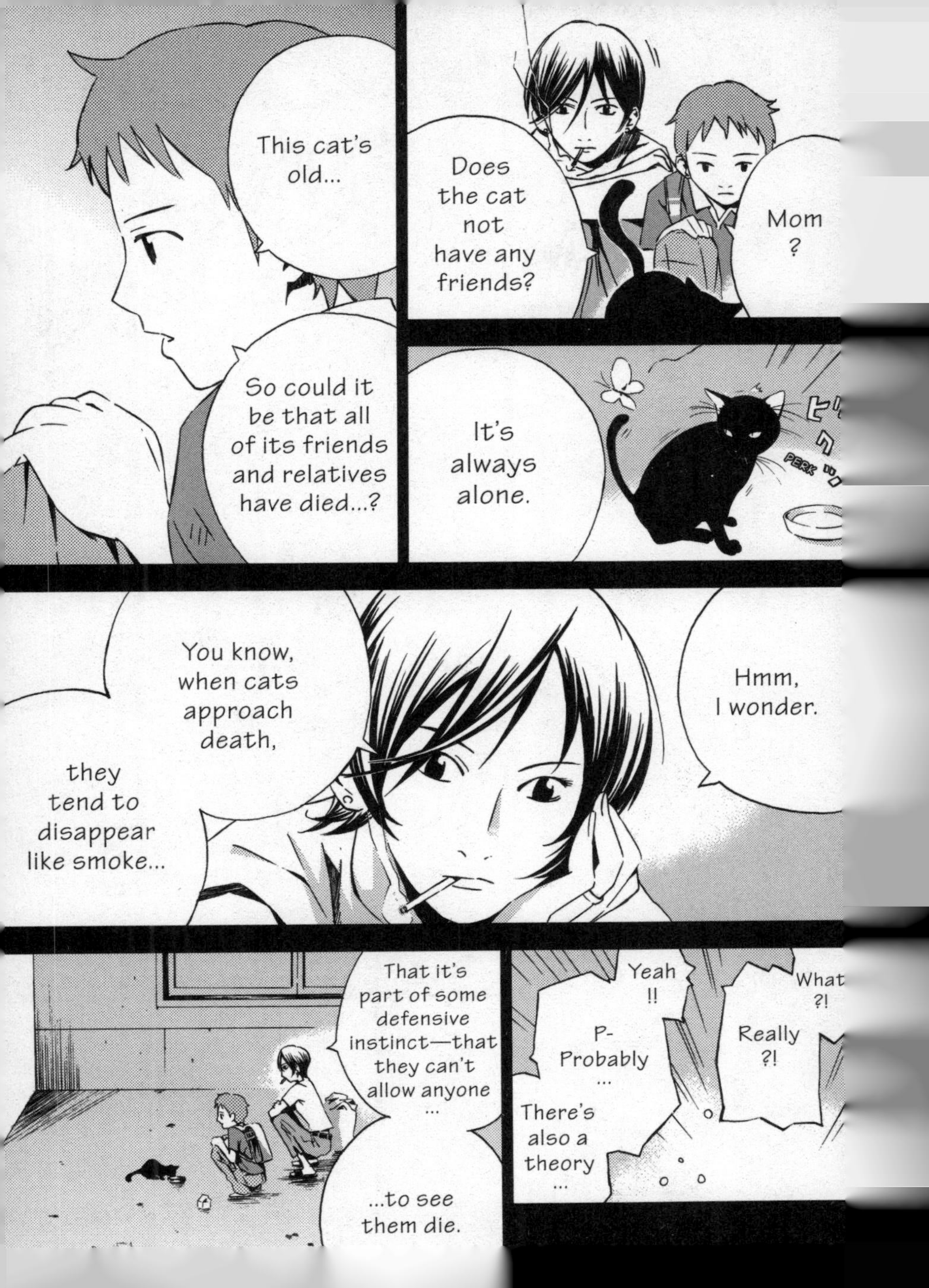

Mom ?
Does the cat not have any friends?
PERK
It's always alone.
This cat's old...
So could it be that all of its friends and relatives have died...?
Hmm, I wonder.
You know, when cats approach death,
they tend to disappear like smoke...
What ?!
Really ?!
Yeah !!
P- Probably ...
There's also a theory ...
That it's part of some defensive instinct—that they can't allow anyone ...
...to see them die.

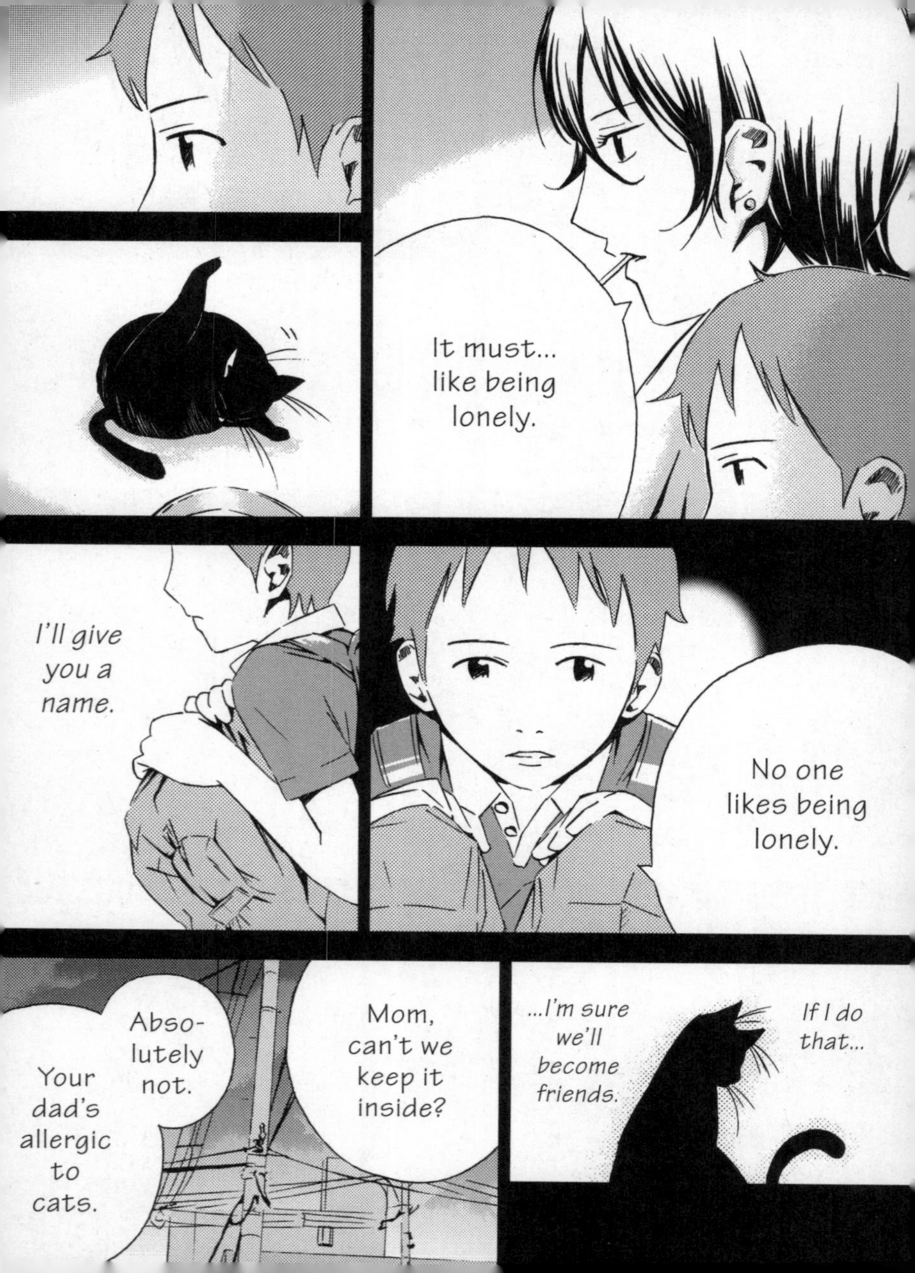
It must... like being lonely.
No one likes being lonely.
I'll give you a name.
If I do that...
...I'm sure we'll become friends.
Mom, can't we keep it inside?
Abso-lutely not.
Your dad's allergic to cats.

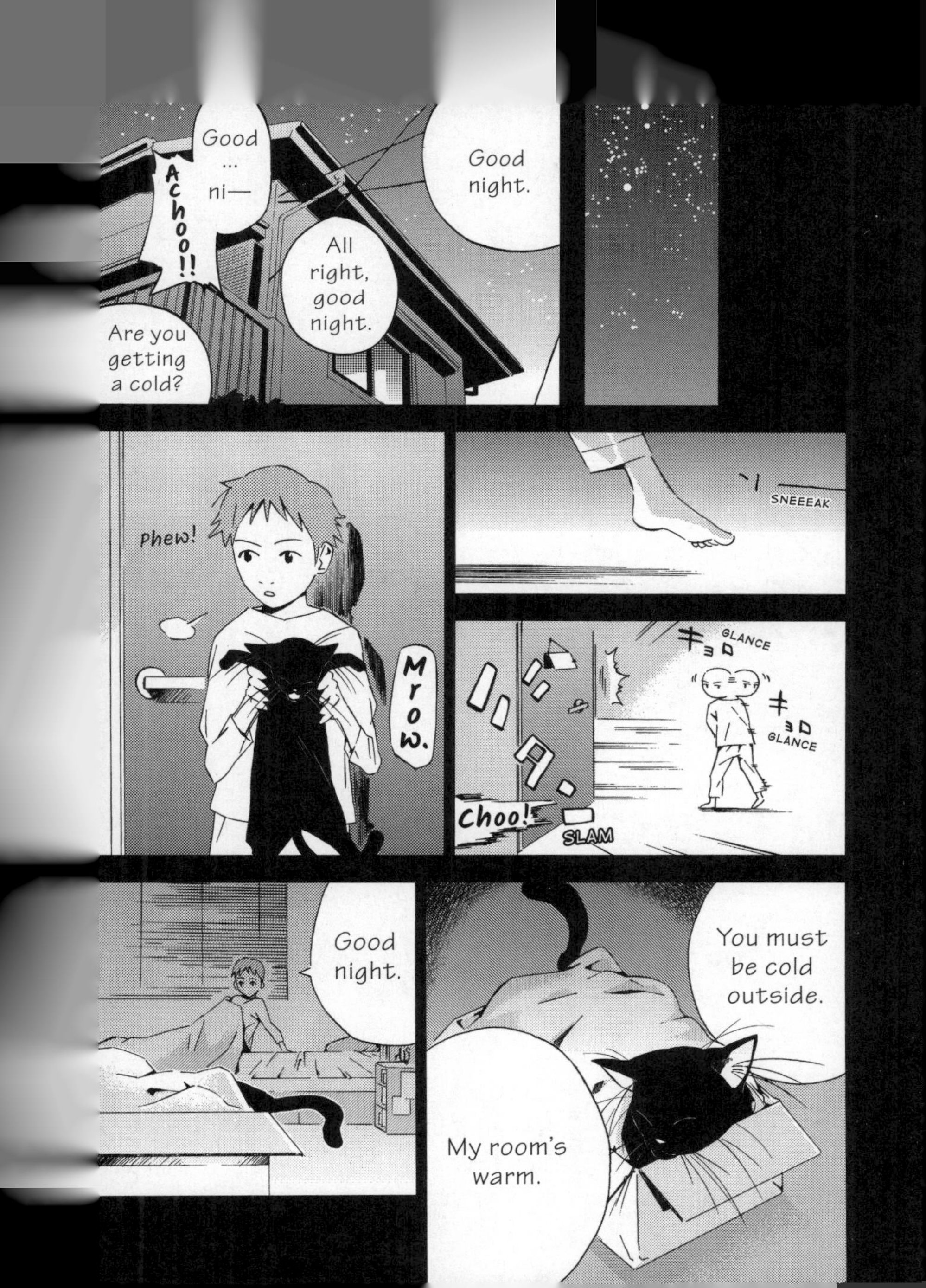
Good night.
Good ... ni—
Achoo!!
All right, good night.
Are you getting a cold?
SNEEEAK
キョロ
GLANCE
キョロ
GLANCE
パタン
Choo!
SLAM
Phew!
Mrow.
You must be cold outside.
My room's warm.
Good night.

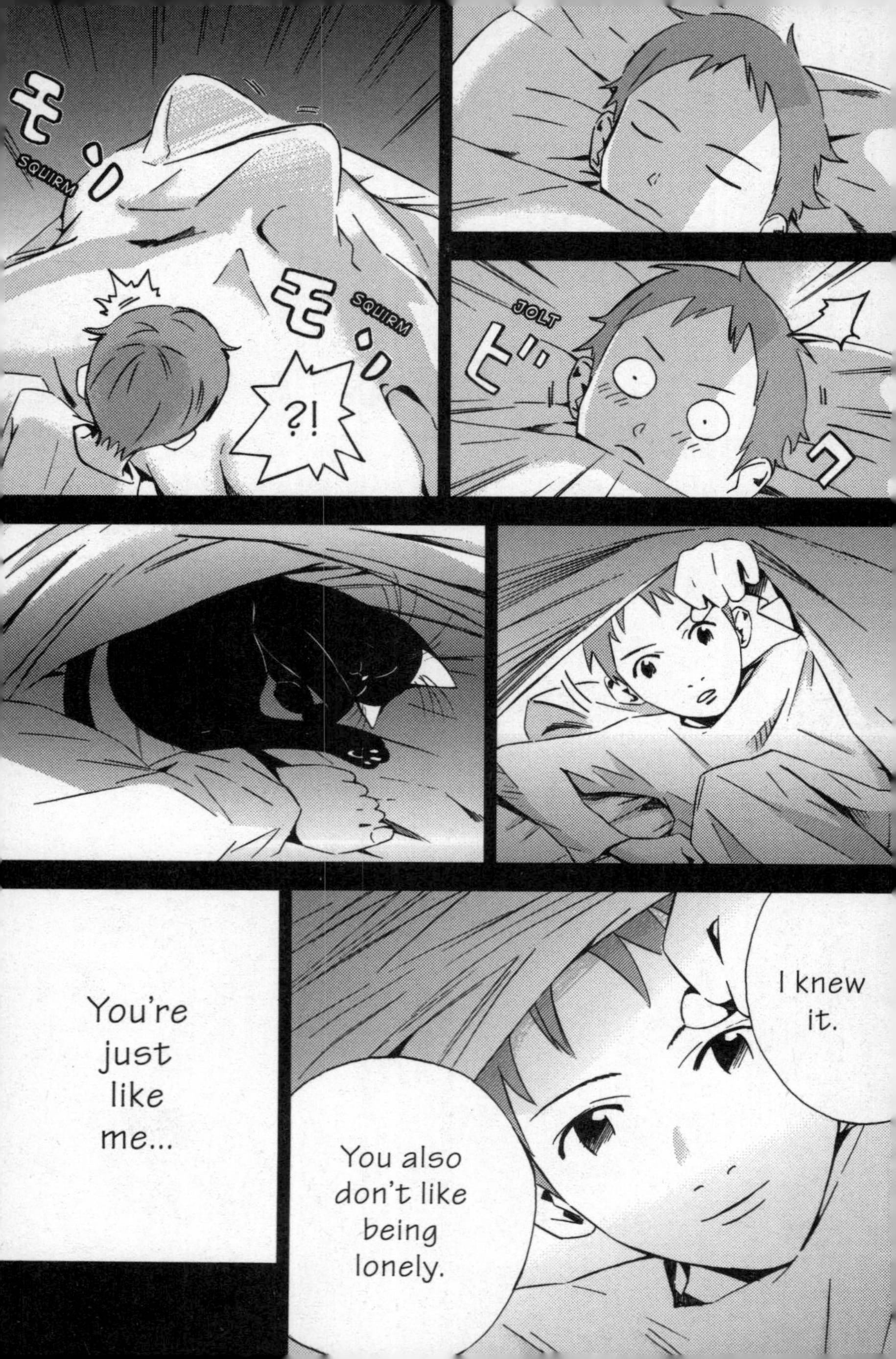
JOLT
SQUIRM
SQUIRM
?!
I knew it.
You also don't like being lonely.
You're just like me...

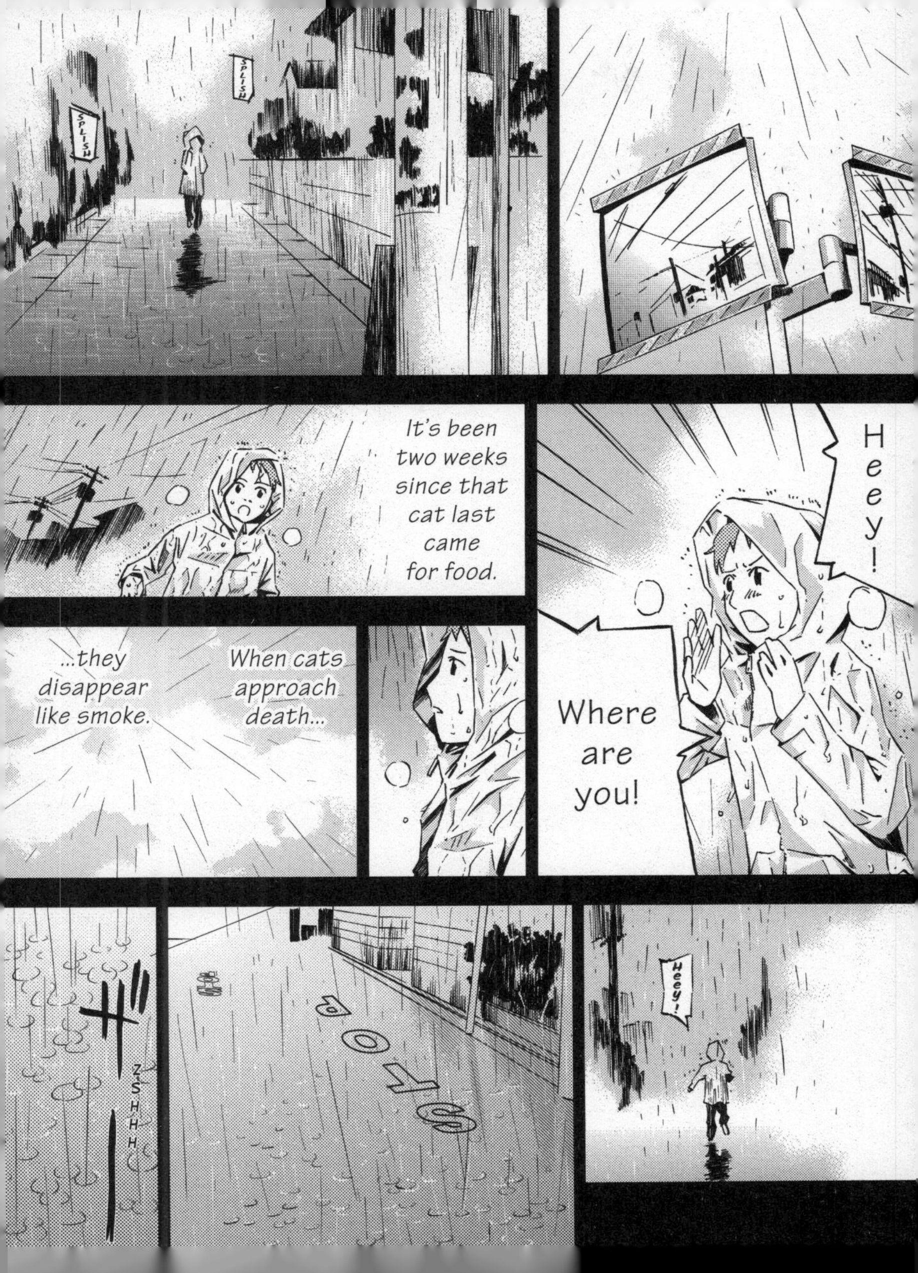
SPLISH
SPLISH
Heey!
Where are you!
It's been two weeks since that cat last came for food.
When cats approach death...
...they disappear like smoke.
Heey!
STOP
ZSHHH

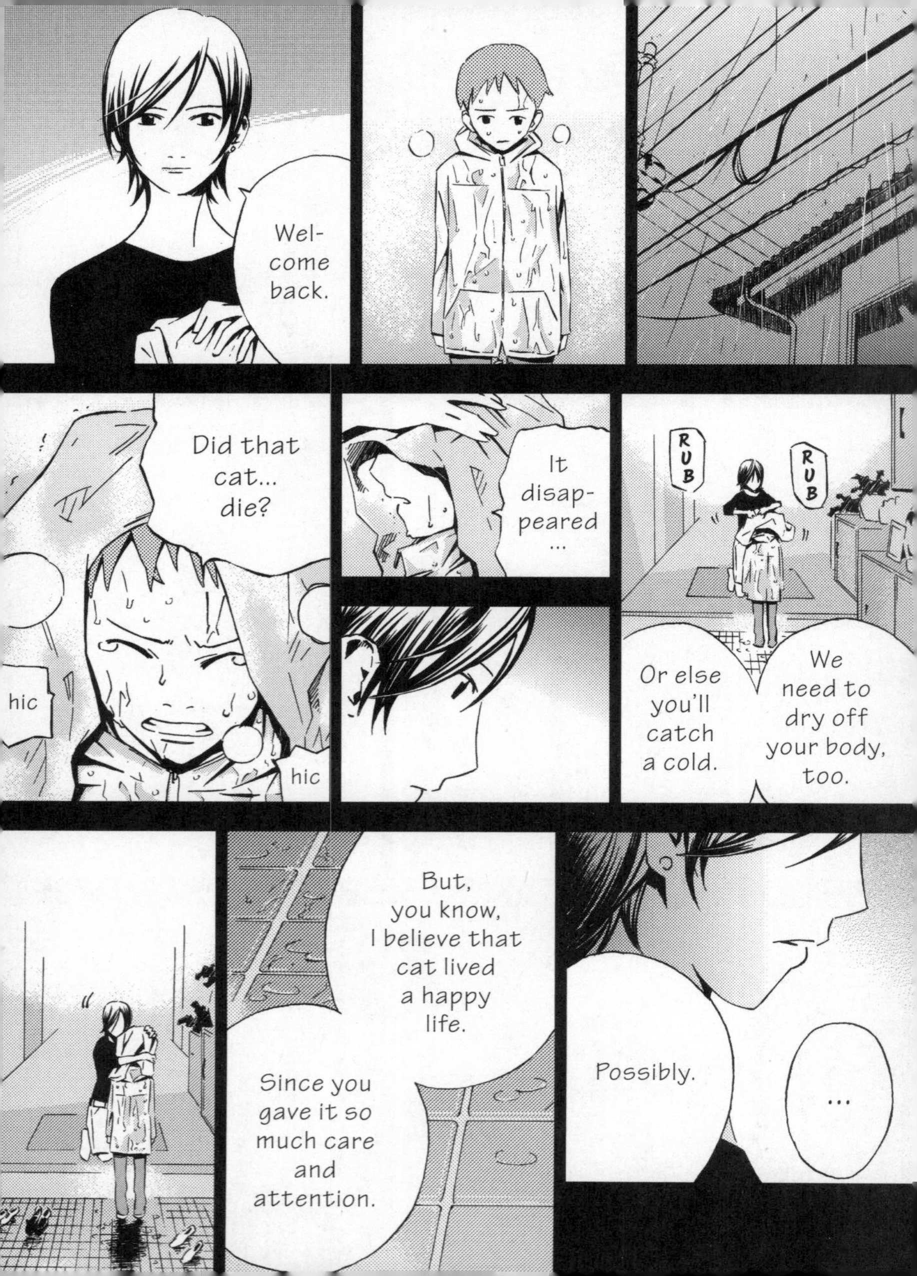
Wel-come back.
RUB
RUB
We need to dry off your body, too.
Or else you'll catch a cold.
It disap-peared ...
Did that cat... die?
hic
hic
...
Possibly.
But, you know, I believe that cat lived a happy life.
Since you gave it so much care and attention.

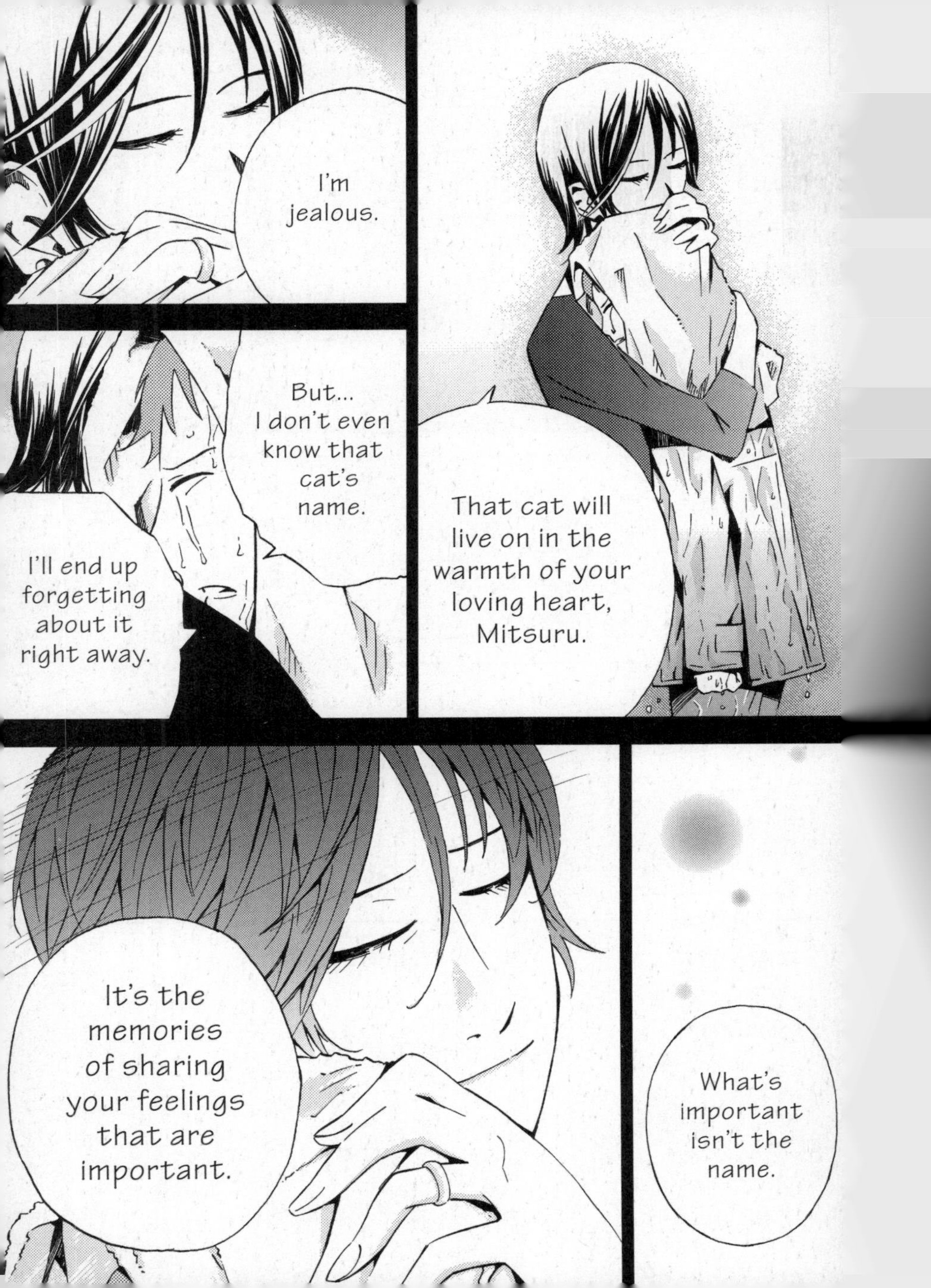
That cat will live on in the warmth of your loving heart, Mitsuru.
I'm jealous.
But... I don't even know that cat's name.
I'll end up forgetting about it right away.
What's important isn't the name.
It's the memories of sharing your feelings that are important.

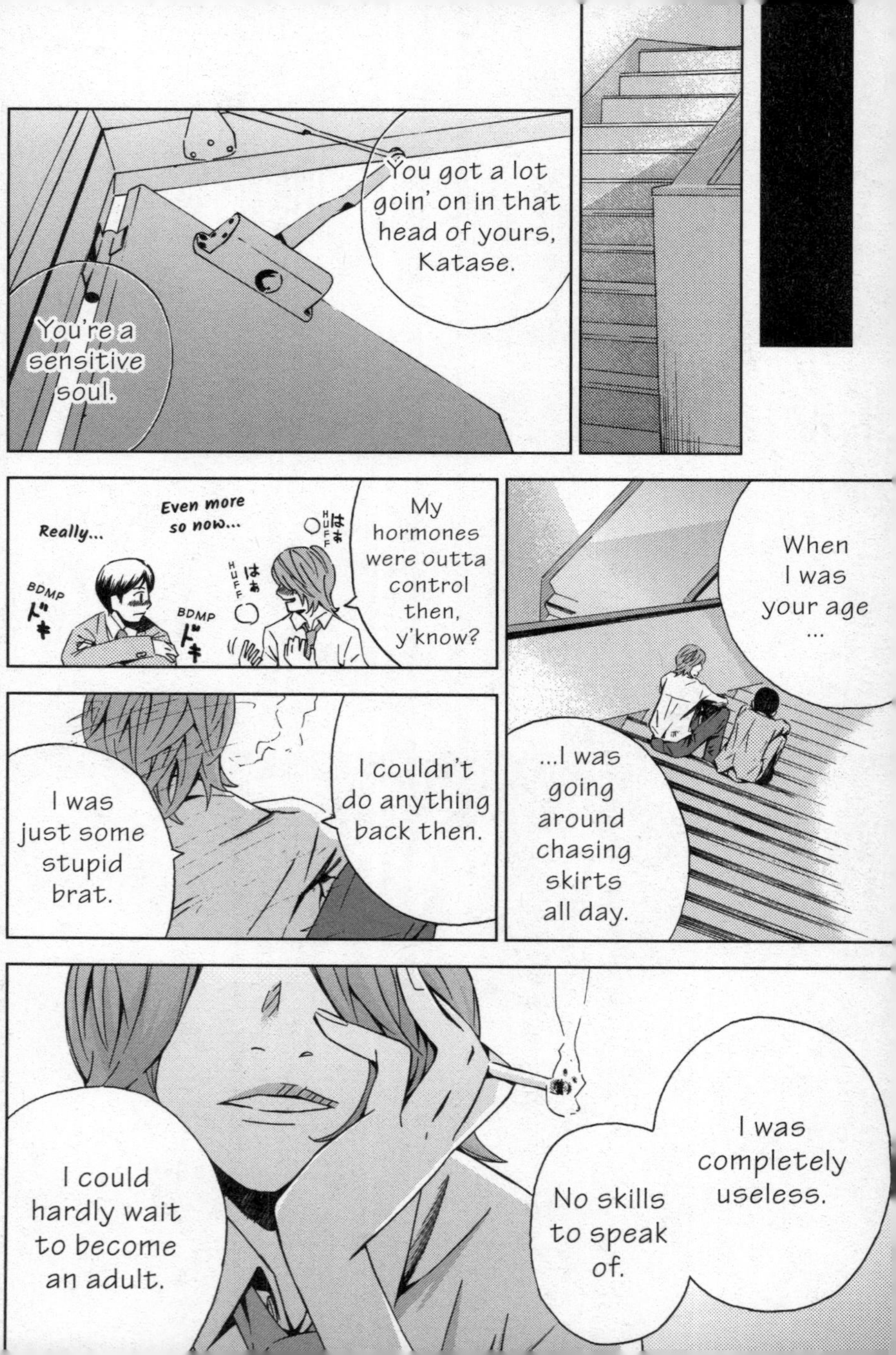
You got a lot goin' on in that head of yours, Katase.
You're a sensitive soul.
When I was your age ...
...I was going around chasing skirts all day.
My hormones were outta control then, y'know?
はぁ HUFF
はぁ HUFF
Even more so now...
Really...
ドキ BDMP
ドキ BDMP
I couldn't do anything back then.
I was just some stupid brat.
I was completely useless.
No skills to speak of.
I could hardly wait to become an adult.

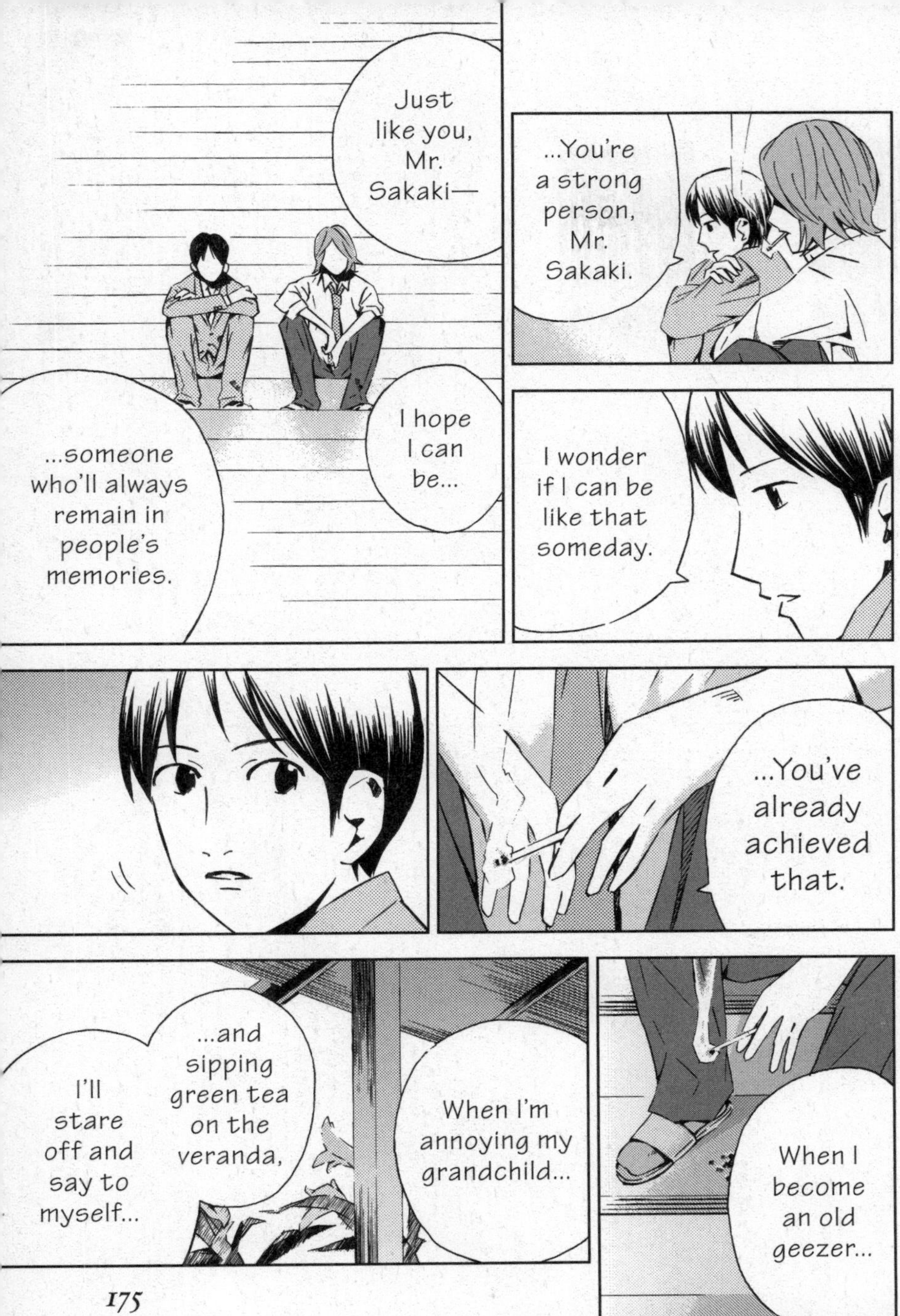
...You're a strong person, Mr. Sakaki.
I wonder if I can be like that someday.
Just like you, Mr. Sakaki—
I hope I can be...
...someone who'll always remain in people's memories.
...You've already achieved that.
When I become an old geezer...
When I'm annoying my grandchild...
...and sipping green tea on the veranda,
I'll stare off and say to myself...

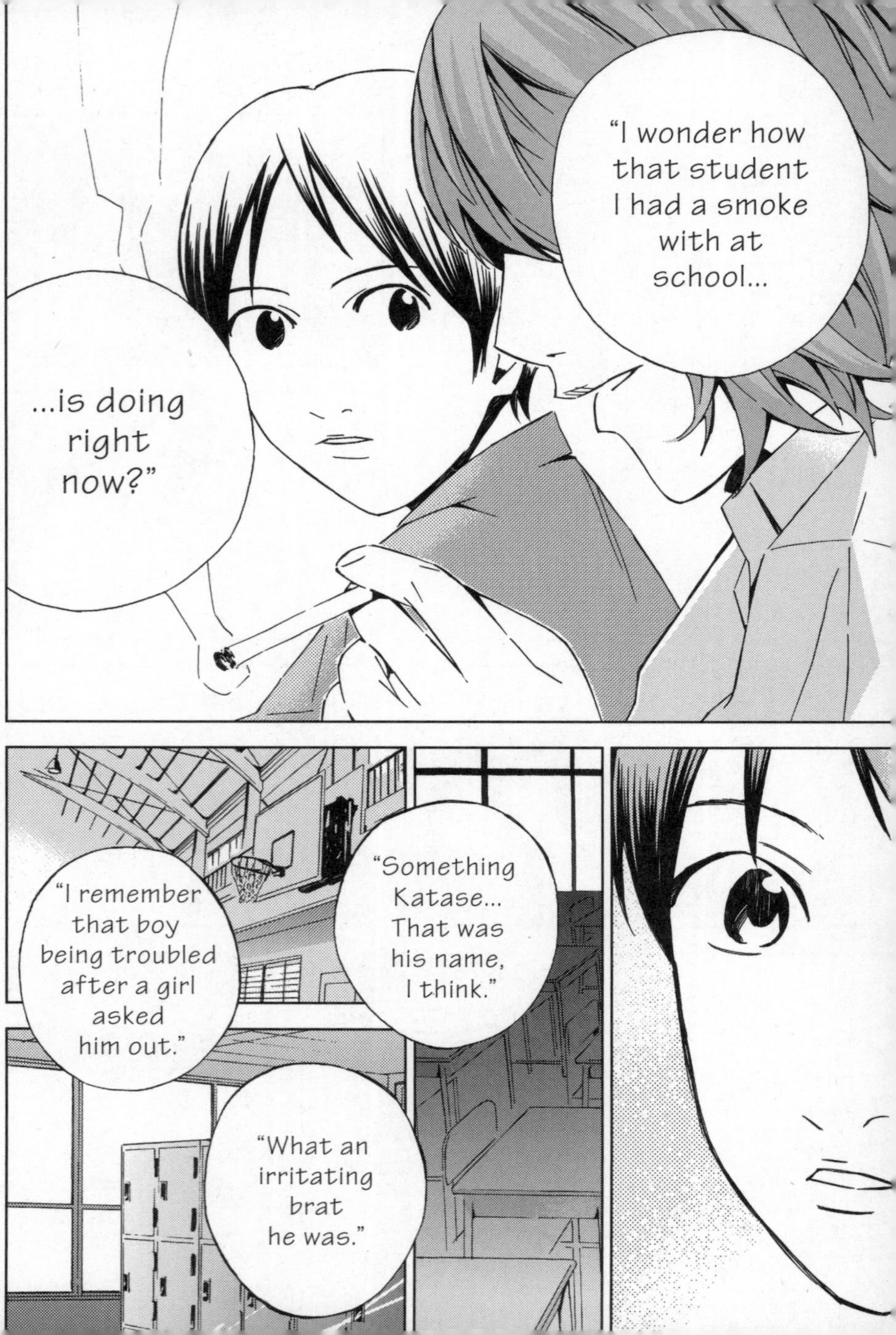
"I wonder how that student I had a smoke with at school...
...is doing right now?"
"Something Katase... That was his name, I think."
"I remember that boy being troubled after a girl asked him out."
"What an irritating brat he was."

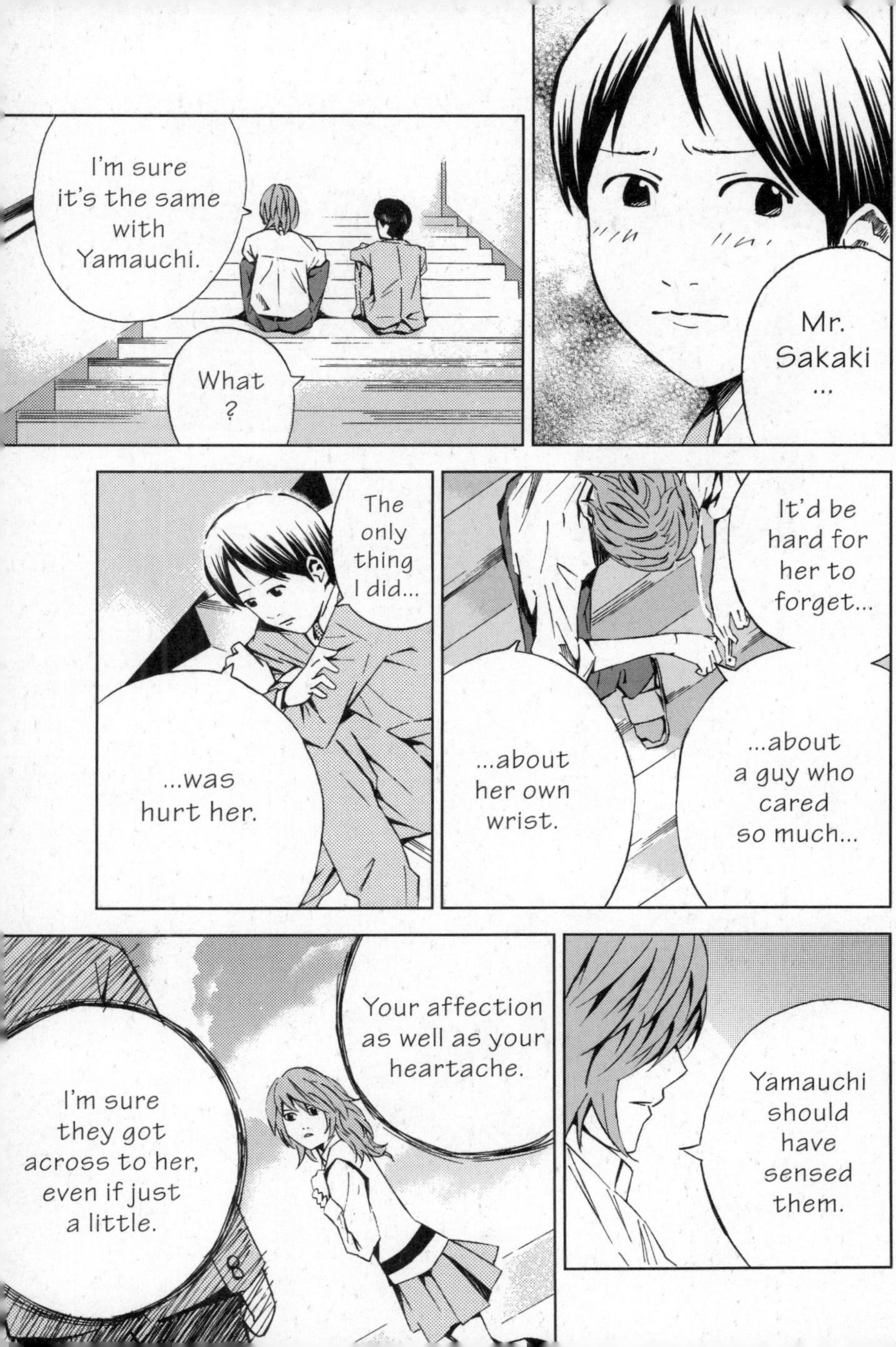
Mr. Sakaki...
I'm sure it's the same with Yamauchi.
What?
It'd be hard for her to forget...
...about a guy who cared so much...
...about her own wrist.
The only thing I did...
...was hurt her.
Yamauchi should have sensed them.
Your affection as well as your heartache.
I'm sure they got across to her, even if just a little.

You were someone that she needed...
...for her to change herself.

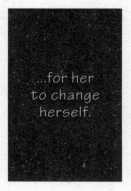

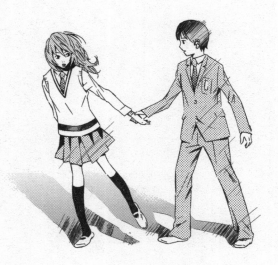

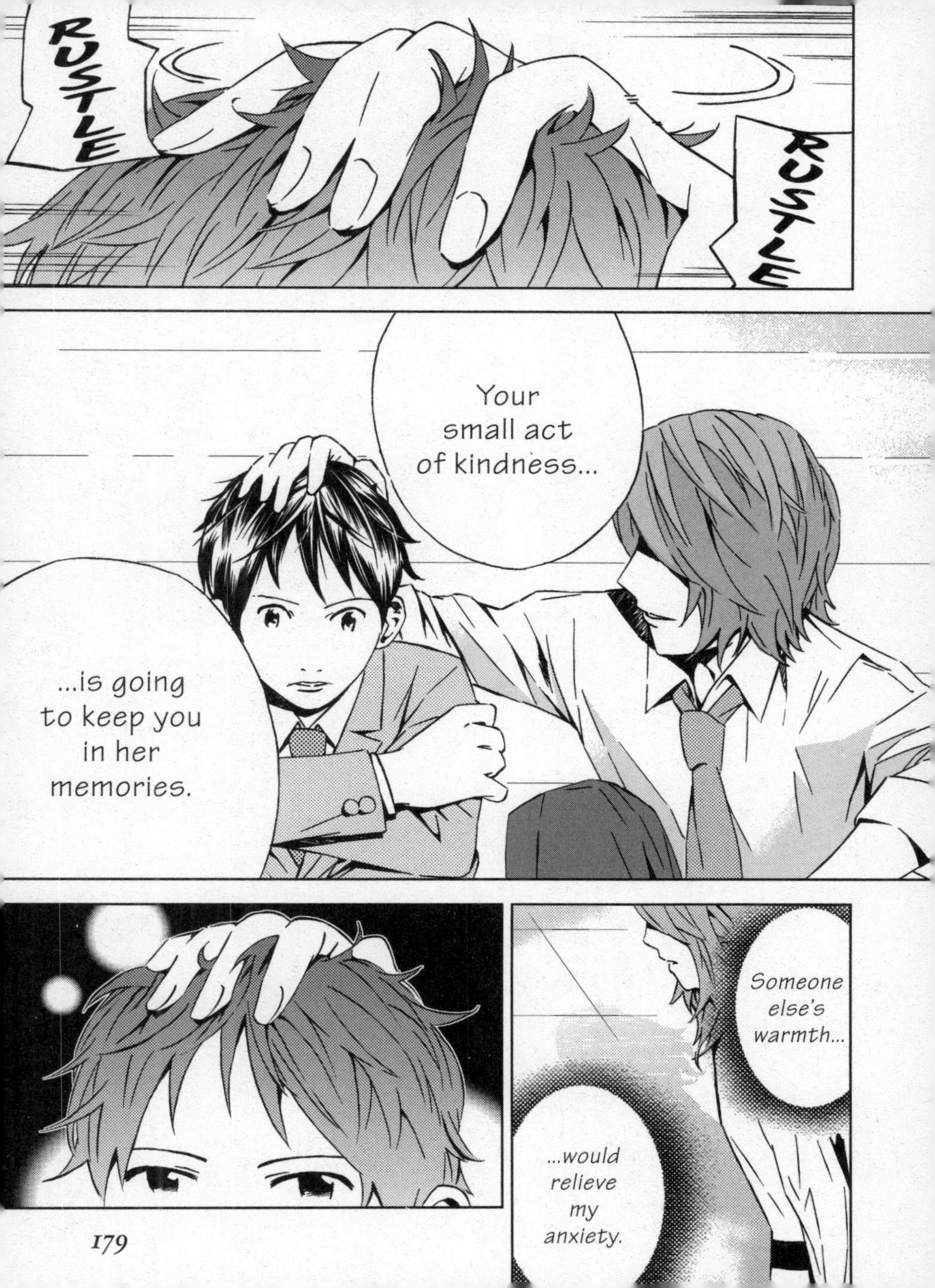
RUSTLE
RUSTLE
Your small act of kindness...
...is going to keep you in her memories.
Someone else's warmth...
...would relieve my anxiety.

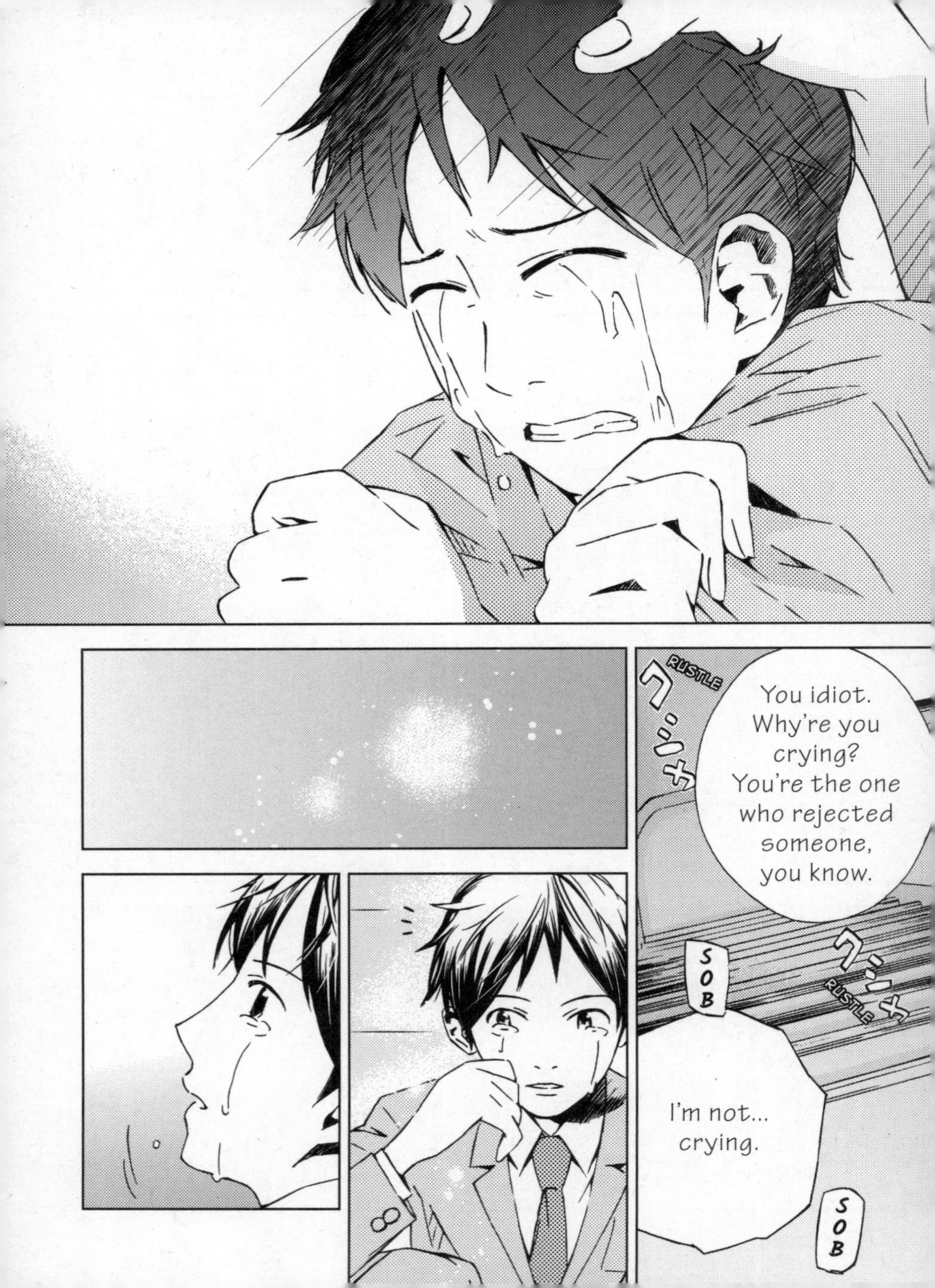
RUSTLE
You idiot. Why're you crying? You're the one who rejected someone, you know.
SOB
RUSTLE
I'm not... crying.
SOB

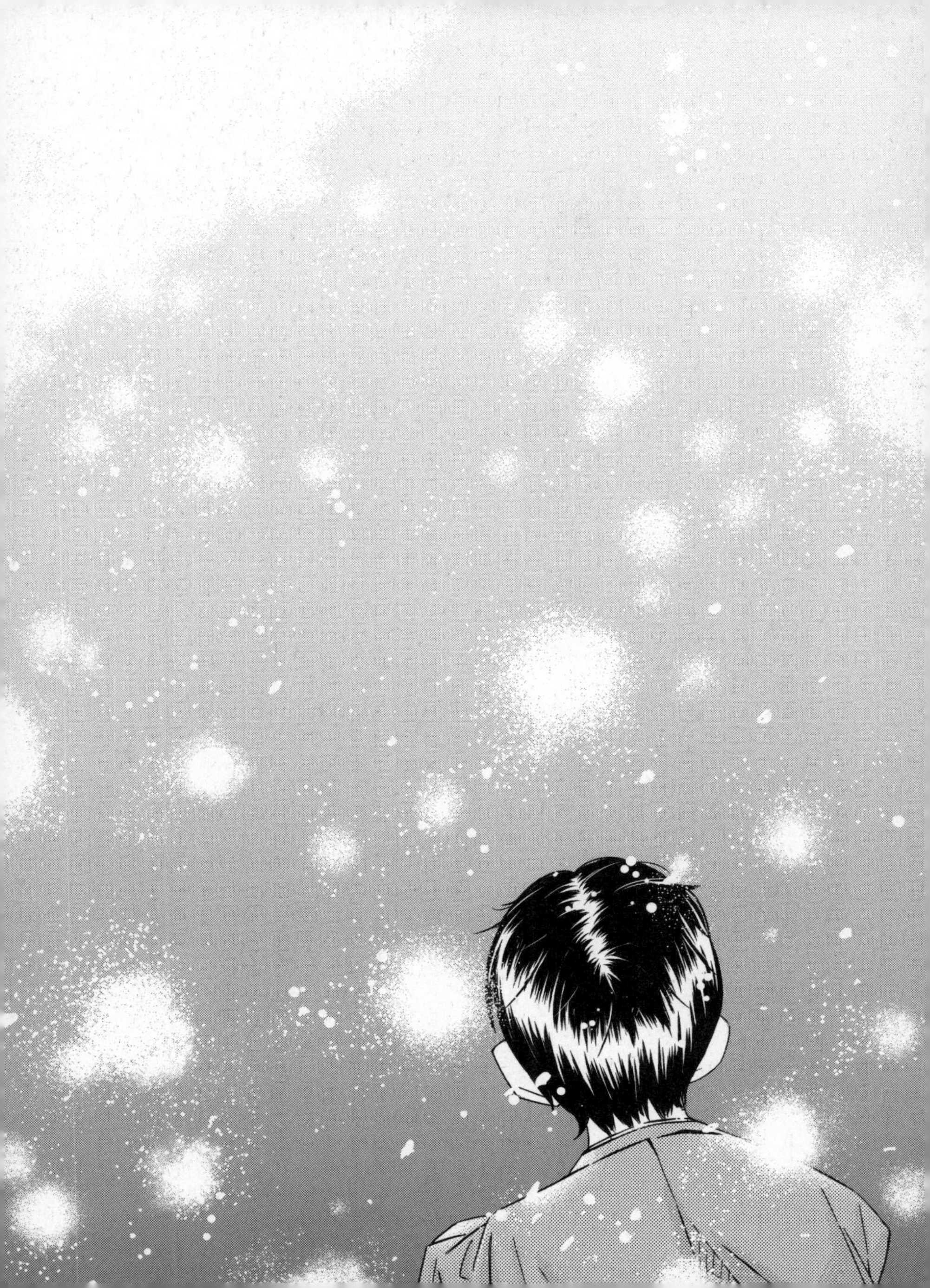

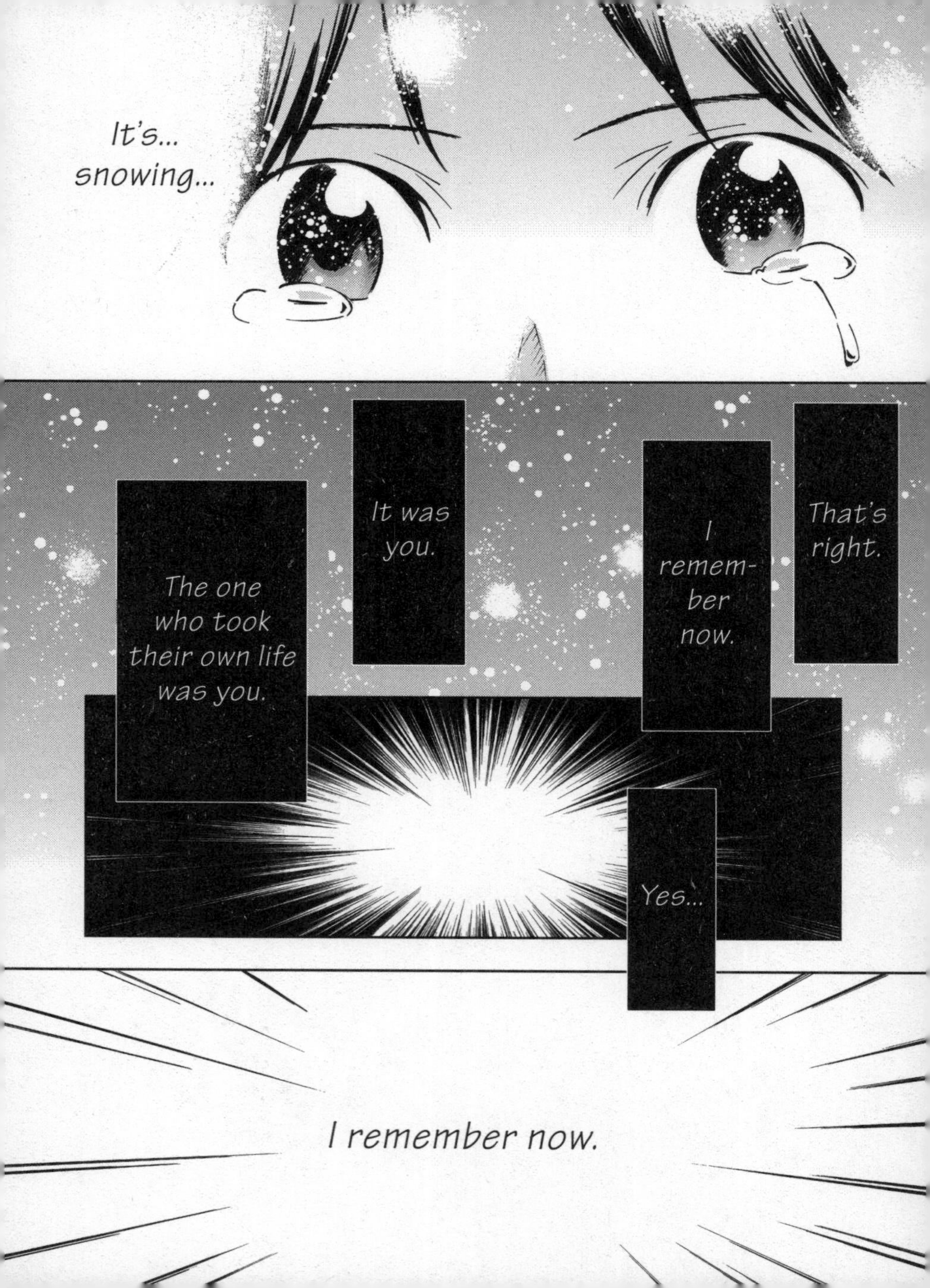
It's... snowing...
That's right.
I remember now.
It was you.
The one who took their own life was you.
Yes...
I remember now.

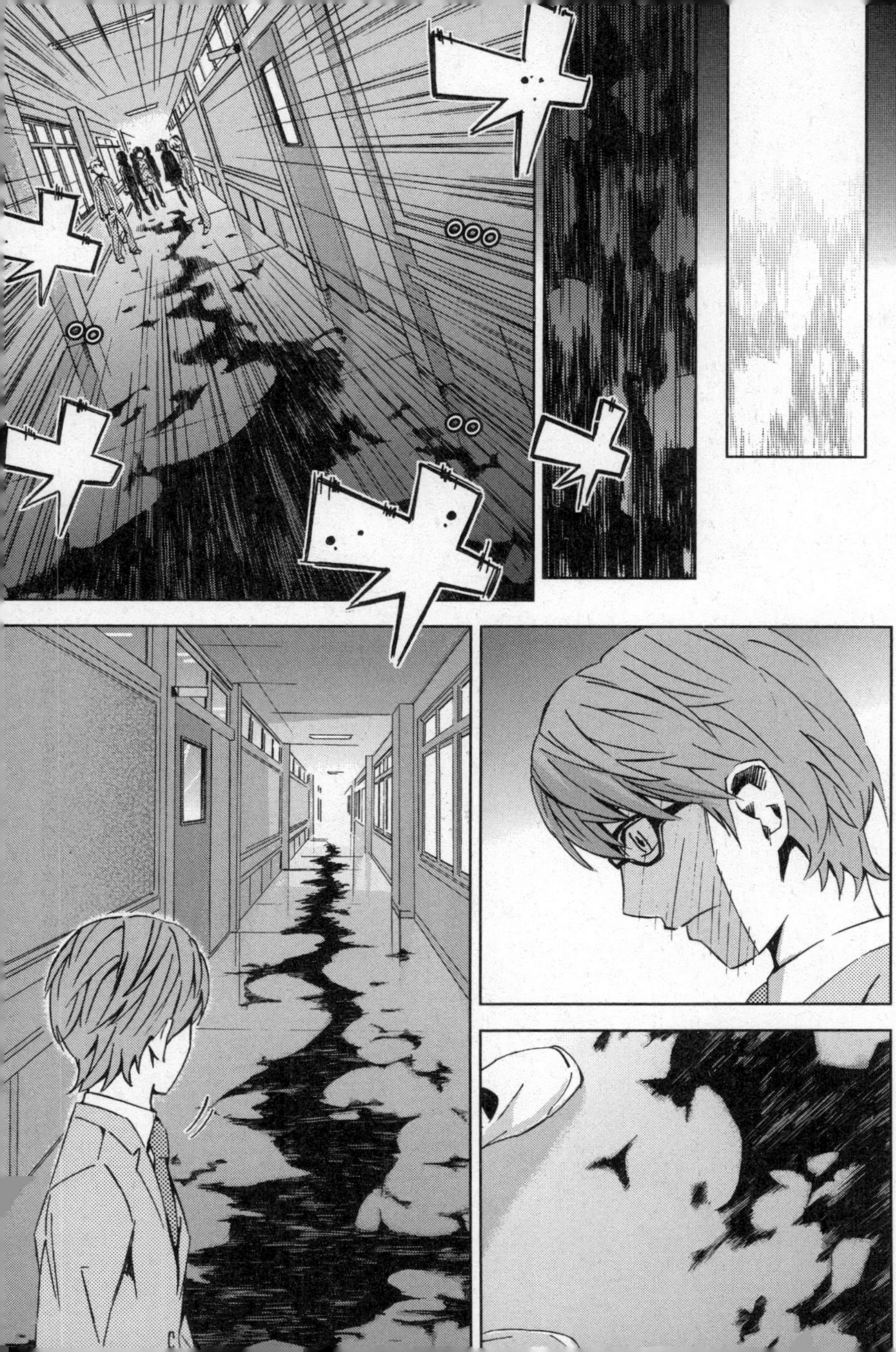

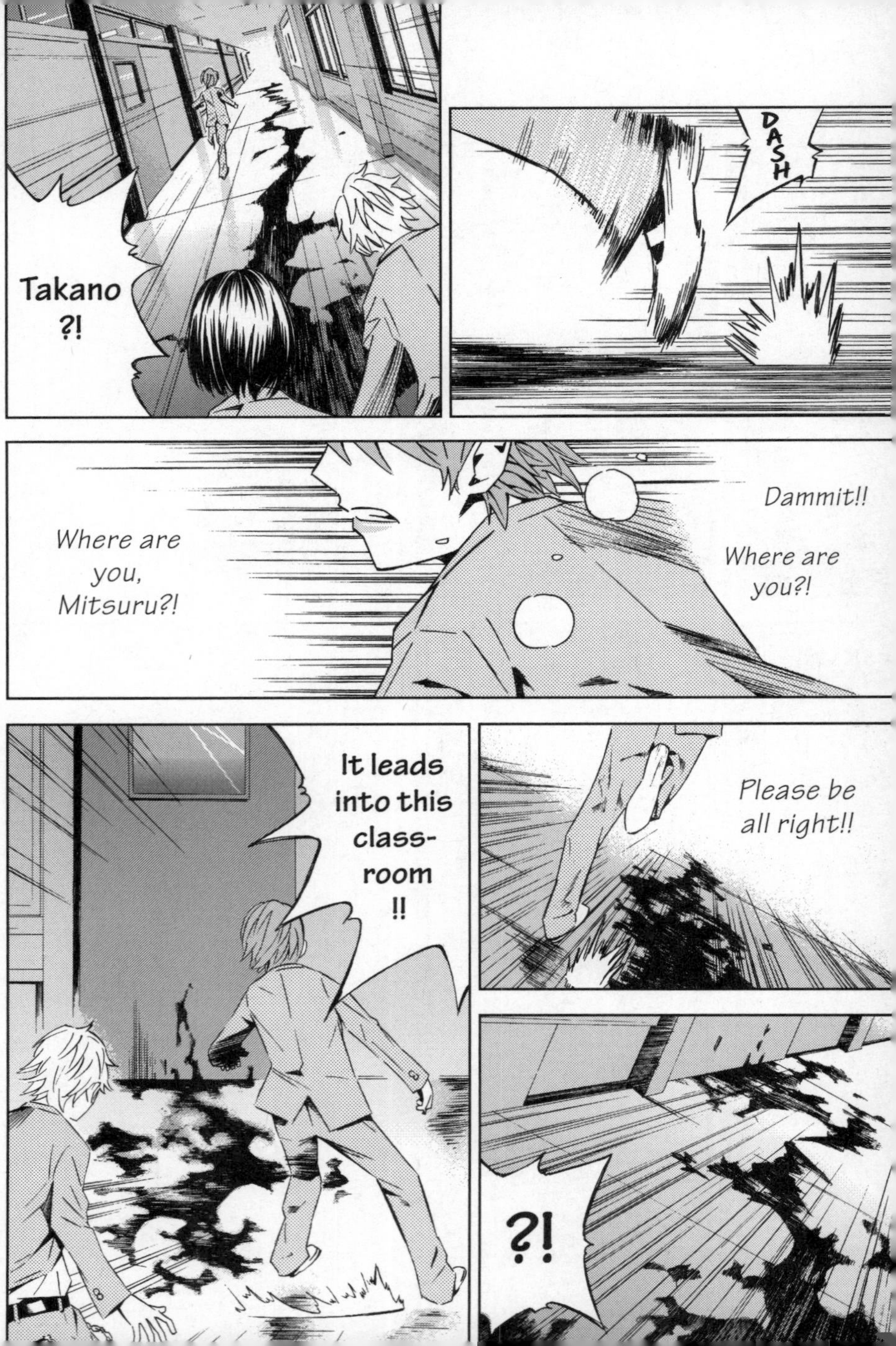
DASH
Takano ?!
Dammit!!
Where are you?!
Where are you, Mitsuru?!
Please be all right!!
?!
It leads into this class-room !!

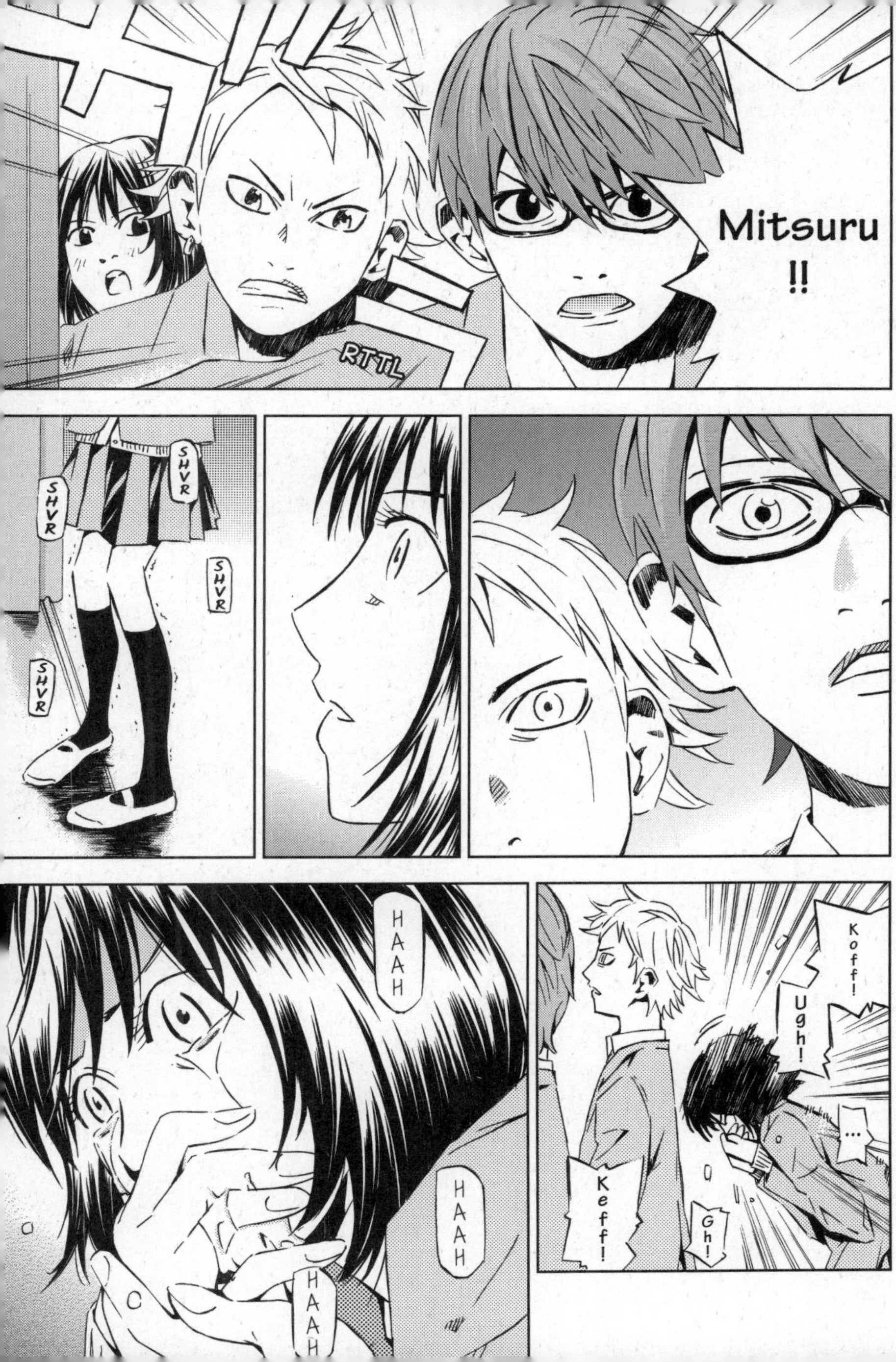
Mitsuru
!!
RTTL
SHVR
SHVR
SHVR
SHVR
Koff!
Ugh!
...
Gh!
Keff!
HAAH
HAAH
HAAH

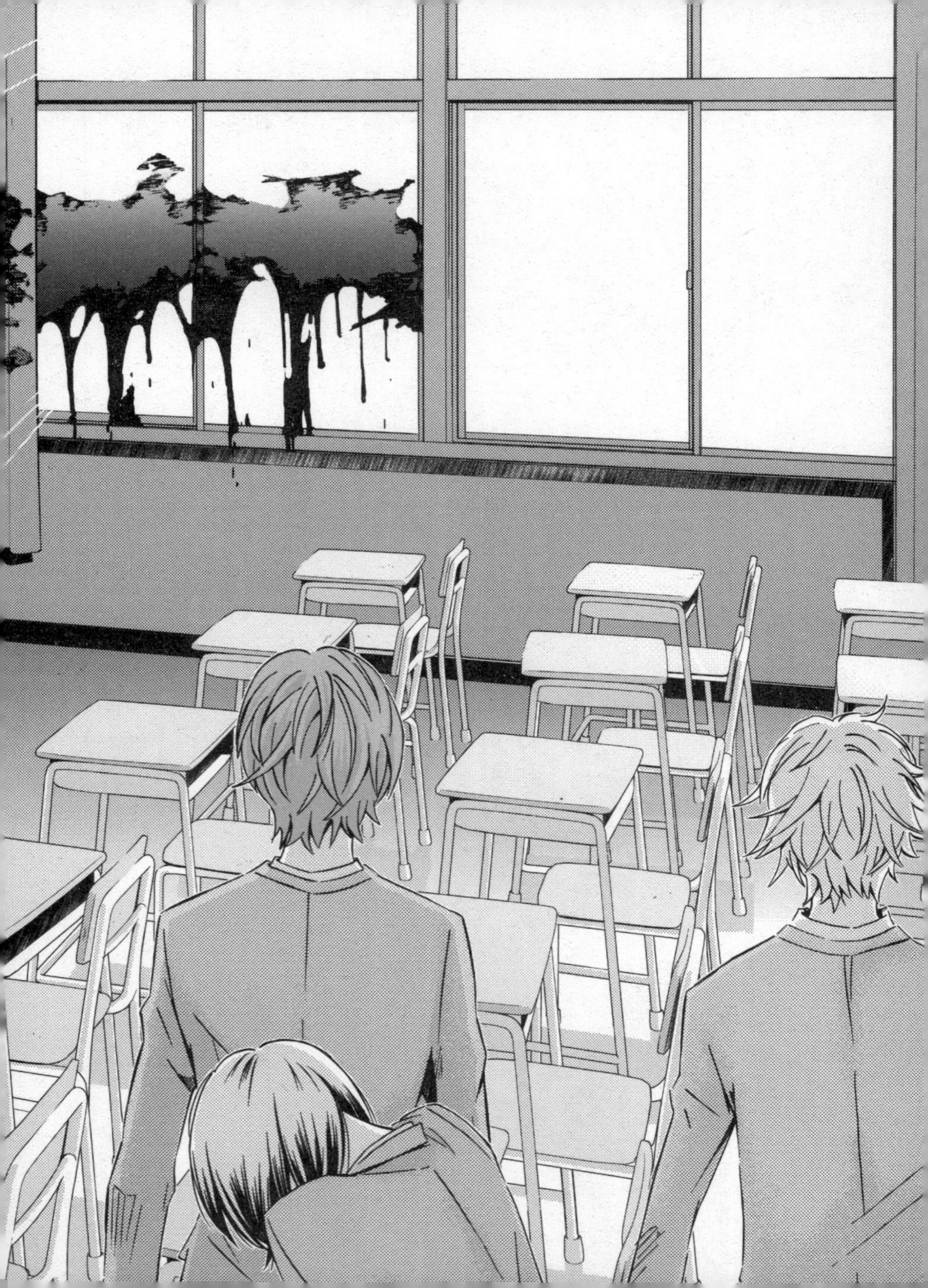

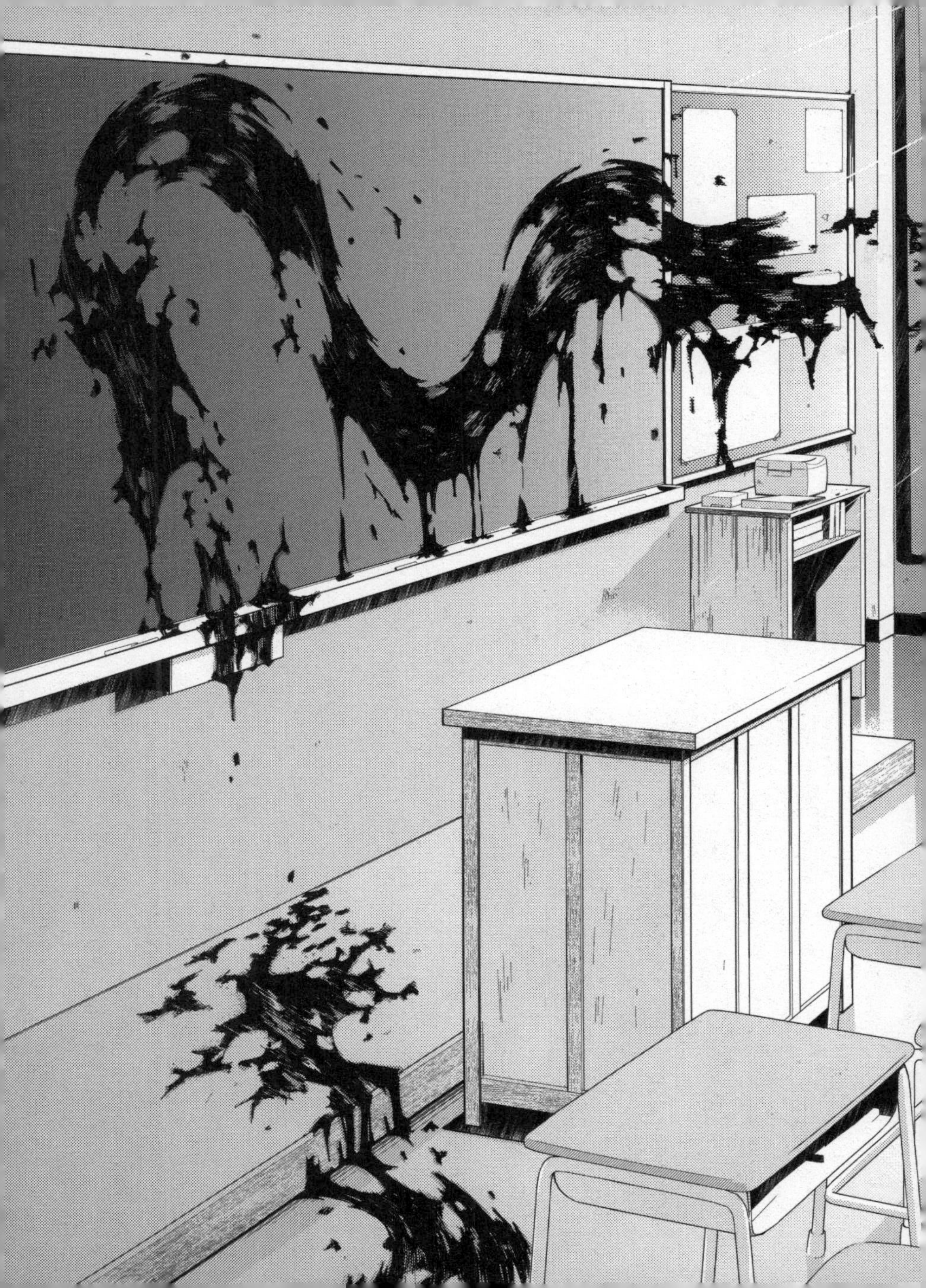

A School
Frozen
in Time

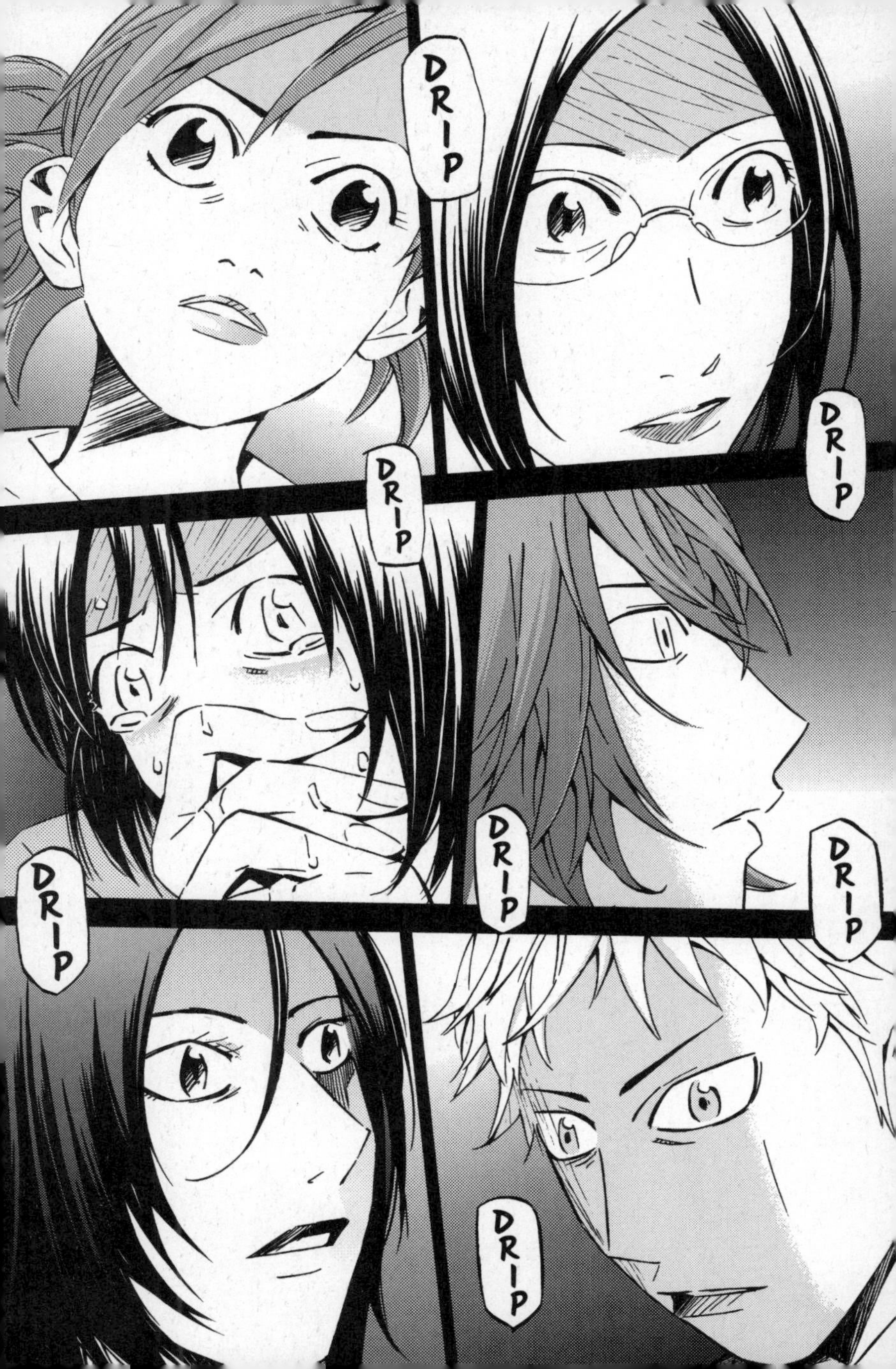
DRIP
DRIP
DRIP
DRIP
DRIP
DRIP
DRIP

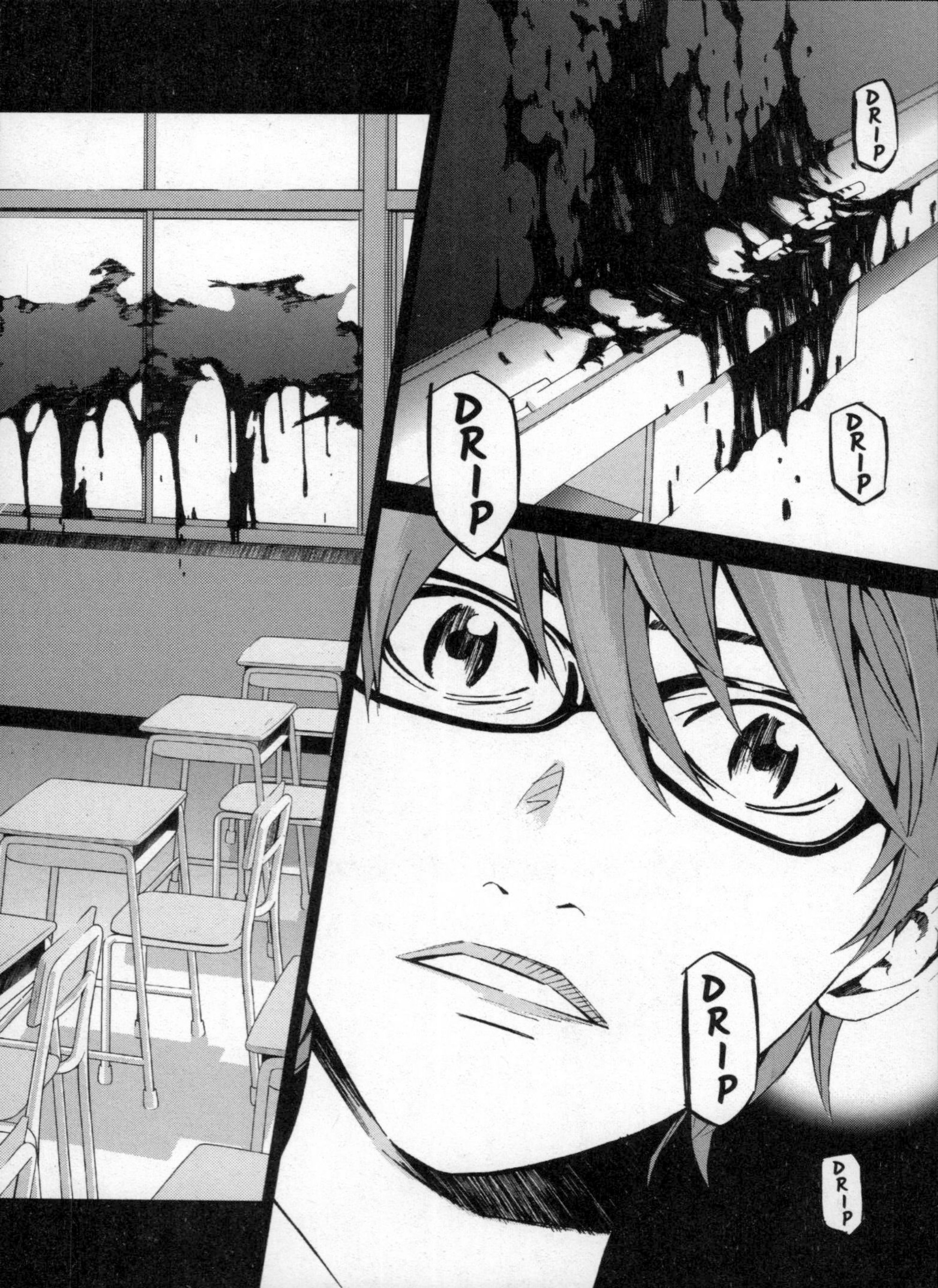
DRIP
DRIP
DRIP
DRIP
DRIP

Chapter 4 It's Not Over

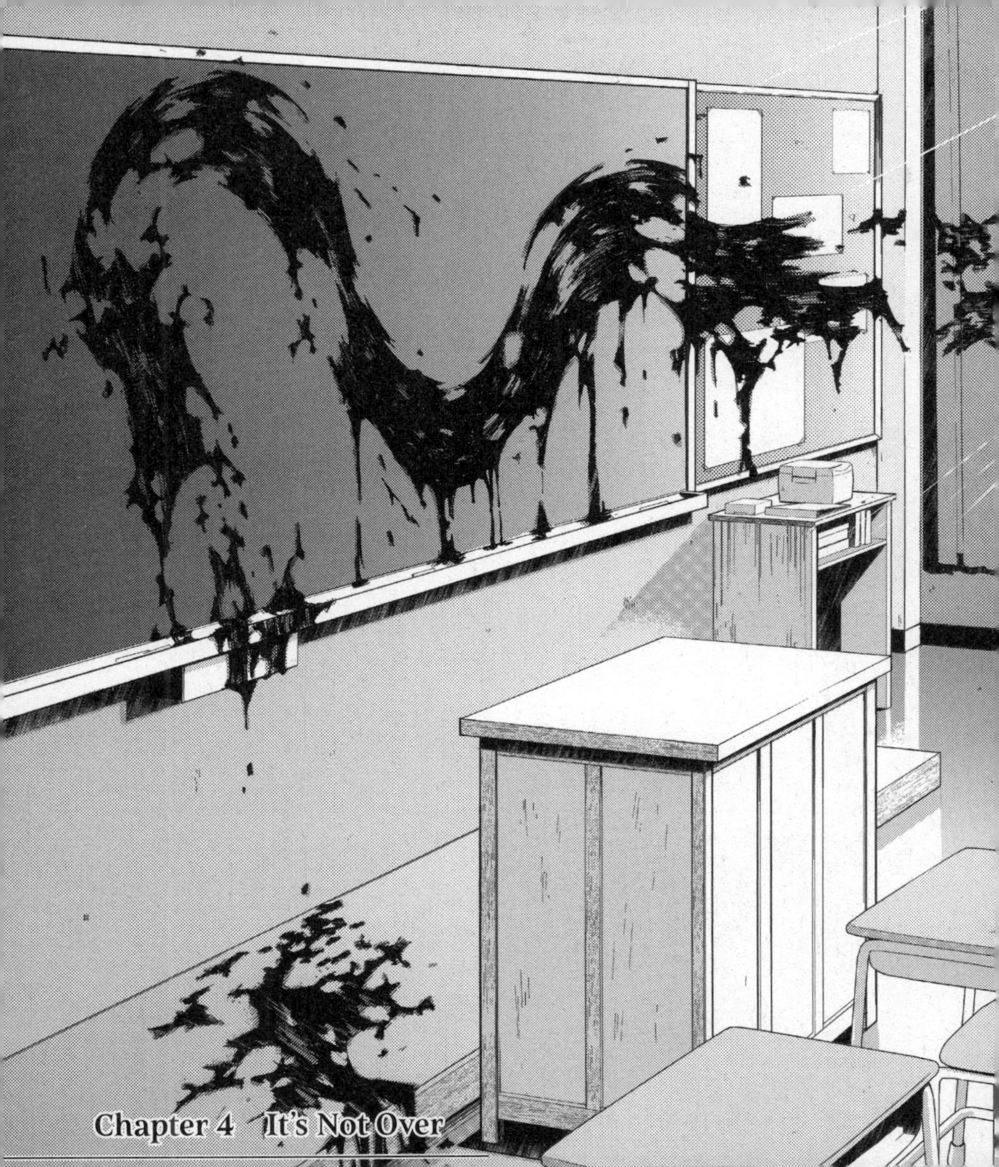

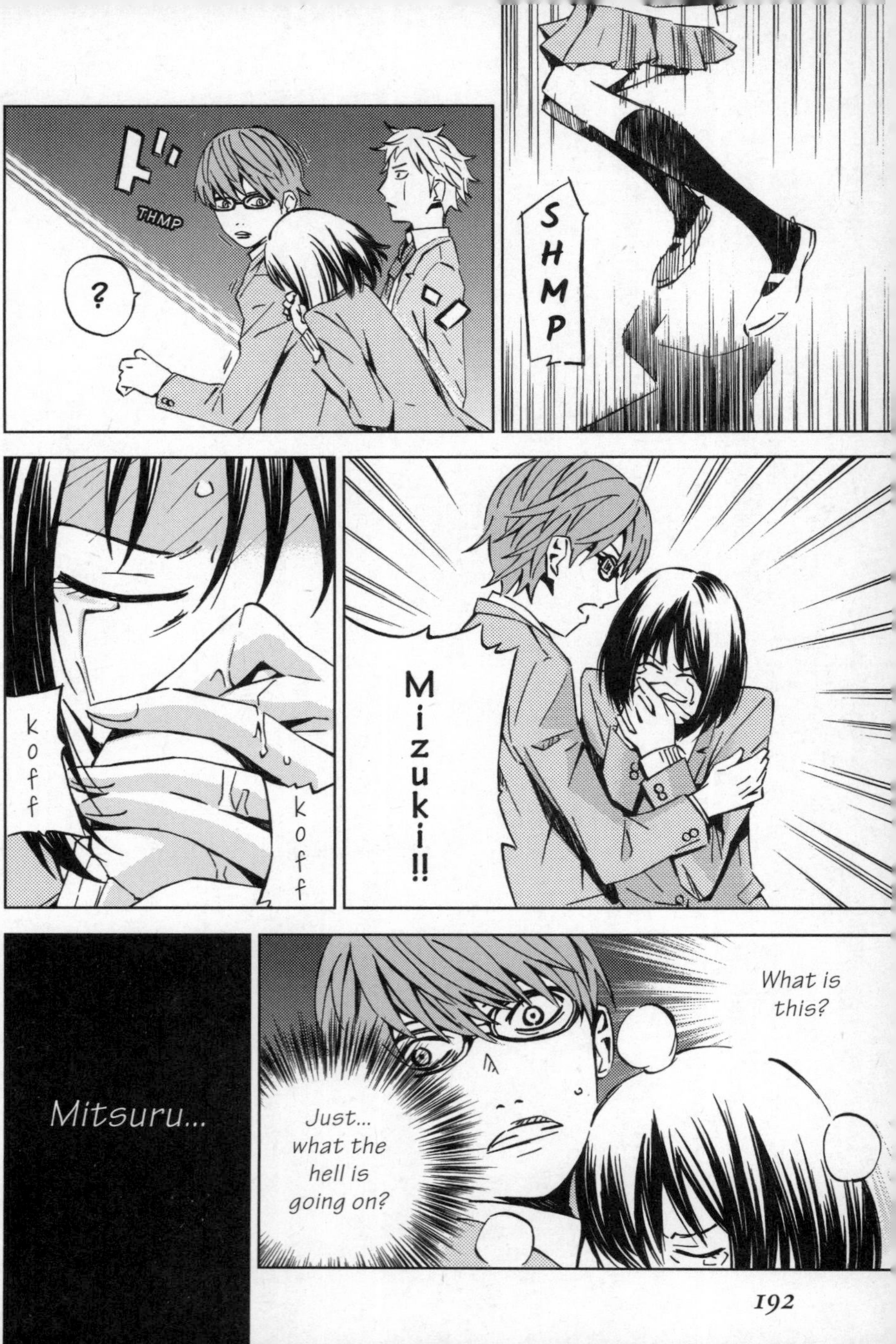
SHMP
THMP
?
Mizuki!!
koff
koff
What is this?
Just... what the hell is going on?
Mitsuru...

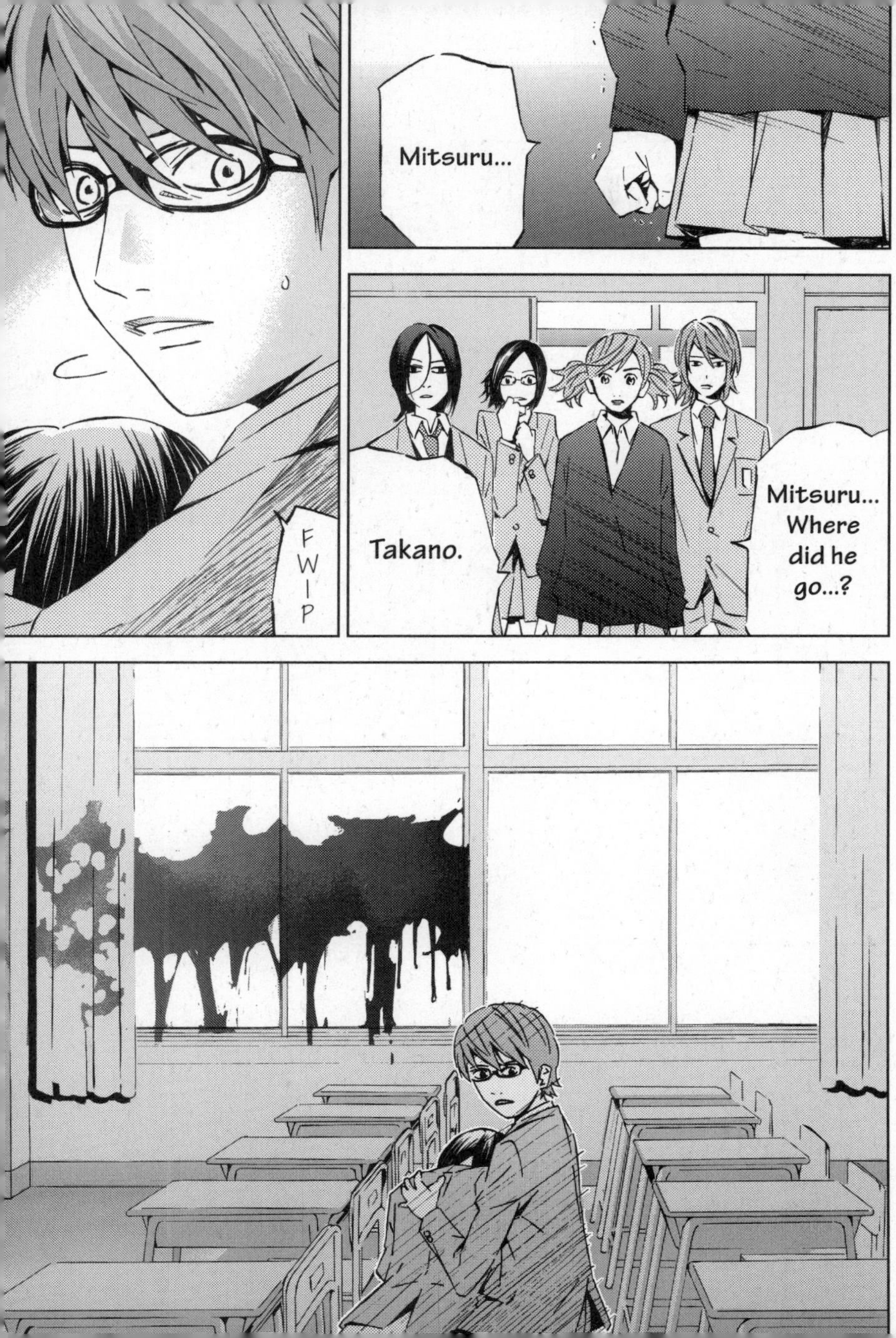
Mitsuru...
Mitsuru... Where did he go...?
Takano.
FWIP

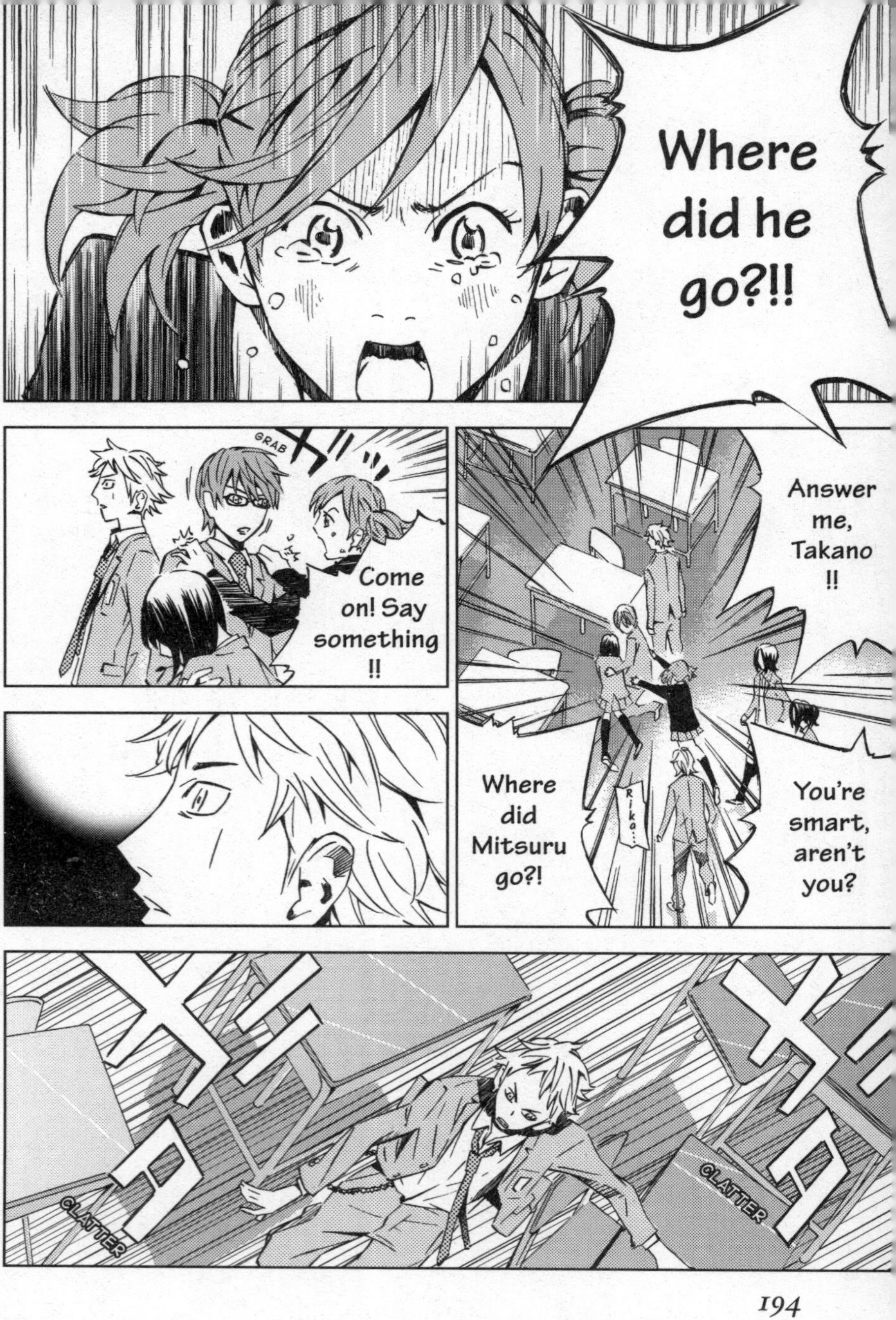

Where did he go?!!
Answer me, Takano !!
You're smart, aren't you?
Riko...
Where did Mitsuru go?!
GRAB
Come on! Say something !!
CLATTER
CLATTER

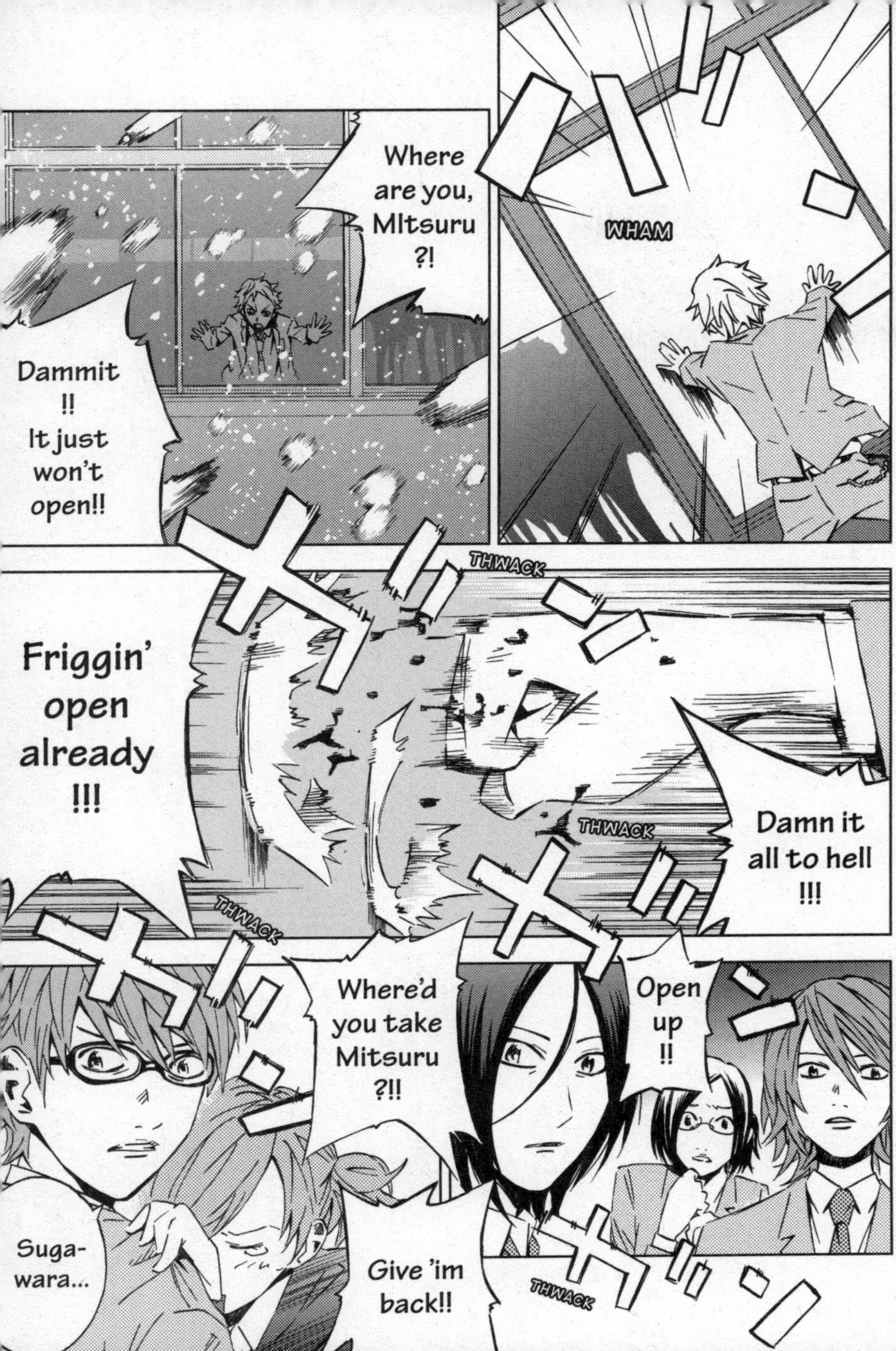
WHAM
Where are you, MItsuru ?!
Dammit !! It just won't open!!
THWACK
Damn it all to hell !!!
THWACK
Friggin' open already !!!
THWACK
Open up !!
Where'd you take Mitsuru ?!!
THWACK
Give 'im back!!
Suga-wara...

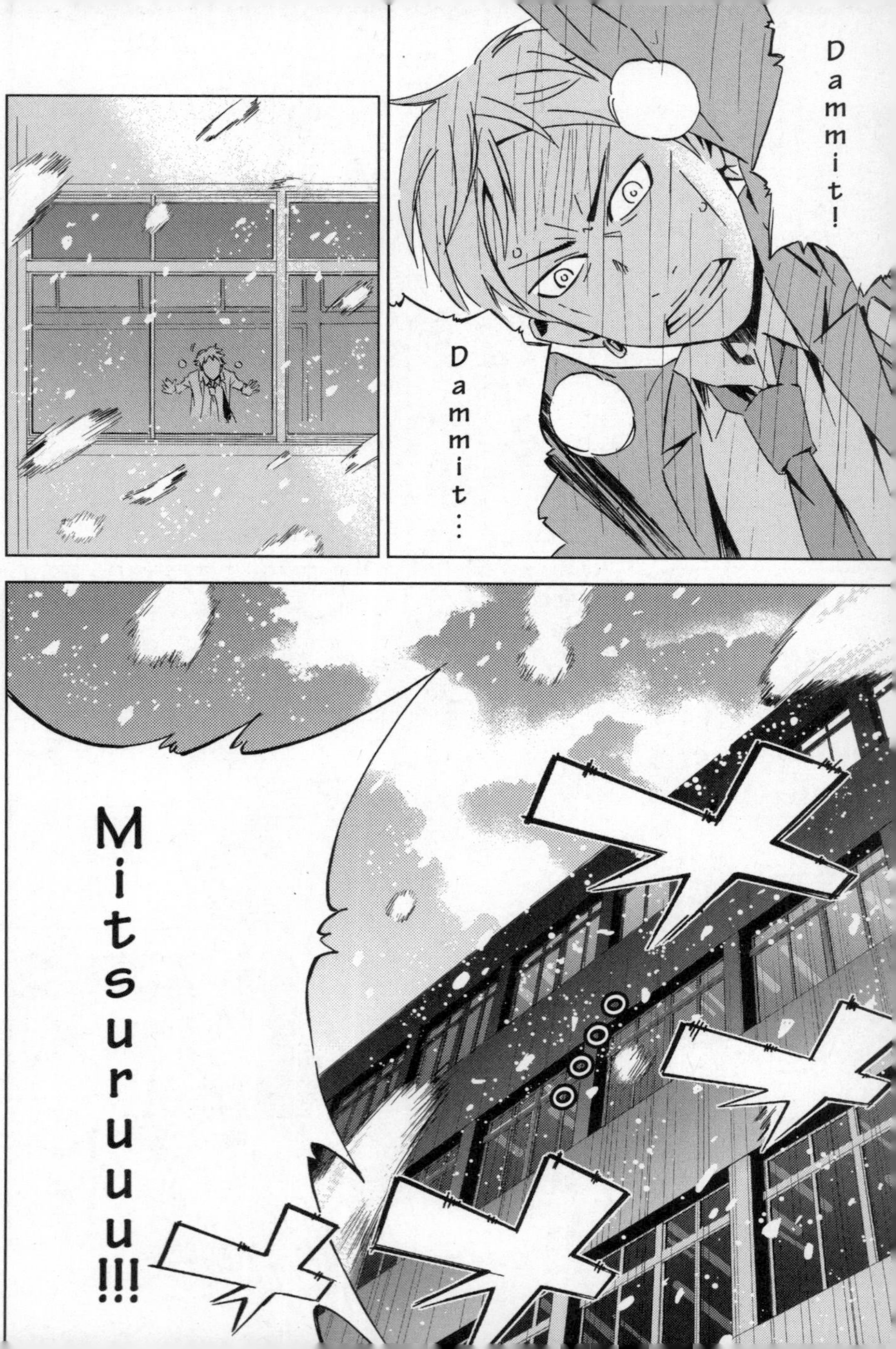
Dammit!
Dammit…
Mitsuruuuu!!!

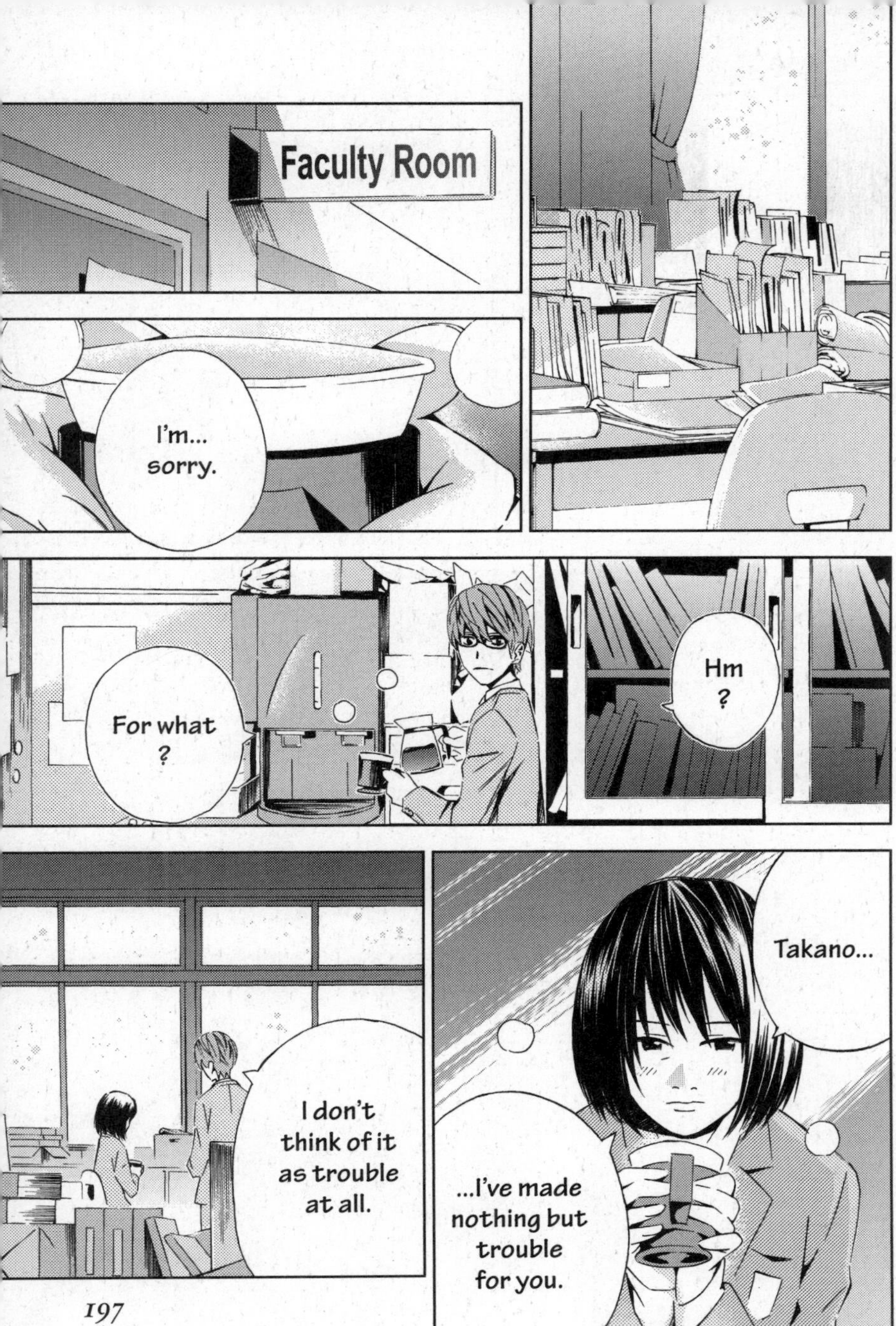
Faculty Room
I'm... sorry.
Hm ?
For what ?
Takano...
...I've made nothing but trouble for you.
I don't think of it as trouble at all.

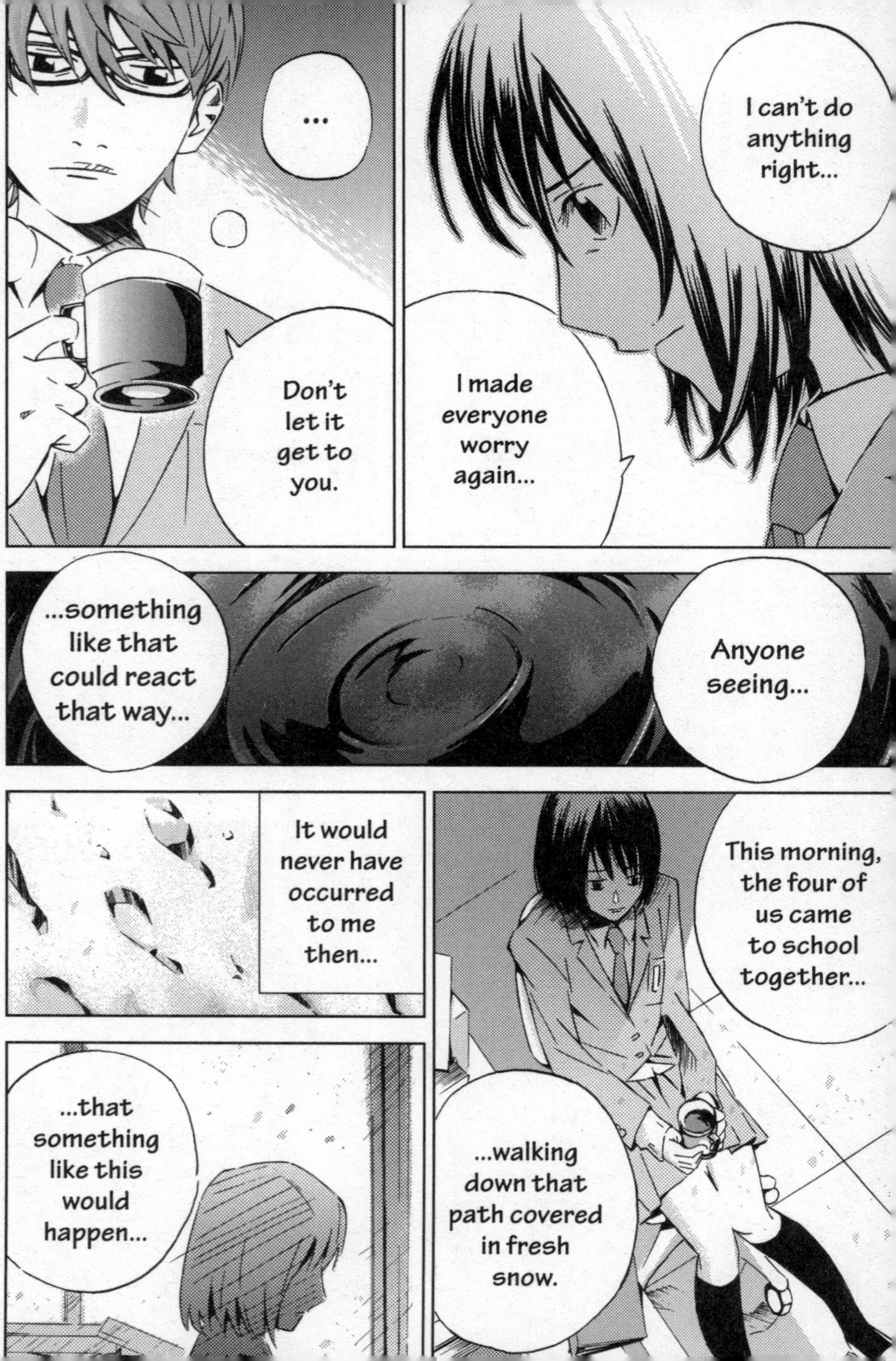
I can't do anything right...
I made everyone worry again...
...
Don't let it get to you.
Anyone seeing...
...something like that could react that way...
This morning, the four of us came to school together...
...walking down that path covered in fresh snow.
It would never have occurred to me then...
...that something like this would happen...

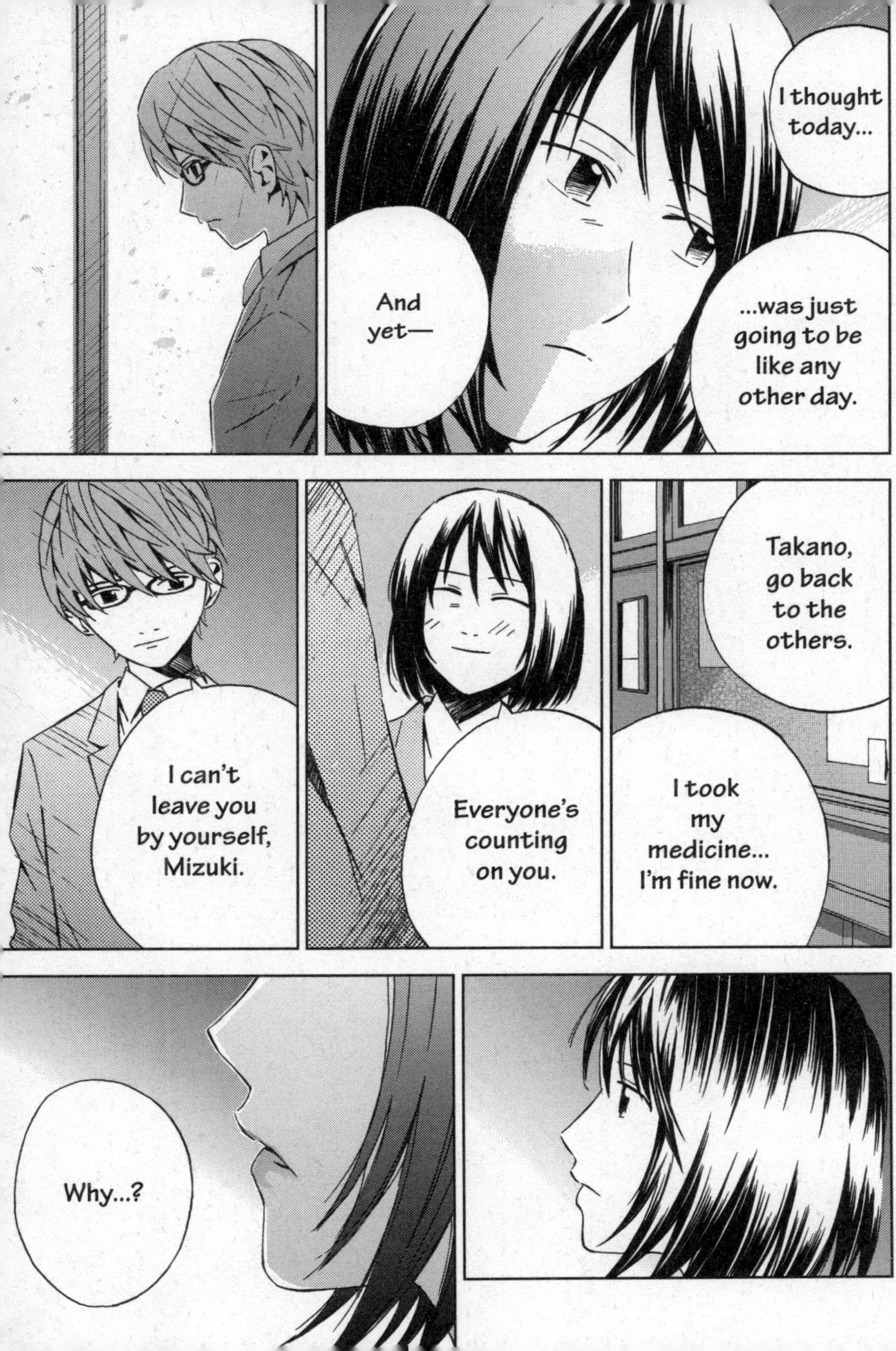
I thought today...
...was just going to be like any other day.
And yet—
Takano, go back to the others.
I took my medicine... I'm fine now.
Everyone's counting on you.
I can't leave you by yourself, Mizuki.
Why...?

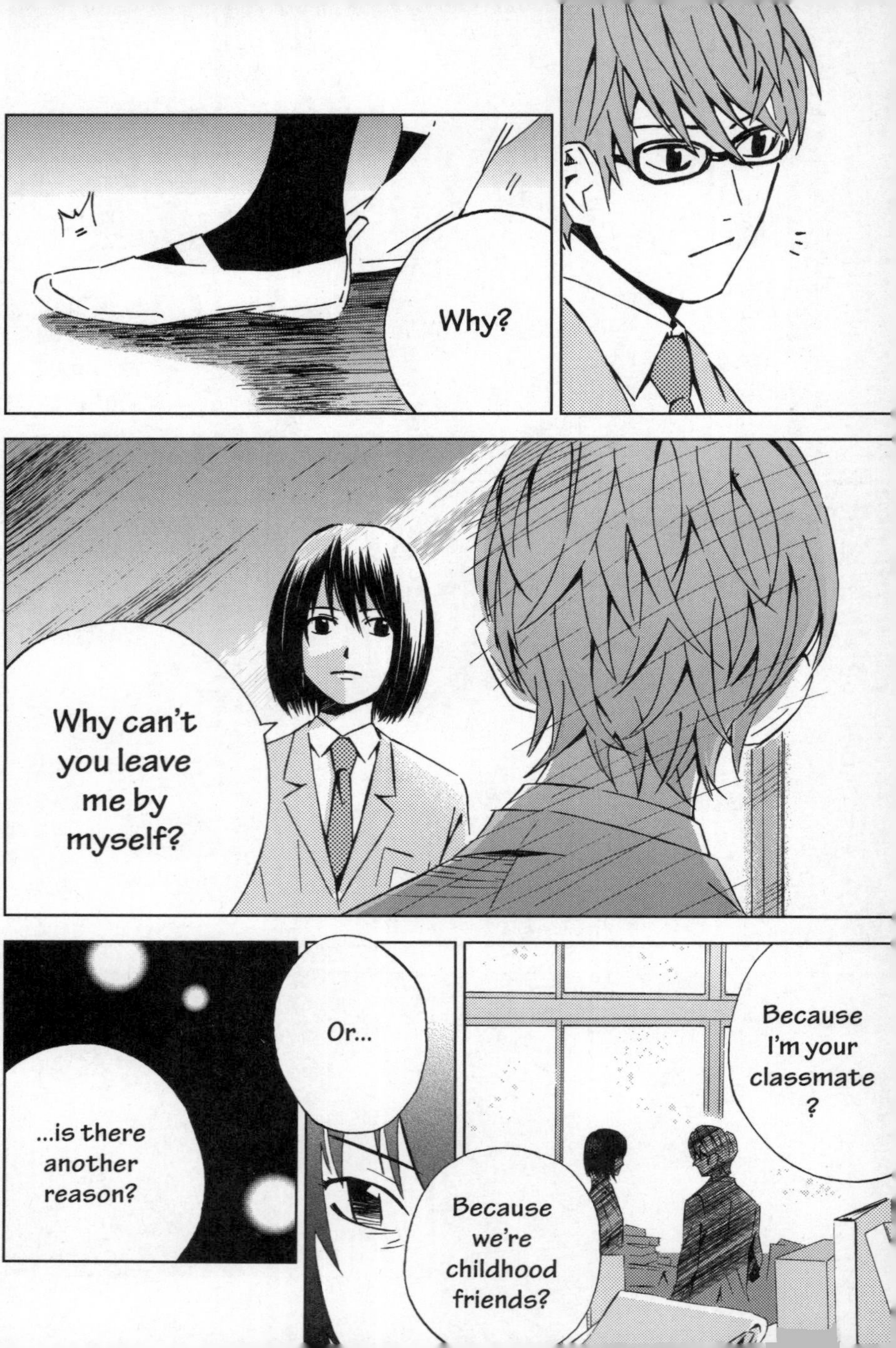
Why?
Why can't you leave me by myself?
Because I'm your classmate?
Because we're childhood friends?
Or...
...is there another reason?

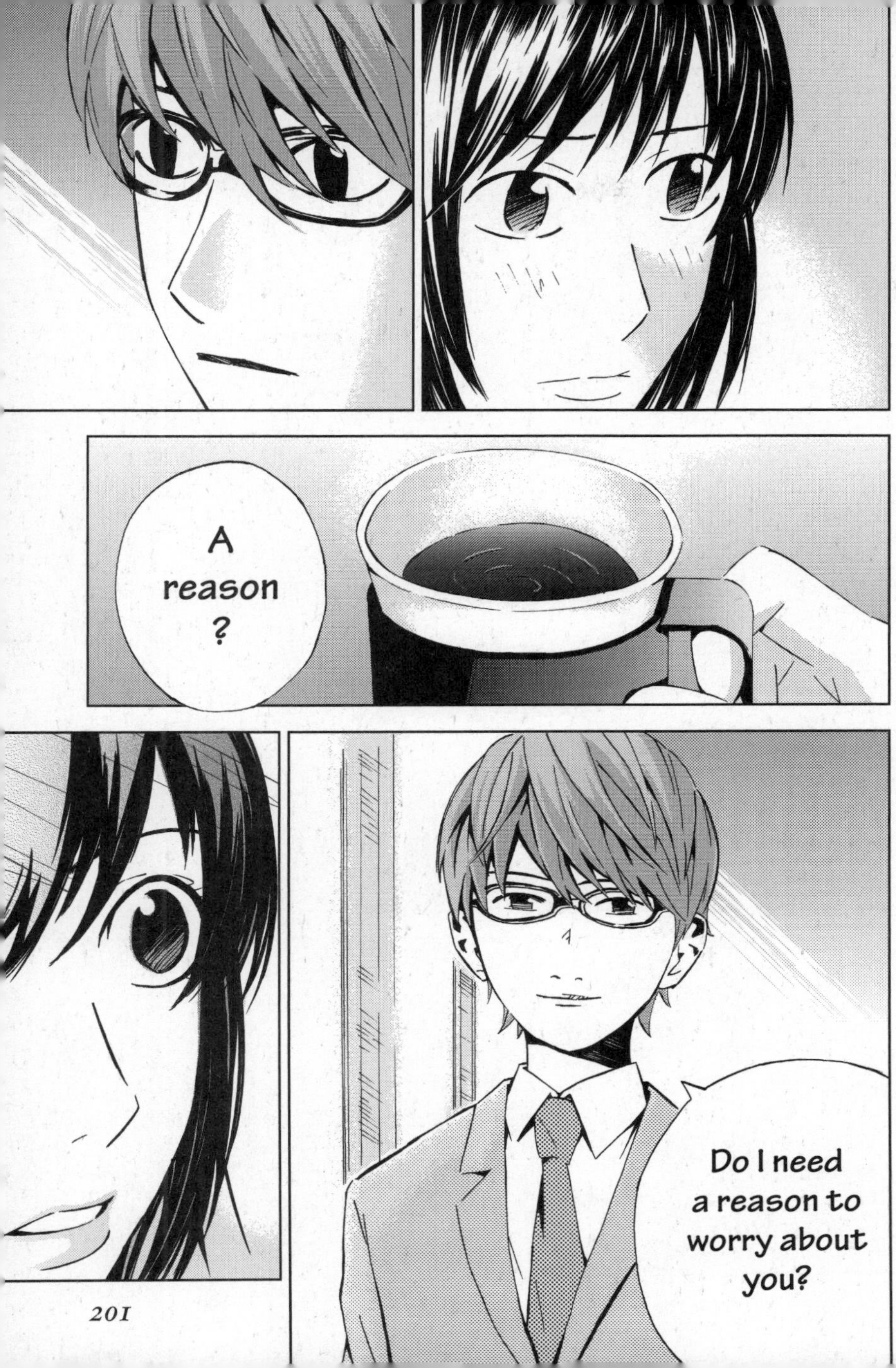
A reason?
Do I need a reason to worry about you?

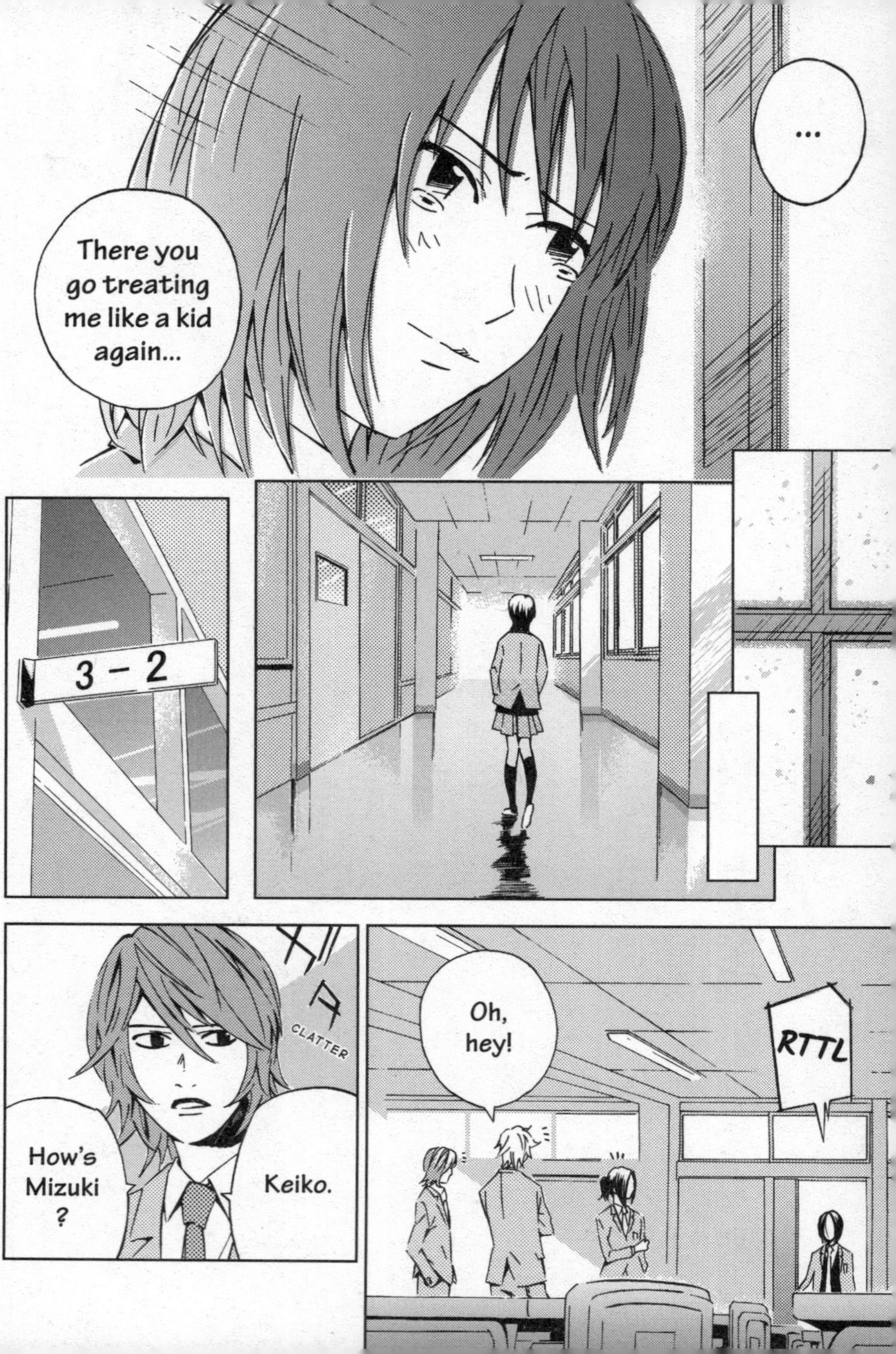
...
There you go treating me like a kid again...
3 – 2
RTTL
Oh, hey!
CLATTER
Keiko.
How's Mizuki ?

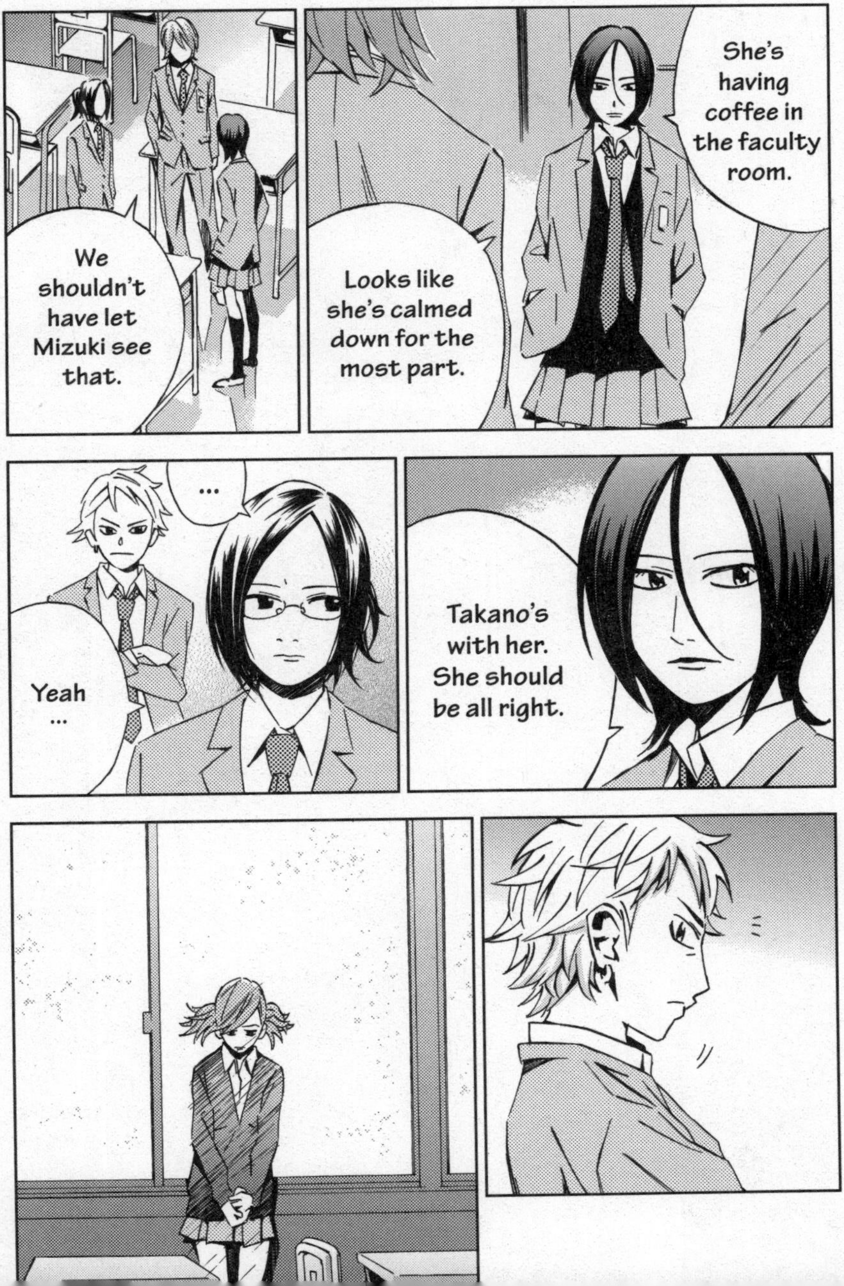
She's having coffee in the faculty room.
Looks like she's calmed down for the most part.
We shouldn't have let Mizuki see that.
Takano's with her. She should be all right.
...
Yeah ...

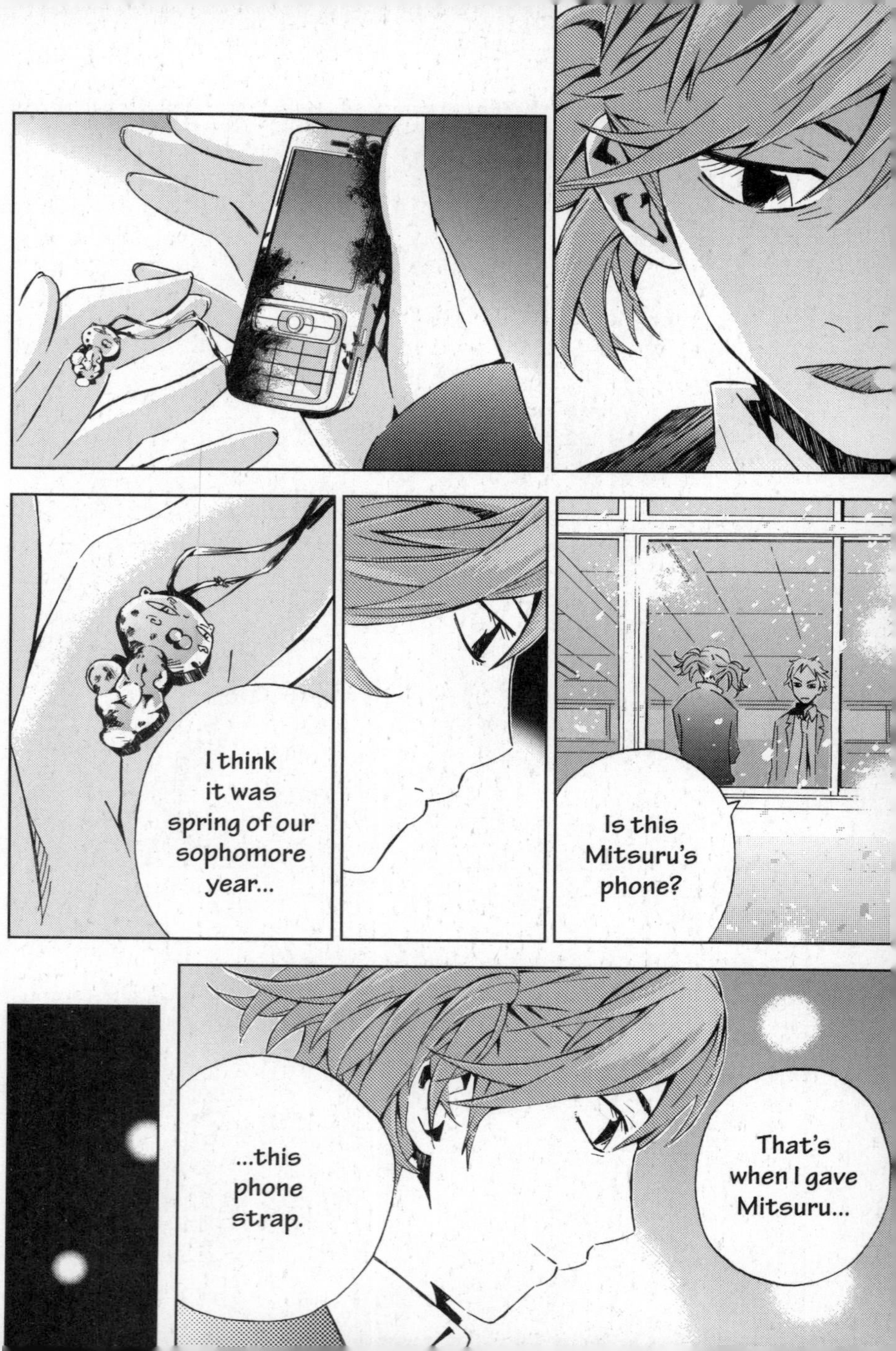
Is this Mitsuru's phone?
I think it was spring of our sophomore year...
That's when I gave Mitsuru...
...this phone strap.

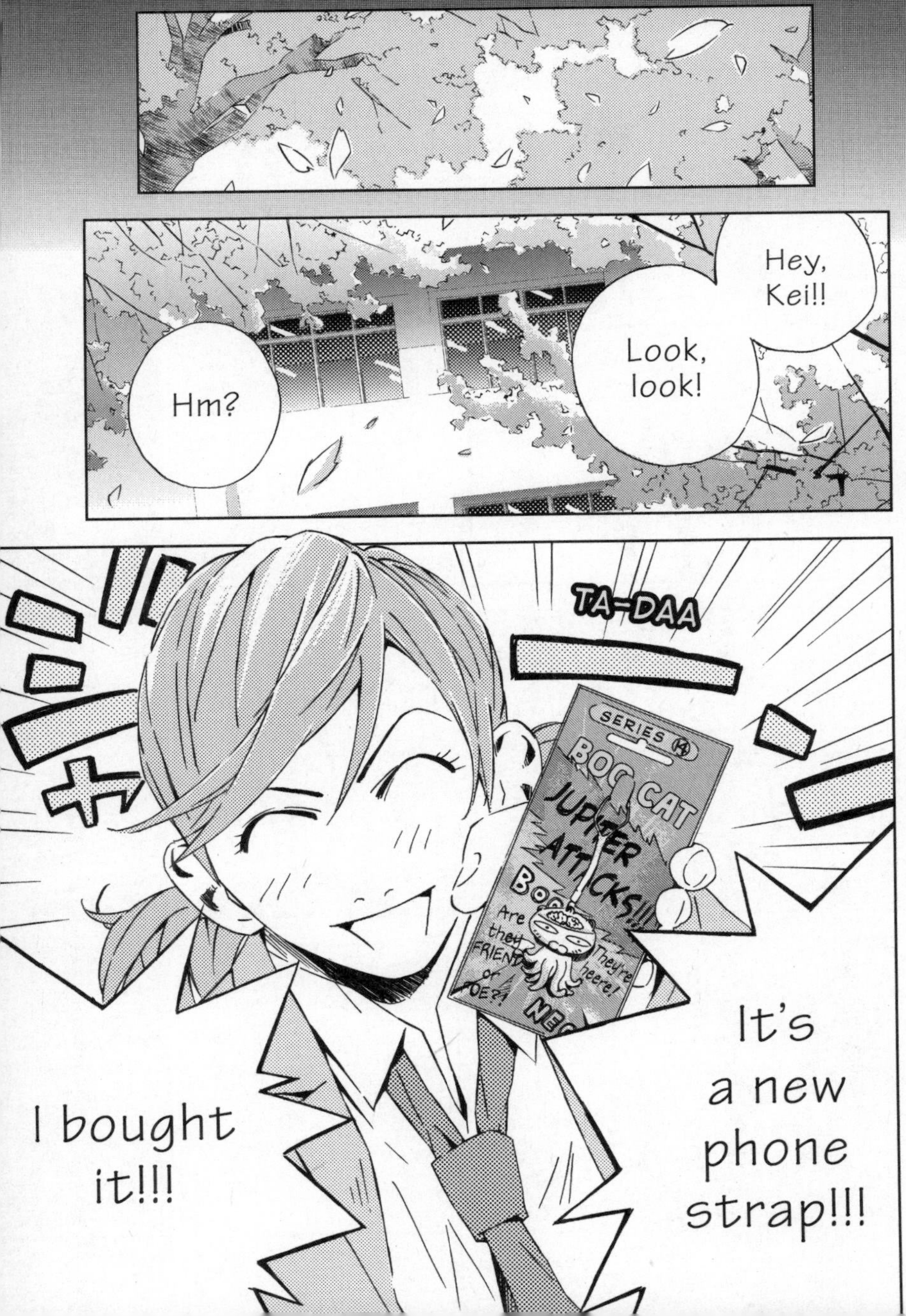
Hey, Kei!!
Look, look!
Hm?
TA-DAA
SERIES 14
JUPITER ATTACKS!!!
They're heere!
It's a new phone strap!!!
I bought it!!!

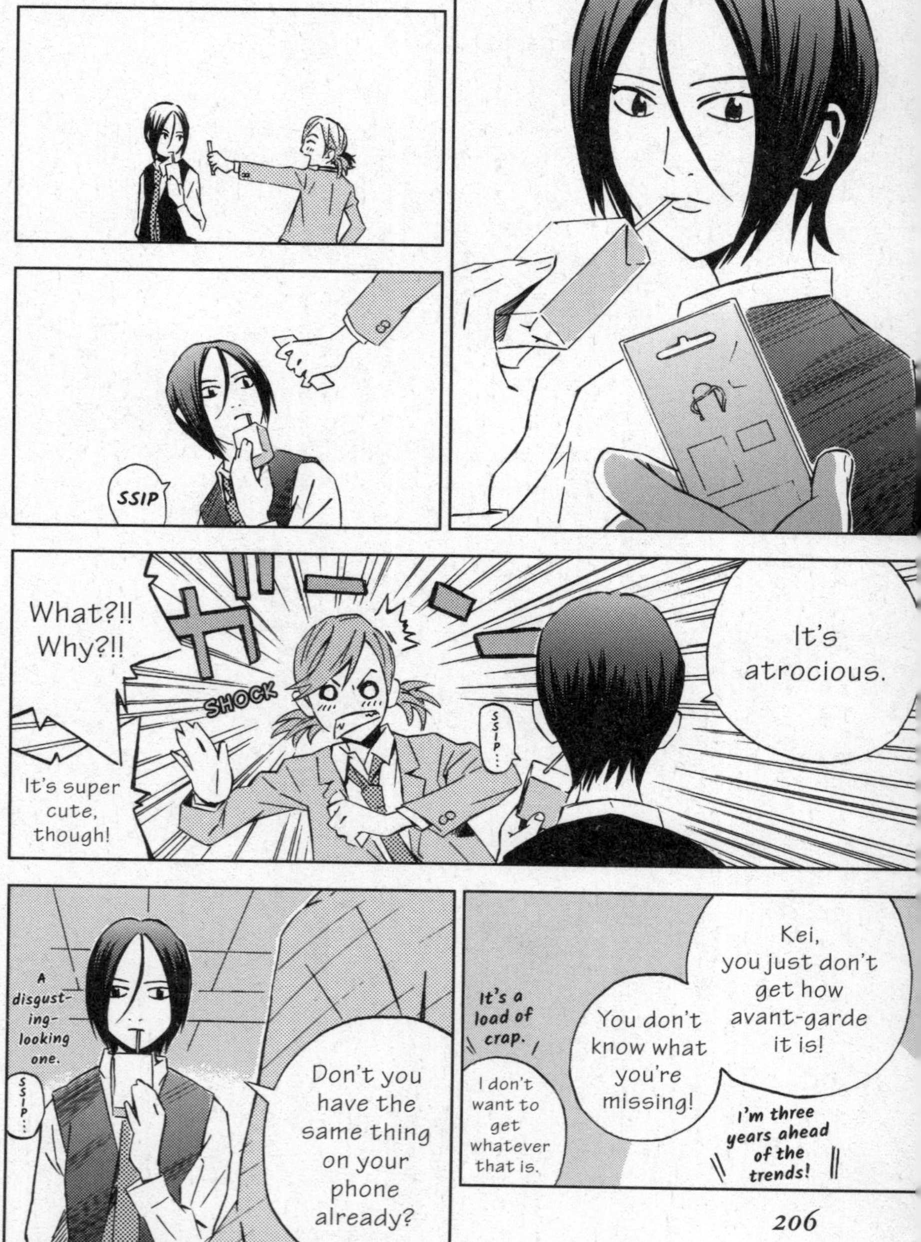
SSIP
It's atrocious.
What?!! Why?!!
SHOCK
SSIP...
It's super cute, though!
Kei, you just don't get how avant-garde it is!
I'm three years ahead of the trends!
You don't know what you're missing!
It's a load of crap.
I don't want to get whatever that is.
Don't you have the same thing on your phone already?
SSIP...
A disgusting-looking one.

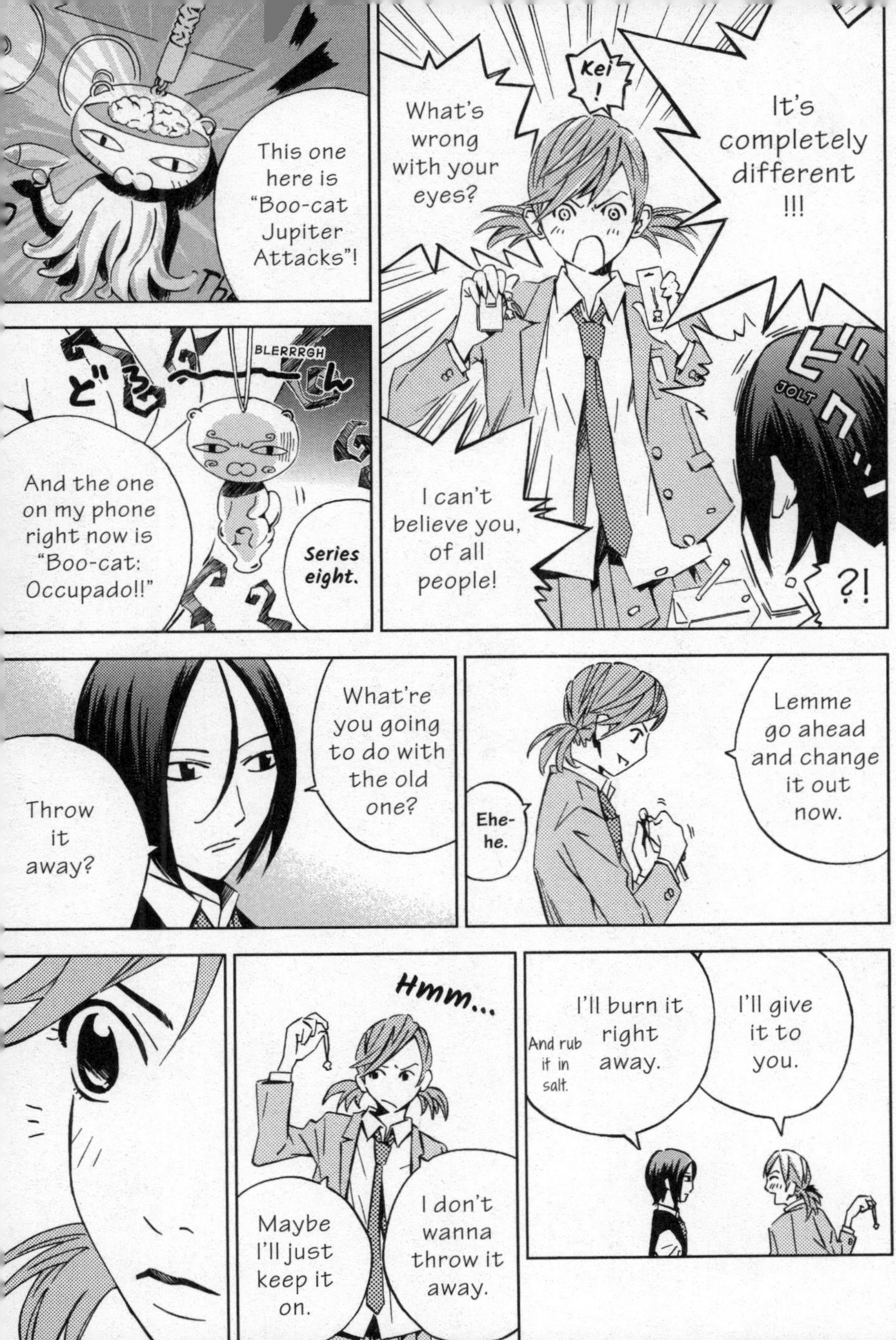
Kei!
It's completely different!!!
What's wrong with your eyes?
I can't believe you, of all people!
JOLT
?!
This one here is "Boo-cat Jupiter Attacks"!
BLERRRGH
Series eight.
And the one on my phone right now is "Boo-cat: Occupado!!"
Lemme go ahead and change it out now.
Ehe-he.
What're you going to do with the old one?
Throw it away?
I'll give it to you.
I'll burn it right away.
And rub it in salt.
Hmm...
I don't wanna throw it away.
Maybe I'll just keep it on.

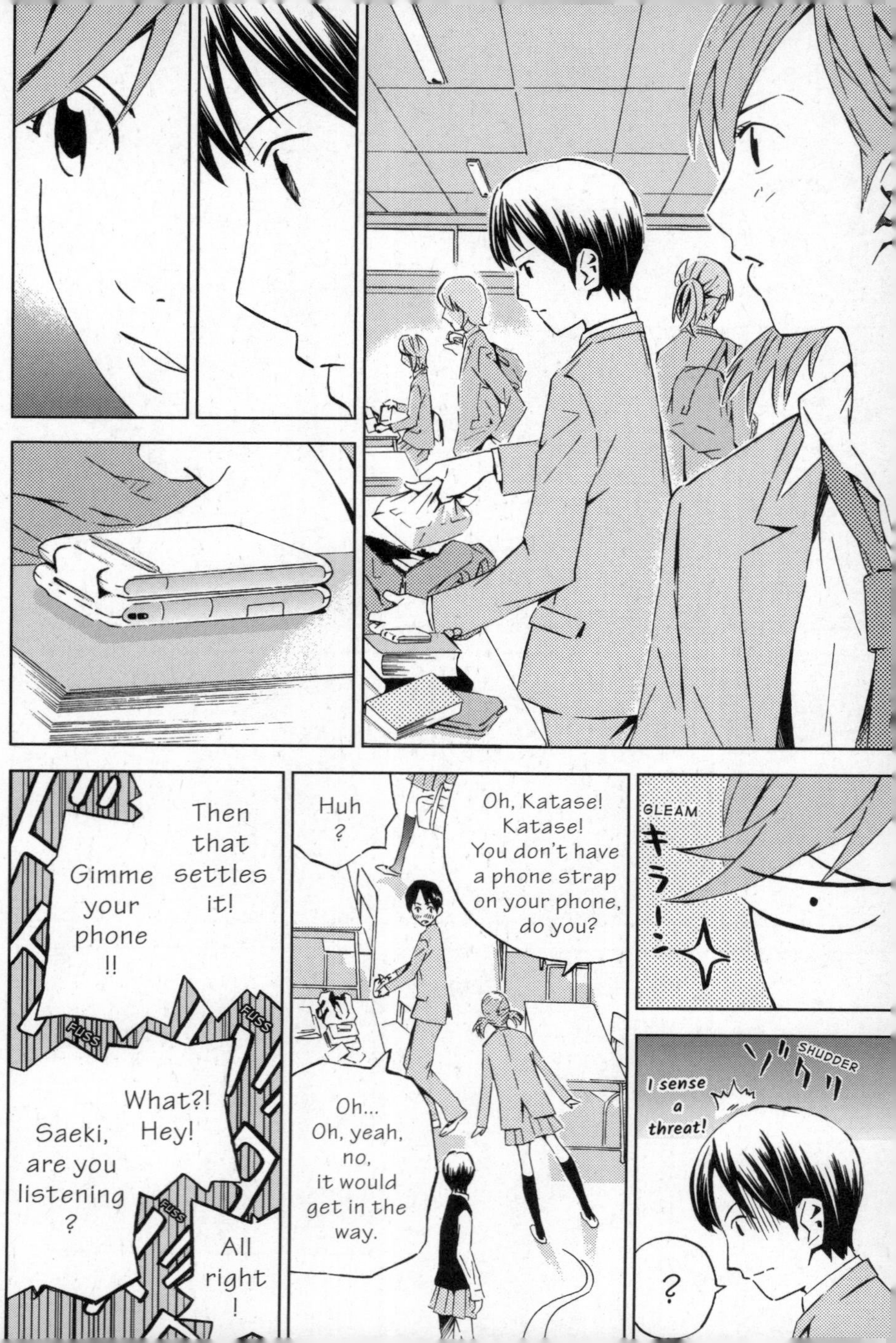
GLEAM
SHUDDER
I sense a threat!
?
Oh, Katase! Katase! You don't have a phone strap on your phone, do you?
Huh?
Oh... Oh, yeah, no, it would get in the way.
Then that settles it!
Gimme your phone!!
FUSS
FUSS
What?! Hey!
Saeki, are you listening?
FUSS
All right!

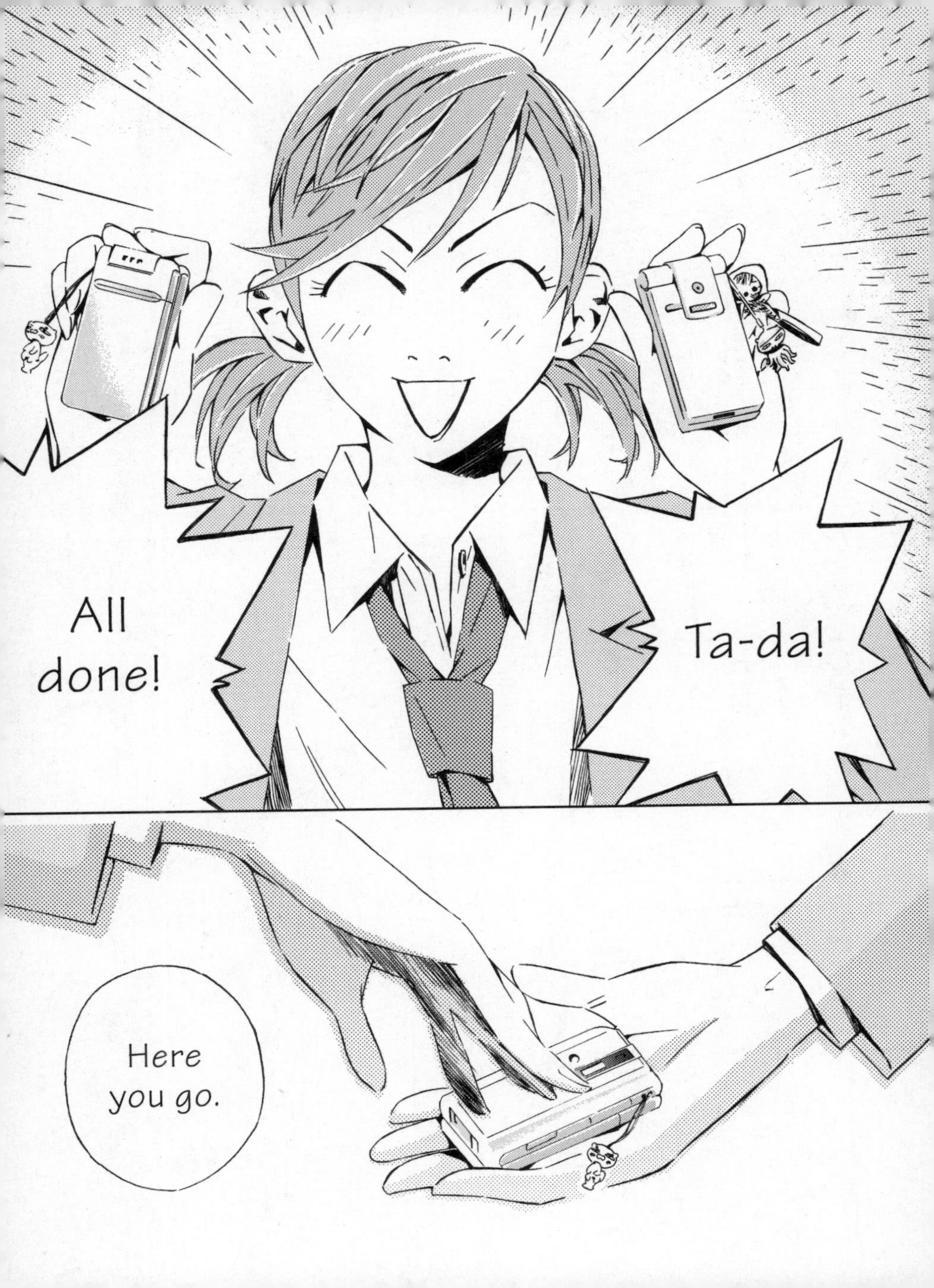
Ta-da!
All done!
Here you go.

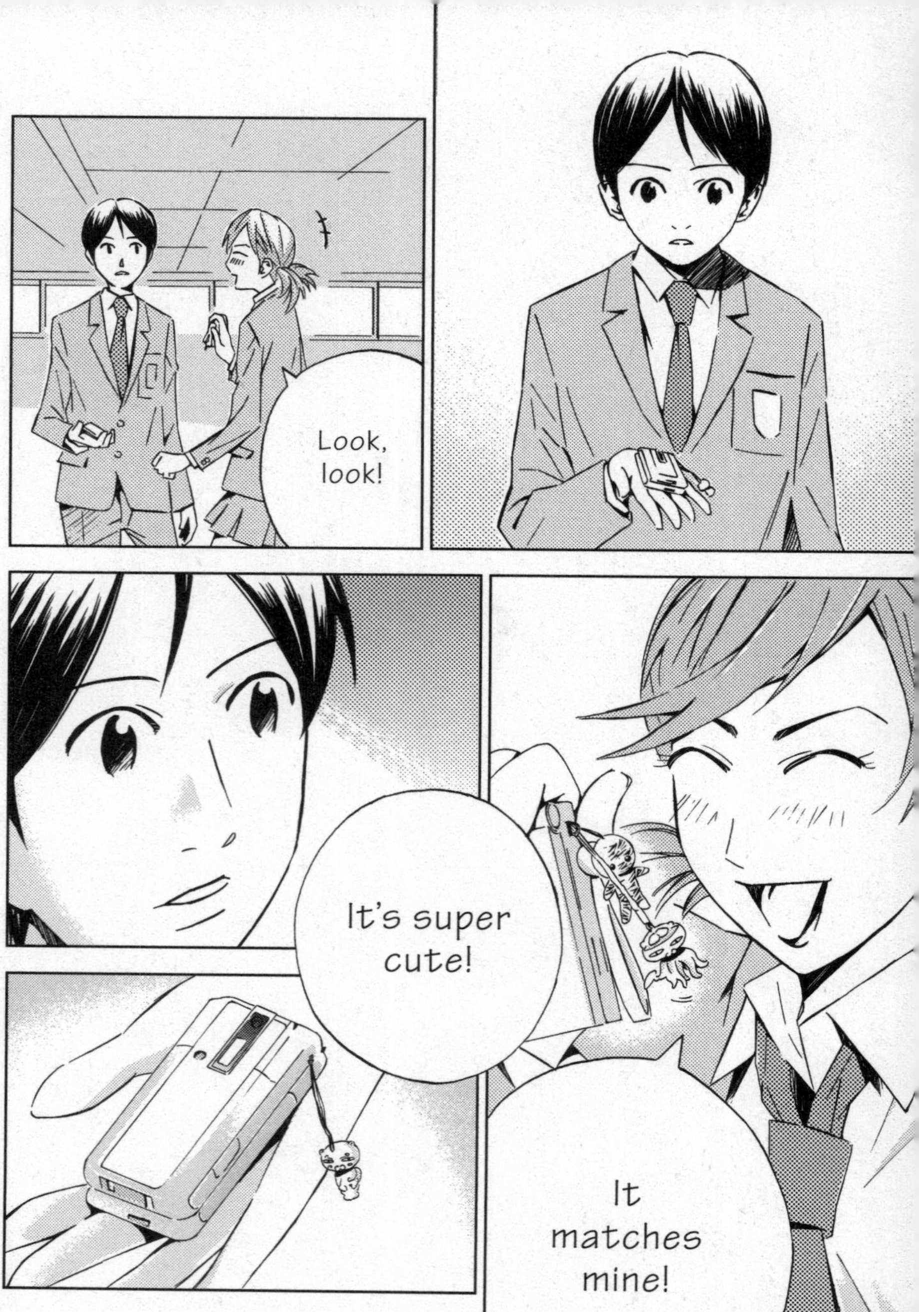
Look, look!
It's super cute!
It matches mine!

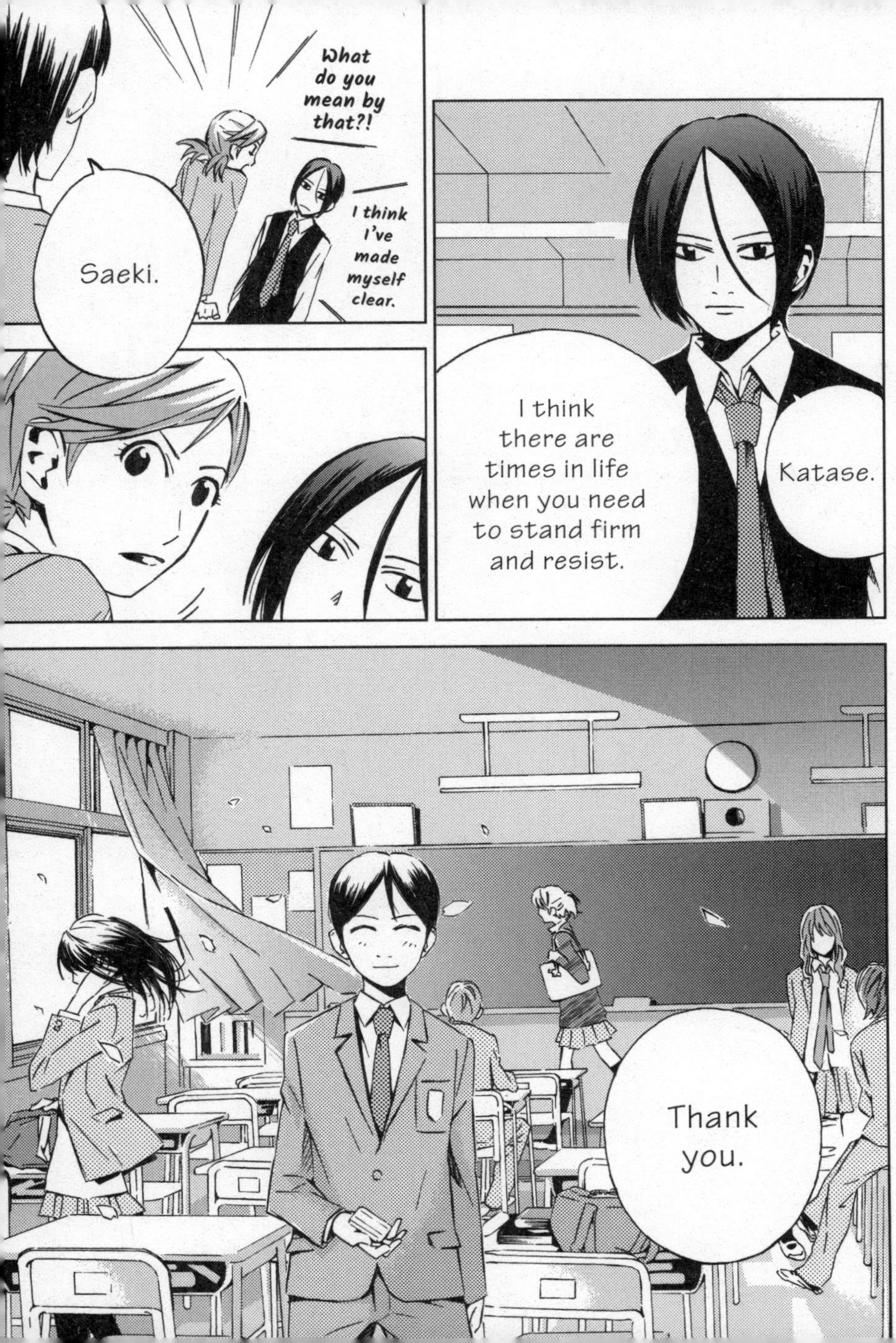
Katase.
I think there are times in life when you need to stand firm and resist.
What do you mean by that?!
I think I've made myself clear.
Saeki.
Thank you.

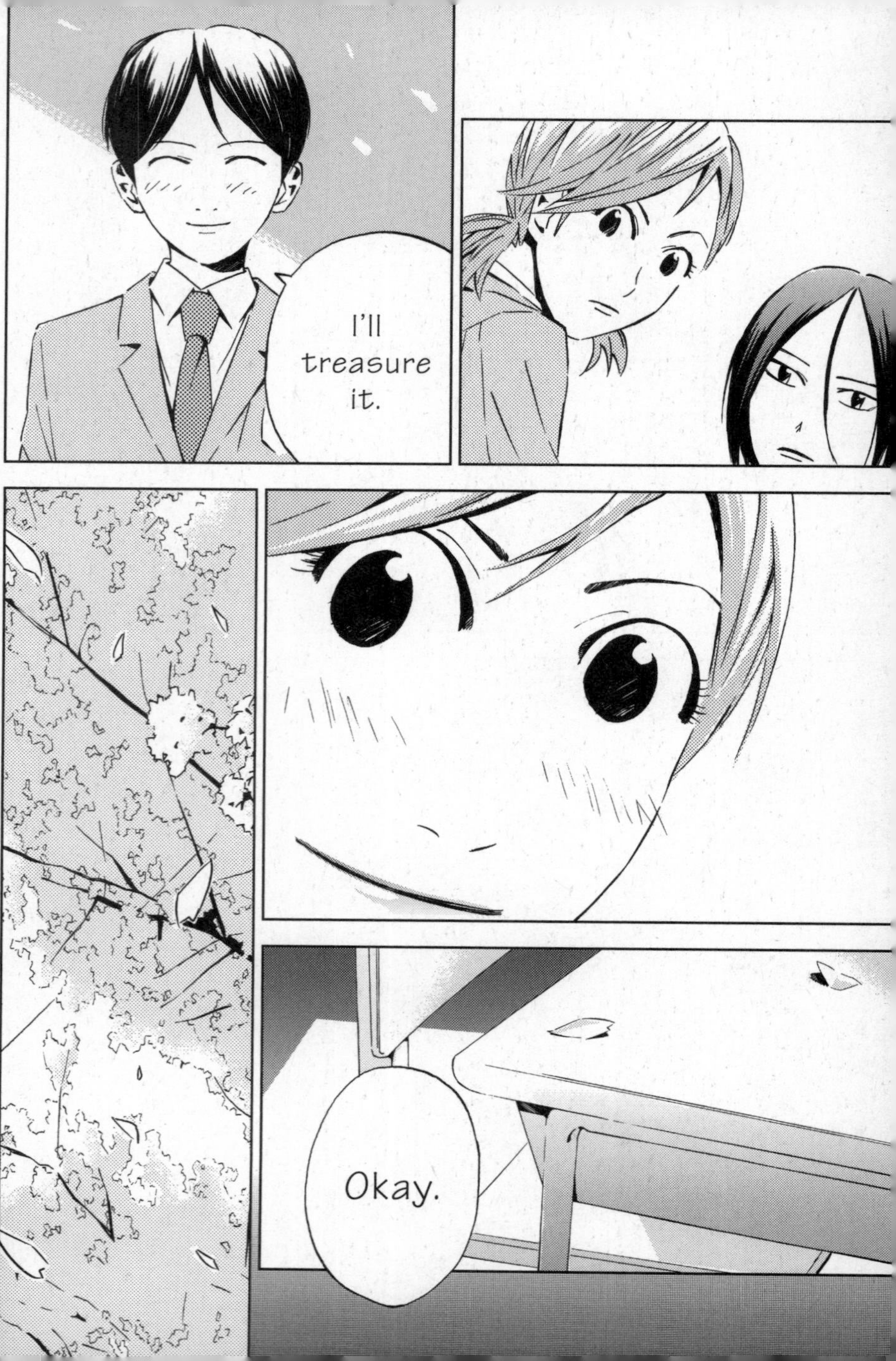
I'll treasure it.
Okay.

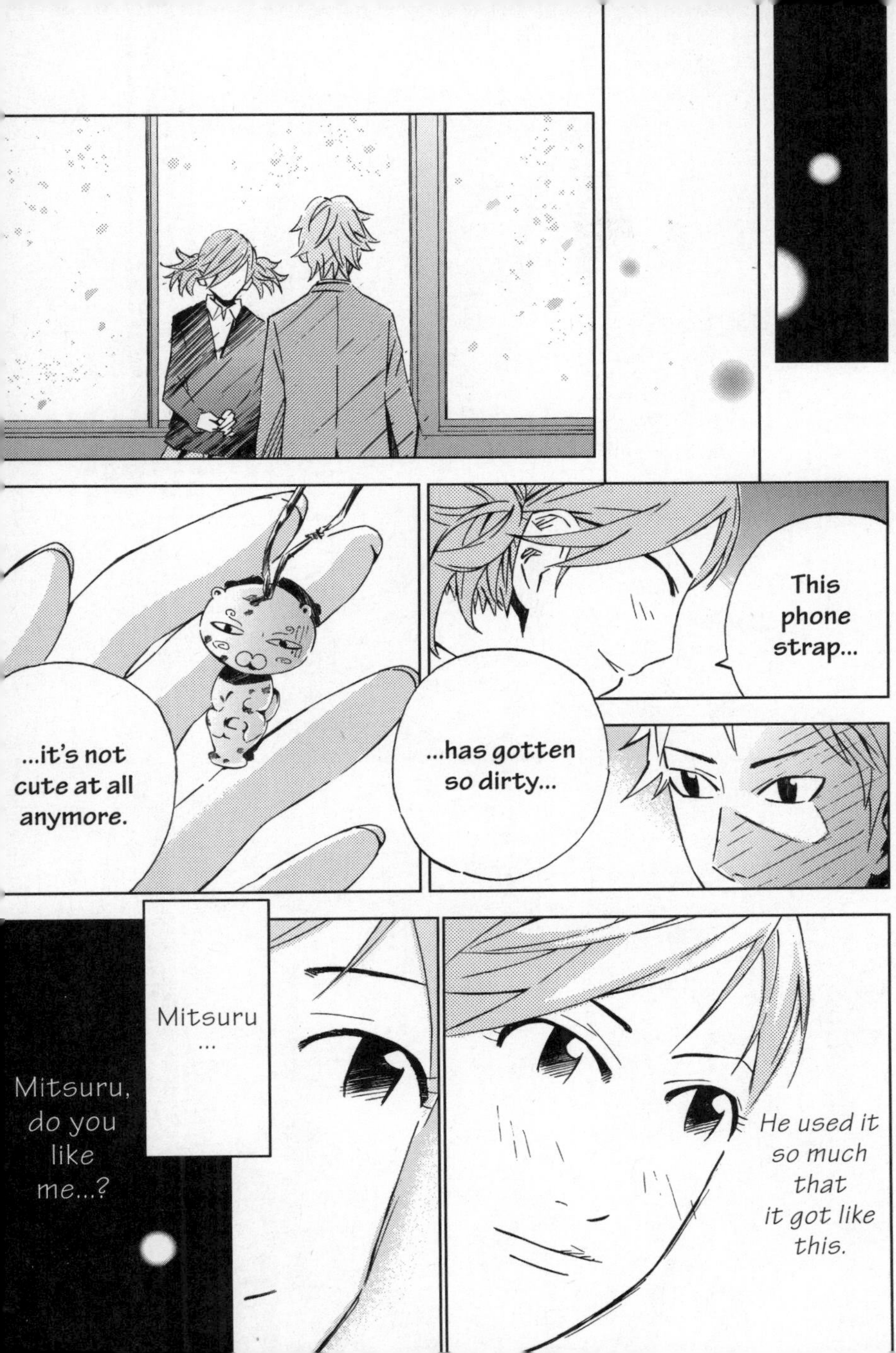
This phone strap...
...has gotten so dirty...
...it's not cute at all anymore.
He used it so much that it got like this.
Mitsuru ...
Mitsuru, do you like me...?

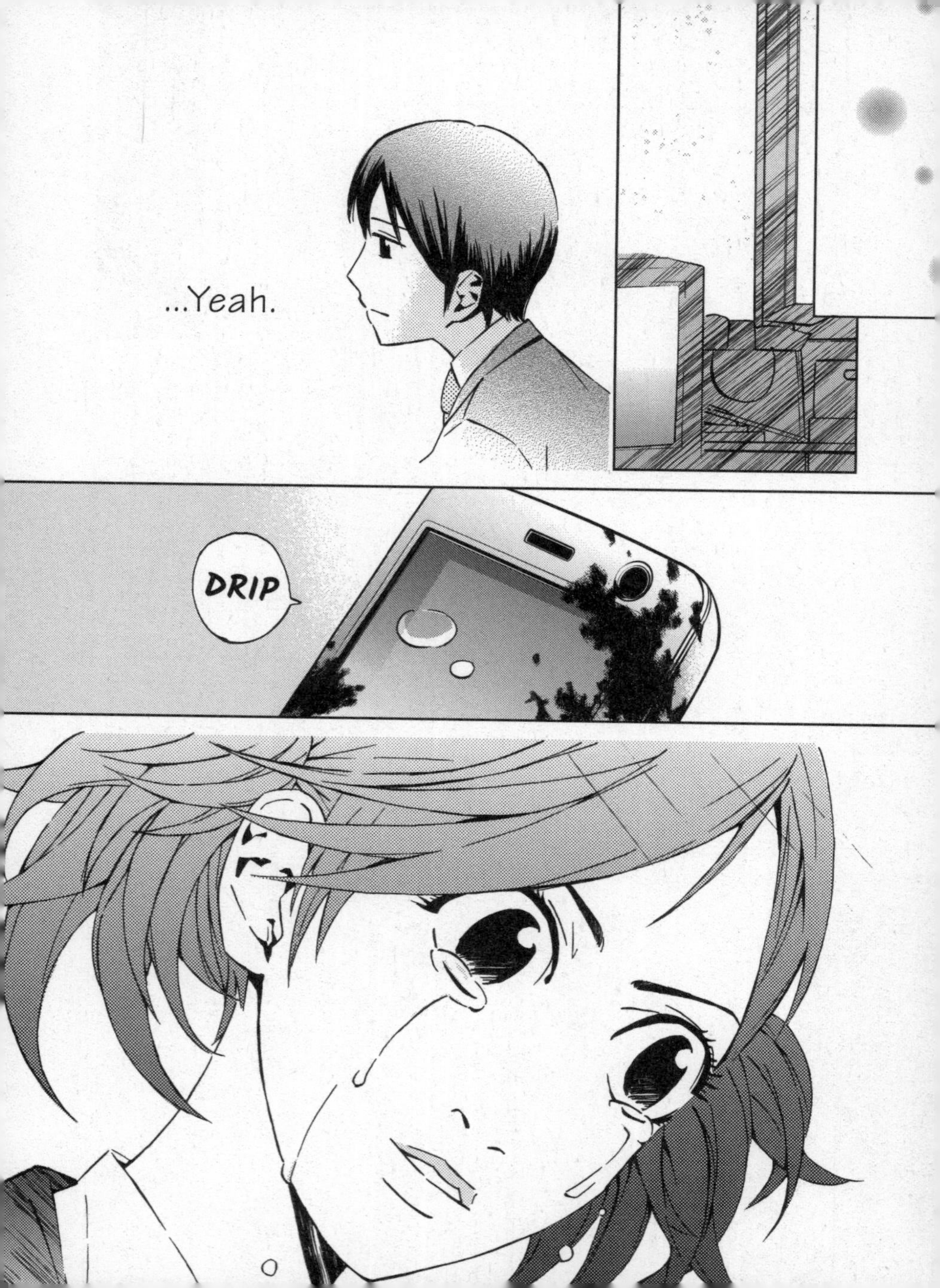
...Yeah.
DRIP

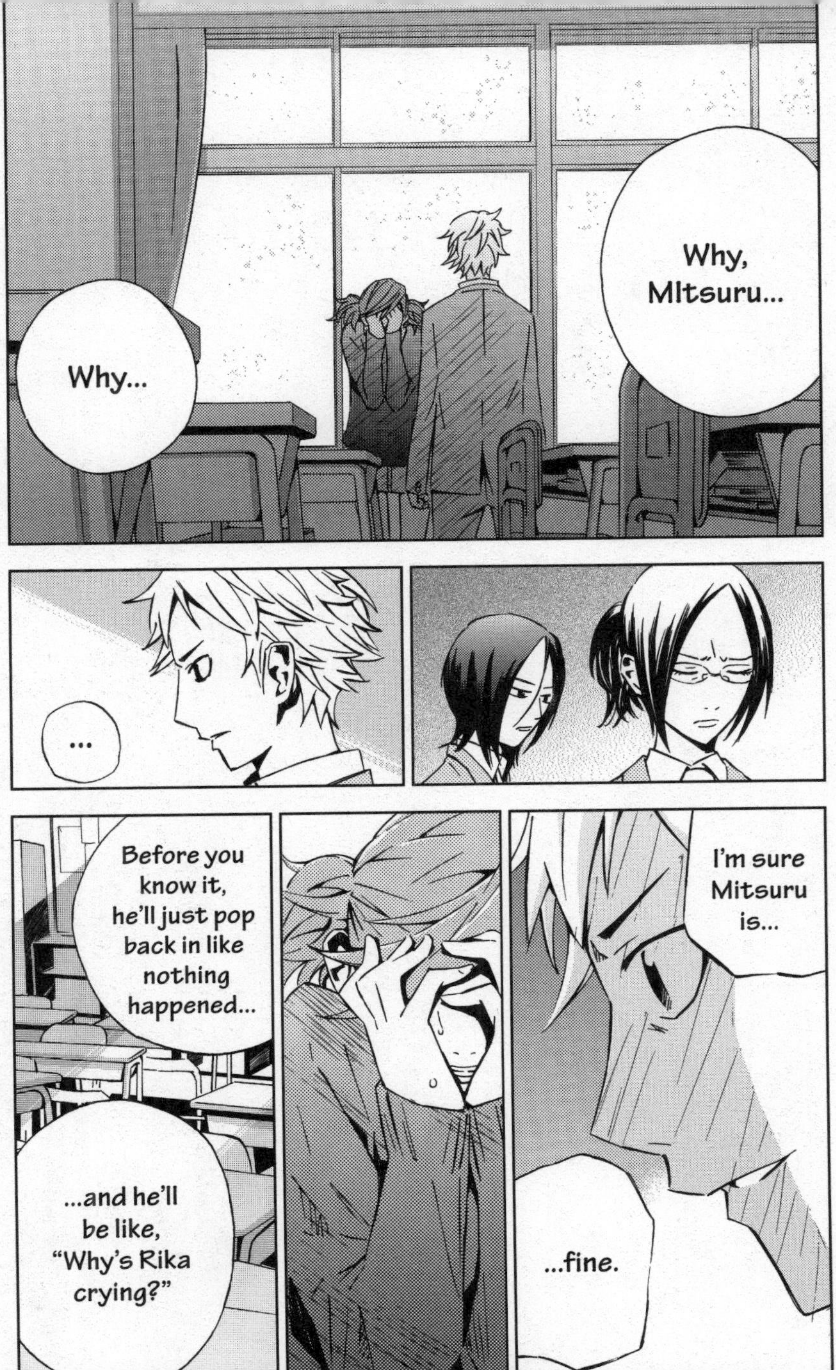
Why, MItsuru...
Why...
...
I'm sure Mitsuru is...
...fine.
Before you know it, he'll just pop back in like nothing happened...
...and he'll be like, "Why's Rika crying?"

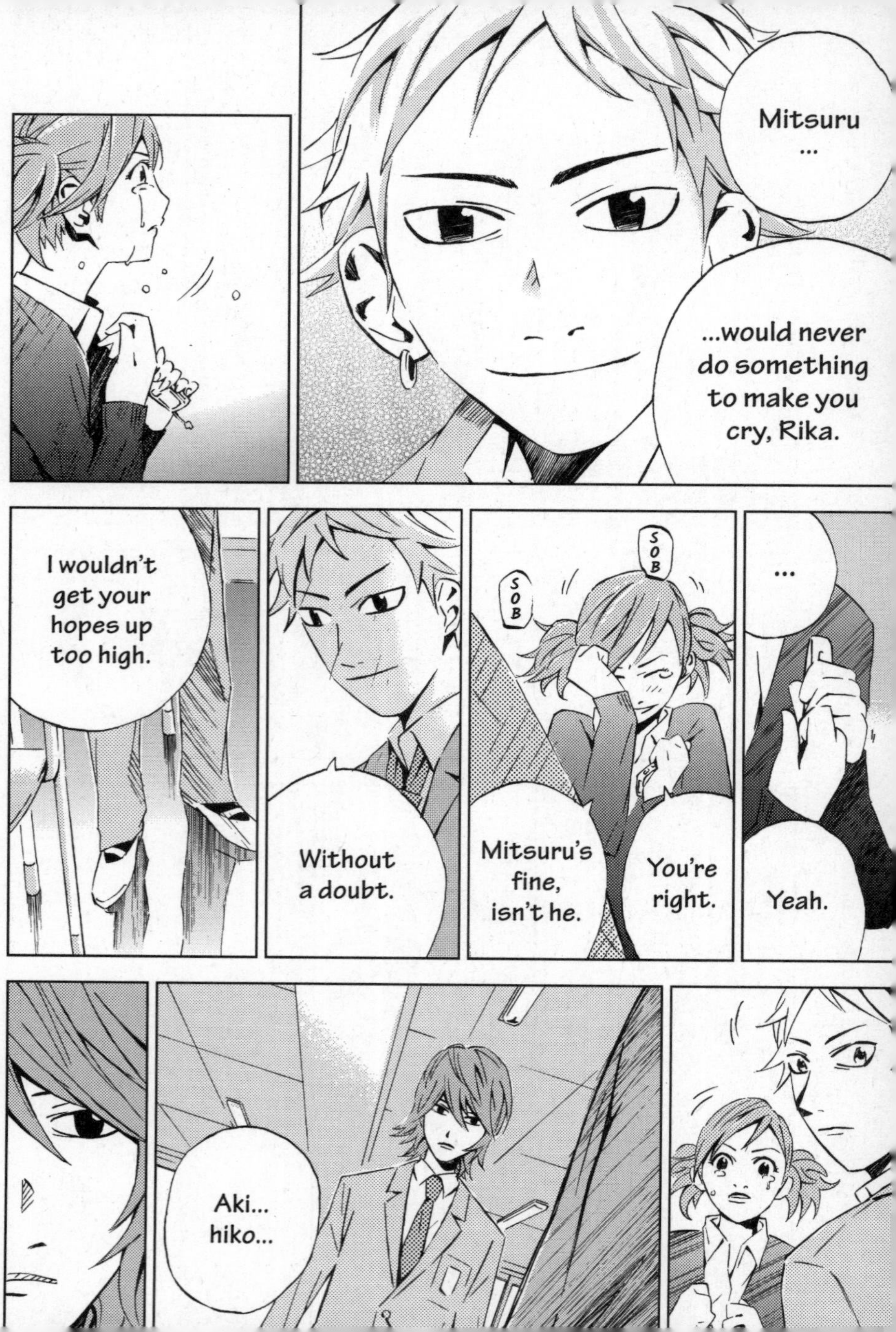
Mitsuru
...
...would never do something to make you cry, Rika.
...
Yeah.
SOB
SOB
You're right.
Mitsuru's fine, isn't he.
Without a doubt.
I wouldn't get your hopes up too high.
Aki... hiko...

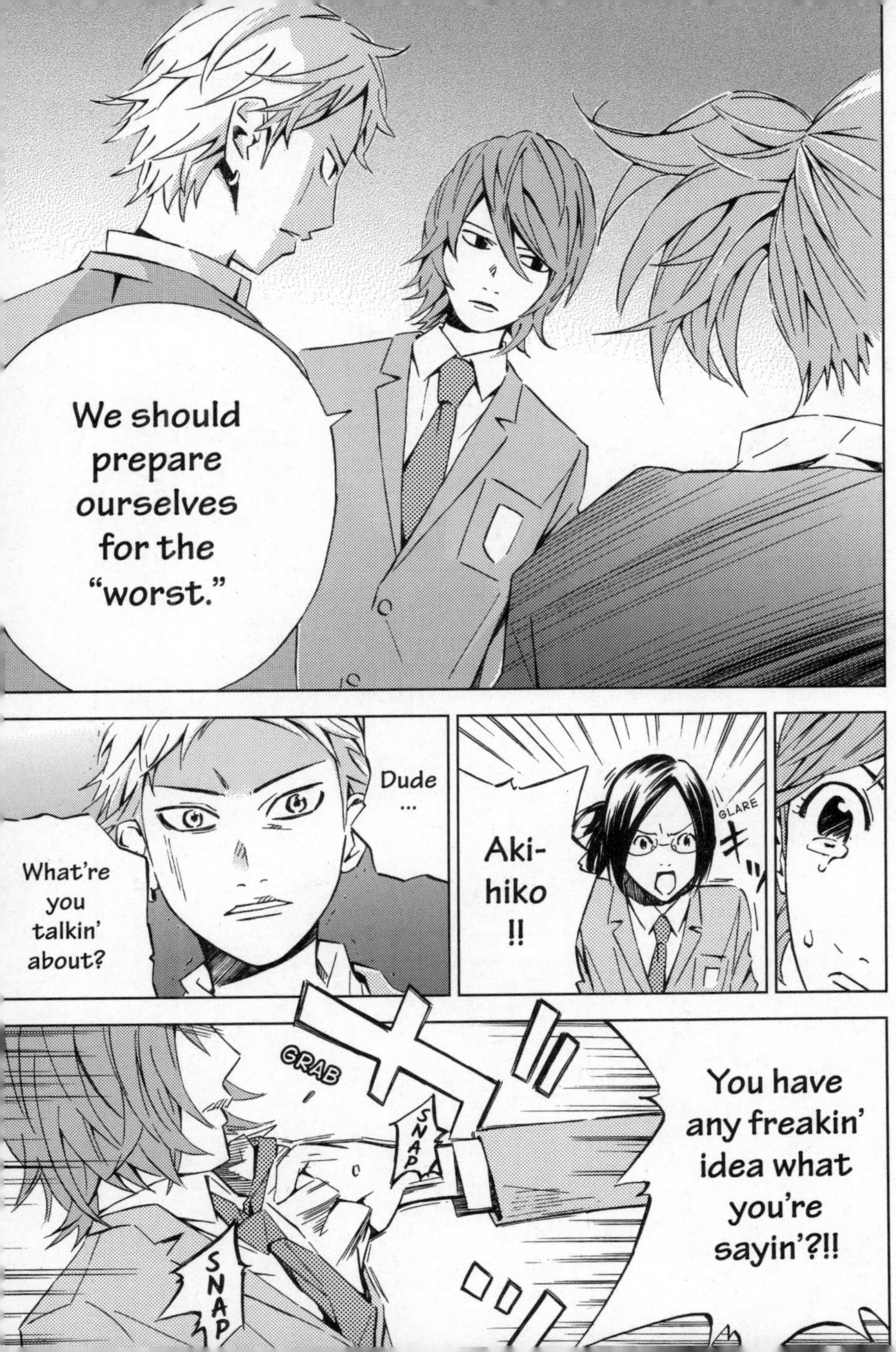
We should prepare ourselves for the "worst."
Aki-hiko!!
GLARE
Dude...
What're you talkin' about?
You have any freakin' idea what you're sayin'?!!
GRAB
SNAP
SNAP

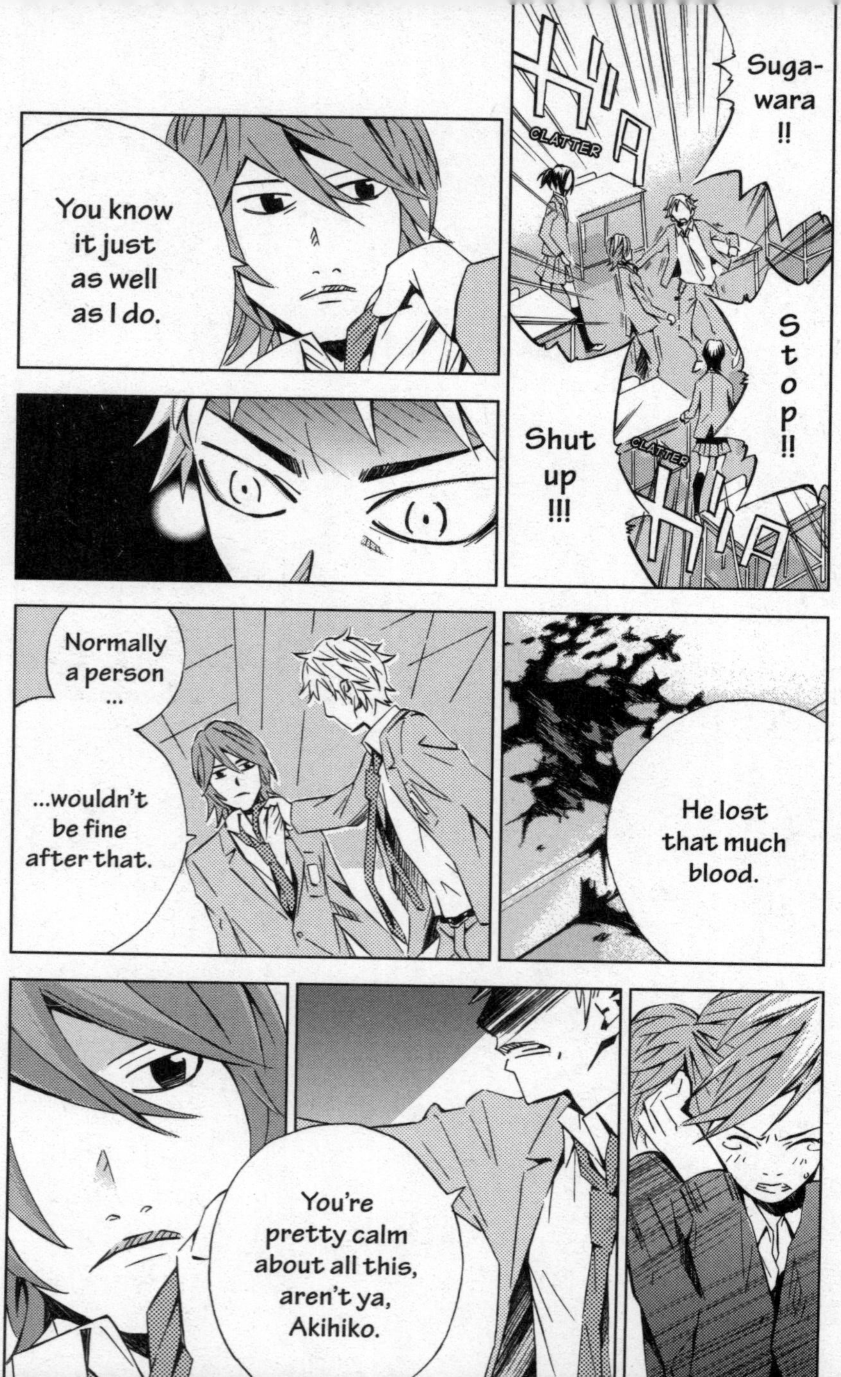
Suga-wara!!
CLATTER
Stop!!
Shut up!!!
CLATTER
You know it just as well as I do.
He lost that much blood.
Normally a person ...
...wouldn't be fine after that.
You're pretty calm about all this, aren't ya, Akihiko.

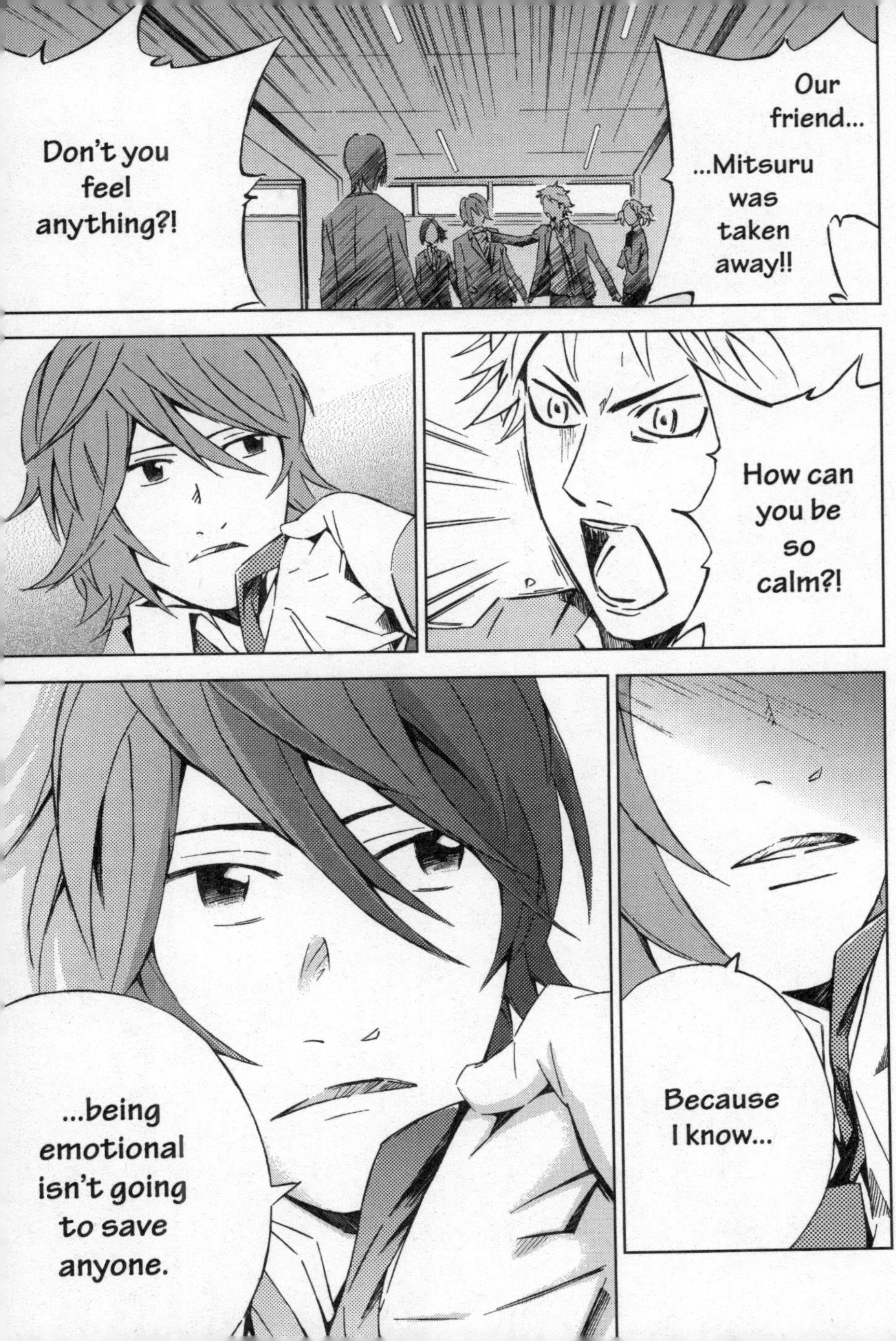
Our friend...
...Mitsuru was taken away!!
Don't you feel anything?!
How can you be so calm?!
Because I know...
...being emotional isn't going to save anyone.

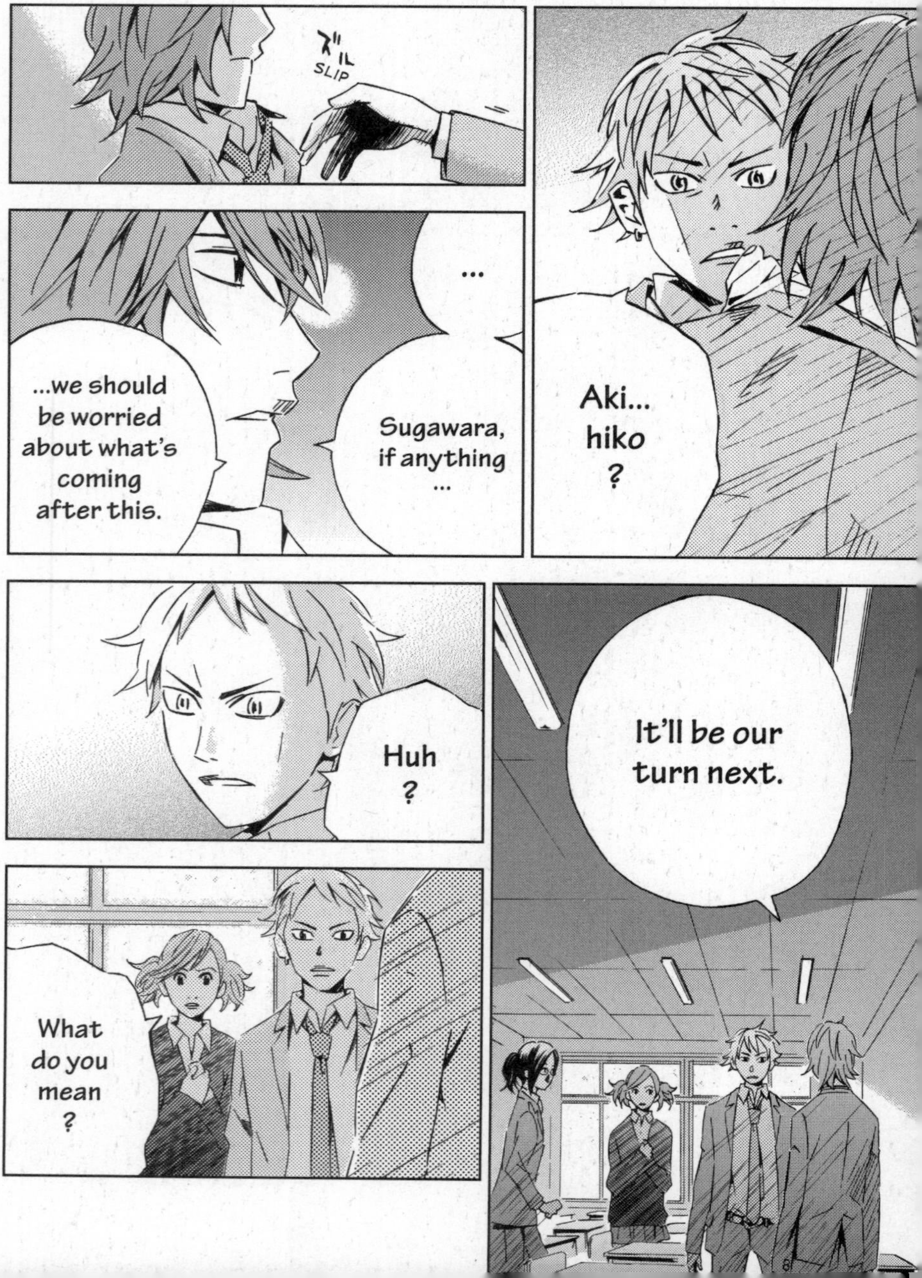
Aki... hiko ?
ズル
SLIP
...
Sugawara, if anything ...
...we should be worried about what's coming after this.
It'll be our turn next.
Huh ?
What do you mean ?

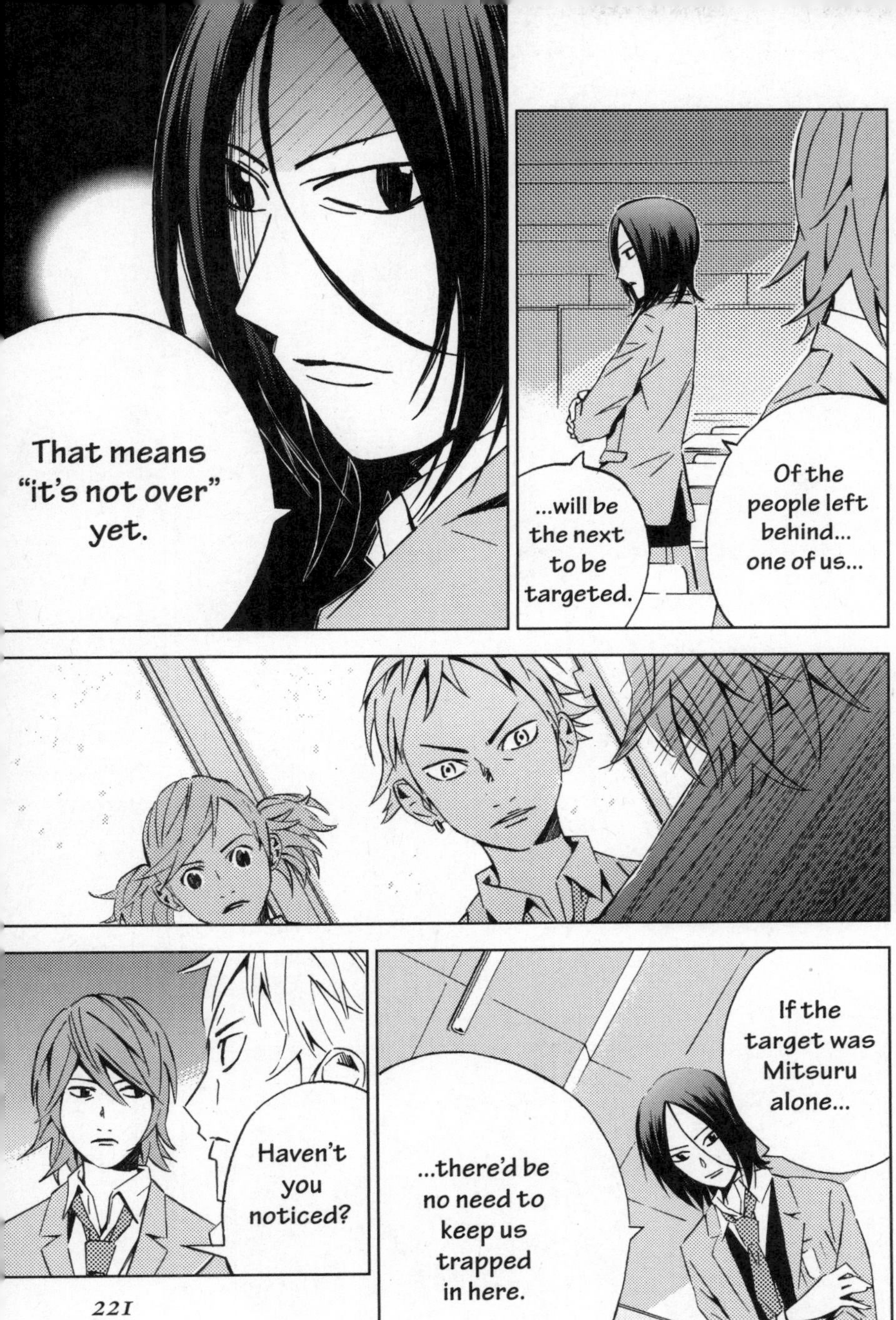
Of the people left behind... one of us...
...will be the next to be targeted.
That means "it's not over" yet.
If the target was Mitsuru alone...
...there'd be no need to keep us trapped in here.
Haven't you noticed?

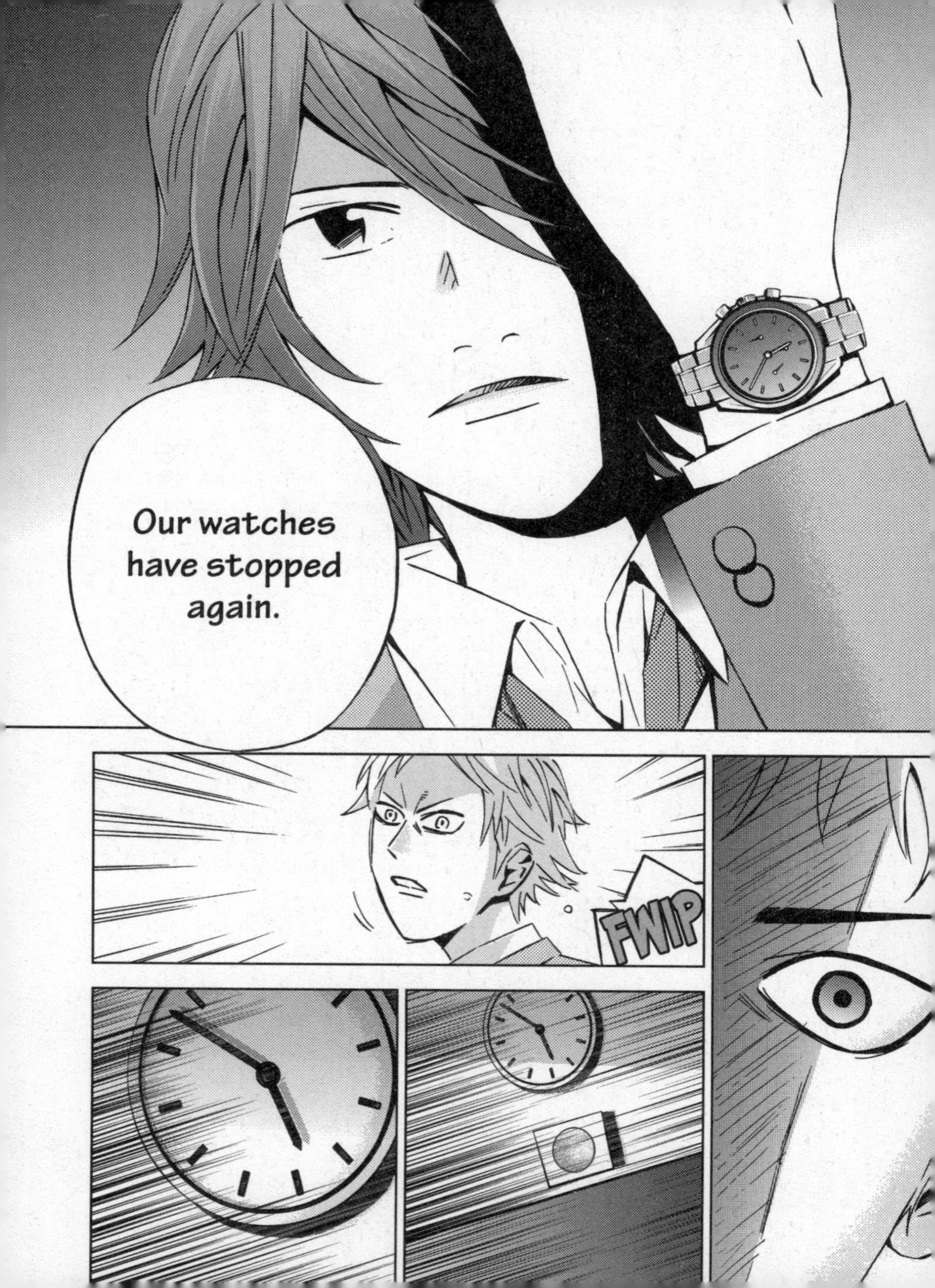
Our watches have stopped again.
FWIP

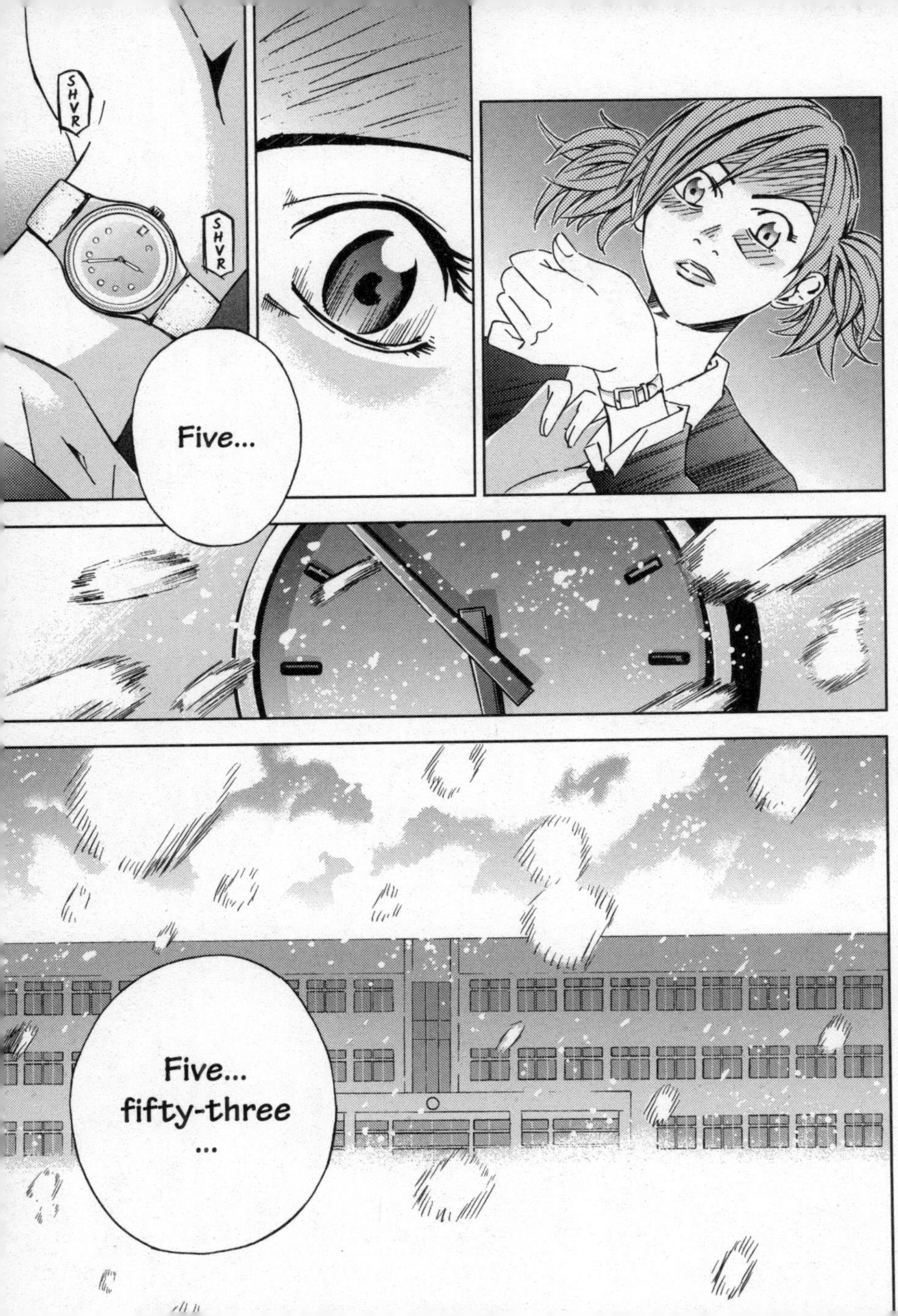
SHVR
SHVR
Five...
Five... fifty-three ...

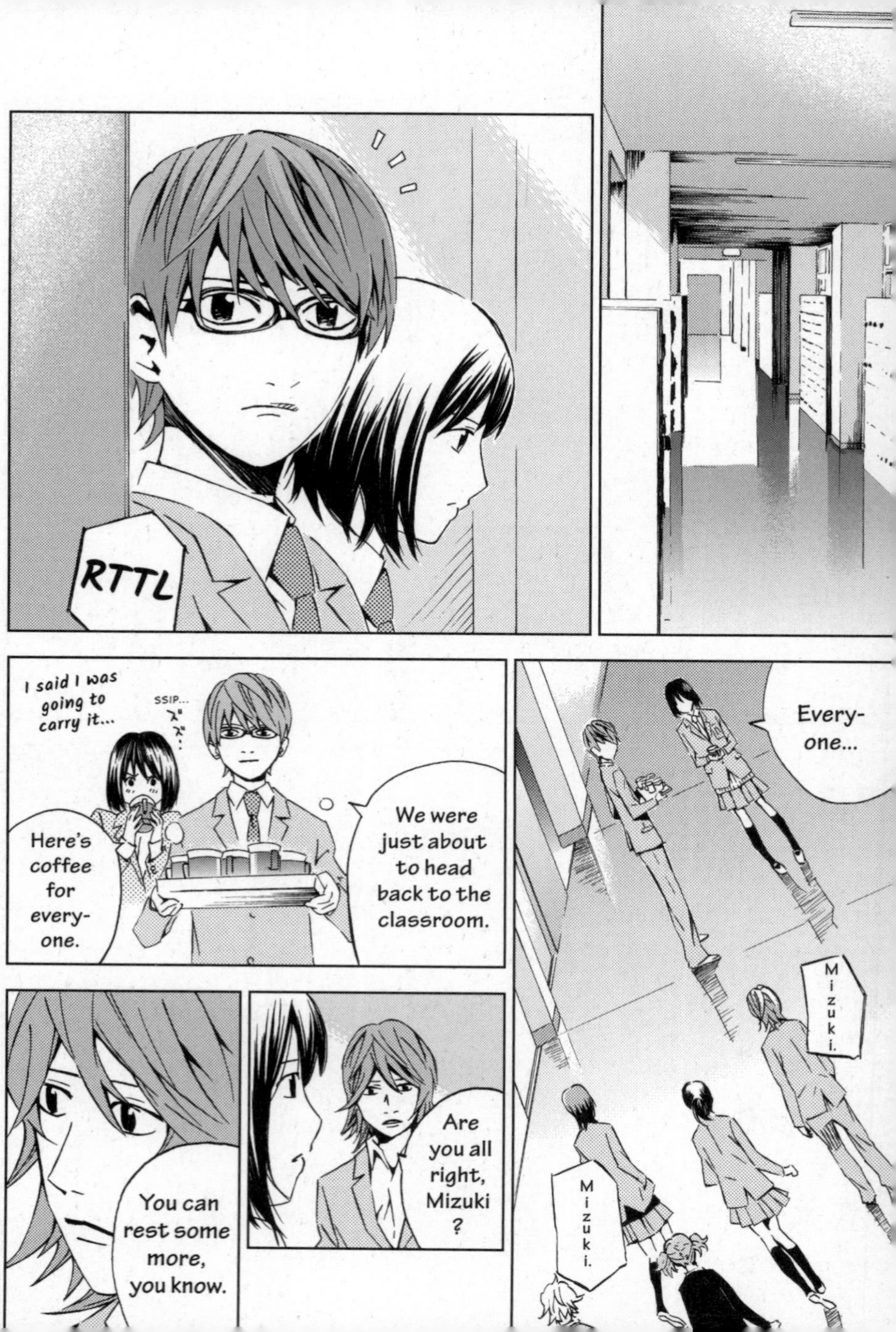
RTTL
Every-one...
Mizuki.
Mizuki.
We were just about to head back to the classroom.
I said I was going to carry it...
SSIP...
Here's coffee for every-one.
Are you all right, Mizuki?
You can rest some more, you know.

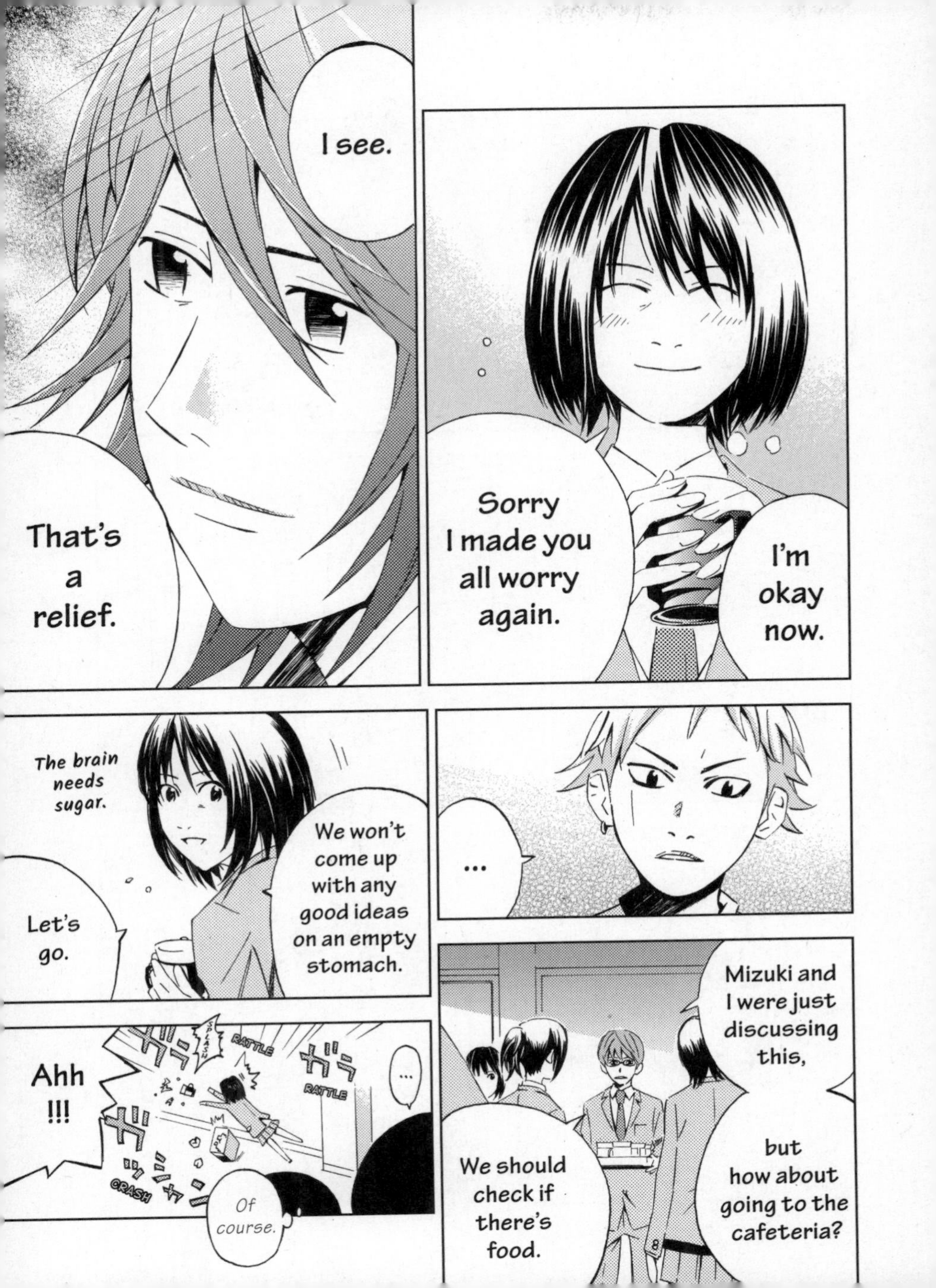
I'm okay now.
Sorry I made you all worry again.
I see.
That's a relief.
...
We won't come up with any good ideas on an empty stomach.
The brain needs sugar.
Let's go.
Mizuki and I were just discussing this,
but how about going to the cafeteria?
We should check if there's food.
...
RATTLE
RATTLE
SPLASH
Ahh !!!
CRASH
Of course.

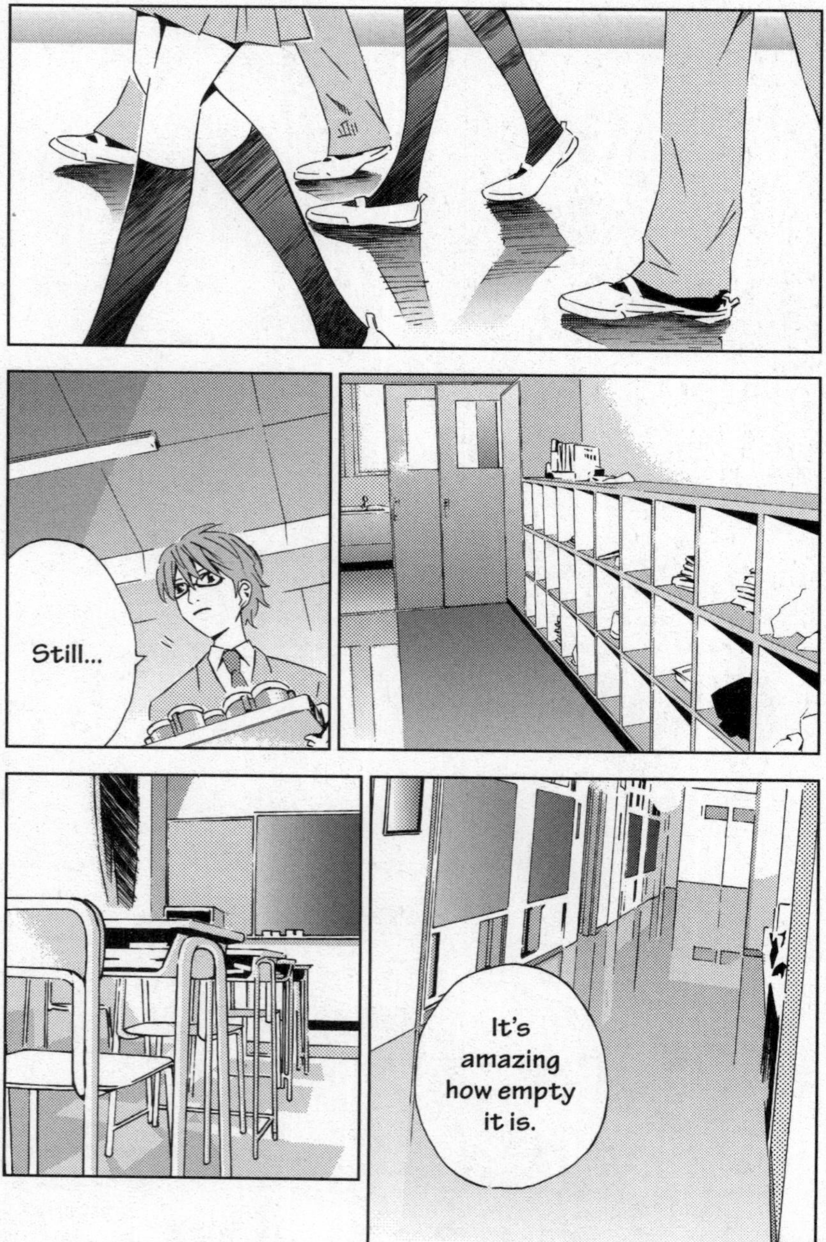
Still...
It's amazing how empty it is.

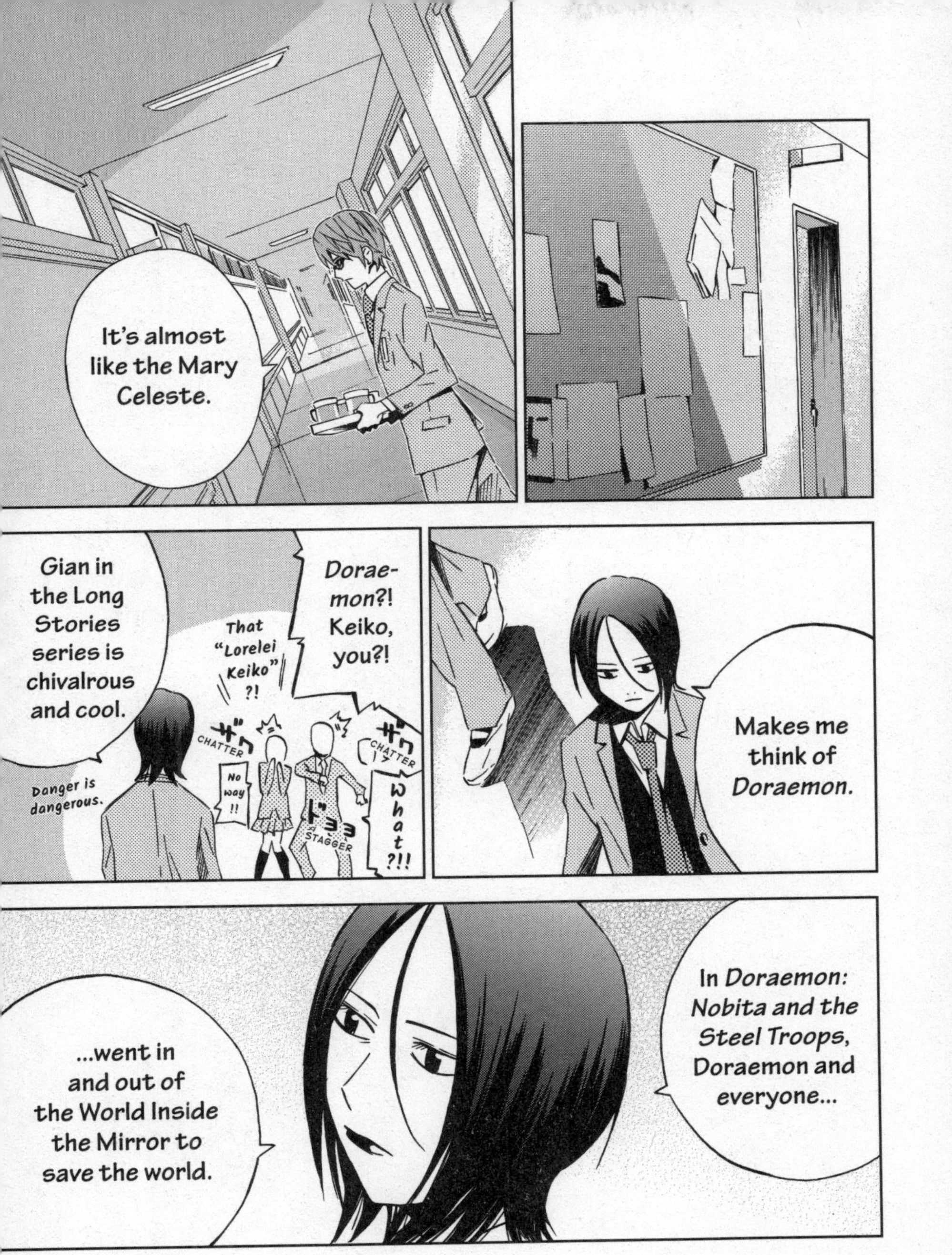
It's almost like the Mary Celeste.
Makes me think of *Doraemon*.
Doraemon?! Keiko, you?!
That "Lorelei Keiko" ?!
Gian in the Long Stories series is chivalrous and cool.
CHATTER
CHATTER
What ?!!
STAGGER
No way !!
Danger is dangerous.
In *Doraemon: Nobita and the Steel Troops*, Doraemon and everyone...
...went in and out of the World Inside the Mirror to save the world.

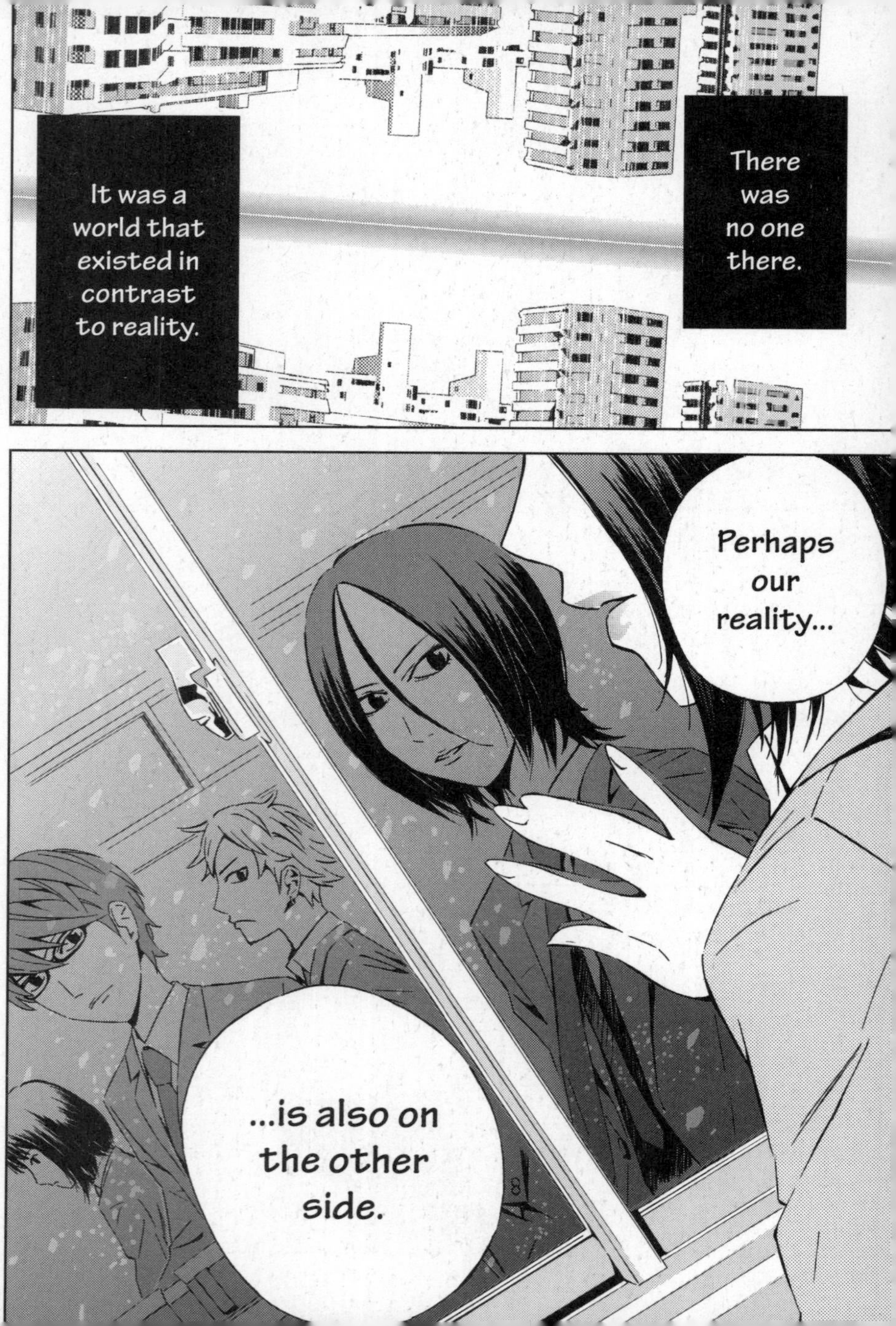
There was no one there.
It was a world that existed in contrast to reality.
Perhaps our reality...
...is also on the other side.

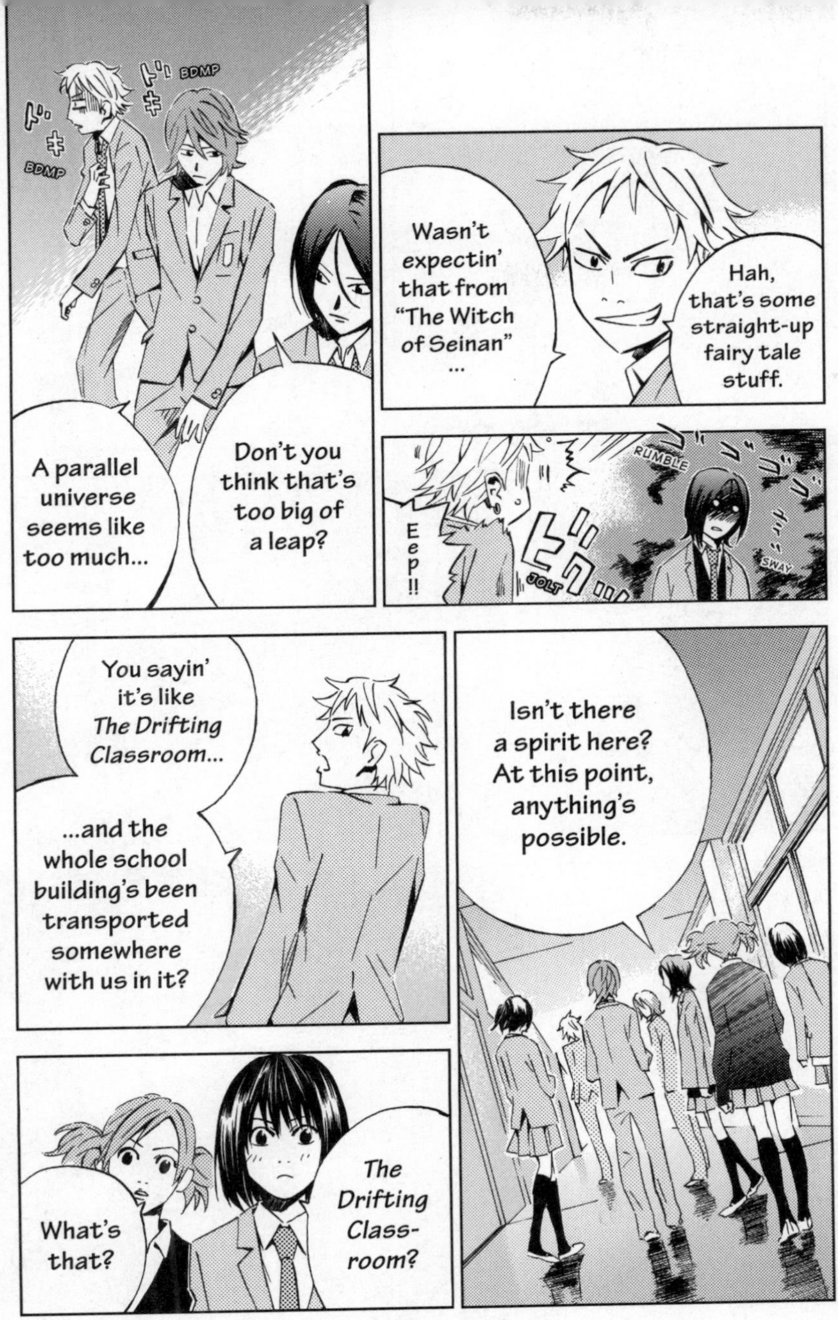
Hah, that's some straight-up fairy tale stuff.
Wasn't expectin' that from "The Witch of Seinan" ...
RUMBLE
SWAY
JOLT
Eep!!
BDMP
BDMP
Don't you think that's too big of a leap?
A parallel universe seems like too much...
Isn't there a spirit here? At this point, anything's possible.
You sayin' it's like *The Drifting Classroom*...
...and the whole school building's been transported somewhere with us in it?
The Drifting Classroom?
What's that?

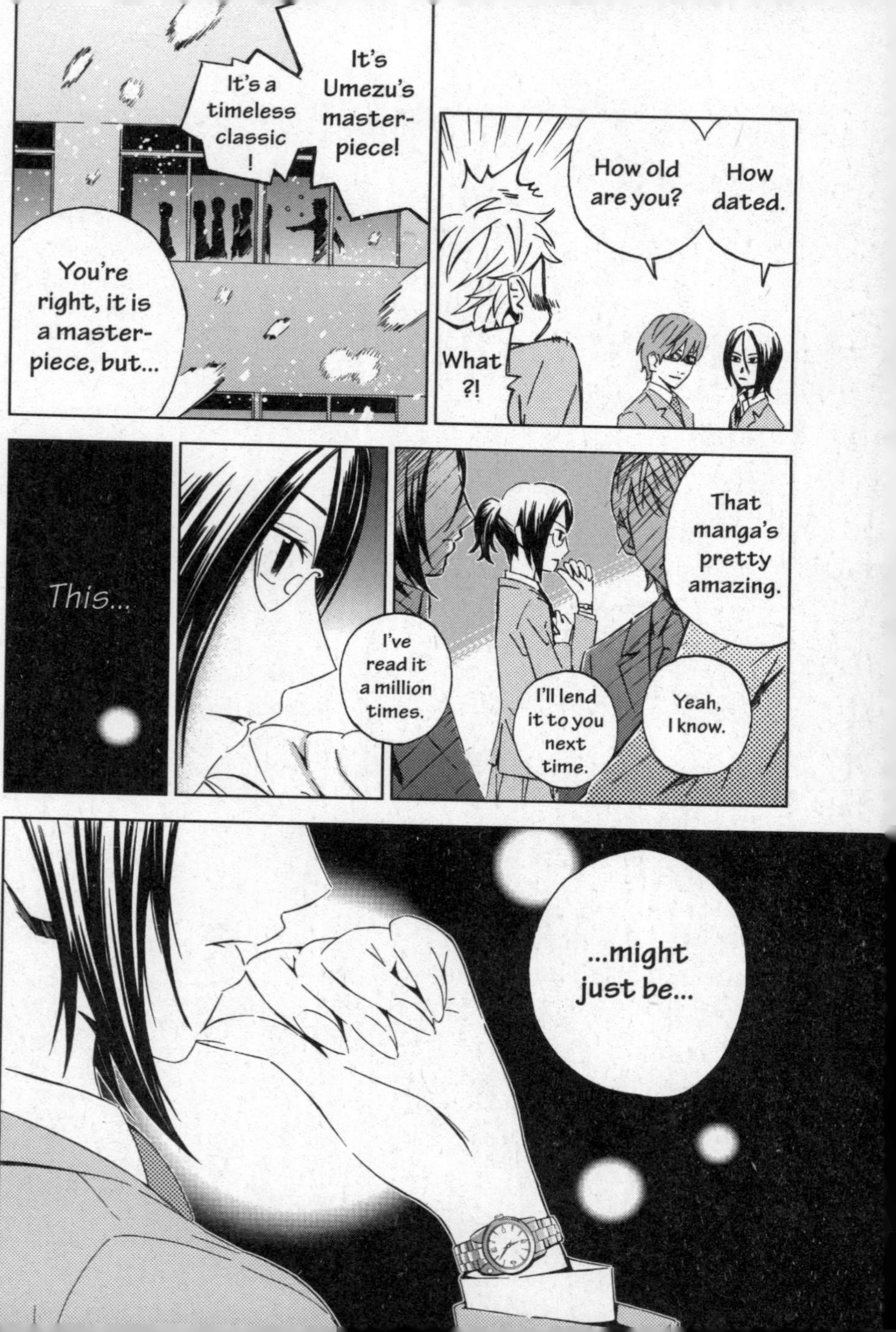
How dated.
How old are you?
What?!
It's Umezu's masterpiece!
It's a timeless classic!
You're right, it is a masterpiece, but...
That manga's pretty amazing.
Yeah, I know.
I'll lend it to you next time.
I've read it a million times.
This...
...might just be...

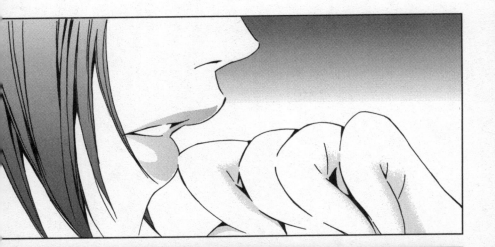

...The Langoliers.

To be continued next volume...

A School
Frozen
in Time

TRANSLATION NOTES

p13 "You could build igloos in this."
In the original Japanese, the igloos Mizuki mentions are *kamakura*. These are igloo-like snow houses that are built during traditional festivals every lunar new year in prefectures such as Akita and Niigata. Each *kamakura* has a snow altar set up in worship of the water deity. During the festivals, visitors are invited into the snow houses and offered grilled rice cakes and *amazake* (a sweet, low alcohol drink made from fermented rice).

p227 "Lorelei Keiko"
Keiko's friends call her "Lorelei Keiko", which is a reference to the Japanese film, *Lorelei: The Witch of the Pacific Ocean*, and its original novel, *Shuusen no Lorelei*, by Harutoshi Fukui. In the film, a young girl with supernatural powers controls a system named "Lorelei" and joins the Navy to save Japan from a third atomic bomb.

p227 "Danger is dangerous."
Keiko is quoting a famous line in the movie, *Doraemon: The Record of Nobita's Parallel Visit to the West*, where Doraemon calls out, "*kiken ga abunai!*" This line sparked debate amongst Japanese speakers on whether or not it was correct Japanese, given its redundancy.

A School Frozen in Time
volume 1

A Vertical Comics Edition

Editing: Ajani Oloye
Translation: Michelle Lin
Production: Grace Lu
         Tomoe Tsutsumi

First published in Japan in 2008 by Kodansha, Ltd., Tokyo
Publication for this English edition arranged through Kodansha, Ltd., Tokyo
English language version produced by Vertical Comics,
an imprint of Kodansha USA Publishing, LLC

Translation provided by Vertical Comics, 2021
Published by Kodansha USA Publishing, LLC, New York

Originally published in Japanese as *Tsumetai Kousha no Toki wa Tomaru 1*
by Kodansha, Ltd.
Tsumetai Kousha no Toki wa Tomaru first serialized in *Gekkan Shounen Magazine*,
Kodansha, Ltd., 2008-2009

This is a work of fiction.

ISBN: 978-1-949980-49-3

Manufactured in the United States of America

First Edition

Kodansha USA Publishing, LLC
451 Park Avenue South
7th Floor
New York, NY 10016
www.readvertical.com

Vertical books are distributed through Penguin-Random House Publisher Services.